W9-BTK-157

WITHDRAWN

# THE UPROOTED
## A Hitler Legacy

### Voices of Those Who Escaped before the "Final Solution"

Ten-year-old Dorothy and her four-year-old sister before leaving their mother for England. It took Inge years to overcome the wrench of parting. (Courtesy of Dorothy Fleming)

# THE UPROOTED
## A Hitler Legacy
## Voices of Those Who Escaped before the "Final Solution"

**Dorit Bader Whiteman, Ph.D.**

Foreword by
**William B. Helmreich, Ph.D.**

✳ **INSIGHT BOOKS**
Plenum Press • New York and London

Library of Congress Cataloging-in-Publication Data

Whiteman, Dorit Bader.
    The uprooted : a Hitler legacy : voices of those who escaped
  before the "final solution" / Dorit Bader Whiteman ; foreword by
  William B. Helmreich.
        p.   cm.
    Includes bibliographical references and index.
    ISBN 0-306-44467-4
    1. Holocaust survivors--Mental health. 2. Holocaust, Jewish
  (1939-1945)--Psychological aspects. 3. Holocaust, Jewish
  (1939-1945)--Personal narratives. 4. Refugees, Jewish--Mental
  health.   I. Title.
    [DNLM: 1. Jews--psychology--personal narratives. 2. Stress
  Disorders, Post-Traumatic--personal narratives. 3. War Crimes-
  -personal narratives.   WM 170 W593a]
  RC451.4.H62W48  1993
  155.9'3--dc20
  DNLM/DLC
  for Library of Congress                                    92-48291
                                                                  CIP

ISBN 0-306-44467-4

© 1993 Plenum Press, New York
A Division of Plenum Publishing Corporation
233 Spring Street, New York, N.Y. 10013

*An Insight Book*

Printed in the United States of America

To my mother and father,
and all those who are no longer
here to tell their story,

and

to my husband and children,
who understood why I had to
write this book.

# Foreword

*The Uprooted* is a book whose time has come. Indeed, reading it, one wonders why it was not written twenty, even thirty years ago. The author has crafted a fascinating story out of interviews with 190 Jews who were compelled by Nazi tyranny to leave Germany and Austria.

When thinking of the Holocaust, it is normal to view it as an event that began in 1939 and whose victims were those who remained in Europe. This book explains how those who left prior to the war were also victims. The trauma and pain of being forced to leave communities in which Jews had lived for hundreds of years still haunt their memories. Many of them felt hesitant to speak about their suffering in deference to concentration camp survivors. They viewed their own suffering as minimal when compared to the agony of those who had experienced the camps and the ghettos. Whiteman's book makes amply clear that the travails of those who were able to escape before the "Final Solution" were both terrible and long-lasting in their effects.

The author has cast her net widely. Her respondents come from all walks of life and from many countries, including England, Australia, and the United States. As they reminisce about what was and what could never be again, we find ourselves irresistibly drawn into their lives, sharing their tragedies, their resourcefulness, their bravery and tenacity, and their kindness to their brethren. We learn of the concern shown by many of those who sheltered the refugees and of the difficulties faced by the immigrants as they learned a new language and new ways in other lands.

Part of what makes this group unique is the fact that they

believed in the value of German culture—its music, its literature, and its seemingly progressive outlook on life. German and Austrian Jewry also considered itself fortunate not to be in Poland or Russia, where anti-Semitism was widespread and often supported by the state. As a result, when the end came, it shattered many illusions.

And yet, despite the hardships that characterized their lives, the escapees rebuilt their lives in new lands. They became acclimated to different ways of life, started businesses, resumed their interrupted education, raised families, and though scars remained, came to terms with what had happened to them. In short, they denied Hitler his final victory by not allowing their experiences to destroy their lives.

*The Uprooted* tells the story of this community in beautiful moving prose. More than anything, it allows its main protagonists to speak for themselves, and when they do, they testify to the capacity of human beings to endure, to overcome, and to live once again.

WILLIAM B. HELMREICH, PH.D.

# Acknowledgments

One hundred ninety people contributed many hours of their time to participate in the study *What Happened to Those to Whom "Nothing Happened at All,"* the project on which this book is based. I owe the greatest debt of gratitude to the participants, who were willing to entrust to me not only the story of their lives, but also their thoughts and feelings about past events. Many participants, too many for me to thank individually, went to a great deal of trouble to obtain names of potential participants and to send documents and photographs, which proved to be most valuable. I am greatly indebted to Drs. Robert Lifton and William Helmreich, whom I consulted at the inception of the project and who encouraged me with helpful advice. I would like to thank the staff of Insight Books for their sensitive understanding of the purpose of the book. Particular recognition goes to the following: Norma Fox, Executive Editor, for recognizing the potential of the study before the collection of data was even completed; Frank K. Darmstadt, Editor, for his pleasant but firm and reliable shepherding of the manuscript through its various stages of development; Barbara Sonnenschein, Associate Managing Editor, and Herman Makler, Senior Production Editor, for their insightful and sympathetic handling of the manuscript through the production process; and Toby M. Troffkin, whose sensitive copyediting reflected a thorough understanding of the material. Profound appreciation goes to Drs. Marianne Anderson, Alice Kaminsky, Jack Kaminsky, Milton Kornrich, and Rhoda Kornrich, and to Ellen Lubarsky, M.S.W., not only for their astute editorial comments but also for their continued interest and warm support. I am grateful to Dr. Diane

Spielmann who, in her capacity as archivist at the Leo Baeck Institute, most graciously provided information on many different topics. Very special thanks go to Blanche Glaser, who appeared every week and helped with innumerable tasks, such as transcribing tapes and organizing files, thereby freeing hours for my research and writing time. I would like to thank Susan Farkas for taping her relatives. I am indebted to Kurt Fuchel, Bertha Leverton, Dorith Sim, and Dorrit Woolf for acquainting participants of escapee reunions with my study. I also wish to extend my thanks to Professor Michael Mitterauer and to Drs. Helga Embacher and Albert Lichtblau, who are engaged in similar work in Austria and whose writings, communications, and encouragement furthered this project. Grateful appreciation goes to the many friends who extended heartfelt interest and encouragement during the long period of isolation while I was writing this book. Profound gratitude goes to my husband, Martin, who extended the kind of valuable assistance and support he has lent to every one of my activities and interests during the course of our marriage. In this particular project his help ranged from providing perceptive editorial comments and engendering highly fruitful discussions of the issues involved to solving practical problems, such as dealing with a recalcitrant computer. In addition, I greatly appreciate his willingness to accommodate his pattern of living in order to help create the time I needed, time set aside from my professional work, to write this book. I thank all those involved for their recognition that the topic of the escapees was one worthy of their assistance.

Grateful acknowledgment is made to the Memorial Foundation for Jewish Culture for a grant to further this work.

# Contents

Foreword *by William B. Helmreich* . . . . . . . . . . .    vii

Acknowledgments . . . . . . . . . . . . . . . . . . . . . . . . .    ix

Prologue . . . . . . . . . . . . . . . . . . . . . . . . . . . . . . .    1

### Part I • Under Hitler

*Chapter 1*
The Moment Our Lives Stood Still . . . . . . . . . . .    13

*Chapter 2*
The Tightening of the Noose . . . . . . . . . . . . . . .    33

*Chapter 3*
Getting Out: The Obstacles . . . . . . . . . . . . . . . .    45

*Chapter 4*
The Sagas of Kurt and Franz . . . . . . . . . . . . . . .    53

*Chapter 5*
Getting In: The Neighboring Cell ............ 71

*Chapter 6*
Leaving: Three Vignettes ................... 89

*Chapter 7*
Kristallnacht: The Beginning of the End ....... 95

*Chapter 8*
Getting There ........................... 109

*Chapter 9*
Three Odysseys .......................... 113

*Chapter 10*
Die Kinder .............................. 127

*Chapter 11*
They Traveled through the Night ............ 139

*Chapter 12*
And Most of All—Smiles! .................. 157

## Part II • Before Hitler

*Chapter 13*
The Nest ................................ 177

**Contents** **xiii**

*Chapter 14*
A Certain Style ........................... 185

*Chapter 15*
Reality or Illusion? ........................ 195


## Part III • The Years of Resettlement

*Chapter 16*
A Placement, Not a Home .................. 207

*Chapter 17*
So Many Reasons ......................... 221

*Chapter 18*
Fragments of the Children's Lives ............ 237

*Chapter 19*
A Meeting of Minds and Hearts ............. 271

*Chapter 20*
The Long Way Home ...................... 289

*Chapter 21*
Not Yet ................................. 297

*Chapter 22*
Internment .............................. 309

*Chapter 23*
Prison, Italian-Style ......................... 331

*Chapter 24*
The Road Upward ............................ 341

*Chapter 25*
The Farmer and the Taxidermist ............. 353

*Chapter 26*
The Energy of Youth ....................... 359

## Part IV • The Emotional Aftermath

*Chapter 27*
Don't Cry, Grandma! ....................... 375

*Chapter 28*
The Assimilated Outsider ................... 389

*Chapter 29*
I Am Glad Hitler Missed One ............... 401

Epitaph: In Memoriam ...................... 415

"Make Believe," *by Gerda Mayer* ............. 417

The Respondents .......................... 419

# Contents

Questionnaire . . . . . . . . . . . . . . . . . . . . . . . . . . . . . 423

References . . . . . . . . . . . . . . . . . . . . . . . . . . . . . . . 431

Index . . . . . . . . . . . . . . . . . . . . . . . . . . . . . . . . . 435

# Prologue

On a summer's day three years ago, sitting at a dinner table in a pleasant house in a small town in England, my cousin talked about the fate of his parents, my aunt and uncle. His father had died in Theresienstadt concentration camp, and his mother—as well as his wife's mother, father, and brother—had perished in Auschwitz. My thoughts wandered to my parents, my sister, my cousins, and myself. "How lucky we were," I reflected, "We escaped from the Holocaust. Nothing happened to us at all."

"Nothing happened" in my mind referred to the fact that my family was able to overcome enormous obstacles, leave Austria after the Nazi takeover, and later resettle in New York. How could our struggle, however harrowing, be compared to starving in a ghetto or arriving in Sobibór in cattle cars and being gassed within forty minutes. Most people who, like me, had been able to escape (I will refer to them as "escapees") adopted a similar attitude. In comparison to camp survivors, the escapees felt that "nothing had happened" to them.

This time, however, I began to think more deeply about the fate of the escapees, those thousands of Jews who were displaced in a migratory wave that changed the constellation of the population they left and the one they joined. I recalled the frantic efforts my parents made to save us—the planning, the scheming, the wrenching goodbyes. I recalled the many years before life took on a semblance of normalcy. I began to wonder about my fellow escapees. How had they managed to flee Hitler? Where did they go after they left the Third Reich? Were they affected in their outlook? Were there still emotional consequences today?

Though there are individual biographies, I found little emphasis on studies of groups of escapees or on the emotional consequences of their experience. Researchers had wisely focused on camp and ghetto survivors because their suffering was infinitely greater and their impact on Jewish history far more important than the story of the escapees. And yet the story of the escapees is one that needs telling. The story is part of the Hitler legacy.

I resolved to collect the stories of those people who were able to escape before the Final Solution started. I titled the study "What Happened to Those to Whom 'Nothing Happened at All.'" Escapees instantly recognized that designation as referring to their self-characterization. The study included those who were able to flee from a Nazi-occupied country, before or shortly after World War II started, to a country of relative safety. Relative safety meant that the dangers escapees encountered there were no greater than those threatening their fellow citizens, dangers such as being in the army, being bombed, or suffering food shortages. Under this definition, those escapees who fled Poland and spent their war years in Russia were not included since many, owing to a number of circumstances (such as being interned in Russian labor camps), did not live in relative safety.

Two important aspects of the study had to be considered at the start: how the information was to be obtained and how the potential participants were to be reached. Since I wanted to contact escapees beyond my immediate area, the interview would have to be conducted by mail. For this purpose I designed a questionnaire consisting of four pages of essay-type questions that could be answered either briefly or in great detail. The questionnaire covered the escapees' lives before and under Hitler, the escape, the years of resettlement, and the emotional aftermath.

To acquire volunteers I used, in the main, the "snowball method," starting with a handful of people and asking them to supply the names of possible respondents. I also placed some announcements of the study at a few escapee reunions. In addition, I "buttonholed" people who, I thought, might become respondents. For example, I struck up a conversation with a swimmer who used the breaststroke, as I assumed she might be European since Americans usually swim the crawl. It turned out that she was indeed an escapee, and she consented to participate in the study. While some people in the study have made outstanding achievements in their fields, I had no desire to contact famous immigrants. On the contrary, I was more interested in how people from various walks of life had dealt with the events. Marty (1991), reviewing *News from the Land of Freedom*, a book about German immigrants, stresses the importance of describing the lives of the not so well-known: "[These descriptions] provide glimpses of the sufferings and occasional triumphs that characterize day-to-day existence, and thus illuminate human existence in ways that special contribution literature seldom can do" (p. 2). It is this day-to-day existence that I wanted to portray.

My procedure was as follows: After receiving the name of a potential participant, I telephoned the person before mailing the questionnaire and explained the purpose of the study; when contacts were solely by mail, the questionnaire was preceded by a detailed description of the study's purpose. The respondents' replies to the questionnaire varied from brief to voluminous. Some correspondents sent additional relevant material: documents, photographs, and old letters, as well as stories and poems they had previously written. After receiving a completed questionnaire, I usually replied with a detailed letter, commenting on the respondent's experiences, asking further questions, and sharing some of my experiences, when appropriate. Frequently, letters sent by escapees following the return of their completed questionnaires yielded more important details than their original responses. This probably was due to their increasing trust that their material would be treated with respect.

The initial concern, whether sufficient escapees would be willing to contribute the necessary time to complete the questionnaire, proved groundless. Those contacted proved eager to tell their story. For example, a week after a circular of mine was placed at a reunion of escapees in England, I received twenty requests for participation from England, Massachusetts, Illinois, California, Delaware, Florida, and Canada, and within three weeks fifty more arrived. One completed questionnaire, hastily penned on yellow legal paper, was sent back almost by return mail. Its author explained that the questionnaire had such an emotional impact on him that he could not wait to get to his typewriter and felt compelled to respond immediately as memories came flooding back. Many of the people contacted assumed spontaneous responsibility to further the project. Several escapees sent photocopies of the questionnaire to escapee friends. Someone, I do not know whom, placed an announcement of the project in an Australian newspaper. Some escapees worried that a delay in their response might preclude their participation. One writer inquired anxiously whether waiting for a broken arm to heal would interfere with ultimate acceptance of his reply. Age did not necessarily create a barrier to participating; "I am willing and glad to answer your questionnaire, but being 91 now, I have to go slow and cannot do too much in one day. But I hope to be able to send my detailed answer in about a fortnight," wrote one woman.

I discovered that the study struck a timely chord. Apparently, a number of escapees had already started or had been planning to pen some notes about their life; The questionnaire frequently provided them with additional impetus and structure. A respondent noted, "I am grateful for your prompting because in essence [in replying to your questionnaire] I have now prepared an outline for a personal history. I welcome therefore these or any other future questions or comments you might have." For others, their responses to the questionnaire became a chronicle to pass to family and friends: "My daughter had known much of my story, but it had never been presented to her in its entirety. Her husband was quite shaken by it all. My granddaughter, for whom it was new, read it all at once even though she is not what is called a 'reader.' My grandson totally empathized with it. But many other people read it also, and I was moved by the waves of warmth which came toward me after they had read it." Chronicling past events frequently had a beneficial effect on the respondent. One commented, "I did not mind answering your questions. In fact, I found them very stimulating. They helped me face up to some things I have not wanted to look at before." Some writers found it quite easy to let memories flow. One woman noted that the information had been sitting in her mind as in a computer and had been waiting for a "printout." Others, while finding it emotionally draining, welcomed the task because it "cleared the mind of past hang-ups."

Particularly touching was the appreciation the escapees expressed for my undertaking the study. Commented one correspondent: "I want you to know how much I admire you for the enormous task you have set before you. In the end you will derive great satisfaction to speak out on behalf of the silent minority in memory of the six million Jews lost in the Holocaust." One man suggested, as did others, that I call him by his first name because after our lengthy correspondence he now considers me *mishpoche* (Yiddish word for family). Several respondents mentioned that they were gratified that I shared some personal memories with them; the fact that I myself am an escapee certainly contributed to the feeling of rapport.

Several people, in declining to participate, wrote that involvement would be too emotionally draining. For example: "It is with regret to notify you that my wife and I are unable to respond. Too many bad memories surface and subsequently cause a slight depressive mood swing. Therefore, we would like to add that we are sorry that we react so sensitively. Thank you and best wishes." And: "I am very sorry. The memories could crack my heart wide open. But thanking you for choosing me for your very worthwhile project." Only one response was received that was opposed on the ideological grounds that energies should be used to pursue current issues. And one person wrote from South America saying he would only participate if he could be assured of the profits of a movie version!

When I began the study, I assumed that I would follow the usual research method of asking all the participants identical questions that would subsequently be analyzed in order to make statistical comparisons. But as soon as I began corresponding with the participants, I realized that such a method would not fit my purpose. I did not wish to make statistical comparisons of this group with any other group of escapees nor to obtain numerical indices to determine "average" behavior patterns. I do not assume that this group of escapees is necessarily typical of any other group. I view the history of the escapees as if it were an enormous picture cut into jigsaw-like pieces. Each person's story, telling of unique or even monstrous calamities, is a small but important part of the total. Every story contributes to a different aspect of the whole picture, which will never be complete. I believed my task—or, perhaps, my mission—was to give a sequential account of the escapees' experiences and their consequences, as seen through their own eyes, and, while organizing the different stories, to examine them for both unique and communal aspects.

It is noteworthy that other researchers in this area have proceeded in a similar manner. Des Pres (1976), in his study of life in the death camps, wrote the following: "I gradually came to see that I would have to stay within the survivor's own perspective. This will perhaps bother the historian, with his distrust of personal evidence; but radical suffering transcends relativity, and when one survivor's account of an event or circumstance is repeated in exactly the same way as dozens of other survivors, . . . from different nations and cultures, then one comes to trust the validity of such reports, and even to question rare departures from the general view. I had little choice, therefore, but to proceed by a dense use of quotations, by constant reference to examples and stories. . . . This book thus becomes a compilation of actual testimony—the voices of many men and women gathered to a critical mass of rage and sorrow and truth. My job has been to provide a medium through which these scattered voices might issue in one statement" (p. vi). Berghan (1984), who conducted a study exploring attitudes and feelings of German Jewish refugees in England, decided to forgo traditional research methods because she saw the need for a more flexible approach. Her stress was on discovering not only typicality but also diversity. She thought it important to focus on individual cases because "an individual caught up in a specific situation is often the key to the better understanding of the generic" (pp. 2–3).

How was the plethora of material I had gathered to be handled? My purpose was to glean material from the records that would be representative of this group of escapees as well as illustrative of the wide variety of experiences. Therefore, every occurrence in this book is based on a search of every record for references to such experiences. For example, when writing about a particular event or emotional reaction, I culled each record and entered the respondent's observation regarding this experience into the computer. For a single event—for example, leaving one's parents—I might collect up to seventy-five pages of information. This information was then organized into categories denoting which experiences were representative of the group and which were unique; selections were then drawn for illustrative quotations or paraphrasing. This process was then repeated for the next event or attitude described. Thus, each of the 190 records was gone over with a fine-tooth comb over and over again.

As a rule, the researcher does not participate as a subject and strives to remain entirely objective. After some very serious thought, I decided to discard this approach. Being an escapee made me a piece of the large picture. As a result, I felt it appropriate to convey some of my own experiences and memories. My personal remarks can be easily identified: I always call attention to the fact that they pertain to me; in addition, they are differentiated from those of the other escapees by appearing without quotation marks.

Preliminary contact was made with 306 persons. The material in this book is based on the accounts of the 190 (62%) who responded to the questionnaire, an unusually high percentage considering the usual 25% response to mail questionnaires and the length of the questionnaire. Of the 38% who did not wish to participate, 16% were followed up. In most cases, cogent explanations were offered for the refusals, such as illness or writing about the experiences for their own use. The remaining 22% were not followed up because of deadline considerations. For the 190 participants, female and male percentages are 58% and 42%, respectively. Current residences of the 190 respondents include Australia, Austria, Canada, England, Germany, Italy, Israel, New Zealand, Scotland, and the United States, with the highest proportion of respondents living in the United States and England. Within the United States, replies were received from residents of fourteen different states. Respondents escaped from Hitler from the following countries: Austria, Belgium, Czechoslovakia, Germany, Italy, Yugoslavia, Holland, Hungary, Poland, and Romania. Dates of leaving the Third Reich ranged from 1933 to 1942, the bulk of the population leaving in 1938 and 1939, with age at leaving ranging from childhood to middle age. (Our oldest respondent, recently deceased, was 95 years of age.) There were 173 persons who responded in detail to the questionnaire; 57 of this group also sent personal writings, printed articles, photos, documents, and poems dealing with their lives, and twenty-three participants recorded their experiences on audiotape. Seventeen did not respond to the questionnaire directly but sent material that related to themselves and to the content of the study, such as personal articles, writings, and comments.

Since this book is based on the escapees' recollections, the question may arise whether memory can be relied on after an interlude of fifty years. Validity is lent to the accounts by the consistency found from report to report. While each story has unusual and unique features, there is overlap in terms of the events recalled, problems encountered, and emotions experienced. In addition, escapees' reports in other studies and biographies (e.g., Berghan, 1984) are congruent with those presented in this book. It can hardly be surprising that events of such magnitude are not easily forgotten but linger, probably forever. In addition, it is important to remember that the purpose of this study is to recount the events as seen through the eyes of those who experienced them. The memories these escapees were left with were the ones that affected them for the rest of their lives.

One of the respondents summarized the purpose of this study in a most perceptive manner: "[The purpose of your book] is the closest to how I feel that education and historians should come to terms with this dark period of European history. It is not sufficient to study only the exodus and the experiences and feelings during the war of those who escaped. It is necessary to take individual case histories right to the present. Anything and everything which has happened to a person escaping as a child from Hitler Germany is directly relevant to a study of the effects on persons uprooted from countries which came under Hitler's power. This applies equally to all experiences and behavior of the persons concerned throughout the entire fifty years regardless of whether this behavior appears to be normal and thus "superficially irrelevant" or directly traumatic and thus "superficially relevant." This is so because the early experiences of uprooting set a course of events going which would certainly have been very different if that experience had not been."

I have listed the names of those who contributed (six participants requested pseudonyms). A numbered list of the full names of respondents is located in the back of the book. Numbered superscripts in the text refer the reader to the appropriate respondents. When not using direct quotations, I made every effort to paraphrase the respondent's words. It must not be assumed, because of the eloquence of many of the responses, that only people with a writing gift replied. Very frequently, a short phrase expressed a reaction quite as clearly and insightfully as an extended one by a more skilled writer. If no attribution is made to a quote, it is for one of two reasons: to grant a participant's request for anonymity or to extend anonymity to those whose quotes appear in the chapters that deal with long-range emotional consequences, sections for which privacy might be the right course.

Being a psychologist and not a historian, I have added only enough historical background to help readers orient themselves to the occurrences at the time. While a number of sources have been used for background material, the following books were most heavily relied on: for the Third Reich, William L. Shirer's *The Rise and Fall of the Third Reich* (1962) and Lily Bader's eyewitness account from her unpublished autobiography, *One Life Is Not Enough* (1956); for the refugee experience of Shanghai, David Kranzler's *The History of the Jewish Refugee Community in Shanghai* (1971); and for the internee experience, Connery Chappell's *Island of Barbed Wire*, Miriam Kochan's *Britain's Internees in the Second World War* (1983), and Cyril Pearl's *The Dunera Scandal* (1990).

Previously published material by two contributors is reprinted in this book with their kind permission: "The Gold Watch," by George Jellinek (copyright 1987 by the New York Times Company), and two poems by Gerda Mayer: "All the Leaves Have Lost Their Trees" and "Make Believe" (1988), copyrights of both poems by Gerda Mayer. Stella Hershan's contribution was subsequently published as "Memoir of Nazi Austria and the Jewish Refugee Experience in America" in the *American Jewish Archive* (1991).

In the introduction to the project sent to potential participants, I included two quotations since they served as an inspiration to me and would also, I hoped, serve as such for others. In many ways they encompass the reason for this book. The first is from Primo Levi's essay "Shame" (1988): "We, the survivors, are not the true witnesses. . . . We survivors are not only exiguous but also an anomalous minority; we are those who by their prevarications or abilities or good luck did not touch bottom. Those who did so, those who saw the Gorgon, have not returned to tell about it. We speak in their stead by proxy. I could not say whether we did or do so out of a kind of moral obligation toward those who were silenced or in order to free ourselves of their memory; certainly we do it because of a strong and durable impulse." (p. 102)

The second is from Betty Hillesum's *An Interrupted Life* (1983), written at age twenty-nine in Holland before her deportation to Auschwitz: "And I shall wield this slender fountain pen as if it were a hammer and my words will have to be so many hammer strokes with which to beat out the story of our fate and of a piece of history as it is and never was before."

In a sense, the story told here represents, if only in part, what at least some concentration camp victims *did* experience before their conveyance to death and what they *might* have experienced in migration and resettlement had not the final agony supervened, for so many of the Holocaust victims were as resourceful, as active, as energetic, and as desperate as those who got away. They differed in only one respect—calamitous chance.

*Part I*

# UNDER  HITLER

## Chapter 1

# The Moment Our Lives Stood Still

In the morning there was hope. By the evening all was despair. The Jewish population of Austria knew full well that tragedy had befallen them. The cancellation of the plebiscite was the moment hope ended.

The plebiscite had been called for March 13, 1938, by Kurt Schuschnigg, chancellor and head of the ruling party of Austria. Its purpose was to establish once and for all whether, as Hitler claimed, the Austrians truly wanted to be annexed by the Germans. For years the Nazis in Germany had propagandized the idea that all Germans should belong to one Reich and one Reich only—the Greater German Reich. The Nazis held that Austria should become a part of Germany and partake in the quest for dominance over less pure races.

Schuschnigg was a dictator, though a benign one. True, there was no freedom of the press or of speech. On the other hand, there was no real danger to anyone; there were no midnight arrests, no cruel lengthy prison terms, no institutionalized anti-Semitism. Nor was there great fear. Schuschnigg's was the entrenched party, the Christian Democrats. Its characteristics were conservatism and Catholicism. Schuschnigg's problem was that a large percentage of the country did not support him. For example, there were the Social Democrats, known as the "Sozis." Workers, liberals, and those for whom Catholicism was not the primary or overriding point of view had belonged to this party. But the Social Democrats had been defeated in an uprising in 1934. They had been ousted by the Christian Democrats, who had even fired their guns into the large apartment complexes in which many Social Democrats lived. They had never forgiven the Christian Democrats. Schuschnigg could not count on support from the Sozis, whose members were seething with anger against him.

Then there were the *Illegalen*, who numbered in the thousands. They were the secret Nazi sympathizers and activists, and they covered a wide spectrum. Some were supporters of Hitler but not engaged in illegal action; enchanted by the image of power, straining at the idea of becoming once again a mighty nation, they supported Hitler in word and spirit. There were also those who were merely hedging their bets, opportunists who wanted to be aligned with whatever side would emerge the stronger. Finally, there were Nazi party members who had been working illegally—planting bombs, infiltrating organizations, and collecting lists of supporters and enemies; they were ready for the great day, convinced that ultimately Hitler would control Austria. That day had almost come on July 25, 1934, when the Nazis invaded the chancellory and shot Engelbert Dollfuss, then chancellor and leader of the Christian Democrats. They let Dollfuss bleed to death on the floor of the Chancellory. But the putsch failed, and Schuschnigg became chancellor. No wonder he hated the *Illegalen*.

So there he was, with a divided Austria. Schuschnigg hated the Nazis and had no love for the Sozis. The Sozis also hated the Nazis. Only the Christian Democrats supported Schuschnigg. Nonetheless, the Jewish population was not overly worried. They believed that most people wanted Austria to remain an independent country, that they were surely too smart to abandon their freedom to the German Reich. And, anyway, the Austrians were known for their easygoing ways; they were notorious for their *Schlamperei*, their lack of organization and purposefulness. They could never stand the Prussians with their obsessive need for structure, their militarism, and even their harsh pronunciation of the language.

To prove to Hitler that the Austrians wished to remain free, Schuschnigg called for a plebiscite: Vote yes and Austria stays independent; vote no and Austria becomes part of Germany. At that dangerous moment, when there was the threat of a Nazi takeover, the

Socialists finally joined ranks with the Christian Democrats. The rift between the two parties was papered over.

March 11, 1938, dawned bright, warm, and windy. The city of Vienna was feverish with excitement and anticipation; the atmosphere was charged to the exploding point. The Jewish population was anxious yet confident; they felt they had reason for optimism. The anti-Hitler forces appeared to be carrying the day. All day long, trucks loaded with young people who favored keeping Austria independent had driven up and down the city streets. They tossed leaflets to the passersby, urging them to vote yes to Austria's independence. The leaflets covered the streets of Vienna like snow. All through the day the wind lifted them high into the air, dropped them, and lifted them again, as if the very air was jubilant over the strength the country was finally exhibiting. Every heart rejoiced at the solidarity shown in the face of the Nazi menace.

Of course, the antagonism between the political parties was still in evidence. Its display filled a woman, a directress of a girl's boarding school, with acute anxiety (Bader, 1956). She later recorded her impressions: "The main scene for the battle between the two parties was one of Vienna's main thoroughfares, the Kärntnerstrasse. On one side of the narrow street the government supporters were massed, waving Austria's red-white-red flags and shouting their slogan: 'Red-White-Red, until we are dead.' The Nazis, armed with sticks and brazenly displaying swastikas, yelled from across the street: 'Ein Volk, ein Reich, ein Führer!' [One people, one state, one leader] Fists were shaken, stones were thrown, police were barely able to keep the two groups separated. Trucks carrying young people shouting government slogans raced through the streets, generating a feverish atmosphere" (p. 272).

But such confrontations seemed to be rare. There were fewer Nazi sympathizers on the street than had been expected. All the anti-Nazis—whose ranks included the Jewish population, the Sozis, and those religious Catholics who disliked Hitler for his antireligious views—hoped that the diminished presence of Hitler's followers indicated an attitude of resignation on their part. Then, suddenly, a rumor, a dreadful, fear-arousing, almost terrifying rumor: Hitler, possibly worried that too many Austrians might vote yes, opting for independence, had ordered the plebiscite called off. Of course, he was not in an official position to do so. He was the head of a foreign government. But his power was so great that Schuschnigg did not dare oppose him. It was clear what was likely to follow; Hitler would almost certainly march into Austria. The anti-Nazis dragged themselves home to safety to listen to the radio; all waited in a state of agonized tension.

The state of suspense heightened the directress's anxiety to a pitch (Bader, 1956). Her recollections continue: "The end to our uncertainty came at seven o'clock, when the waltzes and light cocktail music being played was suddenly interrupted. Schuschnigg, in a broken voice, hardly concealing his tears, was broadcasting that he was yielding to force. His last words, 'God save Austria,' were followed by shuffling and by confused sounds, which made it clear to us that Schuschnigg's speech had been terminated by force. The Anschluss, Hitler's annexation of Austria, was about to take place. We were stunned. With tears in our eyes, hardly able to believe what we were hearing, we had listened to Schuschnigg's farewell. Sobbing, we clung to each other. What should we do now? What decisions should we make? At that moment, we remembered what a friend had told us a few months ago. She was married to a diplomat who for the last few years had been ambassador to Berlin. She spoke in a whisper after she made sure that she would not be overheard. 'I want to give you warning. Should Nazism ever get hold of Austria, don't delude yourself that you could possibly live under it. The only thing to do is to flee. Don't hesitate, flee at once!'" (p. 273)

Yet the directress did not flee that night. The girls who attended the boarding school were mostly Jewish and came from all over Europe. She felt she could not abandon them. She decided to wait until they could be sent home or until their parents came to fetch them. All borders were soon closed, and escape was no longer possible. "So we stayed on," she recalled, "with the terrible feeling that a horrible monster was holding us by our throats, a monster whose strength and ferocity we only vaguely guessed at. The monster as yet was shapeless, its fangs only dimly seen" (p. 275).

But its shape would become clearer every hour and every day. Terror and destruction started that very night. The directress's husband, a physician, was called to a dying patient. He felt duty bound to set out through the danger-filled night. While waiting for death, which was slow in coming, the doctor stood at the window of the sickroom and looked out into the dark of the night. The black of the street matched the somberness of his thoughts. Later he told his wife what he had witnessed: "Suddenly lights in the windows of a big Jewish store across the street were flaring up. Trucks had come to a stop in front of it. Soldiers in German uniforms, bayonets at the ready, rushed out. The doors of the store were broken down, the huge window panes crushed under the blows of the rifle butts. Howling and yelling soldiers swarmed all over the place. Soon they carried out bolts of linen, silken blankets, downy counterpanes. Big bundles were thrown into the receiving hands of soldiers on the trucks. The whole affair did not last longer than ten minutes. Trucks and soldiers disappeared" (Bader, 1956, p. 274). Had not the first dawn shown the scattered goods and upturned counters in the store, the doctor might have thought it all a bad dream. It was no dream. The shapeless monster was taking shape.

The next day dawned on a jubilant Austria. It seemed as if almost every Austrian was wearing a small swastika in his lapel, indicating that he had been an *Illegaler*. Hordes of Austrians appeared in Nazi uniforms, or at least with arm bands displaying swastikas, which had been in closets, waiting for just this occasion. While the Germans were being welcomed with open arms and the radio spewed forth endless speeches by Hitler and his cohorts, most Jews were quite aware that some dreadful fate had befallen them. So was the directress: "It was as if a sorcerer had touched our world with his poisoning wand. Everything around us, as familiar as our own skin, had acquired hostile faces. There was the elderly and rotund policeman, whom I had seen every day on my way from home. Today he wore a swastika and was escorted by an SA trooper. The latter was easily recognizable as such, not only by his brown shirt, high boots, military cap, and red swastika but also by his brutal hooligan exterior" (p. 275). There seemed to be endless rallies and street scenes of hysterical welcome. The streets were filled with people marching and waving flags emblazoned with swastikas. Each flag was a potential threat to the directress, who felt that the very houses, in their display of swastikas (which apparently had been at the ready), showed they had become her enemies.

It was not only the adults who were aware that all of life had suddenly undergone a metamorphosis. The changes were so stark that even youngsters had full awareness of what was taking place. As a fourteen-year-old crisscrossing the city to make deliveries for his mother's grocery store, Meir[134] had ample opportunity to watch events as they were unfolding: "March 12 was a clear, sunny morning when we heard the distant hum of airplanes which very soon turned into a terrifying, ear-deafening roar of 300 German planes with swastikas. They swept low over the roofs of Vienna and covered the streets with tons of leaflets. I picked one up. 'The Führer and the German National Socialist Government greet the German City of Vienna.' Every window was draped with the red-white-red Austrian flag. Sewn on to the flags were improvised swastikas, some barely covering the crooked cross of Schuschnigg's party. On every square flagpoles had been erected. Flags and more flags, a sea of blood-red color, fluttering in the wind in the clear sunshine. Not a cloud in the sky. The radio blared speeches by Hitler, Goering, and Goebbels, which were interspersed with martial music. Over the air came the ecstatic shouts of the masses. Always the nerve-wracking: '*Sieg Heil, Deutschland erwache, Jude verrecke!*'" [Victory, hail, Germany awake, Jews croak!]

"On the way home I made a detour to get a look at the place where Hitler was to enter Vienna the next day. The whole neighborhood, once so familiar, seemed unrecognizable. An ocean of flags, wooden gilded eagles each about five meters high and festooned with golden swastikas, had been erected. Garlands of greenery had been strung along every street. Hundreds of men bustling with feverish activity were all working frantically. Twenty-four hours had not passed and yet all of life had become radically different. Yesterday all had been normal. Today everyone was preparing Hitler's triumphal entry. There was to be a giant rally on the Heldenplatz [a magnificent plaza called the Plaza of Heroes]. Hitler was going to make one of his decisive speeches. Continuing on my way home, I saw the first looted and burned-out Jewish shops, an awful sight. Just before turning into my street I saw the first German soldiers.

"Next day I walked to Mariahilferstrasse to watch Hitler's entry into Vienna. I stood among a huge mass of people bellowing slogans and waiting for Hitler with shiny eyes. Leaders were giving orders and instructions [on] when and how to shout in unison. There certainly was no need to encourage this exuberant and jubilant mass of humanity. Literally chiming in were the church bells, which rang out their salute to the celebrating Viennese. Suddenly, an unbelievable roar: 'Here he comes!' And here he was, Hitler, standing upright in an open car, raising his right arm to shoulder level. He was not smiling but stared straight ahead. He passed quickly and was gone. The climax came when Cardinal Innitzer, his arm raised in the Hitler salute, received Hitler on the steps of St. Stephen's Cathedral [Vienna's famous landmark]."

Meir reached the store before his mother. "Mother had passed Jewish shops which had been smashed, looted, and burned. Vast crowds were roaming the streets, screaming their blood-curdling *Jude verrecke!* Her customers turned their heads away so as not to have to greet her. She was forced to put a sign in the window saying, 'This is a Jewish shop.'"

From the very first day on, everyday life was beset by danger. Arrests started immediately. It was easy for the Nazis to trap Jews; they had long prepared for this day. For one thing, the Jewish Culture Community, whose membership included almost all of Vienna's Jews, had always kept a list of Jewish residences. The Nazis had acquired these lists and therefore could easily locate the Jews they wanted to capture first. Among those they wanted first were the wealthy. In the years before the Anschluss the *Illegalen*, no slackers, had been busily researching their Jewish neighbors' financial status; this secret work had come to light in 1936 (John, 1990). Some workers laboring in a house near Kirtzendorf accidentally came across a card file that listed in detail the fortunes of all the Jews living in the area. This kind of research proved to be a gold mine after the Anschluss, enabling the Nazis to easily locate well-to-do Jews.

How quickly people's fortunes would diverge, how drastically different their fates were to be, became evident on the very first day. At the conclusion of Schuschnigg's speech an eighty-year-old man[141] took a taxi to the train station and boarded the 9:35 for Zurich and safety. The owner[172] of a large chain of shoe stores also tried to board a train to Zurich the same night. At the station he was arrested and later taken to Dachau concentration camp. His wife jumped out of a window and was killed instantly. At her funeral the Gestapo were present, intending to arrest her son, but he disappointed them by not appearing at his mother's funeral.

All those who had been politically prominent in anti-Nazi activities before the Anschluss—as well as members of the press, always a threat to a dictatorship—were immediately at risk. A woman[4] recalled the havoc wreaked on her family: "My father, a journalist, was arrested immediately when Hitler entered Austria. It was terrible. My mother was recovering from a major operation at the time. The phone rang and she was told that my father was under arrest. We spent most of the night burning anything incriminating, such as newspaper cuttings."

Such recollections are by no means rare since arrests were made for innumerable reasons and were frequently engineered by those whose mouths had long watered for booty. Shortly after the Anschluss, Anitta,[43] a fourteen-year-old daughter of an artist, found herself faced by SS men, guns at the ready, who ordered her family to vacate their lovely apartment within three days; most likely a neighbor had coveted it for some time. Another family's ruin, recalled by the daughter,[152] came as quickly and was engineered by the family's customers: "Nazis who had been former customers of my father's looted our flat and evicted us. Then they looted my father's store and closed it down. They arrested my father, and we had no word where they took him. He returned three days later minus front teeth and with black and blue bruises over his body."

Arrests could be precipitated by a careless comment. The father[106] of a young family lived in a small village where he and other regulars frequented the local inn. He made a prophetic but unwise remark: "The Pharaoh was bad to the Jews, and the Jews are still around. The same will be with Hitler." Ten minutes later they came for him. He landed in Buchenwald concentration camp but did get out and managed to reach Shanghai. After the war he returned to Austria. His wife and their two-year-old boy had perished in the camps.

Arrests were arbitrary. The SA went on continual fishing trips—on trams, Jewish places of business, and outside consulates where Jews were standing in line. Stella,[72] while out walking, saw a truck crowded with men dressed in coats and hats. Packed like sardines, they were standing in the swaying vehicle, terror on their faces. The truck swerved around a corner in the direction of the Gestapo headquarters.

Non-Jews wore small swastikas in their lapels. With bare lapels Jews could be easily recognized. Some Jewish men wore medals from World War I, hoping that this would protect them from arrest. It did not. Families suffered acute apprehension whenever members had to leave the house. If they did not return, apprehension turned into well-founded fear. Eighteen-year-old Nelly[73] suspected that her elderly father had been rounded up. For two days the family waited with mounting dread. When he finally returned, he was a physical wreck. He had been thrown into a lorry laden with cattle carcasses and was forced to lie on top of the bones while being beaten. His shattered appearance on his return remains in his daughter's memory. Since the fear of being rounded up was constant, men fitting the stereotype of a Jew—long nose or dark complexion— tried to avoid leaving their homes.[42] The business of the day, trying to find a way to leave the country, had to be left to someone in the family with a less Semitic look.

Being viciously beaten during roundups was not the worst. "A young man of twenty vanished from the street. The family searched for traces of him. They went from one police station to the next. They contacted every one of influence they knew. But the son's name did not appear on any list. He had simply vanished. Some days later a telegram arrived from Buchenwald: 'Your son has been shot while trying to escape. By sending 2.50 marks an urn containing his ashes will be forwarded to you'" (Bader, 1956, p. 275).

Of course, arrests could be instigated by anyone who hoped to become a citizen in good standing with the Nazi party. All that had to be done was call Gestapo headquarters and convey a suspicion, any suspicion, of illegal activities. The directress's friends were denounced in this manner. A few women (among them the daughter of the famous conductor Bruno Walter) had congregated in a private home. Suddenly the bell rang furiously. Six Gestapo men, with pistols drawn, burst into the apartment. They searched the house, arrested the whole party, and herded them onto trucks waiting in the street. Two husbands had arrived at the same time as the Gestapo. Seeing their wives arrested, they pleaded with the Gestapo agents to be taken instead. The women were released, but the two men, caught by the merest chance, ended up in Dachau. It was later learned that a servant who had recently been dismissed had denounced the gathering as a communist meeting and had summoned the Gestapo.

It was not necessary for the SS or Gestapo to come to a person's home. One could be summoned by telephone and a harsh voice would command the person to appear at the police station. Just such a call was received by a young man, Richard.[145] He quickly called his lawyer and, thus fortified, set out for his police precinct. His anticipation on the way was harrowing: Could this be a routine check? A minor transgression? Richard had been careful to stay within the extensive restrictions of all the new laws. With trepidation he crossed the threshold of Gestapo headquarters. He felt somewhat reassured at having his lawyer, someone to talk for him, by his side. But the lawyer was gruffly sent away. They transported Richard to Dachau, where he stayed until the Czech crisis, when all prisoners were sent to Buchenwald.

Every person had the power to denounce any Jew. Anyone who had at any time borne a grudge or envied a possession became a potential source of danger. Long-forgotten resentments served as springboards for accusations that could lead to death. Accusations could come from anyone—teachers, schoolmates, or neighbors who had been *Illegaler*. A minor disagreement in the beauty parlor occasioned deep worry in a woman:[86] "Several years before the Anschluss, my beautician gave me a permanent and burned my neck. I was angry at him and told him off. After Hitler came, I accidentally ran into him on the street. He hissed at me: 'Now I will show you, I will bring you to the Gestapo.' "

Not every threat was acted upon, but each caused terror and prompted desperate discussions in the family as to what to do. Should the caller be pacified? Ignored? Should one's apartment be abandoned immediately in case the Gestapo was about to arrive? In my own home, I remember a phone call that came repeatedly at night to my father. "Doctor," the voice whispered, "do you still have your car? Doctor, how long do you think you will be able to keep it?" There was no place of safety and comfort—not inside one's home nor outside one's home. The radio blared Hitler's speeches all day and all night. I remember our own maid, Mitzi, insisting that the radio be kept on at its highest volume; thus, Hitler's voice resounded through our apartment at all hours. We did not dare object. The maid became fatter as my mother became thinner. I felt she was draining the life out of my mother.

Each house had a concierge, usually a woman, who could be questioned by the Gestapo. A life could depend on a single word from her. It was her job to open the big front door when residents returned home late at night. If she resented her task, Jewish residents might have to pay with their lives. The SS came to our house and went straight to the concierge. "Which apartments have Jews in them?" Of course, our name was mentioned. But the concierge, a good-natured woman, quickly added: "Yes, but that doctor has nothing. Totally poor." The SS left. They would not have done so at another time, but this time the concierge had saved our lives. Since the concierges knew the comings and goings of all the residents, they served as highly useful tools for the Nazis and could be utilized for sniffing out hidden booty. Many concierges needed little urging and quickly went into partnership with the SS and the Gestapo. A man,[30] twenty years old at the time, recalls: "The concierge was appointed warden. Over the next few days everything in my mother's flat was sealed. End of April the SS came again. The concierge had reported every interaction between herself and the tenants. My mother was slapped for having disobeyed the concierge." In May they came again with Eichmann. He was very polite but, at the same time, threatening. The property of every Jew was important. Eichmann, the bureaucrat, insisted on having everything "correct." He requested that a document be signed that ceded all of the family's property to the German Reich. The shock of these visits would have been worse, had the family known about Eichmann's future role.

One of the tasks of the roaming SA was to pull Jews out of their houses and force them to scrub the streets. This served the multiple functions of clearing the streets of the still-remaining pro-Schuschnigg painted slogan ("Vote yes"), humiliating the Jews, and serving as good entertainment for the populace. The age of the Jews or their acquaintance with those rounding them up was no bar to their being chosen, and even escalated the likelihood of their being dragged into the streets. One woman's[20] grandfather and father were both picked up by former employees to scrub streets as well as toilets. On the sidewalk the Nazis, clubs in hand and accompanied by jeering crowds yelling "*Saujud* [Jew pig]," forced bearded old men to do calisthenics.[72] Meir[134] saw a variation of this entertainment: The Jews were forced to put on their best clothes to scrub streets. The laughing bystanders amused themselves by making sarcastic remarks. One bystander hit one of the scrubbers on his behind and made him fall into the dirty water. Another general practice was to force a Jewish shop owner to paint a huge JUDE on his shop window and then charge him an inflated price for the paint. This game too often ended with sadistic violence. The wounds caused by these experiences sometimes festered for years. A former resident of a small town[94] remembers: "My dignity as a human being was shattered to the core." So deep was the injury that some people could not talk about it for years. A mother[162] who was made to scrub the sidewalk on her hands and knees never told her family about this until many, many years later.

There were many things parents did not want their children to see and hear. In my own case my parents' efforts to protect me started on the night of the Anschluss. After supper my father, looking upset, told my sister and me that the meat had been spoiled and that it was necessary to take an antidote. What he gave us was, in actuality, a sleeping pill. My father, afraid that there would be shooting during the night, wanted to protect us from the noise. But in the long run, protection was not possible. A few days later as I was walking home from school, right across the street, in front of the famous Aida patisserie, I saw a crowd of mocking people and kneeling men and women scrubbing the street. I hurried into the house. I had heard about it. Now I had seen it. That made all the difference.

Street washing was not the only source of entertainment for the masses. There was also a tabloid, *Der Stürmer*, which was posted in protected cages on street corners and was meant to educate and enlighten the public on Nazi doctrine. Its publisher, Julius Streicher, was considered so depraved that even some Nazi officials did not want to be seen associating with him. His tabloid depicted caricatures of Jews with long noses and scrawny, dirty fingers reaching for both money and "*schöne Deutsche Mädchen*" [beautiful German girls]. I remember walking in wide circles around the eager crowds standing in line to inspect each new issue. There was also a weekly newspaper, *Der Schwarze Corps* [The Black Corps], published by the

SS. It reported obscene and pornographic news about Jews who had been arrested. Every Jew, of course, was reported to be a criminal and a rapist. Every picture showed the unshaven faces of the accused, utter fright staring at the camera. Most of the crimes involved "abuse of innocent maids" in service with Jewish families; the articles described the most intimate details of sexual assaults. The accusations were lies. But who dared say so? The public believed them to be true. Didn't the paper say so? Most of the accused were sent to Buchenwald or Dachau for "reeducation." Many did not survive their reeducation.

At the time of the Anschluss, roughly 220,000 Jews lived in Austria, 91 percent of them in Vienna (Jelavich, 1987, p. 232). For years Viennese had gone to school with, worked with, bought from, sold to, befriended, and even married Jews. Yet the public suddenly believed everything it read and could not remember what Jews looked like. It became convinced that Jews looked the way *Der Stürmer* described them; anyone blond and blue-eyed could surely not be Jewish. A woman,[90] in her early teens at the time, recalls: "I looked Aryan. I had blond braids and wore a dirndl [a traditional Austrian costume]. I went into a Jewish store. An SS man questioned why I had done so. I told him that I was Jewish. He took me home, and the maid testified that I was Jewish. It shows how asinine they were. Who at the time would say they were Jewish if they were not? I had my mother cut my hair and never wore a dirndl again."

My blond hair and blue eyes offered me some protection. In spring, soon after the Anschluss, I was walking past the Palace of Justice, with its impressive colonnade of statues, and past the Gothic-looking City Hall. These buildings, together with parks boasting statues and multitudes of flowers, still are part of the Ringstrasse that girdles the inner part of the city. Suddenly, masses of people screaming over and over again "Ein Reich, Ein Volk, Ein Führer!" surged into the broad avenue. A car wound slowly through their midst. A small man was standing upright, his arm raised in a Hitler salute. It was Goebbels, surrounded by a hysterical crowd. As quickly as I could, I crossed the street, afraid that someone in the crowd might identify me as Jewish. Yet at the same time I had a sense of elation. "You fools," I thought, "you think you can tell any Jew by his degenerate appearance. Here I am—blond, blue-eyed, and not far from Goebbels himself—and none of you know." I felt I had out-witted the whole crowd. Nevertheless, not possessing the nature of a gambler, I hurried home.

No desirable personal possession of a Jew was safe any longer. People could deputize themselves to acquire whatever goods pleased their fancy. On the night of the Anschluss Stella[72] hastily jumped into her car to check on her mother's home. A band of young ruffians with brown arm bands and red swastikas stopped her. "Is this your car?" "Yes." "Are you Jewish?" "Yes." "Let's have the keys and get out." The men's faces were like stone. Stella was Jewish. She took the trolley home.

There was no shame or embarrassment in taking from Jews. Meir[134] remembers the agonizing tension aroused by conflicting obligations. He had been helping his mother in her store and, at the same time, trying to make contacts that might help him leave Vienna. All day long he rushed from place to place on his bicycle. "Time was becoming short. One day I had to fetch a document from my flat. I left the bike downstairs. When I returned a few minutes later, it was gone. Just disappeared! I needed that bicycle desperately. In my desperation I rang the bell of the concierge's flat to ask him if he had seen any strangers in the house. When he opened the door, I immediately saw my bike standing in his anteroom. It was out of the question to say anything about it. I just reported to him that my bike was stolen a few minutes ago, and he advised me to go to the police!"

Of course, not everyone grasped so crudely what they coveted. At times, it could be done in a more sophisticated manner, as described in the following scenario:[180] A Jewish lawyer had rented out a garage to another Jewish man. A famous physician and Nazi, accompanied by his elegant wife, appears on the scene. The wife wishes to rent the Jewish lawyer's garage. Why should a Jew be allowed to rent a garage? It is unthinkable. She summons the Jewish lawyer. The maid ushers him in. While waiting in the elegant drawing room, he hears the tinkle of glasses, laughter, and soft talk from the dining room. The genteel company is taking lunch. Presently, the elegant lady appears. She wants the garage. The Jewish lawyer demurs. The elegant lady murmurs something about a new order existing now. She summons her husband, a tall, impressive-looking man in an SS uniform. He inquires in rough tones what the problem might be. The Jewish lawyer, to his own amazement, hears himself saying that the garage is rented to someone else, that he must ask the present owner. He adds, surprising himself, "Do we not live in a land of laws?" The Jewish lawyer is as astounded by his own words as the others are. But there is no Hollywood ending. The elegant lady commandeers the garage. For once, the story does not end there. After Germany's defeat, the impressive-looking doctor in the SS uniform committed suicide.

It seems almost petty to steal cars and garages when whole businesses could be confiscated. The first morning after the Anschluss, Stella's[72] husband went into his office. A man with a swastika was seated there. "Who are you?" he shouted. "The owner," Stella's husband replied. "Not any more!" the man bellowed. "Your Jewish company is being Aryanized. Get out at once!" That was the last time the owner was to enter his office. How was it possible to arrange the confiscation of a business and the installation of a *Kommissar* overnight? Stella explains: "You must realize that the Nazis already had their lists of Jewish businesses and homes. The entire matter seemed to have been prepared long before the Anschluss. I suppose that many of the workers had been *Illegaler* and had gathered all the information."

From the moment of the Anschluss, Jewish businesses began being ransacked, closed, taken over by Aryan partners, or placed in charge of an Aryan *Kommissar*. Being assigned an Aryan partner could spell danger. There were, alas, few Aryan partners who did not wrest the business or its profits away from the original owner. The partner/overseer would "discover" that the original owner had embezzled or committed some other crime. With one stroke the new partner could rid himself of the old owner and acquire a new business. That was an everyday occurrence. Franz[15] describes the demise of his family's business: "Fortunately, my father was quick to see the danger when his 'overseer' suddenly appeared at the end of 1938. He simply turned over the keys to him, and the business was confiscated. But he was still free to go home."

The takeover of businesses could be accomplished with appalling dispatch, even at the front door of an apartment. Alan's[141] family business was run by his mother after his father had been sent to a concentration camp: "The insistent ringing of the doorbell and the hammering on the door at that early hour were too reminiscent of my father's arrest six months earlier. There stood a giant of an SS man in the familiar black uniform, accompanied by a civilian. Barking in military style, the former declared himself to be the newly appointed manager of the business, which he was selling to his companion, who hadn't said a word during the whole proceeding. Would my mother accept an offer of 3000 Reichsmark? My mother replied that she would. The deal was concluded immediately on documents which the two worthies had brought. I recall handing over the keys. The SS man and friend left shortly thereafter. The purchase price was of course a joke. I didn't set foot in the place again for nearly nine years, when I liberated it in 1947."

It was difficult for some Jews to comprehend that henceforth they were to be despised, that working hard or being conscientious would not alter that judgment one bit. A woman[190] describes her brother's misjudgment: "My brother was arrested in May 1938. He had a French visa but did not want to leave Vienna until he had put his law office in good order. He did not want the *Kommissar* to say that the Jew had left his office in a mess. My brother was sent to Dachau for six months and then to Buchenwald for three."

There were two types of *Kommissar*s. Some represented the Nazi Party, and filled the party coffers with ill-gained businesses. Others, however, merely represented themselves. They were referred to as "wild *Kommissar*s." The need to negotiate with them was explained by a lawyer's wife:[142] "The Gestapo took my husband ten days after the Anschluss. They also took our passports—so our basic tool for leaving the country was gone. A Nazi lawyer was interested in taking over my husband's law office. The price for the office was to get our passports back. It took three months." The lawyer who appropriated the office was not a *Kommissar* appointed by the authorities; he merely appointed himself. This kind of behavior made the party leaders furious because it interfered with their ability to fill their own treasury. After all, the Aryanization of stores was not just an expression of anti-Semitism; an equally basic aim was to change the economic conditions of the Third Reich.

At a meeting of Nazi officials in October 1938, Reichsmarschall Goering declared that the economy of the Reich was in a desolate state (Bankier, 1990). Foreign currency reserves and raw materials were limited. The economy had to be turned around by "brutal means." All the old measures to push the Jews out of their businesses had been inefficient. Goering wanted a quicker, more radical solution. The "wild *Kommissars*" irked Goering intensely since they Aryanized stores on their own and kept the profits instead of allowing the booty to go to the party. "Under all circumstances the wild *Kommissars* must be stopped," he complained. "The solution of the Jewish question cannot be allowed to become an insurance system for less capable party members. It must be utilized for compensation to the reliable old party members" (p. 27). Another vexing matter was the incompetence of the new *Kommissars*. They seized Jewish businesses and quickly ran them into the ground. There were about 3500 *Kommissars* who were totally useless. Think what a loss this was for the party treasury.

But never mind. Help was on the way. Until the Anschluss, Austrians had always been famous for their *Schlamperei* [letting things slide], but when it came to commandeering Jewish businesses, their efficiency rose suddenly to unforeseen heights. In fact, the Austrians quickly began to overshadow their German brothers who had always prided themselves on their coolly efficient ways. But Minister Dr. Fischböck, an Austrian, appeared on the scene (Bankier, 1990). He informed Goering how Aryanization would be handled. Fischböck reported: "Out of 17,000 businesses, 12,000 to 14,000 will be closed, and the rest, either through Aryanization or through representatives, will belong to the state." "I must say, that suggestion is *wunderbar*," Goering exclaimed. "In that way, Vienna, which one might call a Jewish capital, will be totally cleaned out by Christmas or by the end of the year" (p. 33).

Fischböck was indeed preparing a happy holiday season for Goering and fellow Austrians. But the purpose of his speedy action was not based solely on anti-Semitism (John, 1990). "The National Socialists' anti-Jewish measures in Austria must be seen as a means of self-enrichment by private citizens" (p. 76). Bankier (1990) writes: "Today, when one studies the requests which arrived at the appropriate offices, one can only wonder at the rapacity of a part of the Viennese population. It appears that it took just a few Schillings, or preferably Reichsmark [German currency], to create convinced and constant National Socialists out of a part of the Viennese population.

Anti-Semitism glowed so intensely that they could not wait for the day that '*Jüdische Volksschädlinge* [Jews harming the German *Volk*]' would have to leave, while leaving their '*Gerschtl* [money]' behind" (p. 28). John (1990) notes that anti-Jewish persecution measures in the year 1939 promised the fulfillment of concrete interests, such as "the elimination of Jewish competition as businessmen, department store owners, lawyers or doctors, as well as the obtaining of apartments and valuable furniture" (p. 79).

In the past Austria had seldom been considered a model for Germany. But as far as the Aryanization of Jewish businesses was considered, Austria served as a shining example to the whole Third Reich: "By the end of 1938, the method of Austrian Aryanization was copied in Germany, an example of the infamous leadership role which Austria played during the period of Aryanization. Dr. Fischböck aroused the unlimited admiration of the leaders of the German economy. His program was presented in an exhibition in the summer of 1939. Every interest group had reached its goal through the Aryanizing campaign. Of 26,000 formerly Jewish enterprises, 5,000 had been Aryanized, and 21,000 forcefully dissolved. Small Aryanizers had enriched themselves. Larger businesses had rid themselves of competition and industries had satisfied their expansion needs. The economy in Berlin was greatly affected. The Austrian Aryanization was a kind of example for the rest of the European countries which later fell to National Socialism" (Bankier, 1990, pp. 35–36). John (1990) emphasizes that whenever the Austrians claim that they were not full partners with the Nazis but were the first country to fall victim to Hitler, it must be remembered that "*the* 'Entjudung *[getting rid of Jews]' in the economy, which took five years in Germany, was carried through in a few months in Austria*" [italics mine] (p. 79).

Under the new circumstances, long-standing non-Jewish business competitors quickly saw their advantage. My own mother's situation was a case in point. She had kept the school going with a skeleton staff for a handful of children who would be leaving by June 1938. A business rival saw the school's demise as an excellent opportunity to acquire its forty well-equipped rooms for nothing. My mother handed the school over without a word. It kept changing hands during the war and was finally taken over by the Austrian government. I saw it many years after the war, still government property. It was shabby and run-down, but I recognized the paintings and the grand piano. No compensation was ever paid. On the actual day of the transaction my mother had been given a receipt. That was important; the Nazis insisted on matters being handled in a "correct" way. As long as there was a signed piece of paper, no one could assume that anything illegal had occurred. A man[30] recollects that to obtain his father's release from a concentration camp the family had to sign a document that ceded all claims his father might have and passed all their properties, except his mother's personal belongings, to the German Reich. In the beginning, the Germans occasionally even went through the farce of handing out receipts after ransacking apartments. Recalls one man:[145] "For the robbery of our apartment while we were absent my parents received a card saying that money had been already taken from us and nothing should happen to them in the future." Of course, that promise was to be broken in the near future.

These curious contradictions in the Nazi mentality were pointed out by one respondent:[190] "My late husband's father was arrested. His wife went to the police, said he was a sick man, and brought his 'kidney X-ray.' He was immediately released." The odd combination of the Nazi's legal and extralegal procedures is commented on by a man whose uncle was arrested and sentenced to two years in prison on a fabricated criminal charge. While the uncle served his sentence in a general prison, he received all the privileges non-Jewish prisoners were granted. As soon as he was discharged from the prison, he was rearrested by the Gestapo, placed under "protective custody," and shipped to Dachau; he died there in 1942.

To Stella[72] the city seemed indifferent to human suffering: "Spring 1938 was gorgeous in Vienna. But the newly painted park benches carried black signs: 'Jews not permitted to sit here.' Signs like that sprang up all over the city—on movie houses, on restaurants, on stores." Franz[15] adds his memories: "The sound of boots on the staircase, the ringing of the doorbell at a neighboring apartment, voices, steps going downstairs and a neighbor never seen again. Though, of course, millions of adults claim they saw and knew nothing, curiously enough I saw, knew, and understood what was going on immediately, though I was only twelve years old."

The directress of the school described the terror (Bader, 1956): "News of arrests and brutalities spread. We asked 'why' stupidly in the first few days when told with whispered voices about the Gestapo making their nightly appearances, usually in the small hours. 'Why?' we puzzled. In the beginning there even were answers of a sort. There was usually a dismissed servant in the background or a dissatisfied employee or a pupil taking revenge on a teacher. Soon we learned not to ask 'why' anymore. The number of people who vanished and were never heard from mounted daily. With every passing day the human tragedy around us multiplied. The number of people we knew equalled the number of tragedies we witnessed. The taking away of all possessions counted as nothing. We had to give up our money, homes, jobs, life works, honors, professions. It meant nothing. In those days we realized what it means to live without the protection of the law. Human beings can adapt to fearful situations. They can live through war and fire and still think life worthwhile. To live without the protection of the law is worse. Nothing is left but the naked fear of the hunted" (pp. 279–281).

There were few Jews in Austria who did not wish to leave. I personally knew only one: a rather pompous teacher who immediately after the Anschluss maintained that she would create a circle of scholars and live in seclusion. We children thought she was mad. A few days later she changed her mind.

## Chapter 2

# The Tightening
# of the Noose

In Austria the Nazis struck swiftly and savagely. Brutal practices were put into effect immediately. Anti-Semitic measures sprang up overnight and throughout the country. In Germany, these developments had been much more insidious, gradual, and spotty. It was both the fortune and misfortune of Austrian Jews that the Nazis showed their true colors immediately. In Germany, it was different, more like the slow tightening of a dreadful noose; It took some experimentation in Germany to hone the Nazis' ability to become the masters of brutality. By the time of the Anschluss, they had benefited from years of practice. With Hitler's appointment as chancellor in Germany in 1933, the process began of whipping up the good burghers to a state of fanaticism to carry out barbarous tasks. It is not that there was a paucity of Germans who were ready to participate, but a great amount of work had yet to be done before the full Nazi terror could be unleashed. It took time to eliminate the Reichstag (Parliament) in order to obtain absolute power. It took time to pass laws that granted the state the right to unlimited house search and the unquestioned authority to confiscate any possessions. It took time to provide for the burning of "un-German" books and the nationalizing of the press. It was not until 1934, after Hindenburg's death, that Hitler took over the German state and the command of the armed forces. However, by then he had prepared one of his most essential tools for governing: the concentration camp, the first of which had been

33

organized in 1933. The apex was not reached until the 1942 Wannsee Conference, which decreed the Final Solution.

Preparatory work had to be done to isolate the Jews. A state-organized boycott of Jewish businesses in April 1933 laid the groundwork. This was quickly followed by the dismissal of Jews from the civil service. After all, how could a Jew work for and be paid by the German state? Those in medical or legal branches of the government were discharged. With the nationalization of the press and the arts, the Jews in those fields were quickly dismissed. In September 1935 the Nuremberg laws were proclaimed; the full power of the state's legal system could now be directed against the Jews. The racial doctrine became well defined. Before, it had been expressed in violent clashes, hysterical speeches, lurid newspaper articles; now it became legal as well as "scientific" law. A plethora of anti-Semitic laws were promulgated. Jews were now ousted from medical, legal, financial, and other professions. Because of their "inferior blood," Jews were forbidden intermarriage with Aryans. But worst of all, Jews were put outside the protection of the law; they were denied access to the courts. This resulted in the Jews becoming subject to the whims of every hooligan and fanatic. Fanatics were being produced en masse by Alfred Rosenberg, whose bizarre racial theories became the bible of every Nazi and every schoolchild.

In 1938 another set of harsh anti-Jewish laws befell its victims. By December 1938, Jews were isolated and impoverished. Jews could no longer run any businesses or enterprises. Jews lost their apartments, were denied access to public places, and could be banned from any section of town if local authorities so decreed. The end result of all those edicts, decrees, laws, and ordinances was a total loss of power, entitlement, and protection for the Jews. But all this took time. Five years. From 1933 to 1938 that dreadful noose tightened, tight enough to presage the extermination of Jews some years later.

In retrospect, the hopelessness of the German Jews' position can be easily discerned. Why all the Jews did not leave in 1933 is a question frequently raised. Some of the escapees, who as young-sters lived in Germany, raise that question themselves. Lore[139] comments, "I am surprised that my intelligent father was 'blind' to the extent of the danger for so many years." And Elsa[96] suggests that "adults 'fooled' themselves into believing as long as they could. Who wants to believe such unbelievable developments unless one is forced to face them? Except in my school, things started to get bad only slowly for many people."

Ah, there is the rub. "Things started to get bad only slowly for many people." The gradualness of the change created a false impression that life might still be livable in Germany under restricted conditions. The brutality exhibited later by government officials was absent in the beginning. Writes historian Lucy Dawidowicz (1975): "After the spate of violence, the boycott, and the enactment of the exclusionary legislation in 1933, neither the German state nor the NSDAP [Nazi Party] appeared to have a clear-cut policy with regard to the Jews. In fact, some government agencies continued to deal with Jews in a correct, even courteous, manner, according to the rules and regulations that had prevailed in Weimar. Emigration, for example, was handled by the Reichswanderungsamt [Reich Office of Migration] within the Ministry of the Interior. It was staffed mostly by officials who were not National Socialists but had, before 1933, been members of the Catholic Center and other nonleftist parties. These bureaucrats continued to operate up to 1938 not only according to Weimar legality but also with sympathetic understanding for the problems and priorities of the Jewish organizations in trying to foster a systematic program of emigration" (p. 82).

There seemed to be no acute hurry to leave. People were prepared to wait for an American visa for two to three years. After all, there were few places that were open to immigrants. In addition, there was a worldwide depression. Clearly, jobs in new countries would not be waiting for people who did not even speak the language. It also seemed reasonable to assume that after the many changes of government that preceded the Nazi regime, the most uncivilized of all governments would not last long in a highly civilized country. And even if it did, the foreign governments were bound to contribute to its ultimate fall.

Certainly, unpleasant incidents did occur right from the beginning of Hitler's rise to power. Like warning beacons, these confrontations flared up briefly and were gone just as quickly. Elsa[96] recalls such an occasion: "I remember an incident in 1933 in a *Biergarten*, where my family had their supper most summer nights. A Jewish-looking man was held against a wall while Nazis hit him. Fortunately he was none the worse for it. But I was deeply worried about my father, who had a long nose. But nothing else happened." On the other hand, life went on normally for others. Most Jews were still able to make a living. If a business was confiscated, the owner did not necessarily become destitute. For instance, a pharmacist[109] was forced to rent his pharmacy in accordance with the Nuremberg Laws, but he still continued to receive sufficient income to live in comfortable circumstances. When he died he left adequate resources so that his family was not subjected to any great deprivation.

People seemed to get used to the altered circumstances and began to take them for granted. This was particularly true for youngsters. Eric,[35] for instance, was aware that there were incidents at times with non-Jewish students. But since nothing bad had ever happened to him, he did not much worry about it. He was the only Jewish boy in his class, and his teacher had told his classmates that she would not tolerate any anti-Semitic remarks. Certainly, no teacher in Austria after the Anschluss would have dared to so openly defend a Jewish child. Even after 1935, when Eric was transferred to a Jewish school, it was still possible for him to have a blissful youth: "We had wonderful times in the Jewish school in the thirties. These were the most beautiful years I ever had. The magic of youth sparkled over everything. I still remember those years nostalgically a half century later."

Friedlander (1991) has described how the Nazis, in order to mislead foreign countries—and thereby incidentally misleading the Jews as well—frequently gave the impression that Jews might be able to lead a restricted though fairly safe life in Germany. A case in point was the Jüdischer Kulturbund (Jewish Cultural Alliance), founded in 1933 and encouraged by the German Ministry of Propaganda. It presented operas, plays, and concerts and employed the many famous Jewish artists no longer able to appear on the German stage. There was a grotesque contrast between the worlds outside and inside the theater, between the search for visas and backstage life: Outside the Nazis ruled, inside there was a Jewish audience. The only non-Jews allowed were police, firemen—and Gestapo. Hannah,[160] a talented dancer and choreographer, used every available dancer since unemployed artists were taken by the Nazis into the dreaded Arbeitsdienst (Work Corps). The Kulturbund was not dissolved by the Nazis until September 11, 1941. Six months later the mass killings of Jews began. But even then the Nazis' efforts to deceive the world did not cease. Famous Jewish artists were forced to perform on a specially built stage in Westerbork, a German collection point in Holland, for Jews being sent to extinction. An actress, Camilla Spira, tells of being costumed as an innkeeper's wife with blond braids and singing the operetta selection "At the White Horse Inn, Good Fortune Stands Before Every Door" for a thousand Jewish prisoners who had arrived for one night in transit from Bergen-Belsen to Auschwitz. "It was horrible," she recalls. "For the moment, they forgot everything. The next day the trains took them to their deaths (*Tagesspiegel* Berlin, 1991). The Kulturbund's director, Dr. Kurt Singer, was arrested and shipped to Theresienstadt. The Nazis pretended to the world that Theresienstadt was a pleasant city reserved for Jews. The postcards Dr. Singer and others were allowed to send bore names typical of small-town streets. In actuality, there were no street names, only numbers for blocks; Dr. Singer's was Q410. He died in 1944 (Friedländer, 1991). Hannah[160] was luckier; she made it to the United States.

But for a long time their continued ability to practice various occupations, as well as the hope that the power of the Nazis was transitory, encouraged the German Jews to believe that they could continue to live in Germany. After a while, restrictions placed on the Jewish population and unpleasant and even dangerous confrontations with Nazis left their mark. In order to avoid these encounters, it seemed best for Jews to conduct their social life away from public places. Even within ever-narrowing confines, life continued for a while rather normally—even, in some cases, pleasantly: "My father [a lawyer] continued his work in due course for Jewish clients only," recalls Beate (now Bea).[59] "There were dinner parties and literary discussion." Those who were teenagers at the time tell of music lessons;[59] attending social gatherings organized by Zionist groups;[165] and Saturday meetings at the Jewish Community Centers, as well as Sunday afternoon hikes and sports activities.[70] In later years it would have been unthinkable for a Jewish youth group to meet: They would very quickly have been annihilated by the Brown Shirts, Hitler's storm troopers.

Discerning the future was also made difficult by the fact that some parts of Germany were easier to live in than others. While one family had to abandon their home in a small town in 1935, other families were able to manage, or even live comfortably within a restricted setting, until Kristallnacht, the night of November 9, 1938. Paul,[91] reviewing his diary written in 1938, admits that it discloses a not unpleasant life in Wiesbaden, while the family was waiting for its U.S. visa: "My calendar for 1938 reflects normal activities, such as receiving a new bike in May, a full schedule of violin lessons, sport activities, private English lessons, attending services on Friday nights, excursions on Sundays plus preparation for my bar mitzvah, scheduled in December. In September there is much excitement about Sudetenland and talk of war. In October 'peace in our time' has been secured by the British. Late October we enjoy the annual festival day. . . . Early November continues normal. . . ." We know, of course, what happened in November—Kristallnacht.

As long as it was possible to make a living, the Jewish population attempted to adjust to the downward spiral. Eric[35] recalls: "Despite the disturbing developments, very few if any of us realized what mortal danger we were in. From time to time could be heard the raucous calls of bloodthirsty columns of Nazi storm troopers who sang the Horst Wessel song about Jewish blood spurting from the knife. But we had heard this so often before that we did not take it literally anymore." There seems to be an almost universal desire to cling to the familiar as long as possible—or even when it is impossible. John McPhee (1989) asked people residing on the slope of volcanic mountains why they remained there. "You learn to adapt," answered one resident. "You live with it. Fortunately, trouble doesn't come too often. In the years we have been here, we have had only one major earthquake, two major fires, and one major flood" (p. 257). Isaac Bashevis Singer once said, "God protect us from all the things we can get used to."

With each escalation of restrictions many of the German Jews assumed that the worst had been experienced, that the apex of cruelty had been reached, and that no new outrages would follow. "Periods of violence and draconian measures were followed by periods of relative calm which gave rise to fresh hope that 'the madness would stop.' Thus several thousand Jews who had emigrated in 1933, actually returned to Germany in 1934 because it looked as if the regime had adopted a more 'legal course' after the initial turmoil of 1933 when arbitrariness ruled" (Berghan, 1984,

p. 72). With each escalation some people found life unbearable and left, but others found that it was still possible to live within the restrictions. For instance, when Jews were prohibited in public places, friends met in each other's homes instead. If working as a civil servant was forbidden, the skills could still be applied to private enterprises. After each edict, an adjustment would take place; that hiatus would then be shattered by the next edict. One respondent[16] who left Germany early on mentions that the state-organized boycott of all Jewish businesses in 1933 was the determining factor in her family's decision to leave. But her family was in a fairly good position to do so. They were in comfortable financial circumstances and had relatives in the United States. The famous burning of the books, which took place in Germany in 1933, was not mentioned by any escapee in this study. It is possible to live without books but not without income. The 1935 Nuremberg laws, which promulgated the racial laws and disenfranchised the German Jews, brought home to many the disastrous position they were in. For others, who were still able to live a restricted life, it was not yet the decisive moment. That is not to say that those Jews who remained in Germany refrained from searching for ways out; the passion with which each lead was pursued grew with the increasing recognition of danger. A mother[35] who did not accept an offer to send her son to a foster family in America in 1936 would gladly have done so a year and a half later. The Anschluss, with its vicious aftermath, served as an additional incentive. However, Kristallnacht finally alerted most everyone. After that no additional markers were needed.

Judgment as to whether action should be taken was influenced by each person's analysis of the political landscape. Jews whose evaluation of National Socialism allowed for no hope were more likely to take immediate measures. Those who sustained any measure of optimism, thinking the regime would not last or that it might be possible to live within its confines, delayed coping with the prodigious problems connected with emigration. Both optimists and pessimists had to rely on suppositions and hunches, their personal outlook on life also coloring their decision. In addition, those who were fortunate enough to have relatives or connections abroad were more readily able to consider emigration as a feasible solution.

There were some people who even early on were able to

discern the sinister signs of what was to come. Among them were victims of previous pogroms who would perhaps have agreed with Tennessee Williams when he said, "We have to distrust each other. It is our only defense against betrayal." Mr. Winer[187] had learned to distrust. Twenty years earlier he and his wife had fled across a frozen river with the Bolsheviks firing their rifles at them. After that experience they had no trouble at all recognizing danger and left without delay as the Nazis gained power. Others who were quick to sense the coming events were the ones who had had some personal encounter with Nazi cruelty. In the beginning most Jews were able to avoid such confrontations. But those who had had dealings with the Nazis had already been put into a position so grievous and fear provoking that even the prospect of a stress-laden emigration seemed preferable by far. Loss of livelihood gave impetus to leaving: A Jewish judge[114] was deprived of his position, and there was no hope of his ever working in the legal field in Germany again. Having relatives in America was a further stimulus for his leaving. He knew he would have no profession in the United States, but he would not have one in Germany either. At least he and his family would be safe.

Then there were the children. As attacks on them increased, so did the motivation for leaving. What a fearful specter when parents cannot protect their own! An escapee[161] reminisced about Passover eve, 1935. Until then the family, headed by his father, an esteemed rabbi, had lived rather peacefully in a small town. The thirteen-year-old son, who was one day to become a rabbi himself, was asked by his mother to deliver a package of matzos and a bottle of wine to the farmer with whom the family had dealt all year. The youngster presented the farmer with his mother's thoughtful present. The farmer recoiled and became agitated. "I drink Rhine and Mosel wine," he exclaimed. "I don't drink Jewish wine. Jewish wine is mixed with the blood of Christian children who have been brutally murdered." To demonstrate his point, the farmer unfolded a newspaper and waved it in front of the boy. It was Julius Streicher's *Stürmer*, the same Julius Streicher who was later tried at Nuremberg. And, here in print, right on the front page, was the source of the farmer's information. The boy asked, "Do you believe everything you read in the paper?" The farmer was incensed at such effrontery. "I see that you are very sick," he said. "There is a doctor in Dachau who specializes in such cases with great success. His name is Theodor Eicke [one of Himmler's associates]." When the boy told his mother of the conversation, she said, "The time has come to leave Germany."

One of the most powerful incentives for departure was a family member's arrest. The Heiman family[69] was spurred on by such terror: "The incarceration of my father was absolutely devastating. The impossible had happened. The realization that we must leave or perish had set in. A sense of betrayal, not just insecurity, overtook me. Total disaster."

That potential total disaster was sometimes hidden from view owing to inexperience or naïveté in dealing with political events. Among the Jews grappling with an unprecedented problem there were some who could not face the grim reality. For instance, as the Heiman family was organizing itself to leave, one of the uncles still refused to relinquish his home. He insisted that he was going to build a bunker in his backyard and stay. Fortunately, he changed his mind. The uncle's attitude reflected a lack of realism possibly engendered by a fear of coping with the overwhelming obstacles entailed in leaving.

Indeed, it is quite likely that some people were overwhelmed by the stress. It took an enormous amount of persistence, resourcefulness, intelligence, luck—and, frequently, money as well as connections—to surmount the obstacles in the way of leaving. It required courage to face the likelihood of unemployment, poverty, and loneliness in new countries. It is not surprising that some people faltered at the prospect. A man[88] recalls his mother's tormenting indecisiveness: "Our passports were issued, and we planned to leave December 1937. My mother lost her nerve at the last minute and made my father return the passports to the police. However, my father and I were able to prevail upon her to leave and we got the passports back." A judgment had to be made whether to go into the unknown and try to survive or remain with the familiar and try to survive. Each option raised the specter of untold difficulties and triggered agonizing ambivalence.

What was happening in Germany was beyond the scope of anyone's experience. How excruciating the decision-making process was is described by Yecheskel Leitner (1987). "When Germany and Russia carved up Poland, the dividing line between their armies became the river Bug. . . . Masses of Jewish refugees fleeing the Germans approached the river Bug to cross to the Russian side of occupied Poland. Simultaneously, multitudes of other refugees fleeing Soviet occupation were making their way to the opposite bank. In their misery and desperation, the first group looked upon the second in wonder: How could any person in his right mind try to escape to the Germans? The other group thought just the opposite, since they were risking everything to escape from the Russians. This dilemma demanded a solution. It was decided to seek a rabbinical response from a recognized judge in the Torah court of the city of Brisk. Reb [Rabbi] Simcha Zelig finally rendered his ruling the gist of which was as follows: We have entered only the initial phase of a war which in its characteristics and features—especially to the extent of its unparalleled subhuman bestialities against Jews—is a war beyond human comprehension. Since the developments of these events defy our understanding, concept or rational analysis, one cannot make Torah [body of wisdom and law contained in Jewish scripture] pronouncements on such matters. There can be no Torah ruling on a subject beyond the grasp of human comprehension" (pp. 43–44).

The question of why so many German Jews did not leave immediately might then be answered in part as follows: For some time after Hitler became chancellor, life could still be conducted in moderate comfort, though within restricted limits. As long as life could still go on with a vestige of normality, as long as it was possible to have some income, and as long as there was hope that Hitler was just a passing phase, it seemed reasonable to wait. The increase in restrictive laws, and in more widespread personal encounters with Nazi methods, helped decipher the direction and the finality of the situation. But that took time. Gunther,[1] who was sent out of Germany by his mother, came to a similar conclusion: "As to my guess why so many did not leave Germany while they could, with the benefit of hindsight I would say that people did not believe that the Nazis would endure, that they considered themselves to be as German as non-Jews, and that it is not easy to give up an established career and property in middle age."

Long after the German Jews comprehended the situation in Germany quite clearly, the rest of the world was still not aware of the true nature of National Socialism. I recall my first day in school in

England. My teacher asked me to tell about the events taking place in Europe. My English was halting, but I managed fairly satisfactorily to tell of not being allowed to go to school, of Jewish businesses vanishing, of arrests. I ended by explaining that many people were driven to suicide. Suddenly, I realized that no one understood me. Was I not using the word suicide correctly? Perhaps I was mispronouncing it. I gestured: I put my finger to my forehead as if it were a gun; I pantomimed cutting my wrists with a knife; I walked to the window as if I were about to jump. No one comprehended; teachers and pupils looked at me blankly. It was not the word they could not understand. It was the concept.

Another woman, Bea,[59] had a similar experience as a child in England. In January 1940 a copy of the magazine *Picture Post* found its way to her school. It showed a photograph familiar to her: her father walking down a city street surrounded by SA men. Passing civilians were gaping at him. Dignified, wearing glasses, fixedly looking straight ahead, he walked with a huge placard hanging around his neck. It read: "I am a Jew, but I *do not want* to complain about the *Nazis*." His trouser legs had been cut off, his head bashed in, and his teeth knocked out. Bea recalls that seeing that picture was a dreadful shock. She cried and showed the picture to her teacher, who did not believe that it was of Bea's father and sent her to the headmistress. The headmistress did not believe her either.

No one could believe the unbelievable.

## Chapter 3

# Getting Out:
# The Obstacles

All activities, all conversations, now centered almost exclusively on fleeing. After the Anschluss, there was only one preoccupation: we must get out. Or, rather, we must get out and we must get in. Because suddenly it became quite obvious that there were two sets of obstacles in the way of leaving: the roadblocks the Nazis placed to obtaining permission to leave and the resistance of other countries to admitting the escaping Jews. The Nazis began to torment the Jews by placing every conceivable obstacle in their way.

Practically everyone who had not left immediately after the Anschluss now faced formidable barriers to obtaining the documents required for exit. Nazi officials became kings who kept the supplicants waiting in endless lines. There was always one more piece of paper required or one more signature demanded. Documents, long sought and finally obtained, would be arbitrarily rejected and all appeals denied. The labor had to start all over again—unless it was a passport that had been impounded. That could amount to a death sentence.

Almost all escapees have some memory of those nightmare days. A fifteen-year-old[106] who accompanied her father on his endless rounds recalls her experiences: "My father did most of the work to get our papers together. I remember going with him to get the passport. We would get to the offices at 6:00 A.M. and stand in line waiting for hours. Then they would close the window and tell us to come back the next day. Since our bank accounts had been closed, my father used to stand in line for other people who paid him for it." There was a desperation in that last act. Those lines were dangerous and to be avoided. The SA would regularly raid the long lines in front of offices. Sometimes they only beat the people with fists and clubs. At other times they would cart them off to concentration camps.

Anything out of the ordinary needed special permits. Anitta's[43] father was a portrait painter and needed special permits to emigrate with his paintings, drawings, and supplies. At first, women were less at risk for arrest than men. As a result, Anitta's mother summoned all her strength and persistence to stand in line for hours in the bitter cold. She would come home to her husband and daughter looking exhausted and bruised, but she never complained. It was only much later that Anitta learned that her mother had been beaten, abused, and made to scrub the sidewalks in the bitter cold, while being forbidden to wear any warm clothing. SS troopers came three times, guns in hand, to plunder Anitta's family's possessions. Anitta watched it all, sitting in a corner while holding her guinea pig and dog, which had been dealt a few hard kicks with SS boots. She spent hours in a constant state of fear and alarm waiting for her mother to come home. Miraculously, the SS visits and her parents' forays for the required documents did not end in disaster. Two of her friends were less fortunate. One day when they returned home from school they found their apartments empty and ransacked. They never saw their parents again.

With their usual sadistic mentality the Nazi officials invented and demanded an endless list of documents. For instance, there was the *Reichsfluchtsteuer* (tax levied for fleeing the Reich). Twenty-five percent of a person's total assets, including furniture, had to be paid in cash. This sum was determined quite arbitrarily by the authorities. But where could one raise all that cash? In Austria, Jews quickly began to lose their jobs and their businesses; in Germany, they had been losing them for some time. The tax became a symbol of an unbearable burden. The *Reichsfluchtsteuer* was only one of many essential papers. Among them was the proof that no taxes were owed the government. A form had to be acquired testifying to one's lack of a criminal record. Proof had to be submitted that no dog tax was outstanding—even if no dog had ever been owned!

On the surface, it might appear senseless for a government to demand an unending succession of bureaucratic forms. What could be the purpose of extracting enormous sums of money for the *Reichsfluchtsteuer*? After all, the fleeing Jews were only allowed to take ten Schillings with them when they crossed the border to foreign lands. Thus, the government would ultimately possess all their money, real estate, and household goods one way or another. There were two reasons: One was to torment the Jewish population. The other was the Germanic need to have every transaction conducted through official channels, sealed with proper stamps, and concluded with appropriate receipts. This compulsion prompted the Nazis to keep exact records of even the most inhuman acts. In *The Nazi Doctors*, Robert Lifton (1986) describes the elaborate records that were kept on the retarded children who were put to death in hospitals.

I myself visited a former German prison in Yugoslavia. I saw the whips with which the prisoners were beaten as well as other torture instruments. There were the large wooden poles, riddled with innumerable bullet holes, to which the prisoners were tied before being shot. On the cell walls the prisoners had scrawled messages and tallies of days, which suddenly stopped. Gathered together were the photographs the Germans took of children and adults when they were first brought to the prison. There were also two extremely large books with hard covers, the kind accountants used in Dickens' time. On each line on each page was the name of a prisoner, the date of arrival, and a prison number, all carefully entered in perfect script. Then there was a line drawn crossing out each name, with a final date. And all the lines were of exactly equal length and perfectly parallel to each other. It was a most perfectly kept book of death. Whether Yugoslavia or Austria or Germany, the records were always meticulous.

The difficulties in obtaining the necessary papers had increased over the years. In 1934 it was not arduous to obtain the essential papers to leave Germany.[115] By 1936 there were problems: A man[124] remembers that he had to go to Stuttgart twice to get essential documents. Between the first and second trip the family lost their house and for eight months slept only on the concrete floor of a barn, an outhouse nearby. Since the acquisition of certain official papers had to be done in sequence, speed was of the essence. By the time paper number two could be obtained, paper number one had frequently expired, and the whole process had to be started from the beginning. A former Austrian[145] describes the situation succinctly: "Leaving the country was not exactly easy. Before we had everything ready, two of us were sent to Dachau."

Officials were enterprising in creating delays. Fritz[167] had applied for a passport at police headquarters. He was told to return in two days, at which time he was instructed to obtain an additional document, for which he had to travel to another town. After fulfilling this request, he returned to the office and said to the official: "I have come for the passport of Fritz Steinweg." The official looked at Fritz quite seriously and said, "I have no such thing." Fritz was dumbfounded and repeated his request. The official, shaking his head, gave the same answer. Then it dawned on Fritz. "I have come for the paper of Fritz *Israel* Steinweg." "That's better," replied the official as he accepted the paper Fritz had brought him.

The requirement of endless forms served as an elaborate means of displaying power. I have a personal memory of my parents once taking me to some government office—a necessary trip, presumably, since they always tried to shield me. I recall the building. The interior was gray, grimy, and poorly lit. A long staircase wound its way up several floors. One or two people stood on each step waiting to move slowly upward. They looked cowed and as gray as the walls. No one spoke. Many held papers in their hands. After what seemed like an eternal period, we reached the top. There was a woman sitting behind a cage. She spoke sharply to my parents, who handed her some papers. She appeared irritated and addressed my parents in peremptory tones. My father, who usually guarded his dignity carefully, said nothing. It shocked me, but I knew it was all he could do. We seemed to have obtained what we wanted. My parents turned and quickly walked down the stairs. We did not slacken our pace once we reached the street. Each step taking us further from the building made us feel safer. No one referred to the incident. There was nothing to be said; we all understood only too well.

Besides the power game, there was also the bribery game, a difficult game to play. For one, it was expensive. Many officials were takers. They could demand a pearl necklace or a gold bracelet, not just a few paltry Schillings. For the givers there were always questions: Am I giving too little or too much? Am I giving to one of the few people who refuses bribes, and, as a result, will I end up in jail? If I pay, will I get the paper I need? Once I run out of money, how will I obtain more? I recall overhearing my parents in such a discussion. I do not know which office my mother went to, taking with her a pearl necklace that had once belonged to my grandmother. I do not know how many times she was forced to pay for obtaining other documents, but I do know that the necklace was not the only piece of jewelry that was swallowed up in the quest for papers.

Wherever there is corruption, there thrive shadowy figures who appear out of nowhere and have "connections"—for a price. And there were plenty of those under the Hitler regime. They were able to penetrate where others were too terrified to tread. They were even able to penetrate the well-fortressed Gestapo. Stella's[72] father was wanted by the Gestapo: "My father was out of the country. The shiny, black cars with the red swastika flags still came to our house. When was my father returning and bringing back all his foreign money? The officials in their black uniforms wanted to know. Our passports were confiscated. A young attorney, sporting a small silver swastika, appeared in our lives. He could get almost anything. A passport? No problem. A little expensive perhaps, but it could be done. Papers stating that you owed no taxes whatsoever, something completely unavailable for Jews about to leave the country? Of course. For cash only, however. We got a new passport." But the passport lacked something important: A red *'J'* for *Jude* [Jew]. Stella turned again to the attorney who had been obliging before—for cash: "Our friend with the small silver swastika appeared again. A *'J'* in the passport? Things were more difficult now. He would see what he could do. But it would be expensive. He disappeared with our passport into the yellow castle of Schönbrunn, the former residence of the Emperor, which now housed the government offices. I waited for him in the park a long time. Had he been arrested? With our passports? Finally he returned, looking exhausted, 'I am having a terrible time,' he told me. 'Many of those people for whom I get passports no longer have any money. So they pay in kind. All night long I commit *'Rassenschande'* [shaming the race; the serious crime of an Aryan having sexual relations with a Jewish partner]. He handed me the passport. It now had a big, fat, red *J*. I gave him an envelope. He vanished into the shadows."

Other black marketeers wanted more tangible assets. "I bribed someone for a visa," recollects one escapee.[144] "For my exit permit I handed over my car."[144] Dealing with these furtive creatures presented all kinds of dangers. At times the contact who made the Jews' illegal activities possible disappeared. Without papers, or with wrong ones, a Jew could be imprisoned and never emerge. And then again, the black marketeer might decide not to return an altered passport at all. There was always the chance that he might get a buyer for the passport, thereby bringing in more money than he was charging for just a *J*. Of course, that would leave the original owner without a passport and in despair. By the time a new one could be obtained, all doors would be closed. But that was not the concern of a black marketeer.

My own parents, desperate to acquire some essential but unobtainable stamp, handed our passports to one of those shadowy figures. Yes, yes, he had assured them, he could get that stamp for their passports. In the middle of the night, my mother awoke in terror. Crying and pacing up and down, she was convinced the man would sell our passports—four beautiful, almost ready-to-use passports. She and my father debated the issue. Retrieve the passport, still without the needed stamp, or leave the passport with the racketeer. Would there be a passport with a stamp? Or no passport at all? Their decision: Retrieve the passport. But from where? My father walked out into the night, an action dangerous in itself. After a round of night spots he found the racketeer. He still had the passports. The next day a quest for the stamp began anew. It was clear my parents did not have the talent for black market dealings.

Sometimes it was necessary to use intricate and roundabout means to obtain a passport. One man[31] desperate for a passport hoped that his cousin, a magistrate in Poland, could produce a passport for him. He could. It was an odd passport, valid for only three months, and although a Polish passport, it was not valid for Poland. But at least it was a passport of sorts that enabled the man to leave Germany.

A quick personal memory: I was on board ship, nearing Canada. A man accidentally dropped his passport overboard. Everyone was horrified. Everyone spoke in whispers; we were in mourning. Without a passport the man was no longer alive.

Few people recall the complete list of documents necessary to acquire an exit visa. The names of the documents required in Germany and Austria were different, but the process was the same. "I cannot remember the details of the papers we had to furnish in Germany. There existed of course many taxes such as water tax, *Warenumsatzsteuer* [tax on the sale of goods], *Gemeindeabgabe* [local taxes], dog tax. While not being liable for all of them, the emigrant had to prove that he did not owe any of these taxes."[42]

All escapees remember the nightmarish days spent in pursuit of the exit visa. The obstacles came in endless varieties, Nazi-honed to perfection. They were created by those expressionless creatures with rough or at best, indifferent voices, sitting in cagelike windows. They saw an endless line of gray people passing in front of them. Yet these bureaucrats never tired of doing their duty. They saw that every *t* was crossed and every *i* was dotted. They willingly sent back a supplicant again and again if they spied the slightest omission. No desperate urging stayed them from their course. If they declined a document and thereby a visa was lost, it did not ruffle their feathers. *Befehl ist Befehl* [Orders are orders]. A bureaucrat knows his duty. I have listened to many accounts about the hardships of procuring exit papers, yet never once have I been told, "Oh, but that official in the tax office was helpful to me" or "Were it not for the man in that office, I would have missed an urgent deadline." No one will ever know how many people missed an essential deadline and were thereby condemned to death. Perhaps somewhere there was an official who did not stick to the letter of the law. There must have been. But I have never heard tell of it.

## Chapter 4

# The Sagas of Kurt and Franz

### Kurt: Excerpts from an Account by Ken Schiller

Kurt Schiller[159] was dark-haired, of an intellectual bent, and possessed of a self-effacing but friendly manner. Due to a bout with polio, he had a slight limp. Life preceding the Anschluss had been peaceful for Kurt. There had been just one frightening encounter with anti-Semitism, in 1932. The memory lingered: a lecture at the University of Vienna; a group of anti-Semitic men, armed with steel whips, bursting into the lecture hall and surrounding the Jewish students; a passive professor, embarrassed but unwilling to interfere. A bad dream? No, a terrible reality. But life returned to normal—that is, until the Anschluss.

Kurt was desperate to leave Austria. But how? There were no countries looking for young physicists. He decided to acquire more practical skills; perhaps these would be instrumental in obtaining entry to another country. Learning to become a barber might help to get him into Australia. Spanish might make him more eligible for a South American country. He and three friends met daily in one of the men's apartments to practice both those skills. A boarder, subletting the next room, called Gestapo headquarters to report a communist plot. The unsuspecting young men were lathering each other's faces for barbering practice when three SA men in full uniform crashed through the door. One of them quickly removed his belt and began beating the group. Another held a knife to Kurt's throat. Amid screaming and cursing, the four young men were quickly and roughly ushered into a waiting car.

The drive to the Landesgericht jail was short. At first Kurt shared a small, overcrowded cell with criminals. After a few days he was switched to a larger, even more crowded cell. It held a baker, some lawyers, some businessmen. All had one thing in common: They were Jewish. From time to time, some of them were called out and did not return. Which were the lucky ones sent home? Which were the ones sent to Dachau? The days passed without contact with the outside world. Kurt knew his parents would be frantic by now.

Finally it was Kurt's turn. He was ushered into a small room adjacent to a bigger one. He heard two voices: "The Jew Schiller, is he going to Dachau?" Kurt could not make out the reply. Minutes ticked by. Then the summons came to enter the bigger room. A piece of paper was shoved in front of him: "Sign!" Through a haze Kurt read the form. It said that he was leaving Austria of his own free will. It was a Nazi custom to require people being discharged from jails or concentration camps to state that they had been treated well and that their leaving Austria was simply a matter of preference. Kurt was also told that he was to report twice a week to the police. Most important of all, if he was still in Austria by July 12 he would be sent to Dachau. It was now May. Remember, he was told, no later than July 12—or else Dachau.

Like Mengele's finger, which arbitrarily consigned an Auschwitz prisoner to life or to death, Kurt's fate had arbitrarily pointed to escape rather than Dachau. But how? Where to? He had no exit papers, no visas, no quota number. Then came a rumor that brought hope: One could still get into Switzerland by way of Freiburg, Germany. All that was needed was a German passport. An Austrian passport would not do. But then, Austria was now a part of Germany. Kurt could exchange his Austrian passport for a German one. Yes, Freiburg was the place to go. Austrian Jews were forbidden to travel in Germany, but some risk had to be taken. What followed was a quick goodbye to parents, a quick train trip to Freiburg, a night of fear walking around Freiburg. If the police spied him, that meant Dachau, for sure. Finally, morning dawned and the passport office opened. Now to get the new passport. But too late. Too late. The ruse had been discovered. The police would not change his passport for a German one.

What now? Every day brought the Dachau deadline closer. After much searching, another solution appeared. Kurt learned of a restaurant in Basel that straddled the German–Swiss border. If Kurt could only walk into the restaurant from the German side and exit on the Swiss side, he would become a free man. Kurt hurried to catch a train to Basel. Yes, there was the restaurant, exactly the way it had been described to him. But what to do next? He could not simply walk through the dining room into the kitchen and out into Switzerland. Alone, worried, heart pounding, he had no clue as to how to approach the waitress. Toying with the menu, Kurt noticed the words *Can you help me?* written on the back. He quickly gathered that the waitress had helped others before him. This gave him courage. He summoned her, turned the menu over, looked into the waitress's face. A nod on her part—she knew. She would help. But he must wait until the cook went home. "He is a Nazi," the waitress said. "We must be careful." Immense relief and hope coursed through Kurt. The specter of Dachau might be fading soon. "Wait," he said to himself, "till the restaurant closes. All will be well." Suddenly, out of nowhere two towering figures approached. "Gestapo," they identified themselves. "Where are you going?" "Switzerland." "Have a passport?" "Yes." One Nazi curtly took his passport and disappeared. The other was surprisingly mild mannered, even helpful. Yes, Kurt had to leave the restaurant. But did Kurt know there was a bridge in Strasbourg that straddles Germany and France? One could easily walk across it in the middle of the night. The first man reappeared, and after handing Kurt his passport, both left. Kurt examined his passport. His worst fears were realized: The passport now bore a new stamp: "Validity cancelled." Kurt pondered what steps he could take next. For no particular reason he decided against going to Strasbourg. Soon afterward he heard that all those who had tried to cross the bridge at night had been shot by the Gestapo. The reason: "Shot while trying to escape."

Dachau loomed closer every hour. But Kurt was not yet at the end of his rope. He ferreted out information about another possibility. He learned of a little town called Lorrach, which although located in Germany was not far from Basel in Switzerland. In order for loaded trucks leaving from Lorrach to reach other parts of Germany, a shortcut through Switzerland could be taken. The truck drivers were known to the German and Swiss customs officials and, as a result, were rarely searched. If Kurt could somehow get a ride on one of those trucks! A quick train ride brought him to Lorrach. As Kurt walked into town, he noted a festive atmosphere. It was the annual meeting of the regional fire services. No trucks were leaving. Kurt realized quickly that he could not linger in the little town. Recognition would mean deportation to Dachau. He left.

A bout of despair, and then again a ray of hope. A wire from London informed him that an uncle who had found refuge there was trying to obtain a visa for him. An almost miraculous prospect had come out of nowhere. Oh, but the passport! He remembered that his passport had been invalidated. Without a passport, England might as well be located on the moon!

Kurt quickly returned to Vienna. Time was growing short. The twice-weekly visits to the police were dangerous; each time there was the possibility of arrest. But luck was with him. His date for Dachau was postponed until September 5. Now the quest for the passport began anew. People queued up for days, in constant danger of SA raids. But the risk had to be taken. Without a passport, there could be no English visa. The danger became too great. Kurt's sister began to stand in line for him. At long last, the passport was in his hands.

Then came a telephone call from London: The visa had been denied. It was now the beginning of September. He had a passport and nothing else. It seemed the end of the line. But like a deus ex machina, a non-Jewish girl who offered help was introduced to Kurt. The girl had a fiancé in Denmark. She had found a way to visit him by way of Warnemünde, a small town on the Baltic coast of Germany. From there she had been able to get holiday passes that allowed her to stay a few days at a time in Denmark. Was there a reason why Kurt could not obtain such a pass and then conveniently disappear in Denmark? Indeed, there was a good reason why Kurt could not do so. The girl's passport had been stamped as valid for three years, but Kurt's passport was valid for only one year. That clearly marked him as Jewish. The Danish customs official would never issue him a pass. Any customs official with any brains knew that no Jew, once admitted into Denmark, would return to Germany when his holiday pass expired.

Kurt and the girl knew that Hitler Youth members had been making regular excursions during the summer to Denmark. They were issued special holiday passes and did not need to show their passports. If Kurt could manage to get such a pass, he could smuggle himself out with a Hitler Youth group. But how could he possibly get one of those passes? The girl remembered that she knew a local *Gauleiter* (district leader). She would get him the pass. Kurt waited impatiently for her. She returned with the news that the *Gauleiter* was on vacation. A daily wait for the *Gauleiter*'s return began. The *Gauleiter* returned just in time to issue a pass to the girl in Kurt's name for the last trip of the summer. Kurt joined the group on September 4, one day before the Dachau deadline. The young Nazis boarded a boat, the *Kronprinz*. Like the others, Kurt wore a swastika in his lapel but for him, as a Jew, it was a deadly criminal offense. He sang Nazi songs and gave the Nazi salute. Finally, the boat docked in Gedser, Denmark, and he and the Hitler Youths disembarked. Kurt took a bus to Nzkobing, where the girl's fiancé met him. The news was not good. The fiancé spoke with urgency: "Kurt, it's too dangerous! Go back. Try something else. A man who had arrived the previous week was picked up by the Danish police and returned to Germany."

But there was nothing else left to try; the next day was Kurt's due date for Dachau. The fiancé handed him a ticket to Copenhagen and two addresses of women who might give him a bed for the night. When Kurt found his way there, he found no one home. It was dangerous for him to wander around. With the little money left, he tried a small hotel. The concierge asked for his passport number. Kurt pretended not to understand. Someone was found to speak German to him; again he was told that his passport number was needed. But Kurt knew there was no Danish visa in it. The hotel keeper would surely alert the police. He pleaded fatigue, saying he would produce the passport in the morning. He got up early, left money and departed from the hotel. The bellboy called after him and ran after him to get the passport. In spite of his limp, Kurt ran faster.

It was now Monday morning, and Kurt was able to locate the women whose addresses he had been given. They finagled a Danish

visa, which, however, was valid for only one week. Kurt's uncle in
England worked feverishly, but by the end of the week there was no
visa. The women, who had never had such dealings before, found a
contact and were able to secure another visa, this one valid for six
weeks. However, it was accompanied by a warning that the period of
validity was final. Totally final. Kurt walked the streets, checked for
a telephone message from the British consulate, and went to the
library of the Universitet Institut for Teoretisk Fysik (of which Niels
Bohr was the director). Six weeks passed. Hope was fading. The
telephone rang. It was the British consulate informing Kurt that his
visa had arrived. He could not believe it; he asked the woman on the
other end of the telephone to repeat the message. He said goodbye
to the Danes who had sheltered him, supported him, fed him, and
fought with the bureaucracy for him. He had not known them before
he had arrived. He would never meet them again. But they had saved
his life.

On October 29, 1938, he arrived in Harwich, England. Kurt, who
is now known as Ken, swore allegiance to the King of England, his
heirs, and successors and became a British subject in 1947. In 1956
he was elected a Fellow at the Institute of Physics.

### Franz: Excerpts from an Account by Frank Parker

The renowned pianist Jan Smeterlin had arranged a position in
England for Franz's[137] mother, a professor at the Vienna Conservatory
of Music, as a governess and piano teacher. Franz's brother Georg
had fled Austria and become an engineering student at the Technion
in Haifa where he remained until he joined the British army. But
neither Franz nor his father had yet found a means of leaving Vienna.
His mother's best friend, Grete Frank, a well-known pianist and
friend of the Queen Mother Elizabeth of Belgium, had tried to use
her influence. Franz's parents had received a beautifully engraved
letter from the queen's office, but the results were nil. The wife of
the Czech minister of defense sent friendly inquiries asking naive
questions, but nil was still nil. One day Franz was to meet a pretty girl
at a café. When he arrived, she revealed that an SS captain had been
walking past the café trying to flirt with her. Since she was Jewish, this

struck Franz as funny and he laughed. It was not healthy for a Jewish boy to provoke an SS captain. When Franz left the café, the captain asked him for identification. Now in danger, Franz thought quickly and held out his Weapon's Pass, a document he had received while an inductee in the Austrian army. The SS captain asked Franz if he was still in the army. Franz lied, saying he was on duty this afternoon. The captain stated ominously that he would check this information later that day. For now, Franz could go.

Franz went straight home, packed a few things, and planned to spend the night at his Aryan aunt's house. By chance, on his way, he met an uncle, who took him to an office located on an obscure side street and run by an orthodox Jew. The latter was engaged in smuggling people into Czechoslovakia under the authority of a member of the Gestapo, who made money on the operation. The gentleman inspected Franz's passport and asked him if the Gestapo was looking for him. "No," Franz replied, "but perhaps the SS is." "No matter," said the man. "The Gestapo does not care about the SS." There were two ways to get over the border: One took several hours and was complicated and unsafe; it would cost several hundred marks. The other would cost double but was safer and faster. Franz chose the second, but he had to go home to get the necessary money. The gentleman looked at his watch. It was Friday and after three. "I will no longer touch money," he said. "Bring it tomorrow night."

After an anxious night Franz appeared at the appointed hour. A limousine took him and seven others to the Gestapo headquarters of a small border town. There they changed to a Gestapo car to be driven to the actual border. The officer explained that the border was formed by a road and a railroad track running at right angles, both heavily guarded. Between the two was a swamp that was bisected by an abandoned railroad track. They were to follow the latter, which would lead to a point of confluence with the active track. Once there, local railroad tickets could be purchased to Prague.

The group included teenaged Herbert, a middle-aged woman, and a family consisting of a father, a mother who two weeks previously had undergone abdominal surgery, and their three little daughters, the oldest of whom was only twelve. Franz and Herbert supported the mother, who was unable to walk on her own. The others followed three to six yards apart. They reached the Czech town after an hour, looking conspicuous among the local people who were wearing the national costume. Near the railroad station they found themselves facing two policemen and quickly decided to part and rendezvous at the local inn, a less conspicuous place. To their disappointment the place had been commandeered by the Czech army. The group left quickly. The father insisted he had to find food for his wife and children, who were weakening. They stopped the first man they met to inquire where food could be obtained. The man gave them a long, hard look and asked, "Where do you come from?" Franz was contemplating how to reply when the father volunteered that they had just come from Austria. The man spoke in low tones. "Follow me," he instructed. "I am the town's rabbi." The rabbi sent someone to purchase train tickets and fed the group until just before departure time. At the station Franz had only ten more minutes to wait when two policemen approached, inquiring where he was going. Franz presented his ticket. "I know you have a ticket," commented one of the policemen impatiently. "I want to see your passport." "Of course," said Franz, knowing that his passport lacked an exit stamp, an entrance stamp, and a visa. It was a matter of thinking on his feet or perishing. Franz handed over his passport and with much flourish added a piece of paper on which the mayor of Slana, an unimportant small town in Czechoslovakia, had written a few words. The family of a friend of Franz's owned a textile factory in Slana, and the note from the mayor allowed that he had no objection if Franz wanted to live there. The document contained the mayor's signature and a very official-looking seal. The paper had as much value as one in which the mayor of Massapequa notified a citizen of China that he could come to live in the United States. The two policemen conferred as the train, which was to stop in the station for only three minutes, arrived. "This is my train," Franz insisted. "Please give me my passport." "Well," said the policeman, "if he has permission, he can go." Franz grabbed the passport and jumped into the train.

It would be fifteen years before the family was reunited. Franz, now Frank, graduated from Harvard Law School and became a lawyer. Both Ken and Frank are my cousins.

This sign reads "In this town we do not desire any Jews." Signs reading "Jews and dogs forbidden" went up on stores and park benches. (Courtesy DOW)

Members of the SA (left) and SS (right) posting signs on a Jewish store: "GERMANS! DEFEND YOURSELVES! Don't buy from Jews!" (Courtesy DOW)

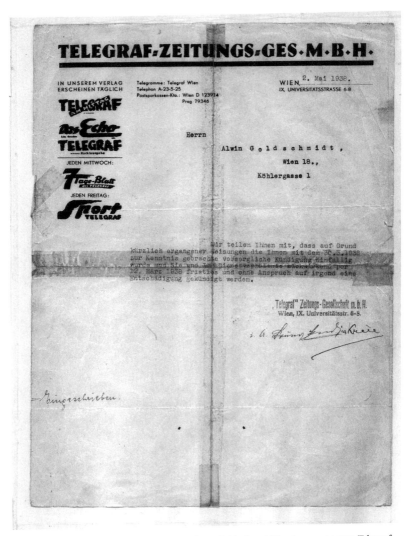

Dismissal notice to Jewish journalist Alwin Goldschmeid by the newspaper *Telegraf*. Dated May 2, 1938, it was retroactive to March 12 of that year (the date of the Anchluss) and barred any compensation. Subsequently, Goldschmeid fled to France, was deported, and murdered. (Courtesy Elli Adler)

Abgelehnt

Für die verehrliche Direktion des

„Deutschen Telegraf"

Wien IX. Universitätsstraße 8

Mit Rücksicht darauf, daß ich seit der Suspendierung vom Dienst und der Inhaftsetzung meines Mannes Alwin Goldschmied subsistenzlos bin, und doch die Vereinbarkeit einer seinerzeitigen Abfertigung oder Entschädigung anderer Art besteht, bitte ich um eine momentane finanzielle Hilfe.

Ich hoffe, daß Sie mir diese Bitte nicht abschlagen werden, umso eher nicht als ich und mein Kind doch gewiß an diesem Zustand schuldlos sind.

Hochachtungsvoll

Maria Goldschmied

Wien, 25. II. 1938

N. S. Wollte nur noch erwähnen, daß ich Arierin bin, und daß dies vielleicht noch eher zur Begründung meines Ersuchens dienen könnte.

Mrs. Goldschmeid's letter to the *Telegraf* asks for some compensation for her husband's dismissal and emphasizes that she and her child, though guiltless, are destitute. To bolster her claim, her P.S. explains that she is Aryan. The penciled reply on top: "Denied." By the same hand, a sarcastic remark at the bottom: "What a nerve!" (Courtesy Elli Adler)

**Block-Nr.** 40     1938     **Besucherschein-Nr.:**

## Geheime Staatspolizei
## Staatspolizeileitstelle Wien

### № 19

Herr
Frau    *Goldschmied Marie*
Fräulein

Amtsbezeichnung *Hausfrau*
   (Beruf)

von der Behörde
   (Firma)

aus (Ort) *18 Kölbl straße*

    Herrn
wünscht zu Frau *dr Floger*
    Fräulein

in der Angelegenheit:

| | | Zeit | |
|---|---|---|---|
| Tag und Monat | a) des Eintritts | b) der Entlassung durch den Besuchsempfänger, bei dessen Abwesenheit durch den Amtsgehilfen | c) des Verlassens des Dienstgebäudes |
| 1) | 1) | 2) | 3) |
| 25. IV. | 9 Uhr 52 Min. | 11 Uhr 10 Min. | Uhr Min. |

Vermerke des Wachhabenden:

*Vom Besucher auszufüllen, nötigenfalls nach Anweisung des Wachhabenden.*

*zu 1) u. 3) vom Wachhabenden auszufüllen, zu 2) durch den Besuchsempfänger oder den Amtsgehilfen auszufüllen, Zeitangabe und Namensunterschrift.*

**Dieser Schein ist dem Wachhabenden am Ausgang wieder zurückzugeben.**

*konnte es aber geheim mitnehmen da gerade unten beim*

This Gestapo ("Secret State Police") document permitted Marie Goldschmeid to visit her husband in a Gestapo prison. The day and time of the visit are noted with emphasis that the permit be returned by the recipient before leaving. Noted on the back and signed by Marie is the following: "I was able to take the paper along because some poor victims were just being beaten up by [the Gestapo]. Without this piece of paper the bureaucrats won't believe that my husband was in prison. This will serve as proof; otherwise, all of the other offices will deny my claim." (Courtesy Elli Adler)

Jews forced to scrub streets much to the amusement of the taunting citizenry. (Courtesy DOW)

Jews queuing for necessary exit papers in front of the police department. The office opened and closed at arbitrary times, prolonging the waiting time sometimes for days or weeks. Similar lines formed in front of every consulate. The SS frequently beat or arrested those on line. (Courtesy DOW)

## Amtsbestätigung.

Die Jüdin *Olga Sara Groszmann*
geboren am *31. 8. 1883* in *Wien*, in Wien, *2* Bez.,
*Praterstrasse* Gasse / Straße / Platz Nr. *26* wohnhaft,
hat heute hier angezeigt, daß sie zusätzlich den Vornamen Sara annehme.

Sie wurde belehrt, daß sie überdies die Anzeige bei der Bezirkshauptmannschaft ihres Wohnsitzes zu erstatten habe.

Unterschrift des Beamten:

J. A.

*Pokorny*

2 6. Juni 1939

This document reads: "Official Certification. The Jewess Olga Sara Groszman, born August 8, 1883, Vienna, living at Praterstrasse 26, has given notice that she has accepted the additional name of Sara. She was instructed as to the requirement to give additional notice of the fact to the District Administrative Office of the district in which she resides." Note that the document is worded as if the titleholder had voluntarily named herself Sara. (Courtesy Charles and Gertrude Deutsch)

---

## DOROTHEUM
Wien, I. Spiegelgasse 16

### Öffentliche Ankaufsstelle

No 29537

nach § 14 der Verordnung über den Einsatz des jüdischen Vermögens.

Johann Israel G r o s s m a n n II.Praterstrasse 26

Von: _____

wurden am heutigen Tage nachstehende ablieferungspflichtige Wertgegenstände angekauft:

| Laufende Nr. | Gegenstand 5953 | Ankaufspreis Reichsmark | Anmerkung |
|---|---|---|---|
| 1. | 6 Gabel 6 Messer mit Silber | -.20 | |

Statement by the Official Purchasing Agency: "In accordance with Paragraph 14 of the regulation regarding the disposition of Jewish property: On this day the following valuables, which are required to be surrendered to this office, were purchased: Six silver forks and knives for 20 pfennig [a few cents] minus 2 percent tax." (Courtesy Charles and Gertrude Deutsch).

# Umzugsgutverzeichnis

**(in doppelter Ausfertigung einzureichen)**

Vor Ausfüllung Merkblatt für die Mitnahme von Umzugsgut durchlesen

## Beförderungsart:*)

### H a n d g e p ä c k

Name und genaue Anschrift des Auswanderers:          Zum Antrag vom _____

Johann Groszmann, Wien, II., Praterstrasse 26/30

| Lfd. Nr.**) | Abschnitt***) | Stück | Gegenstand (genaue Bezeichnung) | Einkaufs- preis | Zeitpunkt der Anschaffung | Bemerkungen |
|---|---|---|---|---|---|---|
| 1 | 1 | 2 | Hemden | | | |
| 2 | 1 | 1 | Sporthemd | | | |
| 3 | 1 | 3 | kurze Hosen | | | |
| 4 | 1 | 2 | lange " | | | |
| 5 | 1 | 2 | Pyjama | | | |
| 6 | 1 | 1 | Nachthemd | | | |
| 7 | 1 | 6 p. | Socken | | | |
| 8 | 1 | 8 | Taschentücher | | | |
| 9 | 1 | 1 | Badehose | | | |
| 10 | 1 | ~~1~~ | ~~Herbstanzug~~ | | | |
| 11 | 1 | ~~1~~ | ~~Flanellhose~~ | | | |
| 12 | 1 | 3 | Kravatten | | | |
| 13 | 1 | 4 | Kragen | | | |
| 14 | 1 | 1 P | Handschuhe | | | |
| 15 | 1 | 1 p. | Hausschuhe | | | |
| 16 | 1 | ~~1~~ | ~~Regenmantel~~ | | | |
| 17 | 2 | ~~1 p.Schuhe~~ | | | | Ersatz |
| 18 | 1 | 1 | Hut | | | |
| 19 | 1 | 1 | Chromnickel taschenuhr | Matal | №3473444 | |
| 20 | 1 | 1 | Schirm &Stock | | | |

*) Anzugeben ist, ob die Sachen befördert werden sollen:
   a) in Möbelwagen, in besonders gedeckten Güterwagen, als geschlossene Sendung in anderen Beförderungsmitteln oder in Behältern bzw. Liftvans, die zollsicher verschlossen werden können;
   b) als Reisegepäck, Expreß-, Eil-, oder Frachtstückgut;
   c) als Handgepäck.
**) Die laufende Nummer darf nicht geändert und nicht mit Zusatz, wie z. B. a) und b) versehen werden.
***) Vgl. Nr. 4 des Merkblattes.

This is a request, submitted in duplicate by Johann Groszman, for permission to take some items of clothing with him when emigrating (i.e., two shirts, three short and two long pairs of trousers, six handkerchiefs, a pair of gloves, a hat, etc.). A pocket watch is described as being made of chrome, since a more expensive one would not have been permitted. The following items—a warm suit, flannel trousers, a pair of shoes, a raincoat—seem to have been disallowed. (Courtesy Charles and Gertrude Deutsch)

DEUTSCHES REICH

REISEPASS
Nr 193201

NAME DES PASSINHABERS

_Johann Israel Groszmann_

BEGLEITET VON SEINER EHEFRAU

UND VON        KINDERN

STAATSANGEHÖRIGKEIT:

DEUTSCHES REICH

Dieser Paß enthält 32 Seiten

The idea of marking all Jewish passports with a _J_ was suggested by the Swiss and put into effect by the Germans. Note "Israel" inserted between the first and last names. The Nazis decreed that all Jewish men were to be called Israel. (Courtesy Charles and Gertrude Deutsch)

The dining room of the Stern School for girls about 1929. After the Anschluss, Lily Bader, the school's owner and director, sold the forty-room school to a former competitor. Subsequently, the state appropriated the school, and no compensation was ever paid. After the Anschluss, Jewish businesses were "Aryanized" or sold for a pittance. (Author's file. Lily Bader is the author's mother.)

P 56.640

31. Aug. 1939

(Dienststelle)  (Ort und Datum)

(Aktenzeichen)  (Straße)

## Steuerliche Unbedenklichkeitsbescheinigung
(Gültigkeitsdauer: zwei Monate ab Ausstellung)

Gegen die Auswanderung des(r) _____ _____
(Beruf oder Stand, Vor- und Zuname)

_____ , _____ am 25. 11. 1879 in Wien ,
(Wohnung)

und seiner Ehefrau Olga Sara geborene _____ , geboren am 31. 8. 1883

in Wien , und seiner Kinder _____ , geboren am _____

_____ , _____ , geboren am _____

habe ich keine Bedenken.

_____
(Unterschrift)

Lager-Nr. 954. Kleinkonzept. 1938. — A 4 (Unbedenklichkeitsbescheinigung). — Staatsdruckerei Wien. (St.) 1844 39

A Tax Payment Clearance Certificate. This was one of the innumerable and difficult to obtain documents which had to be submitted to receive an exit visa. Since it was valid for only three months, in many cases it expired before other necessary documents could be procured. Then the entire process had to start all over again. (Courtesy Charles and Gertrude Deutsch).

Dr. Michael Siegel, a well-known attorney, was seized by the SS while defending a Jewish client. He was marched barefoot down the street with his trouser legs cut off, his head bashed, and his teeth broken, carrying a sign: "I am a Jew, but I will never again complain about the Nazis." (Courtesy Hulton Deutsch Collection Limited and Bea Green)

## Chapter 5

# Getting In:
# The Neighboring Cell

One might well have asked those who were finally able to obtain their emigration papers, "Now that you have broken through the wall with your head, what will you do in the neighboring cell?"

The first cell was the problem of collecting the necessary documents to leave the Third Reich. The neighboring cell involved the problem of finding a country to go to. The difficulties of being admitted to a foreign country matched, and even superseded, those of getting out of the Third Reich. In theory, the Jews had the legal right to emigrate from their countries, even though the Nazis made it next to impossible. The Jews possessed no legal right at all to enter another country. An escapee[20] recalls those turbulent days: "There were terrible difficulties; trying to get into different countries, leaving loved ones behind, going to and fro for this and that, leaving all belongings, closing our business to be allowed to go."

Meir,[134] whose bicycle had been appropriated by his concierge's son, continued in his quest to find a way out: "The pursuit of a visa was on. There never was a lack of rumors, as everybody tried to find a way to get a visa, any visa, to enable one to go to a country, any country, ready to take Jews. Visas were also necessary merely to pass through a country. Visas became more precious than gold. At all foreign consulates long, very long, queues of Jews began to form under the malicious eyes of the police, who were there to enforce 'law and order.' Sometimes a troop of SA rowdies would fall upon such a queue, dispersing the waiting people in all directions, beating and clubbing them to a pulp, arresting and kidnapping at random.

Sometimes Jews waited in line for whole nights. Needless to say, most of the time all the queuing was fruitless."

There were endless frustrations: "transit visas that could not be obtained, tickets that could not be used, war action that cut off emigrations."[33] There were plenty of restrictions that put almost insurmountable obstacles in the way of obtaining asylum. Who needed so many Jews? Who wanted refugees during the depression era? No one, it seemed. The world has now developed a consciousness and somewhat of a sense of responsibility for fleeing masses, but no sanctuary was offered to the European Jews during the Nazi epoch.

People were not finicky in their choice of countries. No place was considered too far. Some distant regions, such as Tibet, had no procedures for immigration. Whenever Hitler invaded a new country that previously had promised asylum, the search had to start all over again. The countries approached for visas by the group of escapees in this study were Argentina, Australia, Belgium, Bolivia, Brazil, Canada, Chile, Cuba, Czechoslovakia, Ecuador, England, Finland, France, Holland, Italy, Liechtenstein, New Zealand, Palestine, Paraguay, Peru, Philippines, Portugal, Santo Domingo, Scotland, South Africa, Spain, Sweden, Switzerland, Trinidad, and the United States; the international city of Shanghai was also approached.

Each country carefully defined the qualities it expected in an applicant. Desperate dialogues took place in consulates, day after day. Would-be immigrants may well have heard the following:

Clerk to harassed-looking applicant with gray complexion: "You are a scientist? What kind? We only accept eminent scientists, as well as artists with international reputations. Are you known throughout the world? Have you made an outstanding contribution to science? No? Unfortunately, in that case England cannot invite you."

"Are you an agricultural worker? No! But that is what we need in New Zealand! We do not have much use for your profession. We cannot accept your application for a visa."

"Do you have anyone who will deposit two hundred pounds in your name in Australia? You don't? Then how do you expect to get a visa?"

Or consider the following agonizing exchange:

"Do you have a sponsor in the United States willing to sign an affidavit stating that you will not be a burden to the state, that your sponsor will take care of you should you fail to get a job? Well then, you can enter the United States. But, of course, not until you receive a visa."

"How do you get a visa?"

"You get a quota number, of course."

"A quota number?"

Clerk, frustrated and irritated: "You don't know what a quota number is? Really, sir, you are most ignorant! The United States allows a specific number of people from each country to immigrate. At the time of your application, you will be given a number. When the turn for this number comes up, and if you still have your sponsor, you will be issued a visa. Unfortunately, the quota from Austria and Germany is oversubscribed. Your number will not come up for two years!"

"Then give me a quota number from a country like Sweden or England. They don't emigrate en masse to the United States. There must be numbers left from their quota."

"There are. But such a step would be against our policy. You must wait two years."

"Two years! But we will all die!"

"Next, please."

Imaginary conversations? Yes and no. There were variations on this theme being played out at every consulate in the Third Reich. But it occurred most frequently at American consulates. The United States was the most sought-after country in the world. The lines in front of the consulate were endless and moved at a snail's pace. A young man failed to mention to his brother the need for obtaining a quota number. His brother queued up only two days later, but it cost him over a year in waiting time. The standards at the American consulates were exacting. Each affidavit sent from the United States was carefully examined to determine if it guaranteed sufficient funds for the immigrant. Fears and hopes accompanied every trip to the consulate: Will I get into the consulate today? Will the amount of money guaranteed by my not-so-rich relatives be sufficient? Will my quota number come up soon? It rarely did. The atmosphere at the

American consulates was not one that welcomed the poor, the huddled masses. It was known to be cold to the point of indifference. The staff was not merely unhelpful; they appeared to want to slow down the pace by creating unnecessary and petty precautions.

My own parents trekked repeatedly to the American consulate. The answer was always the same: "Your file has not yet been processed. You must wait your turn." My parents were certain that there was some mistake. People who had registered long after them were passing them by. The clerks behind the desk were singularly unhelpful. The wait for the quota number was interminable. At the rate we were progressing, we would never survive. At night I heard my mother pacing the floor, back and forth, back and forth, sighing. (To this day I find it unbearable to hear anyone sigh.) It was essential to leave immediately. But how? My mother had applied for and obtained a position as a maid in England. She was, therefore, entitled to an English visa. Based on this visa, her family was allowed to enter England. But there was an "if"—a very big "if." The English visa was only a transit visa. To be able to land in England, we would first have to prove that we had an ultimate destination. In that lay the dilemma. We could only go to England if we had a quota number from the U.S. consulate. And we could only survive waiting for our quota number if the waiting period was spent in a safe haven. It was essential for us to get to England. We needed both visas to survive. A lucky encounter solved this apparently unsolvable predicament. My father ran into a patient who was working at the U.S. consulate. She made a brief search for our file. An unused cabinet held it. She took the file from the wrong filing cabinet and put it in the right one. Shortly after that we received our quota number. On such simple actions did lives depend.

None of the difficulties encountered at the American consulates discouraged the would-be immigrants. Everyone hoped and searched for an American sponsor. The lucky ones found one. Having a relative in the United States was one of the best ways of obtaining a sponsor. Some people dug deep into their background and discovered one. Others had relatives who had recently arrived in the States who made it their business to help find a guarantor for those left behind.

The urgent need to get a visa prompted would-be émigrés to pursue even the most unlikely leads. Our American contact had been obtained through a number of fortuitous events: Some years before the Anschluss my parents had traveled in Norway and had encountered two American schoolteachers. After the Anschluss my parents wrote to them, asking them to sponsor us. The teachers were unable to raise the money needed, but as luck would have it, they contacted a synagogue where a new president was about to be installed. The president was eager to find a worthwhile project and decided that rescuing us was a worthy task. The members of the synagogue contributed funds to save an unknown family.

Relatives went to great lengths to help. Charles[28] explains: "My wife's relatives in America were guardian angels. They pooled their meager resources and deposited all the money they were able to collect in a bank as a guarantee that we would not become a burden to the state. As soon as the government had checked to see if the proper funds were available, they withdrew the money and deposited the same funds in another bank as a basis for additional affidavits. The result was the rescue of fourteen relatives."

Connections in high places proved to be as good or perhaps even better than a relative in a foreign land. It seemed that the "right person" could untangle the thorniest bureaucratic knot with the snap of a finger. A former consul[79] to Norway had befriended the Greek consul. The ex-diplomat was in the happy position of quickly obtaining a Greek visa for his daughter. Not surprisingly, connection with royalty was an extra plus. The Danish wife[13] of an Austrian scientist wanted to gain admission for her family to Denmark. It was not a simple matter, but because her father had been a Danish civil servant, he was able to enlist the cooperation of the King of Denmark in obtaining a visa for his daughter's scientist husband. All this was necessary in spite of the fact that the scientist had worked with Niels Bohr in Sweden and had been decorated by the Swedish government for his work in plant genetics.

Connections were vital, but they did not necessarily have to be with the highly placed. Simple people, such as a concierge at a consulate, could prove to be very effective. Fifteen-year-old Susan[53] and her family had already booked passage on a ship, but they needed to have their passport stamped at the Chinese embassy. They obtained quick entrance because Susan's mother was able to speak Czech to the doorman at the Chinese consulate. He wielded power over who was allowed entry. It is strange that speaking Czech would prove a boon to opening doors to the Chinese consulate. Probably a hefty tip gave an additional push to those doors.

Fame was now a doubly valued commodity. Far from being ephemeral, it was worth its weight in lives. Escapees in this study who had a prestigious family member vividly recalled their fortunate position: A man whose grandfather, a social scientist, had an international reputation found it relatively easy to obtain entry to England. The daughter of an eminent cardiologist,[7] whose patients had come to Vienna from countries around the world, recalls that her father received affidavits from three former patients in various parts of the United States. A famous Jewish man may have had worth in the United States, but he counted for less than nothing in his native country.

Sometimes it took a combination of fame and knowing the right people to produce results. The wife[172] of a scientist describes this extraordinary combination: "My father had been sent to Sweden by Freud, where he met with one of Freud's friends, Professor Gunner Holmgren, head of the Karolinsky Institute, which grants the Nobel Prize for medicine. This man came to visit us in 1937. Because my father was busy with patients, my husband showed the professor his laboratory. The two became very friendly. In 1938, as soon as I picked up my passport, I phoned Professor Holmgren in Stockholm. It so happened that the professor's brother was the foreign minister. We had the Swedish visa within eight hours. I still marvel at all the lucky coincidences."

But there were also strangers, ordinary people, who extended help for humanitarian reasons without asking for payment of any kind. Such people with connections to government officials came to the rescue of Richard,[145] a young man who found himself in a dreadful position. While still in Dachau, he was told to leave Austria within a week of discharge or be rearrested. "My uncle sent my papers to a friend in England, who passed it on to someone in Australia whom we did not know. This stranger procured landing permits which were needed for immigration to Australia."

It was often impossible to tell which government would take a benevolent attitude toward supplicants and which would plot in secrecy to exclude them at all cost. Application for entry to the wrong one could delay departure until it was too late. Switzerland was a case in point. It extolled itself as a country with a mission to help refugees (Wickers & Wacker, 1990). Officially, it represented itself in the following way: "Switzerland is a refuge to those who have been driven out of their countries. In this way we not only express our thanks to the world for our centuries of peace, but also give recognition to the great contribution the homeless refugees have made" (p. 2). Covertly, the attitude was quite different. The *J* for Jew had been inserted into the German passports at the request of the Swiss consul. In this way Jewish refugees could be quickly singled out. The *J* would guard against the danger of an unsuspecting official mistakenly turning a transit visa into a permanent one. But worse, Dr. Heinrich Rothmund, the Swiss chief of police in charge of foreigners, decreed which refugees were to be rejected at the border: "We accept those who flee from their army units. We also accept war prisoners who are not in a position to travel on. We also accept political prisoners as every political refugee is under a death threat. Do we turn back only the Jews? This conclusion seems to force itself on us" (pp. 4–5). Dr. Rothmund was made of stern stuff. He cautioned against sympathy in the case of Jewish children. "There are already quite a few [Jewish] children in our country. Therefore, it is necessary to state in each case quite clearly: there can be no permanent sanctuary [for Jewish children]. This has to be explained to their parents. One may not flinch from turning back [Jewish children] under any circumstances. We have to be quite determined to think of our own young growing people. Our compromising [in letting Jewish children in] could lead to their [the Swiss youths'] misfortune" (p. 2).

On the other hand, immigration policies of countries could suddenly become more favorable through unexpected circumstances. In the case of Cuba, favorable circumstances were due to Rabbi Shuster.[161] He had arrived in Cuba on a transit visa. Rabbi Shuster knew that only those who possessed quota numbers to the United States were admitted there. But what about the Jews still in Europe who had no American affidavits? Was there no way to get any of them to Cuba? Most refugees in foreign countries chose to lie low and stay away from officials. Not Rabbi Shuster. He saw the graft and corruption in the country, and he conceived an extraordinary idea. He asked a businessman friend to arrange an appointment for him with Colonel Batista, president of Cuba. The rabbi strode into his office and requested that Jews be brought from Germany to Cuba. The president referred the rabbi to his brother-in-law, Señor Gonzalez, the minister of immigration. The rabbi found him playing cards. Undeterred, the rabbi made his request. Señor Gonzalez, continuing with his game, answered, "For a thousand dollars per head, bring them all over." Rabbi Shuster worked day and night organizing a committee that raised large sums of money. The refugees came by the thousands in all kinds of ships, large and small.

There were countries that opened their doors to those with specific occupations. Least desired were professionals and business people. Skilled workers stood a better chance. As a result, courses such as dressmaking, glass grinding, and candy, hat, and flower making began to proliferate. Besides arranging for the various visas, Gerda's[100] family members were engaged in learning various trades. Her mother took a course in facial massage, her father in making facial creams, and her sister in sewing hats. Chocolate making was another escapee's[54] choice. Charles,[28] who was striving to obtain an English domestic visa for himself and his wife as a couple, enrolled in a Gestapo-permitted course for becoming a butler. He learned how to clean shoes, prepare the table, and serve wine. Classes were held in an abandoned café opposite Gestapo headquarters. The Gestapo inspected the place several times, keeping Charles in a constant state of fear. The course ended quickly. Otto,[42] who after the Anschluss had been expelled from his last year at medical school, searched for some practical skill. He enrolled in the Institute for Beauty Care. His report card confirmed that he passed face massage and hand care with the top grade of "very good," entitling him to present himself as a Specialist in Beauty Care. Needless to say, most courses proved useless. Because of the increasing necessity to raise cash, some people used their own expertise to give courses. Hilda's[162] father, who owned a matzo factory, taught fine pastry baking. Charles's[28] father-in-law, an experienced upholsterer, gave courses in mattress and pillow making.

The most important lesson of all was learning English. Besides burning her customers' hair while learning hairdressing, Stella[72] was struggling with English: "We took English lessons, making sharp *sss* sounds out of 'the,' and tried to force our lips to produce a proper

English *w*." English, unlike most other courses, was of immediate value: It made the reading of foreign newspapers possible. An article appeared in an English paper written by the daughter of the Lord Justice. Miss MacKinnon was calling on the English people to assist the Austrian refugees. Gertrude[29] wrote to its author and enclosed a snapshot of her little boy. Miss MacKinnon answered and became an adviser and guide. Long lines of women lined up to take English lessons with Gertrude.

Knowledge of English was also helpful in corresponding with strangers in the United States. Fred[39] relates: "I wrote letters in what I assume must have been broken English to at least twenty or more persons with the same last name as mine. I obtained their addresses from a Manhattan phone book at the American embassy." He had no luck. In contrast, Dorrit[188] recalls her friend's successful efforts: "One of my schoolmates by the name of Waxman wrote to Franz Waxman, the prominent film musician. No relation. Amazingly, he sent affidavits for the whole family. She had known his name only from the movie credits."

Families who in the early days had pledged to leave together began to acknowledge that their devotion to each other was an impediment to survival. In a fairly typical case[137] the mother of a family went to England, one son managed to get to Israel, and another crossed illegally into Czechoslovakia; the father at first had no options but later was able to join his wife in England. Friends felt disloyal when they were forced to abandon mutual efforts to leave. Kurt[159] and two friends had pledged to stick together. At one point Kurt's friends realized that only Kurt had a chance to reach England. They persuaded him to leave, but Kurt felt he was deserting them. In fact, later Fritz and George were forced to split up, too.

There were other soul-searching and possibly life-saving decisions to be made. Whether to be baptized was one of these. Stella[72] and her husband considered this option. "We had been told that South American countries will let you in. But you have to have papers stating that you are Catholic. Catholic? Well, you could buy those papers. They were a mere formality, of course. It did not mean that you really converted. Just a means to get out of the country and be safe. One late afternoon my husband and I found ourselves in a dim loft. A handful of shabby, dejected people were gathered there. In front was a lectern on a podium. A priest appeared. He had a white collar, a black robe. His large golden cross sparkled on his chest. His face was kind, illuminated with a warm smile. He went to each of the huddled figures and talked to them in a low voice. I showed him a picture of my little daughter. His smile deepened. 'I would love to get this little soul.' Something within me stiffened. He went to the lectern, raised his arms. 'Now we shall kneel,' he said, 'and learn how to cross ourselves.' In the darkness I glanced at my husband. He looked at me. My knees had stiffened. They were rigid. We slunk out."

It was important to be worldly-wise. Naïveté could be costly. A man recalls his family's lack of experience. The family[51] had applied to the French embassy for a Tunisian visa and went to pick it up. When they presented their passports, they were told the papers had disappeared. Later they learned that they should have inserted a considerable sum of money. Some consulates made the procedure much easier: Joseph[144] remembers that the receptionist at the Ecuadoran consulate let you know what you had to pay and passed the baksheesh on to the official who then offered the visa.

Amidst the running for documents and visas there was the constant concern about money. Loss of jobs and the expenses involved in obtaining documents impoverished many people.[134] Youths planning to emigrate to Palestine tried to raise money for those too poor to pay the fare. It was agonizing to be short of funds when even small amounts could be of pressing importance. In spite of her helpful connections, Emma[142] was short of money and her brother needed a guarantee of a hundred pounds deposited in England before he could enter that country. The trouble was that they did not have a hundred pounds. Then Emma's husband remembered an Englishman he had met while working in England. He lent the money, and Emma's brother got to England two days before war broke out.

Funds in a foreign country could be a life saver. But under the Nazis all such capital had to be turned over to the authorities. Fail-ure to do so resulted in the death penalty. Therefore, many people obeyed orders and notified the appropriate Nazi officials of the existence of their funds. However, many people decided not to do so. Gerda's[100] family made a pact never to reveal the existence of their

Swiss bank account, not even under torture. Businessmen who had traveled abroad[185] and people whose relatives resided in foreign countries were in a good position to hide funds. Because of the unpredictable political situation in Austria, my own parents had deposited some money in secret accounts both in Norway and in Switzerland. They decided that if they relinquished one account, the second one would probably not be suspected. While we were in Austria, however, these funds were not helpful. Since the mail was censored, it was not possible to inform possible guarantors that we had resources that would prevent us from becoming dependent on them, but hints were made in letters. For example: "We will not be a burden to you. Our Aunt Rosie in New York will help us." The message was not understood by the recipients. They had never lived under a dictatorship. In their innocence, they believed that we really had an Aunt Rosie.

It was common knowledge that the Jewish population was short of money. The human vultures would emerge and buy their possessions for a song. The ticket agents took advantage of a perfect opportunity; they claimed that nothing cheaper than first-class berths on luxury steamers were available and insisted on selling only round-trip tickets to Jews, who, of course, needed only one-way fares. Or after claiming that they were all "sold out," ticket agents could be persuaded by gifts to miraculously discover a "recent cancellation."[144]

Illness was one of the unforeseeable obstacles that could suddenly halt all plans and place a whole family in danger. A youngster[187] in a family that had acquired visas and tickets for leaving Romania suddenly suffered a near-fatal appendicitis attack. After the child's three-week hospital stay the family had to make arrangements all over again. The Germans took over Romania within months of the family's departure. They just made it, but there were countless others who failed to get out before the Nazis' arrival. Those with a lingering illness found all doors closed; they, together with selfless family members, perished. Lottie's[165] mother suffered from multiple sclerosis. All countries rejected her. Lottie was sent to England, but her father decided to stay with his wife. He was deported to a concentration camp two days after she died.

Age, like illness, was a major barrier to emigration. Those

beyond middle age were considered undesirable by most foreign countries. When parents were too old to begin anew, the children were left in an agonizing quandary. Franz[15] remembers: "My paternal grandmother posed a problem: She was old and born in Czechoslovakia—a most unpromising combination for obtaining a visa for the United States, and in fact she was refused. What were my parents to do? Apply for a visa themselves and leave her? Not apply for one and face almost certain death sooner or later? Such issues now became everyday, practical problems in need of prompt solution." Otto[42] pursued a hopeless quest to find a country that would accept his parents. They had no money abroad, no guarantors, no suitable occupation. They perished. Some elderly people simply felt that without a foreign language, money, or prospects of any sort the task of resettling was too overwhelming. It is a sobering thought that all those who escaped from Hitler are now the same age or older than their parents were at that time. Were these events to recur today, these escapees would all be considered too old to be rescued.

Beyond money, connections, and occupation, there was one factor that was all-important. It could not be obtained through effort or bribery and without it everything was lost. That factor was luck. One had to be lucky not to be arrested, as Dorrit[188] discovered. On a hot July day in 1938 she and her friend wanted to go swimming. But all public swimming pools in Vienna barred Jews. Unwisely, the girls took a a trolley to Baden-bei-Wien, about an hour's ride away, where Jews were still permitted to use the pool. While the girls were dressing to return home, they heard a commotion and realized that the Nazis were raiding the pool and herding the Jews into trucks. They hastily left the dressing room and ran for their lives.

If one was arrested, the life and death outcome frequently depended entirely on luck. Luck was with a babe in arms[46] who, together with her mother and sister, was caught in a roundup. Because of a severe ear infection the baby was crying. Her mother begged to see the Gestapo official in charge, and to her surprise they recognized each other. Her husband had once given the official's brother a job. The family was allowed to leave. A similar event was played out at another jail. Stella[72] relates: "My friend's husband, a lawyer, was arrested. While he was being held at the police station a sausage vendor appeared at the jail. The crowd of arrested people jostled each other to buy a sausage. My friend's husband was not hungry. He drifted into a conversation with a policeman, who told him that he had trouble getting a divorce. The husband gave him some legal advice, and the policeman arranged for him to be dismissed."

The most important piece of luck was to find a sponsor able to provide a visa. Sometimes such events were sufficiently coincidental to be part of a Hollywood movie. Norbert[14] had no prospects of emigrating. He was working in his father's store when an American man who had lost his way entered. Norbert offered to walk him to his hotel. On the way Norbert revealed that he was Jewish and had no chance of leaving. "How old are you?" the man inquired. "Twenty-one," Norbert replied. With apparent interest, the man inquired whether he had been born in July 1917. When Norbert answered yes, the tourist, who introduced himself as Mr. Selsberg, grew pensive. He asked Norbert to meet his wife. At the hotel the couple talked briefly with each other. Mr. Selsberg then turned to Norbert and offered him an American affidavit. Many years later Mr. Selsberg disclosed the reason: In 1917 Mrs. Selsberg had fallen and suffered a miscarriage. Its consequences prevented her from having children. The lost child would have been born in July, close to Norbert's birthday. The couple believed that meeting Norbert was a sign from God. He was a substitute for their lost child and thus they had to save him.

If no visa was obtainable, luck was even more essential. Not only was it needed to find a bribable person, one had to be even luckier to find one who would actually honor the commitment. Alice's[128] father had been unsuccessful in obtaining a visa. Finally, he took the desperate step of buying exorbitantly expensive, clandestine transportation to Venice. The border officials had been bribed by the travel agent. In the early morning hours, when the train crossed the border, passport control bypassed their compartment. It was the last such arrangement. The next group escaping by this route was caught.

And even when sponsors and visas had been procured, luck was still necessary to obtain passage. Joseph,[144] unable to persuade his parents to try for South America, had obtained a visa for himself to Ecuador. But he despaired of getting timely passage. After sending his daughter off to England, he was leaving the train station when he ran into a man he had met at the Ecuadoran consulate. Both had obtained their visas the same day. Joseph mentioned that he expected war to break out. He was frantically looking for an escape route and asked the man what chances he had to get to Ecuador. To his surprise, the man revealed that he had booked passage for his family on the SS *Horatio*, which was sailing on July 16, 1938, but that he could not use the tickets because he had to wind up some business affairs. He was on his way to return the tickets to the shipping agent. Overjoyed, Joseph accompanied him to the agency and took over his passage.

When all papers were in hand, it was time to leave relatives and friends. Under normal circumstances warm handshakes and good-bye kisses ease the pain of parting. Those loving gestures would have been particularly reassuring to escapees, who left frequently with the grave suspicion that they might never see their relatives and friends again. But good-byes were a luxury that few could afford. The last days and hours were usually filled with anxiety-arousing activities. It was not that people were taking many possessions with them. Most people simply walked away and left all their furniture behind. Or they packed belongings into huge boxes that were to be shipped once they were overseas. The packing was either done under the eyes of a Nazi official or checked when completed to ensure that only items permitted to leave the country had been packed. The strain of having a Nazi official looking over one's shoulder weighed heavily. In actuality, the huge crates in which the escapees packed their furniture rarely left the Third Reich: Either some official stole them or, as happened in the case of my own family, the goods were auctioned off, with the proceeds going to the Party.

I myself recall a rather subdued, grim atmosphere as my mother was gathering the few things she valued and planned to take along. This activity had to take place in a surreptitious manner. Our cook, Mitzi, who had been with us since I was born, had become an ardent Nazi. A lonely woman whose husband had deserted her and whose only child had died young, she had succumbed to the flattering description bestowed on every German woman. She had become "*eine schöne Deutsche Frau* [a beautiful German woman]." Identifying herself with the victorious Nazi party gave her a personal identity she had never had before. She insisted on listening to the Nazi officials' speeches, and Hitler's or Goebbels's screeching voices rang through our house from morning to night. Mitzi loved me dearly. On the one hand, she wanted to stay with the Jewish child she loved. On the other hand, she wanted to be a faithful Nazi. Mitzi began to hatch a plot. If my parents left, she would keep me with her and turn me into an "honorary Aryan." The plan was only a figment of her imagination, but it was nevertheless a great danger to us. My parents feared that Mitzi would denounce them to the Gestapo on some pretext in order to snatch me away from them. As a result, my parents desperately tried to prevent her from knowing the exact day of our departure. On that day, my mother hastily prepared the few items she wished to take along. She asked me to fetch the family photograph album and place it beside the few other items she was sorting. I remember the album quite clearly: It was of green leather and fastened with a golden clasp. "Later," I said, and promptly forgot about it. My mother, preoccupied with more important things, said no more about it. Years later I missed that green album as an English lord might miss the paintings of his ancestors, had they been removed from the grand staircase.

For most, the good-byes were wrenching. Joseph,[144] who left for South America, remembers how painful it was to leave his old parents behind. As Valerie[151] departed with her husband, her mother looked out the window and cried; Valerie tried not to think that they might not see each other again. Otto,[42] only twenty-three when he left, has the moment clearly etched in his mind: "I said good-bye to my ailing mother. My father came to the railway station. We pretended that this was only a temporary parting, but both of us had the foreboding that this was forever. It was a heart-rending moment. I cried bitterly when the train left. This scene is vivid in my memory, and I cannot write about it without emotions."

My own father's optimism had made me feel secure about our chances of leaving. One afternoon I walked into the family room, which was usually empty during office hours. I was startled to find my father and his best friend there. As I stood hidden in the doorway, neither noticed me. My father, wearing his white physician's coat, had obviously just been called out of his office. The friend was telling my father that he was leaving. The two men remained silent for a minute. Then they embraced and, to my great shock, tears filled my father's eyes. I quietly left the room.

There were many subterfuges used to cover one's disappearance. When Dorrit[188] left with her mother, they carried no luggage. Her mother had a very big handbag, and Dorrit brought her school satchel with a change of clothes, a doll, and a toothbrush. She also carried her violin case. The boy Franzl, with whom she always played, came by and asked where they were going. "To the dentist," Dorrit answered. They tried not to attract attention.

Menacing danger surrounded the escapees until the border was finally crossed, and it frequently took extraordinarily quick thinking not to falter at the last moment. Alice's[172] scientist husband proved himself equal to the task: At the airport an official searched the couple's luggage so slowly that they were bound to miss their plane. The Ulmans had come this far to a large extent through the help of two heroic women. One was Dr. Ella Lingens, a non-Jewish physician who offered her apartment to Jews on the run and was eventually caught and sent to Auschwitz. The other was Muriel Gardner, a young American woman, who told her own story in *Code Name Mary* and was probably the inspiration for Lillian Hellman's *Julia*. The Ulmans had been hidden by Dr. Lingens. Muriel Gardner, who only recently had supplied Manfred, a well-known Jewish socialist leader, with an empty apartment until he could be equipped with a passport, had also provided Alice with money and an affidavit. Having been helped by Ella and Mary, Professor Ulman did not want to falter now. He knew how to outfox the recalcitrant official by appealing to his "*Befehl ist Befehl* [an order is an order]" mentality. "You know," said the professor, "the Führer wants us to leave Germany. If we miss the plane, we cannot obey him. The tickets took our last money. And you will have to be responsible for our not leaving." That was the kind of language the official understood well. In a hurry, he snapped the luggage shut. The couple ran to the plane. The propellers were turning. One has to live through such a narrow escape to be able to imagine how they felt.

Dorrit[188] remembers the exact moment she crossed the frontier: "We arrived at the border during the night. I think it was Aachen. I was jolted awake in time to see the Gestapo taking my violin case from the overhead rack and examining it. He put it back and passed on. Some foreigners on the train had hidden money for Jews and now returned it to them. As we crossed into France, all the passengers began to shout from sheer joy."

My own family too was aware of the looming danger until the last minute. I have a clear image of our leaving in my mind's eye: My family is at the airport. We are to fly to London in order to avoid crossing Germany. At the gloomy airport a pair of SS men in their black uniforms and high boots, the death's head symbol on their hats, are pacing. Everyone speaks in low voices. My parents, sister, and I are ready to board. Each one of us is carrying a small overnight case and the ten marks we are allowed. The two tall SS men approach us. They demand our passports and begin to search us. My father has accidentally overlooked three pennies buried in a deep trouser pocket. The SS men triumphantly retrieve them and begin to discuss whether my father has broken the law and should be removed. My heart stands still, but I cannot believe that they will take my father. Not *my* father. An endless moment passes. Finally one nods for us to leave. Relieved, we board the plane.

My father frequently told me that never before or after did he experience greater happiness than on that lift-off. My mother and I looked green and yellow, respectively. The plane was not pressurized and we were deadly sick. My father was aglow. But for years afterward I had nightmares about those two SS men.

Not everyone found the actual moment of leaving joyous. Charva,[63] who departed with a group of young people for Israel, describes her last moments in Germany: "We walked to the pier in drizzling rain. We carried twenty kilograms on our backs and ten marks in our pockets. In my arms I carried my mother's pillow, made of diapers should my baby be born prematurely. Passersby shouted to our sad group: 'Look, it is the *Saujuden* [pig Jews] who have to run. Look at that one over there. She has a parcel in front and one on her back.' That meant me."

It is always wise to learn a lesson from the past. Reading and rereading the descriptions of the experiences of all those who escaped, I felt I should formulate some principles, some general themes that might teach me to handle future catastrophes should they occur. After all, one can never tell what the future brings. The next time, I wish to be prepared. I have come to some conclusions, and I am quite willing to share my newfound knowledge. Here are the general principles to prepare for catastrophe: First of all, be sure to be born in a country other than the one in which your parents hold citizenship. That will give you dual nationality. If one fails, the other may hold. Have an eminent father or mother who possesses a great deal of money. It helps to be a world-renowned scientist or musician. Be skilled in a trade scarce in foreign countries, such as plumber. If connection with royalty is not available, cultivate high government officials. Have no disease proscribed by foreign countries. Remain under forty years of age. Possess the stamina to stay in line for hours. Be extremely resourceful and intelligent. Most important of all, have a great deal of luck. With all these attributes, you will stand a fairly good chance.

## Chapter 6

# Leaving:
# Three Vignettes

The circumstances of leaving were different for each person. Each parting was poignant in its own way. But some of the elements in the following accounts are contained in most other escapees' chronicles as well: fear, an unexpected turn of events, persistence, luck, and pain.

### All of a Sudden:
### Excerpts from an Account by Stella Hershan

Friends began to leave. Some without papers. We waited for our affidavit from America. Suddenly it was fall, November 1938. Shortly before the year was over our affidavits arrived from America. Now we could buy the tickets for the SS *Queen Mary* to take us across the ocean—with our last money.

The Swiss official carefully examined all the issued visas. "You may stay in Switzerland for eight days," he explained as he wrote it into the passport. "But it cannot be extended. You understand?" We understood.

"When do you want to leave? Tonight?"

"Tonight?" My husband looked stunned. "No, I don't think . . ."

"Why not?" I asked quickly. "What are we waiting for?" The Gestapo? I did not say it, but we all knew what I was thinking.

"All right then," said the Swiss official as he stamped the passport. "Eight days beginning today. Bon voyage!"

At home, we packed a small overnight bag. I dressed my daughter. She had a new traveling outfit. Tied to her blonde hair was a matching hat that tied beneath her chin. She gave us a big smile and settled in her daddy's arms. Our train to Zurich left late, and it was after midnight when we walked out of my parents' house. We still locked the gate in front and tossed the keys over it onto the snow on the lawn.

I don't remember any longer how we went to the Westbahnhof [West Train Station]. A taxi? The trolley car? I don't know. The main thing was not to draw too much attention to ourselves. We did not talk about our fears. People had been turned back at the border, we knew. The train station was swarming with people. Our tickets were for a sleeping car. Our last money. The very last. One could not take any money out of the country anyway. I put the baby to sleep. We sat up and waited. In the morning we arrived at the border. Nazi officials stepped into the compartment.

"Your passport." The voices were as cold as their faces. No human emotions showed in them. My husband handed them the passport. They took it, studied it for a long while. Then they disappeared with it. We sat frozen. This surely was the end. We would be taken off the train. The official came back, returned the passport, and asked for the tax statement. My husband handed it to him. It fluttered in the air. He studied it. For a long while. Then he handed it back. Stretched out his hand. "Heil Hitler." We saw his broad back as he walked out.

Outside the window we saw dejected, pathetic figures carrying small suitcases like ours being led away. We did not dare to breathe. The baby woke, cried a little.

Slowly—we did not notice it at first—the train started to move. We stared at each other unbelievingly.

New officials came into our compartment. They spoke in a Swiss dialect and smiled at the baby as they inspected our passport. We were in Switzerland. I think the first thing I did when the train gathered speed was to put on some lipstick. In Nazi Vienna, one did not dare to draw attention to oneself. My gray face looked at me in the mirror. How did I feed the baby? Change her? I can't remember. "We are safe!" I said to my husband. "We really are safe!"

## Working Against Time:
## Excerpts from an Account by Lilly Friedman

One morning my father called me into his study. From the tense look on his face I knew something important was about to happen. He started by saying that he had thought it would never be necessary to bring up the subject, but circumstances now made it essential. "You were given birth by an American mother in Vienna, and we adopted you when you were six weeks old." Slowly he added, "We don't know what may happen to mother and myself. But we can save you. I have been told by the United States embassy that you will soon be issued an American passport." He paused and studied the effect of this startling news. I was an American citizen. That made me feel more secure. That I was adopted did not have much impact on me. As far as I was concerned, I had a loving father and mother.

The first time the Brownshirts came, it was evening. They came like locusts. While we watched helplessly they tore the fixtures from the wall, the mantelpiece from the fireplace, and stripped the apartment bare. Before they left, they gave us a receipt for everything taken. That made everything "legal." The second time they came, it was at seven o'clock in the morning. I was still half asleep when my father entered my room. He tried to sound matter-of-fact as he explained that two policemen were taking him and his brother to the station for routine questioning. He left without carrying anything. Not even a toothbrush. When he did not come back, another brother offered to go to the police station to make inquiries. He did not come back either. We learned through the grapevine that all the Jewish men in our neighborhood had been taken to the local jail. The official version was that they had been taken into custody for their "own protection."

We waited an endless wait. After two agonizing weeks, we received a postcard. It said: "I am well." But it was sent from Dachau. At least he was alive. Now we could begin the impossible task of getting him out. My mother made every attempt, grasped at every straw, followed every unlikely lead, pursued every rumor to help him. "Aryans" with "connections" appeared, who for a hefty price arranged visas to foreign countries. My mother bought visas to Santo Domingo, Honduras, Madagascar, Shanghai. They all turned out to be worthless. A friend suggested that she go to Gestapo headquarters in

Berlin. In spite of the danger involved, she went. She returned empty-handed. The postcards, thirteen lines long, came every two weeks. Now they came from Buchenwald. My father and his brothers had been transferred. In veiled language, the men appealed to spare no money or efforts to get them out.

My mother and I had to vacate our apartment within two days. It had been requisitioned by a high-ranking SS officer who fancied it. We carried with us what we could and fled to a relative's apartment. The months crept by. My father and two brothers had been incarcerated for seven months. With each passing day their chances became slimmer. Just as there seemed no more hope, we were told that men who had a visa for the United States were being released. Did we have friends or relatives in America? I thought of my birth family and wondered if they would help. It was a shot in the dark, but we had exhausted every other possibility. It was our last chance. My mother had kept the adoption correspondence and rummaged among her old papers. We located the brother of my biological mother and wrote to him. Then we waited, checked the mail daily, and hoped. A few anxious weeks passed. One morning, miraculously, a letter arrived from America. "Uncle Izzi" was willing to send an affidavit for my parents and myself. No words can describe our gratitude and relief.

The first condition for my father's release had been met. We had a foreign visa and a country to go to. But our quota number would not come up for six to twelve months. We would never survive that long. My mother had relatives in London who were in a position to procure a transit visa for us. Armed with these documents, and after much pleading, the Buchenwald gates opened, and my father and his brothers were freed. Shortly after that, prisoners were no longer released from concentration camps.

## The Gold Watch:
## Excerpts from an Account by George Jellinek

It hangs, suspended in a glass enclosure, near my record-playing equipment, and that means that I see it every day. A gold pocket watch probably from the 1930s, emphatically unfashionable today but not old enough to be "antique." The hands are stopped at 6:40. In all likelihood, it was P.M., because I don't remember ever rewinding it since the watch passed into my hands at the railroad station in Budapest on April 15, 1939, the last day of my "early life."

My train to Hamburg via Vienna was to leave around noon. I spent the last hours with my family, and I passed the time in a kind of numb disbelief. My father, thinking of everything, had planned, months before, that I should get used to the idea of "being away from home." He asked my aunt in Belgrade to invite me for a week's visit. "At least Yugoslavia is another country," he said, "it will serve as a transition." It did not work out. I got homesick and, after five days, I came home. My father looked at me with a mixture of bafflement and anguish. "You got homesick? What will you do in April?"

So there I was, at age nineteen, preparing to leave a home that had given me all the love and security that are so easy to accept and so foolhardy to take for granted. The [Hungarian] government provided a glimmer of hope for the ever-optimistic Hungarian Jews, but not enough to convince my father that I, of military age, had any kind of future in Hungary. At least outwardly, he seemed more fearful of the war than he was of the Nazi threat. Hence his decision that I leave for Havana. I did my best to prepare myself mentally for a new life of adventure, independence, and uncertainty. Unfortunately, I was then qualified only for the last of the three.

And then, my father took me to the railroad station, supporting me all the way, telling me how important adult decisions were, how I must learn to rely on myself now that he would not be there to guide me. My mind was full of doubts about my ability to make my way from one city to another, let alone to start a new life in a new country, another continent, among strange people. What would become of me without his strength, his foresight, his resolute and protective hand? What if I never saw him again? I remember nothing more until the time came to say goodbye. And then, this man who had sternly guided me through my early life and now was saving me for a later one, looked around, searching for one more thing he could do for me. And he took his gold pocket watch and quickly, wordlessly pressed it into my hands as I entered the train. My tears did not stop until I reached Vienna.

We never saw each other again, and I had to become a parent

myself before I could realize fully what must have passed through
my father's mind not only at that moment but through all the months
between his decision to let me go and my actual departure.

Through my intense homesickness in the Havana period (1939–
1941), we corresponded regularly. After Pearl Harbor, all communication between us ended. In time, Hungary was taken over by Hitler's
army, and my parents were swallowed by the Holocaust.

I had to reach middle age before I fully realized my vulnerability at nineteen, the unknown dangers, the innumerable ways in
which my life could have gone off the track. The gold watch seems
like the embodiment of all that kept me together through those years.

## Chapter 7

# Kristallnacht: The Beginning of the End

## Official Explanation of Kristallnacht as Given by the Nazi Party

"Legationsrat [German Counsel at the Legation] von Rath was shot in Paris by the Jew, Hershel Grynszpan, on November 7, 1938. Von Rath died of his injuries and on November 9, in a spontaneous outburst, the German and Austrian population vented their rage against the Jews. To avoid further violence, the authorities took a large number of Jewish men for their own protection, into custody" (Bankier, 1990, p. 26).

## Statement by an Escapee Who Had Been Incarcerated in Buchenwald Concentration Camp for Some Time before Kristallnacht

The Nazis asserted that Kristallnacht was the unpremeditated, impulsive act on the part of the German population resulting from Von Rath's murder. The testimony of a concentration camp inmate, that Buchenwald was being prepared four days in advance of the event, puts the lie to the German claim.

Richard Roberts,[145] concentration camp inmate: *"Four days before Kristallnacht,* [italics mine] in anticipation of new transports, we had to put up some 20,000 beds in empty huts. We were ordered to separate these beds from our part of the camp with barbed wire. We did not know what was happening outside our camp. Later we learned that the Germans claimed that as a reprisal against the murder of Mr. von Rath 20,000 Jews were sent to Buchenwald. What a hoax!"

## Excerpts from Escapees' Recollections of Kristallnacht

### Murder

"The SS invaded our[69] home and threatened us with pistols, which they waved in front of their helpless and frightened victims. [They were searching for the father of the household, who, at that moment, was not at home.] They ransacked the house, made a shambles of the place, and carted away 'anti-state' material. They went next door to another Jewish home and, in their frustration, shot father and son on the spot. The killing of neighbors left me almost in a state of shock. There, but for the sake of luck, went my father, my mother, or even I."

"My[156] father was taken by the Gestapo. Three days later he was dead."

### Arson

"The synagogue in Düsseldorf was burning brightly. High flames shot through the roof. Books and notebooks were strewn all over the street."[35]

"We[64] saw the red sky in the background and realized that our synagogues were in flames. In Fürth they were located in a courtyard, the center of many of our activities, religious and otherwise, and a place where our ancestors had worshipped for hundreds of years."

"On my[109] return to Frankfurt the day after Kristallnacht, I saw the synagogue on fire, but had no idea about the thousands of arrests."

## Round-Ups

"A pounding on the door of our[64] home. Brownshirts forced their way into our apartment. Among them was my dad's comrade in arms from World War I. While we quickly dressed, the men screamed at us and cursed us. We were rushed out of the house and marched through town in total darkness, accompanied by the yelling, screeching, and heckling town population. They had been alerted to this so-called 'spontaneous action.' They rushed all the Jews to a square. Many had been beaten up, some had been thrown down the stairs. The Nazi thugs took their clubs and inflicted injuries and death on old and young, the sick and the infirm alike. We stood there helpless."

"Storm troopers came twice to our[174] apartment, but as I was hidden by friends, they did not find me. Thinking that by early evening the day's 'action' was over, I came home. On the third visit to our house, they found me. Together with many others, we were herded to so-called 'assembly-points.' Old and young men, beaten and injured, were eventually pushed into lorries and taken to the local SS barracks, where they were again beaten, herded into small rooms, and 'interrogated' for the next two days. Eventually we were separated into groups. One was sent to Dachau concentration camp, whilst a few others were released. For some unknown reason of fate, I was in the latter group. On November 12, I was released on signing a paper that I would be leaving the country within two months. I signed, although I did not know how I could manage this, with all borders closed."

"They arrested my[152] father. There was no word where they took him. He returned three days later minus front teeth, with black and blue bruises all over his body."

## Concentration Camps

"Papa was in Dachau. Uncle Karl and cousin Ernst were in Buchenwald. Uncle Josef in Sachsenhausen. On November 21 we got the news that Ernst had died in Buchenwald. Aunt Emma learned that her husband also had died at Buchenwald, and a few days later she was notified that her brother had died as well."[91]

"My[69] father was promptly arrested and shipped off to Dachau, which was literally overflowing with prisoners after Kristallnacht. There was not enough room for all of the concentration camp inmates. They finally let my father go after six weeks, with the warning: 'The next time we catch you, you won't get out.'"

"My[109] father was arrested and sent to Buchenwald. For four weeks my mother and I lived with my aunt, whose husband had also been sent to Buchenwald. My father was very subdued after his return. He did not speak about his experiences in the camp. I think he was afraid."

## Jail

"I[168] saw a lorry with several men coming down the street. One man in uniform, wearing a steel helmet and holding a gun in his hand, sat at the back. I believed that they were coming for my dad. I never thought their interest would go further. The vehicle stopped at our house, and three men in civilian clothes approached my father. They asked whether he was a Jew and placed him under arrest. Another man approached me and determined that I was a member of the family. When he found out that I was seventeen, he ordered me to come along too. We all went inside our house and ran into my uncle. They arrested him also. I heard one Gestapo man remark with satisfaction that they had gotten three people when they had only expected one."

"A friendly neighbor hid me[174] for most of the day. When we thought arrests were over, a new wave commenced. I was dragged along with others to the local Gestapo headquarters."

## *Mayhem*

"In the shop there was absolutely nothing left. All the shelves which were not broken were empty. Anything that could be of any use had been taken away. The rest had simply been dumped on the floor and had been broken or smashed. When I went into what had been the tap room, the scene that greeted me was one of utter chaos. The whole place was a shambles. There was not a table or chair that was not broken. The floor was covered inches deep in litter, broken glass, and smashed furniture. In what we called our best rooms, there was some solid, heavy oak furniture. The big sideboard had been overturned and was broken. It was the same in the other room. The piano had been overturned and the table and chairs had been smashed. Whoever had done that had also tried some old-fashioned burglarizing. A panel out of my father's writing desk had been knocked out. My father used to keep his box with petty cash there."[168]

"I[189] remember cowering in the dark. We did not dare to turn on a light in the apartment. We heard the smashing glass and porcelain in another apartment. People were being beaten, and they were screaming."

"The SS men found my[168] uncle and set about him. My uncle, while he was an old man now, had been quite a boxer in his younger days and was able to parry most of the blows. This incensed the SS man even more. A Jew was not supposed to put up any resistance. To vent his anger he picked up the first thing at hand, which was a flower pot, and smashed it over my uncle's head."

## *Evictions*

"Some former customers of my[152] father came and at gunpoint looted our apartment, evicting us. They also looted my father's store and closed it down."

## *Extortion*

"My[64] dad was sent to Dachau. In order to gain his freedom, mother and I were invited to 'visit' a Mr. Kandel. His ultimatum forced us to turn over my dad's business and car for a fee of twenty marks—about ten dollars. We were told that any reluctance on our part would mean my father's certain death."

## *The Populace*

"The streets of the town reflected a horrendous sight. Burning synagogues filled the air with smoke. The jeering crowds enjoyed the rounding up of all male Jews. They were jubilantly supporting the carnage."[174]

"We[64] were marched through town in total darkness to the yelling, screeching, heckling by the town population, who were all alerted to this so-called spontaneous action."

## *A Hero*

"Our[64] little rabbi was singled out for special abuse by the Nazis. As children, we had often poked fun at him. Truly, that night [because of his dignified behavior] this four-foot ten-inch man grew into a giant in the eyes of all of us."

## *The Hiding*

"I[39] had the good luck to slip out of the house just as the SA came toward the house. I was scared. My father and I proceeded into the city to a hiding place. We camped out in a vacant apartment downtown. We remained undiscovered, possibly in some way aided by a cooperating concierge."

"My[87] father was arrested, but because he was only half-Jewish, they let him go. He saw the brutality at Gestapo headquarters. He was afraid, so he traveled around the country for weeks. We hid with a 'mixed' family. After I left, my father was accused by a neighbor of listening to foreign radio stations. He was about to be arrested again. He committed suicide."

## Women and Children

[We[64] were lined up in the town square.] "It was a bitter cold morning. I remember sharing a pair of gloves with my little friend Eva, who was nine years old—six years younger than myself."

"Some Nazis came into our[66] apartment and overturned the china closet. Because we were only women and children, that is all they did."

"My[47] father and seventeen-year-old brother had gone into hiding, so the hoodlums took my mother and aunt. I was left behind. Hiding behind a curtain, I looked out of the window, and what I saw made my heart stand still. They had dragged my mother into the street and forced her to kneel on the sidewalk. They strong-armed her into scrubbing off some white paint on the ground. It had been spilled by the mob when they had scribbled the word *Jude* on store windows. Two hours later she came through the door, wet and exhausted, fear written all over her face. She put her arms around me and cried."

"Grandpa, as he did every evening, came to sit at the foot of my[43] bed to listen to me reciting the *Sh'ma Israel*. Then he sang for me 'Rozhinkes mit Mandelen.' That night he didn't leave and I recited the *Sh'ma* and he sang 'Rozhinkes mit Mandelen' again. It wasn't too long until we heard the march of boots in the halls, loud nasty voices, doors and windows breaking, screams, clubbing and pleading, while I recited the *Sh'ma* over and over again, alternating with grandfather's lullaby. It was dawn when the screams, pleading, and clubbing finally let up. I fell asleep before he left the room. The next morning all Jewish families were gone, their apartments ransacked."

"A horde of about ten Nazis in uniform made us[96] open the door. They destroyed furniture and broke glassware. They piled everything into a heap and hurled my seventy-five-year-old grandmother on top of it. I will never forget the scene."

### Foreigners

"Foreigners were not protected. I[64] remember one Swiss friend screaming, 'I am Swiss,' and the Nazis hitting him, saying: 'You are what? You are a Jew'!"

### Help Extended

"My[15] mother received an anonymous telephone call, telling her that my father should not take any streetcar, bus, or taxi. He arrived home safely."

"The superintendent came to speak to my[43] grandparents. He instructed them not to turn on the lights or walk around, but for all of us to keep quiet and go to sleep. The next morning all Jewish families were gone, their apartments ransacked. We noticed that there was no *J* on our door." [Someone had removed it to protect the family.]

"I[183] spent the night in Dr. Ella Lingens' apartment." (Dr. Lingens, non-Jewish, spent two years in Auschwitz for protecting Jews.)

### Postscript

#### *Memo from Gauleiter (District Leader) Odilo Globocnik after Kristallnacht (Bankier, 1990)*

I. These are my orders:
   a. All Jewish stores are to be closed and keys are to be brought to the police station. All damaged windowpanes are to be replaced by the Jewish owners of the stores.

    b. The furniture in apartments vacated by Jews is to be placed in a separate room, which is to be sealed. The apartments are to be given to party members in return for payment of appropriate rent.

    c. With respect to apartments and businesses, where the safety of merchandise cannot be guaranteed, the goods must be transported immediately to the appropriate rooms at the district or regional offices, which have been set aside for this purpose.

II. From the actions [of Kristallnacht] the following advantages have accrued [conclusions by Gauleiter Odilo Globocnik]:

    1. Of the 5000 [Jewish] individual and small businesses to be shut down, *in accordance with the plan* [italics mine], about 4000 were closed very quickly, thus improving and strengthening the economy of the Aryan retail store owner.

    2. The inventories will be ceded to Aryan businessmen, the market price being determined by a departmental commission.

    3. Food products which spoil easily will be handed over to the NSV offices.

    4. Through our action [during Kristallnacht], about 2000 party members have received appropriate small apartments.

*Minutes of Meeting of Goering with Nazi Officials after Kristallnacht, November 12, 1938 (Bankier, 1990, pp. 31–32; my translation)*

GOERING: Gentlemen. I am finished with this kind of demonstration. They do not harm the Jews, only myself, since I am in charge of the economy. When a Jewish stores is destroyed and the merchandise tossed into the street, the insurance companies compensate the Jews. The results are that not only are the Jews not harmed but, in addition, consumer goods belonging to the *Volk* [nation] are being destroyed. If in the future you carry out demonstrations, which may be necessary, then I would ask you to lead these in such a way that they do not bite into our own flesh. It is simply crazy to clean out a Jewish warehouse and burn it and then a German insurance company has to carry the damage. And all the time while I need

the merchandise, whole warehouses full of clothes, and who
knows what else, are being burned. And I need these things
urgently! You might as well burn the raw material when we import
it. . . . I would have preferred that you had killed 200 Jews, instead
of destroying such good merchandise.

HILGARD (*representative of the insurance companies, discussing the
need to pay for destroyed but insured Jewish businesses*): We do a
great deal of international business. We cannot afford to under-
mine confidence in German insurance companies. If we do not
meet our obligations, it will be a black spot on the escutcheon
of the German insurance companies.

OBERGRUPPENFÜHRER HEYDRICH: Simply pay the insurance. Once it is
paid [to the Jews], it will simply be requisitioned [by the Nazi
party]. This way we will formally save face.

HILGARD: I believe what Obergruppenführer Heydrich has just said is
the correct solution.

### Pronouncement by Hermann Goering

Hermann Goering, November 12, 1938. Conference on the
Jewish Problem. Point 7: A one billion-dollar fine will be levied on
the Jewish Community as a penalty for the destruction of stores and
apartments on November 9 and 10 [Herzstein, 1974, pp. 96–97].

Lea (on stool) with three of her five siblings. The three girls in this picture were sent to England. Lea's brother, mother, and two younger siblings died together in camps. Lea's father returned from the camps after the war to children who had difficulty adjusting to a new life with him. (Courtesy Lea Taub)

Elli and her parents in 1928. In 1939, Elli was sent to England. Her journalist father was caught in France and was believed to have been deported to Auschwitz and murdered there. Her mother survived and lived in England, but could not get over the loss of her husband. (Courtesy Elli Adler)

**Deutsches Rotes Kreuz**

Präsidium / Auslandsdienst
Berlin SW 61, Blücherplatz 2

**ANTRAG**

an die *Agence Centrale des Prisonniers de Guerre, Genf*
— Internationales Komitee vom Roten Kreuz —
auf Nachrichtenvermittlung

**REQUÊTE**

de la *Croix-Rouge Allemande, Présidence, Service Etranger*
à *l'Agence Centrale des Prisonniers de Guerre, Genève*
— Comité International de la Croix-Rouge —
concernant la correspondance

1. Absender    ERNA STEIN, PRAG XII.
   *Expéditeur*  SCHLESISCHE STRASSE 116

bittet, an

*prie de bien vouloir faire parvenir à*

*Verwandtschaftsgrad:* .. TOCHTER.

2. Empfänger    GERDA STEIN PER ADRESSE
   *Destinataire*  MURIEL AGNES SHADWICH, FRÜHER
   FAIR MEADOWS BROADSTONE, DORSET

folgendes zu übermitteln / ce qui suit:

(Höchstzahl 25 Worte!)
(25 mots au plus!)  GELIEBTE GERTI — VOR MEINER
ABREISE 1000 KÜSSE — BETE TÄGLICH
FÜR DICH. — HABE MUT — SCHREIBE AN
SCHWESTER VON ELLY — HELLA —
HABE NUMMER VIERHUNDERTEINUND-
SECHZIG. — DATUM 20 X. MUTTER

(Datum / date)                    (Unterschrift / Signature)

3. Empfänger antwortet umseitig
   *Destinataire répond au verso*

Gerda's mother's last message before deportation to the East. Sent through the Red
Cross, it is dated January 11, 1943, and includes her prison number: "Dearest Gerti—
before my departure 1000 kisses—Pray daily for you—Have courage—Write to Elly's
sister—Hella—Have number 461. Date 10/20. Mother." (Courtesy Gerda Mayer)

RED CROSS ENQUIRY/MESSAGE

Stamp of issuing Red Cross:

ENQUIRER
DEMANDEUR

Name/Nom ............ FELDMANN

First Names/Prénoms ...... Lily

Address/Adresse ............ c/o F.R.Dept., B.R.C.S., 8 Sh. Malika Farida, Cairo.

Original Home Address (in the case of a Displaced Person) /Domicile dans son propre pays:

Relationship of Enquirer to Addressee/Degré de parenté du demandeur avec personne recherchée:
.............. Daughter

The enquirer desires news of the Addressee and asks that the following message should be transmitted to him:
Le demandeur voudrait des nouvelles de la personne recherchée et désirerait lui transmettre le message suivant:

.............. Anxious for news of welfare and whereabouts.

Date ............ 8.8.1945.

ADDRESSEE
DESTINATAIRE

Name/Nom ............ FELDMANN

First Names/Prénoms ...... Marianne

Date of Birth/Date de Naissance ...... 18.9.1898     Place of Birth/Lieu de Naissance Wien, Austria.

Nationality/Nationalité ...... AUSTRIAN     MOSAISCH

Single — widow(er) — divorced     (Delete all irrelevant matter).
Célibataire — veuf (ve) — divorcé (e)     (Barrez les mots qui ne servent pas).

Profession/Profession ...... PRIVATE

Last known address/Dernière adresse connue:
.............. WIEN II, PRATERSTR. 15, AUSTRIA.

THE ADDRESSEE'S REPLY TO BE WRITTEN OVERLEAF (NOT MORE THAN 25 WORDS)
LA RÉPONSE DU DESTINATAIRE (25 MOTS AU MAXIMUM) PEUTÊTRE ÉCRITE AU VERSO.

PSSN / SQIF / 6-45 / 5.000

Inquiry by Lily Feldmann to the Red Cross, dated August 8, 1945, asking for news and the whereabouts of her mother. Lily's mother had been deported and perished. (Courtesy Charles and Gertrude Deutsch)

Official Check

PR 0257216

MANUFACTURERS HANOVER TRUST COMPANY
INTERNATIONAL DIVISION. PAYING AND RECEIVING DEPARTMENT
44 WALL STREET, NEW YORK 15, N. Y.

1-30
210

DATE 12-30-63

PAY $347.64**

TO THE ORDER OF
LILY FELDMANN
C/O CHARLES DEUTSCH
812 RIVERSIDE DRIVE
NEW YORK 32, N. Y.

AT THE REQUEST OF
CREDITANSTALT BANKVEREIN
WIEN, AUSTRIA

INSTRUCTIONS
L 12/20/63. GS/407
SR.

ORDER—ISRAELITISCHE KULTUSGE-
MEINDE, SCHOTTENRING 25, WIEN
1.
RE. "ENTSCHADIGUNG NACH DEM
OFG" EQUIVALENT OF S 9.053.60.
REP. $348.64, LESS OUR COMM.
$1.00.

AUTHORIZED SIGNATURE

⑈:0210⋅0030⋅0000 0⋅0002⑈

A check received by Lily Feldmann as compensation for her mother's murder. Her mother had been transported to Lodz and disappeared there. The Austrian government considered the amount of $347.64 sufficient compensation. Lily never cashed the check. (Courtesy Charles and Gertrude Deutsch)

David (front row, center) is pictured here in Germany with his parents, aunt (back row, right), and two brothers before his departure to England. David now resides in the United States and his brother (at David's right) in Israel. His other brother, mother, father, and aunt were all murdered by the Nazis. (Courtesy David Ross)

Six-year-old Maritza with her parents and maternal grandfather in Prague. Shortly afterward, she was sent to England. Her grandfather was shot on a Prague street five months after the photo was taken. Her parents were gassed in Auschwitz. (Courtesy Maritza Jasper)

## Chapter 8

# Getting There

For some escapees, once permission to leave was obtained and the transit and final visas were in hand, the actual journey was uneventful. But it was never simple. The exhilaration of having escaped combined with trepidation and anxiety about the future made leaving a formidable event. This was even true when the travelers were headed without detours to the most desirable point, namely, the United States.

By the time escapees reached an embarkation point, they were willing to board any ship, no matter how decrepit. Certainly, Olga[32] and her family were willing to embark on any vessel that might take them to the United States. They arrived in Barcelona from Stuttgart after a circuitous route took them through Lyons and Marseilles. They held the secret conviction that no ship would ever appear. To their surprise, it did materialize, and the family finally walked up the gangplank. True, it was no luxury liner, only a freighter that had seen better days. In fact, it had been sunk during the Spanish Civil War, then refloated and subsequently used in the banana trade. To the refugees who were to board her in Lisbon and Tangier, no ship had ever looked better.

Olga's family had only to cope with an aged ship and lack of money. There were many others for whom the journey was much more difficult. The surreptitious crossing of frontiers became an everyday occurrence. Desperation led to desperate methods. Edith[106] recalls the Gestapo summoning her father to appear. "He left the same day and tried unsuccessfully to get over various borders. He finally swam across the Moselle River into Luxembourg."

Belgium appeared to offer a temporary haven. The problem was to get in, which was no easy task. Immediately after Kristallnacht, Berta's[152] father found a guide to lead him across the border. "My father had escaped to Belgium secretly. There were paid guides to conduct refugees over the border at night. Mother tried to escape to Belgium after father and I had left. It was a dark night; the terrain was rough. She could not keep up with the group's fast pace and became separated. In the distance she saw the lights of a farmhouse and decided to take a chance. After giving her ring to the farmer, he put her in his basement. Another guide took my mother over the border the next night. I greatly admire her courage."

But then the Germans invaded Belgium. For those who had gotten into Belgium it was now a struggle to get out. "I have escaped twice," asserts a woman.[116] "Once from Germany to Belgium in 1933. It was a night of terror. I was seven years old and remember crossing the woods of the frontier at night. I arrived with my mother in Antwerp, where my father had relatives. Again, on May 10, 1940, when planes were over our heads and bombs were exploding, we fled Brussels, and our trip was full of anguish and fear. There was no time to think. We went to Bilbao, Spain, where we stayed for a month, waiting for a ship, the *Margues de Cosmillas*. Then off to Cuba. We stayed there for four months and finally arrived in New York."

Another family of more comfortable means took a different route after the invasion of Belgium. Armand[104] recalls their circuitous passage: "We went by car to the Belgian–French border. There my father bought a truck and hired a driver. The French confiscated the truck. Fortunately, my father was able to buy a Model A Ford, and we crossed from Vichy France to Free France at 11 P.M. By midnight the border was closed. From there we went through Spain to Portugal, where we stayed until my father was able to obtain one of about one hundred visas issued by the United States for political asylum. In 1940 we came to the United States by a Portuguese ship."

Since Czechoslovakia bordered on Austria, illegal escapes were frequently negotiated successfully across its border. Ernest,[30] twenty years old at the time, was under pressure to leave Austria while awaiting a British visa. His parents had some non-Jewish friends with connections. They were able to arrange an illegal border crossing into Czechoslovakia for Ernest at a cost of two thousand Reichsmark. After a tension-filled escape, Ernest crossed the border in August 1938. He was stopped and challenged by the Czech police. Why was he in Czechoslovakia? Where was his Czech visa? The picture of the SS began to loom in Ernest's mind. And then he had an inspiration. He pulled out a letter with an impressive insignia from the British embassy and presented it to the policeman. Ernest explained that he was in Czechoslovakia only temporarily. The letter was proof of his immediate plans to leave for England. The guard looked impressed and permitted Ernest to proceed. Ernest sighed a deep sigh of relief. The relief had to do with the fact that the guard did not understand English: The letter stated that Ernest's application for an English visa had been denied.

Illegal escapes were also taking place across the Swiss border, and some escapees made their way to freedom by way of Italy. It was well known that the Swiss were ruthless. They tracked down Jews who climbed mountains to enter Switzerland, picked up those who swam Lake Geneva, and returned them without mercy to the German authorities. Even children were turned back. But the desperate efforts of the Jews, with the aid of professional guides, succeeded at times in outwitting the authorities. Among strange journeys that of Kurt's[122] father ranks high. Mr. Maurer was hiding in a monastery outside Rome. One of the monks, who was about to be transferred from Rome to Spain, died of a heart attack. Kurt's father was dressed up in the monk's clothing and was flown in the monk's place to Spain.

When Susi,[48] her brother Gerhard, and their parents left Vienna in August 1938, they did not anticipate that the journey would last almost three years, always just a jump ahead of the Nazis. They zigzagged in and out of Czechoslovakia, Hungary, Yugoslavia, and Italy many times. Their ability to stay alive was partly due to Mr. Friedman's scent for knowing who was bribable. The first bribe helped them get out of Austria in a chauffeur-driven car that was flying a Nazi flag. A second bribe to a priest, who practiced his trade in a Serbian Orthodox church high in the Serbian mountains, resulted in a backdated baptismal certificate. With this document and a bribe to a German official in Sarajevo, a passport was obtained devoid of the *J*, a necessity for crossing borders undetected. A fourth bribe, to a guide at the Czech–Polish border, came to naught when the Germans invaded Poland on the night of the family's planned crossing. This was fortunate. Had the family reached Poland, they would have perished under the Germans. A more successful bribe helped the family, disguised as tourists, escape to Slovakia. One guide chauffeured the children across while another skied with the parents across the mountains. Subsequently, a gendarme who saw the family walk along the road was "persuaded" to let them pass. On a train trip through Slovakia, Susi's father distracted a railroad official from looking too closely at their papers by means of a strategically placed sum of money. A stay in Budva, south of Dubrovnic, was made possible by a police commandant known to overlook strangers' presence for a price. The family reached Turkey in October 1940 on one of the last runs of the Orient Express. Fear of being denounced prompted a twenty-four-hour trip to Mersin, a small town across from Cyprus. A little baksheesh helped get them out on a freighter to Palestine. Mr. Friedman's amazing resourcefulness can best be illustrated by an incident worthy of a French farce. The family was staying in a pensione in Budapest when the police arrived. Gerhard had entered Hungary illegally and thus had been hidden in his parents' room. Mr. Friedman handled the situation with his usual aplomb. "It was early morning. Mother was still in bed and Gerhard was getting dressed when the police marched in and questioned the identity of the young man. Father, feigning embarrassment, explained that he was impotent and that the young man was his wife's lover. The police expressed sympathy and left."

The following brief descriptions of illegal border crossings may make these events sound rather simple: "We waited in a railroad station"; "We went to meet our contacts"; "We crossed the frontier at night." But in actuality the hazards at each step brought extraordinary tension and anxiety. Every minute at a railroad station enhanced the possibility of being questioned by local police and being returned to Germany. Every walk through a city increased the possibility of being recognized as a stranger—and denounced. Walking through no-man's-land, evading the periodic searchlights, listening for patrols—such activities made fifteen minutes seem more like fifteen hours. No one can guess how many of those who attempted to reach a safe country failed to reach their goal. And, indeed, at each step some who were struggling toward freedom were eliminated. And yet, difficult as the border crossings were for many, there were others who had to overcome even greater obstacles at every step of the way. Their lengthy odysseys are worth telling.

*Chapter 9*

# Three Odysseys

### The Wandering Jews:
### From an Account by Liesel Lederer

The family had foresight. Liesel's father realized immediately that there was no future in Vienna after the Anschluss. He was fortunate in one respect: He was a Czech citizen. He did not need the approval of Austrian officialdom to leave the country, nor did he need a visa to enter France. The whole family—mother, grandmother, eighteen-year-old son, and fifteen-year-old Liesel—left Austria hastily and settled in Paris. With optimism, but also with some unease for Hitler was still quite near, the family started a new life.

In May 1940 the Germans rolled into Belgium and Holland. Alarmed, the family watched the Germans get closer and closer to Paris. By early June it was again time to leave. They packed a few pieces of clothing, locked the door on their possessions, and left Paris.

There was only one possible direction for them to go–south; they needed to go south, away from the invading Germans. The family caught one of the last trains out of Paris. They did not ask where it would go; they would simply remain on it until the last stop. The train discharged them at Bourbon L'Archambault, a small spa in the center of France. It was teeming with refugees.

On June 7, 1940, France surrendered to the Nazis, and an armistice was declared. There was sorrow everywhere. The village people cried and lamented but comforted themselves with the thought that the *vieux maréchal* [Pétain] would not do anything that was not beneficial to France. Liesel's family was not so sure and became increasingly apprehensive while waiting to see where the line would be drawn between Vichy France and Occupied France. They realized that if they were to find themselves in Occupied France, they would be facing a death sentence. Finally, the expected announcement came: Bourbon L'Archambault was declared slightly south of the *ligne de demarcation*.

It was again time to move on; the demarcation line was too close for comfort. Once more a few belongings were packed. By train, by hired car, and sometimes on foot, Liesel and her family slowly worked their way south to Marseilles. Yet it had become clear that no Jew would remain safe in any part of France. A new destination had to be found.

News spread like wildfire: Brazil needed immigrants and was ready to issue permits to those willing to work in the country's interior. But only Catholics were welcome. Marseilles was a port, a wide-open town. Everything was for sale. The refugees knew that any document could be purchased; its quality, based on the skill of the forger, determined the price. The family might be in France, but Czech baptismal certificates could be manufactured in Marseilles. Did the Brazilian consul realize that the papers were forged? If so, he did not say. He accepted them without question and issued visas. The family booked passage on a French boat, the *Alsina*, which was to leave for Rio de Janeiro on January 2, 1941. The family was joyous. All their troubles were now over. Again a new life was about to begin.

When the vessel reached Dakar, the North African authorities issued an edict that had been received from the Vichy government: No French ships were to leave the harbor and passengers were forbidden to disembark. And so the ship sat in the port. And sat. And sat. The passengers, who were at first perturbed, began to despair. Days turned into weeks; weeks turned into months. Rumors appeared daily: The passengers would be allowed to continue; no, they would not be allowed to continue; they would be interned in Dakar; no, they would not be interned. Worst of all, the passengers suspected that they would be returned to Europe. Ever-changing news kept the passengers in a state of agitation. In actuality, nothing happened at all, except that food got scarcer and desperation mounted. Suddenly, after three months, the *Alsina* began to move out of Dakar. The family was once more on its way.

But the vessel slowly turned around and retraced its way to Casablanca. There the Jewish passengers were unloaded to be transported into the desert. They found themselves in an internment camp at Sidi El Ayachi, a former Foreign Legion post. The camp was already filled to the brink with several hundred refugees. Now the waiting began anew. In the exhausting desert summer heat there was much hunger, much suffering. Liesel's father became part of the camp government the inmates had organized to negotiate with Moroccan authorities. The aim was to obtain permission to leave and to continue the journey.

The refugees began to collect all the valuables from those who still had any. One could not count on the goodness of human nature; it was wiser and more reliable to depend on the officials' greed. With part of the obtained funds, the Moroccan authorities were to be bribed to issue exit papers. The rest was to go to the Brazilian consul. It took many weeks to reach the proper officials of both countries. It took more time for negotiations. But finally the proper documents were issued. Passage was arranged from Spain to Brazil.

First, the passengers had to reach Spain. The group undertook a harrowing trip through the Sahara Desert to Tangier, then crossed through stormy seas to Spain. In Cadiz the group was joined by many other refugees who had somehow made their way to Spain. They set off on a rather dilapidated Spanish ship, the *Cabo de Hornos*. The family found shelter on the steerage deck, which was provided with wooden bunks, four rows high, with people crowded closely, one next to the other. But the passengers had recovered their optimistic spirits and began to prepare themselves for their new lives. They spent time studying Portuguese and allowed themselves to plan for their future. Excitement was at a fever pitch when the ship pulled into the harbor of Rio de Janeiro. A thrill ran through the passengers when they spied the famous coastline, graced by Sugarloaf Mountain.

The passengers could hardly wait for the next morning when they were to disembark. As they descended the gangplank with eager excitement, hopes, and expectations, the blow fell. The small contingent—the group that had been together from Marseilles, through Morocco, through the Sahara Desert, to Rio—was given the news: The consul in Casablanca had no authority to renew their visas; permission to enter Brazil was denied.

The small band of people, who had been used to disappointment, were not prepared for this one. There was weeping. There was shouting. There was numbed silence. There was anger and despair. There was pleading. There were suicide threats. Their utterances were to no avail; they fell on deaf ears. These Jews were not to enter Brazil. The *Cabo de Hornos* sailed on with its cargo of refugees. Slowly it made its way along the South American coast. It was heading back to Europe. The passengers' fate seemed sealed. They would be delivered into the hands of the Nazis and sure death.

But despair was to turn into hope. As the ship continued on its journey, the whole world learned about the plight of the passengers. An angel of mercy appeared out of nowhere. He did not look like one. And his name was rather odd for an angel. Nevertheless, Congressman Sol Bloom was the rescuing angel. He gave his personal guarantee that all who had not been allowed to land in Rio and were still on the *Cabo de Hornos* would eventually be able to enter the United States. On the basis of this promise, the Dutch government permitted the refugees to land in Curaçao in September 1941. The refugees were hungry and dirty. They had nothing left but the clothes on their backs. The members of the Curaçao Jewish community welcomed the arrivals and fed, clothed, and cared for them. In December 1941 the American visas were issued, and Liesel and her family arrived in New York the following January. They had left Vienna in April of 1938. They had left Paris in June of 1939. They ended their journey in January 1942. The journey had taken three months short of four years.

### No Port in the Storm:
### From an Account by Gerald Grandston

He was only six years old, but he knew all about Kristallnacht. On that day he had heard his grandfather tell his father that the synagogue had been burned to the ground. While he spoke, his grandfather had cried. Now his father was telling him that they would travel on a big ship to Cuba. From their small village he and his father journeyed to Bremen. There they boarded the *St. Louis*.

As soon as the ship sailed, the adults began to enjoy themselves.

That was not difficult to understand. They were tasting their new freedom in the comfort of a luxury liner. Not that the passengers had a lot of money to spend. They had only been allowed to take a very small amount. But the passage had been prepaid, and they were heading for a new life.

Gerald preferred to spend his time with the sailors. They were fun and willing to share their meals of wurst and bread with him. It was quite amazing that they would do so. The crew were all "Aryan" Germans! In fact, there were some Gestapo agents on board watching the crew. But in spite of their presence, both Captain Schröder and Purser Müller (both Germans, of course) were helpful and kind to the Jewish passengers. The trip was uneventful. Passengers were free to relax for the first time in months, or even years, in any way they saw fit.

Arrival in Cuba changed all that. Of the nine hundred or so passengers, only thirteen were allowed to disembark. No one knew exactly why those few were so favored. Perhaps their visas were more genuine than those of other passengers. Many of the refugees on board had been in concentration camps. The Gestapo would occasionally grant a release; frequently, a sizable bribe was involved. But after such a discharge the prisoner had to commit himself to leave the country within forty-eight hours. It was also likely that some of the visas on board had been purchased through bribery. Possibly, some of the passengers possessed transit visas to Cuba but had no visas for further destinations. In that case, the Cuban authorities would not have permitted them to enter Cuba. Or perhaps those who were able to leave the ship had connections in Cuba. It was impossible to guess why only thirteen people were allowed to disembark.

Gerald immediately noticed a change of atmosphere. He saw small groups of people meeting and debating and noticed that some were even crying. Everywhere he looked, there were passengers talking, discussing. He noticed that his father was very worried. He considered a question his father had asked distinctly odd. "Gerald," he had asked, "if I jump into the water, would you hold on to me and lie on my back while I swim to shore?" Gerald's father was the most unathletic person in the world. Even Gerald knew that there would be two deaths immediately—his and his father's.

There were rumors, rumors, rumors. One in particular stood out: America was planning to give asylum to the ship's passengers. It relieved the panic for the moment, but the travelers learned soon enough that the ship's crew had purposely spread the rumor. They had wanted to prevent mass suicides.

The Hamburg–American Line ordered Captain Schröder to return to Germany. The captain knew full well that to do so would be to deliver his human cargo to certain death. In spite of orders and in spite of the presence of Gestapo on board, Captain Schröder proceeded to American territorial waters around Miami, hoping against hope for asylum for his passengers. He was to be disappointed. It was reported on board that the chief immigration officer of Miami had flatly stated, "The Jews will not be able to land in Miami nor in any other American port." Other American officials seemed to share that view. The Coast Guard escorted the *St. Louis* out of American waters.

The captain again received orders from Germany to proceed to Bremen. Again he delayed and stalled for time. He was still hoping to find a refuge somewhere, anywhere, for his terrified passengers. He continued in a westerly direction, all the while allowing the ship to circle again and again over the same area. Little food was left and it was necessary to institute a rationing of water. The passengers had run out of funds. The German crew, no doubt influenced by their captain, showed the greatest compassion for the passengers. They used their own money to buy beer for them. Gerald remembers sailors giving cigars to his father.

Finally, the captain's stalling brought results. An English newspaper, *The Daily Express*, brought the plight of the *St. Louis* to the attention of the world. The Government of the United Kingdom consented to accept 280 of the destitute and fearful passengers. There was a condition: Guarantors had to be found to insure that the refugees would not be a drain on the economy. The other six hundred-odd passengers finally were to be given asylum by Belgium, France, and the Netherlands.

The *St. Louis* finally docked in Antwerp, and all but those going to England disembarked. German crew members, the presence of the Gestapo notwithstanding, leaned over the railings and applauded the departing passengers. "Good luck to the Jews," they cried. "God bless the Jews." From the ship the refugees proceeded to Belgium, Netherlands, and France. It was June 1939. In May 1940 the Germans invaded those countries and began the deportation of all Jews.

In June 1939 Gerald and his father traveled on to Southampton, England, on a German ship, the *Rhakatis*. It was a cargo ship that had been converted from a troop carrier. Gerald slept in the hold, which had bunks in it. The atmosphere became as oppressive as it had been before Gerald had left Germany. This ship had a different kind of captain. The young stewards assembled to sing: "You think you are getting away, Jews, but we will kill you in the end."

The *Rhakatis* discharged its passengers in Southampton. Gerald experienced an enormous feeling of relief and elation when smiling British policemen helped them down the gangplank. He knew only two words of English: "Good morning." He was so happy that he went around saying them to everybody all day long.

The *Rhakatis* was sunk as a troop carrier in 1943 by the British navy.

## The Promised Land:
### From an Account by Meir Neeman

Meir, at nineteen, had been searching desperately for a way to leave Vienna, legally or illegally. His rounds of consulates had been fruitless. Therefore, he was doubly impressed by a large sign posted on a street corner: "Jews, go to Palestine." For years Meir had been a member of a Jewish youth organization. Nothing could appeal to him more than to go to Palestine. Of course, he knew that entry could only be a clandestine affair because Palestine was a British mandate and the British had strictly curtailed Jewish immigration. Yet rumors circulated that an organization was seeking candidates for entry into Palestine. Meir found that the rumor was true: The Zionist Betar Movement was organizing young people for illegal entry. The movement was particularly eager to help boys between seventeen and nineteen. Not only were they the most targeted group for Nazi hunts, but they were needed on kibbutzim. Meir and the members of his youth group were the appropriate age. Fifty of them organized themselves into a cadre and planned to emigrate under the wings of

Betar. To prepare themselves for the rigors of what was to come, they desperately needed a meeting place. There was no possibility of so many young Jewish men meeting in a clandestine fashion. Meir was living alone in a conveniently located flat that could serve as a meeting place. The problem was the concierge, whose approval had to be obtained since he had the power to denounce the boys to the Gestapo. The caretaker's reaction could not be anticipated. Meir hoped for the best. His father had always stressed the importance of a good relationship with the concierge, and substantial bonuses at Christmas time had helped the friendship.

Meir rang the bell with trepidation. The caretaker opened the door. A *Blutorden* (Blood Medal) was pinned to his lapel. The *Blutorden* was awarded to Austrians who had served illegally in the Nazi party before the Anschluss. So the concierge had been one of them! A true and active Nazi, an *Illegaler*. All the while, though, he had not disdained taking money from a Jewish tenant. But Blood Medal or not, Meir had no choice but to take the concierge into his confidence. He explained that he and his friends intended to emigrate to Palestine, and in order to work out the technical details they were planning to meet in Meir's apartment. The concierge accepted the explanation in a surprisingly civilized manner. After this, Meir felt relieved and calm. He and his friends could now meet to complete preparations for their journey.

The date of departure was postponed several times and finally fixed for June 9, 1938. At long last Meir received final instructions detailing the provisions to be carried and the clothes to be worn. He was cautioned not to bring money, jewelry, or books and to report to the Südbahnhof (South Train Station) without family or friends. If anyone questioned him, the official explanation was to be given: "We are students going on a Mediterranean tour." Meir followed instructions carefully, but others did not. He found hundreds of people milling at the station. Relations and friends had not been able to restrain themselves from accompanying the boys. There was much activity. People were coming, going, and exchanging hugs and words of comfort. To his astonishment, Ireni, Meir's girlfriend, was there to greet him. She put her arms around Meir's neck and kissed him in front of all the people! Meir felt a little embarrassed but proud that she had been brave enough to come to the station all on her own and in spite of the terrible danger to which everyone was exposed. Police and SS troops were patrolling as if to make clear who was boss. In spite of their presence, someone started to sing "Hatikva" [the Jewish anthem]. First somewhat hesitatingly, then with full strength, all those present joined in. They sang it with full voices, in Nazi Vienna, and in front of the SS troopers!

The young men were hustled onto a special train. From the windows they blew their last kisses and sent their last good-byes. Shrill whistles and some commands rang out, and the train slowly and silently pulled out of the station and out of Vienna. The youths sat very quietly on hard wooden benches and tried to collect their thoughts. From time to time SS guards passed through the wagons, ordering total silence. The train wound its way through the country-side. After five hours it briefly slowed down, only to pick up speed again. Almost immediately someone noticed a Yugoslavian flag! The train had finally crossed the border into Yugoslavia. They had left behind families and happy times, but they had also left behind hell. They fell upon each other, laughing and crying. They were safe, away from that hell and on their way to Palestine. A happy future lay ahead.

The train continued on its way, stopping several times for long periods in Yugoslavia. At every stop, soldiers cordoned off the entire train. The boys were not permitted to leave their compartments except for a few who were allowed to refill the water canteens. At noon the train pulled into Zagreb, Yugoslavia's capital. An astonish-ing sight presented itself to the passengers. Hundreds of Jews were awaiting the train. They rushed to the windows, crying, laughing and shouting "*Shalom!*" They forced bread, cheese, sardines, salamis, and bottles of wine on the travelers. Some tried to catch outstretched hands. Some knelt down, kissed the rails, and blessed the group for going to the Holy Land. No one could deduce how the waiting throng had learned of the train's arrival. But one thing was sure. The Yugoslavian authorities would make sure to prevent a repetition of that scene. Yet in spite of their efforts, hundreds of Yugoslavian Jews turned out again in Belgrade to welcome the train. The police prevented them from approaching, but shouts of "*Shalom!*" reached the travelers.

During the second night, the exhausted refugees fell into a deep sleep. They were delighted to find themselves in Greece by the next

morning. The Greek authorities were no happier to see them than
the Yugoslavian officials had been. As if they were dangerous
criminals, Greek soldiers cordoned off the train at every stop. These
soldiers behaved worse than the Yugoslavians, even refusing requests to refill empty canteens. The train moved on through
steaming countryside, passing Salonika, a city from which, a few
years hence, thousands of Jews would be deported to their death. In
Athens the boys left the trains for buses, all the while closely watched
by soldiers. They were quickly whisked out of town; the Greek
authorities were as eager as the Yugoslavians to rid themselves of the
group. By late afternoon the buses stopped, and the young men
dismounted onto a flat and stony field. They were to wait until the
ships carrying them to Palestine were ready. A camp of some sort was
set up. The food in the camp was meager: tea, soup, and some slices
of bread. The drinking water was tepid and tasted foul. It was brutally
hot during the day. It took all the boys' strength to walk to some
sparse trees at the edge of camp. The nights, however, were cool,
agreeable, and refreshing.

A week passed with no clear information as to departure. In the
morning of the seventh day, orders came to break camp. There was
not much to pack, and with their few belongings on their backs the
youths hiked an hour to a small village. Located on a bay, it
comprised a few wretched whitewashed houses and huts. As the
group marched onto a little wooden pier, they noticed a few fishing
boats and some sailing vessels but nothing that could be called a
ship. The "fleet" that was to take them to Palestine consisted of one
vessel, which more or less resembled a ship, and two wooden
barges. The view was not reassuring. After three days the more
seaworthy ship departed, leaving the boys divided between the
remaining two boats. The boys were now completely cramped and
had to reduce their living space to a minimum. It was hard to tell
how many were on board each of the two small vessels. The guess
was well over a hundred. The sun shone relentlessly; the air was
sticky, hot, and still. The Greek sailors looked like pirates, but
they were efficient enough to keep the boats afloat.

There was danger on the seas, not just from capsizing but from
prowling British patrols. If the British had their way, no group of
young Jewish men would enter Palestine. Entry had to be accom-

plished illegally, or not at all. The captain in charge of the illegal transport kept careful watch for British warships. Since there was danger of being spotted by the British, smoking at night was strictly forbidden. The small glow of a cigarette might betray their position.

The long awaited shout of "Land in sight!" finally came one evening. Over a hundred pairs of eyes stared at a vague outline. A glow of lights seemed to be going up the slope of a mountain. To their immense relief and delight, the refugees realized that they were seeing Haifa! But before this news could be celebrated, an order to lie flat and remain silent was passed from mouth to mouth. A British warship had been spied. There was no doubt as to its identity. To avoid the British ship, the barges with their forbidden cargo turned and sped with all the power they could muster toward the high seas. Outside the three-mile zone, the barges would be safe in international waters. To avoid detection, the engines were turned off once they reached the open sea. Throughout the night and the next day the ships drifted in perfectly still waters. No food was distributed, only a ration of tepid water. Toward evening the engines were restarted. Again the lights of Haifa beckoned. Again a British destroyer passed by, this one much closer than the one before. The British had probably observed the Greek ships during the day and were now trying to intercept them. The captain repeated his former maneuver. Again he turned around and headed out to sea. Again he spent the next hours drifting in the smooth sea under the blazing sun. Again there was no food. Youthful optimism did not falter.

Late in the evening the engines started up again. This time the vessels seemed to be heading slowly in a different direction. It was pitch dark, the only light coming from a star-studded sky. After two hours the engines stopped abruptly. A lone light in the distance pierced the darkness, flashing on and off, seeming to signal a message. The faraway light beckoned again. That seemed to be the message the sailors had waited for. They lowered two rowboats and directed five boys to climb into each one. With the sailors rowing, the little boats disappeared into the darkness while the remaining passengers waited with trepidation. The boats returned faithfully, continuing their journey between ship and shore. As Meir neared land, the sailor motioned to him to jump into the water. As noiselessly as possible, Meir slid off the boat. The water reached his hips, lapped against his backpack and filled his high leather boots. As he stepped ashore Meir realized with suddenness that he had just set foot onto the promised land. He was in Palestine!

He was in Palestine, but he was not yet safe. There was no time to celebrate. Almost immediately two men on horseback appeared, armed with rifles, their ammunition belts slung across their shoulders. They looked like Hollywood cowboys, but they were talking in Hebrew and German. They hurried the arrivals to march farther inland. Progress was slow as the boys lumbered with their water-filled boots through deep sand dunes. They had not eaten for three days and felt weak. They trudged over moving sands, their feet sinking deeper with each step. The horsemen rode around them like cowboys, urging them to go "*schneller, schneller* [faster, faster]." The boys struggled on until they reached a little eucalyptus grove. Only then did the horsemen, bidding them "*Shalom,*" depart.

It was now about five A.M., and the first light of morning was dawning. It was too dangerous to rest. As soon as the horsemen disappeared, two armed men approached, this time on foot. They accompanied the boys to waiting buses. This part of the journey passed quickly. By eight o'clock, Meir was in Tel Aviv.

He was still not safe. The group of young men had been cautioned to disperse quickly in order to avoid detection by British army patrols. Meir, accompanied by just one friend, was now on his own. It was imperative for the two boys to find their sponsor as quickly as possible. Meir, without a map, was forced to approach strangers and ask for directions. He was acutely aware of being an easy mark with his unwashed and unkempt appearance. There was certainly no one else in Tel Aviv who wore a black raincoat and dirty leather boots on a sunny June day. The boys finally found their way to the Café Noga, located in a fashionable district. As luck would have it, their sponsor was out. They knew no one and had no place to go. There was nothing to do but to sit down on the curb and wait. They sat down on the curb, and both fell asleep, only to be awakened by a barrage of questions fired at them by a stranger. He spoke first in Hebrew and, getting no response, addressed them in a number of other languages. When he came to German, Meir decided to reply. It was a risk, but so was sitting on the curb in a black raincoat. Meir explained, as he had been instructed, that he was a student on an educational Mediterranean tour. The stranger invited the two young men to follow him to his flat. They worried about his identity. Was he a detective? Was he simply a hospitable friend? They felt they had little choice; their appearance made them feel too conspicuous. The stranger offered the young men a hot bath and a meal. Then with an intense look, he asked: "Now tell me the truth. Who are you?" And so Meir told him that he had landed at night on some beach and that a bus had brought him to Tel Aviv. The stranger was overjoyed. Such a large number of refugees had never landed before. As if he could not absorb the extraordinary news, he repeated to himself over and over again: "Three hundred at one landing!" Warning them to stay indoors because of the roaming British army patrols searching for illegal immigrants, their host ran to pass the good news to friends. As if to verify the warning, a British army truck with soldiers in steel helmets passed the house.

In the evening Meir and his friends were taken to Maccabee House, the meeting place for illegal arrivals, for a joyful reunion with their travel companions. The boys were sent to various kibbutzim. Meir was absorbed into Kibbutz Kinrot. At long last his journey was over. He had found refuge. He had arrived.

## Chapter 10

# Die Kinder

Many goodbyes had been said—or left unsaid. Legally or illegally, hundreds of Jews had found some means of escape. But the greater portion was still left in the Third Reich. As the Germans marched first into the Sudetenland, and later into the rest of Czechoslovakia, the number of those desperately searching for a way out increased. War threatened, yet refuge was still impossible to find. The search from consulate to consulate had become a maze with only dead ends. No exit. It became clearer and clearer many would not find sanctuary. Parents whispered to each other: "*Die Kinder! Was machen wir mit den Kindern?* [The children! What do we do with the children?]"

Parents did not know how best to protect their children. Was it better to try to hide the grim reality or speak openly about the dangers? The fact was that for their own protection, even young children had to be instructed. Under the Nazis, youth was not an extenuating circumstance. Five-year-old Gerd[58] learned to recognize the signs "*Juden unerwünscht* [Jews not welcome]." He had been told never to enter the neighborhood toy and sweet shops except after hours and through the back door. He was mindful of other people living in ways very different from his. For instance, the doctor's house always had a swastika flag hanging down in front. His two sons, until recently Gerd's playmates, would shout "*Juden-schwein* [Jew pig]" at Gerd. Paula,[17] only six, had been taught not to leave the house without an arm band marked *J* for *Jude* and always to carry her identification card, which bore her fingerprints. If small children failed to grasp the realities, there could be serious trouble. Magie[52] recalls: "Our mother took in laundry and sewing. We had a seamstress who came to the house to help. In my childish way I asked her why she ate so much. She threw her sewing down and told my mother that she would never again work for Jews."

Obviously, it was impossible to prevent the children from knowing at least some of the truth. Still, it was difficult to know just how much to tell them. Marion[85] found it disturbing to live with half-truths. She was only seven when the Nazis came to power, a sheltered, naïve child. Sometimes her father had to go into hiding, and even though her mother reassured her, she worried about his safety. When she asked, she was only told that the Nazis did not like Jews and that the family would try to go to America as soon as possible. Franz[15] felt it important to know the full extent of the danger and appreciated his parents' openness, which he credited with helping him avoid a number of potentially dangerous situations. Franz was a *Mischling* (a mixture of Jew and Gentile). Two of his grandparents were Jewish. He learned to manage this status: "According to the Nuremberg laws, I was a half-Jew of the first degree. This confused and perplexed people: Is a half-Jew a Jew? How much is the other half worth? I soon learned to take advantage of any confusion or puzzlement shown by anyone in order to clear out as quickly as possible while I was ahead. I was, after all, an outlaw, free to be beaten up anywhere, at any time, by anyone. I quickly became adept at finding my way through back alleys and my sprint developed to racing team level."

I learned from personal experience that possessing knowledge may have the potential of endangering the family. Before the advent of Hitler I had been told that my parents had placed some money into foreign bank accounts. At that time, even though it was against the law, it was a much-practiced custom. But under Hitler, it became a capital crime. Yet my parents decided to reveal only the existence of one of the accounts to the German authorities. The second account was their nest egg for resettling. It would prevent us from becoming destitute. I was told that if I were questioned by the Gestapo, I should never reveal any knowledge about my parents' finances. If my interrogators were to tell me that my parents had confessed to having funds in foreign countries, I should recognize it as a ruse used by the Gestapo to obtain evidence against my parents. The knowledge weighed heavily on me. I feared I might put the family at risk. I would have preferred not to know. But having been told in pre-Hitler times, my parents could not shield me from that knowledge now that circumstances had changed.

While parents tried to offer some sanctuary for their children at home, they had no influence as to what happened to them during school hours. Franz[15] describes his final year at the *Gymnasium* (high school): "I was persona non grata. I had no friend. No one spoke to me except in insults. Everyone avoided me." A girl[41] attending an exclusive girls' school fared no better: "Jewish pupils had to sit apart. The others began to appear in the uniform of the BDM [a Hitler youth organization] and to this day it makes me sick to my stomach when I see white knee-length socks on young girls. It was particularly amazing to hear my non-Jewish schoolmates talk about how they would betray their parents if the situation arose and the Führer wished it."

Young children fared no better in school. One day when six-year-old Gerda[40] trudged to school as usual, she found that nothing was to be "as usual" that day. First, she was not allowed to hang up her coat with the others but was told to place it at the other end of the room on the so-called Jewish coatrack. She was then told to move her books from her usual seat to the *Judenbank* (the Jewish bench) in the back of the room. The school atmosphere became so charged with venom that some children found attendance beyond bearing.

Teachers did not provide protection for the Jewish children. On the contrary, they would encourage an atmosphere of hate and whip up their pupils against the Jewish students. I recall one of my own teachers—tall, blond, and beautiful and idolized by myself and many of my classmates—entering the classroom the first school day after the Anschluss. She wore a swastika in her lapel and treated the children with icy disdain and contempt. We sat frozen in our seats. Another "Aryan" teacher who had never been able to keep discipline entered like a ferocious animal. This was her moment of revenge. We dared not move. After school we disbursed as quickly as possible. Boys would organize forays and beat up Jewish girls as they were leaving, and we knew that our teachers would not attempt to stop them. Many children fared far worse than myself. For instance, one teacher asked all the Jewish boys to stand up and, over the derisive jeering of the other children, told them to go home and not come back.

Even though parents attempted to "act as normal as possible" in front of their children,[4] worries and fears became more pervasive with time. Franz[15] describes the emotions felt: "The terror all around us; the sudden arrests and disappearances; the beatings, the thefts, and vandalism of Jewish property affected family relations. The stress was obvious. Tempers flared. I would characterize my family's principal emotions as fear, anxiety, and depression but not terror, hate, or sadness. For terror incapacitates one from acting rationally, and this was not the case. And hate and sadness are luxuries for which one must have the leisure and freedom of not having to see to one's everyday and long-term survival." Youthful innocence was lost amidst a dangerous world. Dorli[41] remembers a change in herself: "I grew older and more serious for my age as I saw my parents worrying and talking about who had committed suicide, who had gotten away, and so on. My life was full of talk of permits and visas and guarantees and guarantors. Laughter and jokes disappeared. Everyone was nervous and tense and thus perhaps less tolerant than before." The uncertainty as to where and when the next menace would arise and the constant conferences among the adults, from which the younger children were excluded, became increasingly oppressive. Six-year-old Maritza's[75] worst memories are of hearing and seeing the elderly relatives in anxious huddles, which she felt were somehow connected with her future. Elli[4] adds: "We spoke in whispers even at home." But in spite of the strain, the remnants of home life are remembered with nostalgia. Inga[78] reminisces: "We were badly affected, but family relations even improved. We clung together. It was cozy."

Some of the younger children who had been born in Germany had lived almost all their lives under Hitler and were not even aware that their life was abnormal. Susi[146] seemed to have been afraid of Hitler for as long as she could remember. She simply took it for granted that Jews were second-class citizens. Margarete[55] knew that her father's store had been taken over by the Nazis. Every time she heard the line in the Horst Wessel song, "When Jewish Blood Spurts from Our Knives," she was afraid. She vaguely knew that there was something "wrong" about being Jewish but did not exactly understand what it was. A woman[52] remembers that she used to see the strain on her mother's face but did not know that there was anything abnormal about that. She had no normal times to compare it to. And Inga[78] was so young she didn't understand anything. She was miserable because everyone else was too. While these very young children generally could not express their concerns in words, it affected their behavior. One woman[126] was prone to temper tantrums as a little girl. She remembers having one because she did not want to go to England; she wanted to go to the zoo instead. Kurt's[51] emotional reaction did not emerge until he came to England, when he was haunted by frightful nightmares and could not go to sleep without checking that every door was bolted.

After a while there was no more deliberation as to what children should be told. The youngsters witnessed the deterioration of their families. Jobs were lost, money was not available, apartments were appropriated sometimes by force. Nothing remained the same. Peter[130] returned home from a friend's house only to find two Gestapo officers padlocking the front door. His mother and sister, each holding a small suitcase, had been awaiting his return. They found refuge at his cousin's house. The children[85] experienced the loss of their home as a terrible blow, particularly since moving meant landing in inferior quarters. "We moved from our pretty flat in a desirable residential neighborhood," recalls Beate,[59] "to a fairly grotty one." Kurt's[51] new home consisted of one small room in someone else's home.

It was not only that the physical environment changed. The children noticed that their parents were constantly being humiliated. In European society, where parents (and fathers in particular) had commanded a great deal of respect from their children, this was a double shock. Susi[146] had always seen her parents as all-powerful and observed that they now were helpless to change things. Kurt[51] learned that his father was fired from his job at the bank; his father was told that he had "a birth defect." Heinrich[170] was aware that the family could no longer buy food for themselves but had to rely on the good graces of the janitor's wife.

Twelve-year-old Gerda,[123] who lived in Czechoslovakia, was aware that family values once taken for granted were now being lost. To a twelve-year-old this was disturbing. "Word reached us that a Jewish family had converted to Roman Catholicism in order to emigrate to Latin America. I am indignant: 'How can they do such a thing?' But my parents are sad and thoughtful and say nothing at all. And I realized they are wondering whether, given the chance—the wonderful chance of emigration—they might not be tempted to do the same." Gerda, apprehensive about her family's circumstances, must have been hoping for some reassurance when she asked her father, "How long can we live if you don't work?" "Half a year," came the reply. Her father's promptness in replying surprised her. She realized he had given the matter some thought.

It was also quite evident to the children that their parents had been deserted by their non-Jewish friends who, in previous days, had contributed to making family life stable. All kinds of honorary non-Jewish "uncles" and "aunts" suddenly vanished. Former business associates or even strangers were suddenly in possession of the family business. Even where no risk to themselves was involved, friends refused to extend help. A good-bye at a railway station highlighted to Susi[146] how alone and abandoned her family had become. Her father, under the threat of arrest, had finally obtained a visa for a foreign country, and now they were waiting for the arrival of the train that was to take her father to safety. The train was not due for another two hours, two interminable hours in a public place where every single person served as a potential source of danger. The waiting passengers on the platform had begun to recognize the family as Jewish. Sub rosa remarks and threatening gestures began to fill the air with menace. It became too dangerous to remain in the station. The family quickly left. But where to go now? Restaurants were forbidden to Jews. Roaming the streets in the dark was an invitation for arrest by any roving patrol. Why, of course! There was one obvious solution: The family's nearest and dearest lifelong friend lived near by. They could spend the two hours in safety at his house and then rush to the station just in the nick of time to catch the train. Susi's father called his friend, spelling out his dire need as clearly as was prudent over the telephone. The friend regretted that he could not be of help; unfortunately, he had retired for the night and receiving visitors would be inconvenient so late in the evening. Susi's father explained again: It was essential; he needed a place to stay for two hours. Did his friend not understand? And then came the reply: "You are a Jew. Why didn't you leave long ago?"

Lore,[139] then thirteen years old, describes the inevitable dissolution of family life: "The situation worsened so slowly and insidiously that I hardly noticed. I accepted the ever-tightening adjustments and restrictions. During the last years in Leipzig, our lives and surroundings were gradually being dismantled. My father had been arrested and released twice. He was no longer permitted to practice law. We children were no longer able to go to school. Our servants had left, since 'Aryans' were not allowed to work for Jews. We moved twice—into smaller and smaller apartments. Our elegant furniture disappeared, either 'sold' for a pittance or requisitioned. We were only allowed to shop in stores owned by Jews, and there were fewer and fewer of those. Our names were officially changed to include the middle name *Israel* for men and *Sarah* for women. I remember how strange and awful it felt to read for the first time '*Lore Sarah Loewenheim.*' "

At times the roles were reversed, and children had to protect their parents. A memory of my own returns; it is about a shopping trip I undertook for a friend. I had been invited for the weekend to a friend's place outside of Vienna. My parents were apprehensive, but my pleading prevailed. Martha's home consisted of two modest rooms above a *Gasthaus* (a simple eating establishment). By evening, when all stores were closed, her mother ran out of food. We had to purchase some downstairs, but there was a problem. Martha and her mother both had black hair. Being blonde, I volunteered to enter the *Gasthaus*, with all its potential dangers. I walked downstairs slowly, with pounding heart. I crossed the room with its brown peasant benches and tables, where exuberant men, many in Brownshirt uniforms, were talking and singing patriotic songs. In front of them were steins of beer resting on thick, round paper coasters. The informal atmosphere worried me. In this kind of room it was exceedingly dangerous to be Jewish. There was a strong possibility that someone might strike up a conversation. My thoughts were filled with various alternative replies, should I be questioned. I looked fixedly ahead as I stated my order, hoping that my voice would have a natural ring. Finally, the waitress handed me the order. Not suspecting that I was Jewish, she smiled at me. If she only knew, I thought. I paid and bounded up the stairs, two at a time. My relief, when I returned to the small rooms, was tempered by a sudden insight: "Martha's mother is poor. Her legs are swollen into huge stumps. She walks slowly with a swaggering gait, from swollen leg to swollen leg. She seems helpless to organize a small meal." I was suddenly certain that Martha and her mother would never get out. The thought was shattering. I quickly buried it and returned to our little feast. I have often wondered if Martha made it. Martha, Martha Taussig, are you there?

Events continued to escalate and became intolerable. It seemed that they could not get worse. And then came Kristallnacht. Whatever sense of security might still have sustained the children was ripped away as they watched their fathers being arrested. Sometimes the SS came in the morning, before the day started. Dora[173] remembers that her father was taken at 6:30 A.M.. A solitary Viennese policeman came to do the job. But not with the usual Viennese *Gemütlichkeit*. He briskly ordered her father to come along. No, he could not take anything with him. No, not even a toothbrush. He would not say where he was taking him. The next day, before the family could locate her father, he was shipped to Dachau.

Sometimes the SS arrived at midday. One youngster recalls that they asked for his father when he was at work. Before the SS men left, they ordered that his father be called home. The boy's father came home. The family hoped the SS would forget and not return. They waited in prolonged agony. The SS remembered. They came and arrested the boy's father. The boy was devastated. The neighbors' children jeered and called the boy unkind names.

Sometimes the SS came in the dead of night. Lore[139] has a clear memory of the event. "I woke up in the middle of the night to see two Gestapo men searching my room for my father. From that moment on the horror was clear and ever present." With the arrests, the children's security was entirely shattered. With their fathers gone, the children's complete isolation stood in stark relief. They longed for their fathers' return, but if that wish was granted, they faced another psychological blow: the sight of their fathers after the Nazis had done with them. Beate[59] was in bed when her father came home after having been caught. She heard her father's footsteps going past her room, but, contrary to custom, he did not stop to greet her. "After a while I got up and saw my father's bloody clothes hanging outside the bathroom. I crept down the corridor, knocked at my parents' bedroom door, and went in softly. My father had the bedclothes pulled right up to his eyes. He did not want me to see that he was bloodied and his teeth had been knocked out. He had been beaten by the Nazis."

With husbands in prison or hiding, a heavy load descended on the women of the families. They had to face the SS and the Gestapo without support during the repetitive house searches. Wives took all kinds of risks in their indefatigable efforts to snatch their husbands from the Gestapo and the jaws of death. Right after Kristallnacht thousands of Jews were sent to concentration camps. The ingenuity exhibited by the women in their dealings with the Gestapo was astonishing and reassuring to their children. Margarete's[54] mother went to the Gestapo—a dangerous act in itself since it could precipitate arrest—and obtained her husband's release by offering American dollars, which she had hastily obtained from relatives in America. Ernst's[141] mother had already handed her husband's business over to the SS in a quick transaction while standing in the doorway of her home. When her husband was sent to Dachau, she found some sort of underground political connections—Ernst does not know how—and obtained a spurious steamship ticket to a nonexistent ship leaving for Shanghai. Probably a bribe was involved to induce the Gestapo to accept obviously fraudulent documents. Maritza's[75] mother became resolute in the face of her husband's indecision. The issue was whether six-year-old Maritza should be sent from Czechoslovakia to England ahead of her parents. Maritza had never heard her parents argue. Her mother would not relinquish her stand. Maritza must be sent to England immediately. Her mother's insistence saved her life. Her parents did not survive.

The situations that children had to handle grew increasingly more complex. Susi's[146] father, who had escaped to England, was being sought by the SS. The family was fearful of his flight being discovered. When that ominous and insistent ring of the doorbell sounded, both mother and daughter knew its meaning. The door was opened with trepidation and there they were—two SS men. Where was her father, the SS men demanded. While they spoke to her, they held a gun against her mother's head. Susi, ten years old, had been taught to say "I don't know" if she was questioned by the Gestapo. But these men would not take "I don't know" for an answer. They insisted and badgered. Susi strayed from the script and lied boldly: "I

don't know. All I know is two men like you came and took him away."
This was not Susi's first encounter with the SS. An automatic act of
courtesy nearly precipitated a catastrophe in the girl's life. Even in
those anxiety-producing times, Susi did not forget her manners. She
had been taught to politely pick up any object dropped by an adult.
Walking home, she happened to pass an SS man. She noted some
coins on the ground and automatically picked them up, handing
them to the man in the black uniform, black boots, and black hat
with its skull insignia. He took the money, briefly glanced at it,
and then accused her of having pilfered some. Perplexed, Susi
assured him that she gave him all the money she had found. He
ordered her to follow him into the hallway of the nearest house. In
the darkened hall he stepped behind her and attempted to strip off
her clothes. In a flash Susi recognized his intentions. Susi had broken
her arm when she was thrown off a swing by a former friend whose
SS father did not think Jews should be permitted on swings. She
turned around and with her left hand took her right arm, the one in
the cast, and hit him on the head. As she ran away with all the
strength she could muster, she heard him call, "You don't have to tell
anyone about this." It ws lucky that he chose not to silence her
forever. A reflex reaction on my own part caused me considerable
anxiety. I recall an SS officer who, mistaking my blond hair and blue
eyes as being "Aryan," smiled at me. Without thinking I returned his
smile and immediately was overcome by guilt and fear, guilt because
I had smiled at the devil incarnate and fear because I dreaded his
reaction should he guess that I had dared to smile at an "Aryan."

While at first it was Polish-born men in Germany and Austria
who were shipped to Poland, the net soon began to widen to include
their wives and children. It mattered not that most of them had never
been to Poland. Nor did it matter that they had become citizens of
Germany and Austria long before there was any talk of a Third Reich.
And it mattered even less that Poland did not want to take back their
former citizens. Hitler stripped all of them of their German citizenship and dumped them in Poland. Nine-year-old Siegfried[110] and his
family—his father and mother, his younger brother and older sister,
and his blind grandfather—were ordered to appear at the police
station. They had been allowed one little suitcase and a few marks in
German currency. It was a Friday evening, the time when those who

were religious would ordinarily be preparing for Sabbath. But this Friday Siegfried and his family would be forced to violate their usual custom and travel. They would travel on Friday evening and they would travel on Saturday. And when they reached Zbaszyn, inside the Polish border, they would be dropped off like so many sacks of flour. Over 20,000 other deportees, who were penniless would be abandoned in that small, unprepared town, which was loath to shelter them.

Children were now being included in the regular roundups. Dora[173] was one of them. When her parents were taken in, the janitor felt sorry for the fifteen-year-old girl and hid her. But the Nazis were clever. Just when Dora felt safe, they came around a second time. When Dora arrived at the police station, she spied her mother. The police were not yet prepared for the large number of Jews the Gestapo was bringing in. So Dora just stood in the jail. She stood holding her mother's hand. In the confined space all the women just stood. For one long whole day. By evening the police, not knowing what to do with them, sent them home.

Dora was lucky. When Eric's[35] father came out of Buchenwald concentration camp, he was desperate to get Eric out of the country. Of all the terrible sights he had seen there, one ranked high: young children in the camps. It was clear that if the children were to be saved, they had to leave. Immediately. It was now or never. And so the parents said to each other, "*Was machen wir mit den Kindern?*"

## Chapter 11

# They Traveled through the Night

During the dark hours of 1938, stunning news came from England. Britain had declared itself willing to extend a temporary haven to Jewish children living under Nazi oppression. Perhaps this was merely a rumor. There had been dozens of rumors—no, hundreds—in the past year. Perhaps finally, after all this time, one of the great powers was offering massive help. The rumor turned out to be true.

A number of circumstances had led to this new development: Kristallnacht had at last shattered the indifference of individuals as well as governments. Voices began to be raised: if the adults cannot be saved, then at least let the children be saved. The clamor to help the children so impressed the British government that on November 21, 1938, the House of Commons decided to permit Jewish children to come to Great Britain. There were provisos: The children had to be under eighteen years of age and certified to be healthy. The children's stay was envisioned to be only temporary; a guarantee of fifty pounds for possible remigration was required. Additional help would be needed to process the thousands of applications, which would surely start streaming in; the Refugee Children's Movement was created for that purpose. The Quakers played an important role in arousing the conscience of governments and people alike. They helped find guarantors and battled bureaucratic obstacles. Other organizations and individuals pledged money, collected goods for the children, and prepared places for them to stay. The processing of applications began. Photographs and a health certificate had to be obtained for each child and submitted to the British Home Office.

The Home Office checked the documents and referred them to the Record Office to secure entry permits. The papers traveled to Passport Control, where they were stamped and returned to their places of origin. The government genuinely desired to simplify procedures. It even eliminated the need for passports for the children: Simple travel papers would suffice. But in spite of all their efforts, the process still took time (Turner, 1990, pp. 47–49).

The most important aspect of preparing for the children's arrival was to find placements for them. Foster parents had to be found. A guarantee for each child had to be arranged either through an individual or through a fund newly created by former prime minister Stanley Baldwin. Housing had to be made ready for those children who had no foster parent to go to. Deserted summer holiday camps, Dovercourt at Harwich and Pakefield near Lowestoft, were hastily prepared. Dorothy de Rothschild provided a house on her estate for thirty-five boys, complete with a headmaster and his family. Volunteers helped man the phones, which rang ceaselessly. Potential foster parents called. Refugees importuned and pleaded to have their nephews, nieces, friends' children placed on the list of the next transport. Government officials, already overwhelmed by requests and paperwork, were urged to further increase their pace. And all the while, the clock kept ticking away (N. Wollheim, interview, January 1990).

Activities had to be coordinated with the Jewish officials working on the other side of the Channel. They were the ones who had to locate the children and organize their exodus. How was this task to be accomplished? Endangered children were in Austria, Germany, and in newly occupied Czechoslovakia. On November 28, 1939, in Vienna alone there still remained 35,000 Jewish children. And Poland, which was being mentioned with increasingly ominous overtones in Hitler's speeches, also had a large Jewish population. The Jewish communities, in all but Poland, were in complete shambles; the *Kultusgemeinde* (the Austrian Jewish community) barely managed to exist. Many Jewish officials had been arrested. The records of Jewish communities had been impounded by the Gestapo. Arrangements had to be coordinated from city to city. While the bulk of the Jewish population in Austria was centered in Vienna, the German Jews were scattered in many cities, small and large. The number of children overwhelmed the available facilities (Turner, 1990, p. 40). How were the limited places to be apportioned among thousands of children? Who would contact the children, organize collection procedures, arrange railroad schedules, and, last but not least, deal with the SS? And topping all those difficulties was the pressure of time. Now. The children must leave now. Tomorrow might be too late.

The German emigration officials would also have to be dealt with. They had to grant permission for the children's departure. In addition, their cooperation in organizing transportation was essential. The emigration official in charge was in Vienna. His name was Adolf Eichmann. Who would be capable of facing Eichmann? Norman Bentwich, one of the originators of the Refugee Children's Movement, knew the right person for the task; he chose Gertrude Wijsmuller (Turner, 1990, p. 40).

Resourceful and intrepid, Mrs. Wijsmuller (1961) was a Dutch woman who had been active in refugee affairs. She immediately set out for Vienna and demanded an interview with Eichmann. With sangfroid, she detailed the British government's willingness to accept 10,000 Jewish children. Eichmann's attitude was disdainful. Why was she, an Aryan, bothering about Jewish children? Mrs. Wijsmuller argued her case, and in the end Eichmann gave permission. A train was made available for the first group, consisting of 600 children. The rescue activity was referred to as *Kindertransports*, and those who were rescued still refer to themselves, when discussing the events fifty years later, as *Kinder*. But, of course, Eichmann made a stipulation. All of the 600 children would have to be out of the country within the next five days! If the time limit was not met, the deal was off. With calculated irony Eichmann chose the day for the journey: Saturday (Shabbat!). By permitting only five days to organize a transport for 600 children, Eichmann, in his sadistic way, had placed an enormous obstacle in Mrs. Wijsmuller's way. Within the hour of Mrs. Wijsmuller's meeting with Eichmann, parents were lining up with their children for applications. With everyone working through the nights, Eichmann's conditions were met, and the transport departed just in time (Turner, 1990, p. 42).

In Berlin a young man of twenty-eight was willing to put his family's and his own interests aside for the sake of the Jewish children. He had long been active in the Jewish Youth Movement.

More recently, Norbert Wollheim's organizational capacity had been demonstrated in his work with Jewish men who had originally been rounded up on Kristallnacht and recently released from Oranien-Saxenhausen concentration camp. Dr. Otto Hirsch, the executive director of the Central Board of Jews in Germany, turned to Wollheim for help, asking him to take charge of those *Kindertransports* that would emanate from Berlin. Wollheim hesitated. He had been trying to find avenues of escape for his own family. Dr. Hirsch pleaded that Wollheim's expertise was urgently needed and that after a year's time every effort would be made to help him find a haven for his family. Wollheim consented. The task was indeed formidable. "Because of all the technical problems, it was very difficult to pull the transports together. I was inundated by a tremendous heap of papers. These were the permits which had arrived from England all at once. In order to get the cooperation of the German authorities I had to emphasize again and again that the children's emigration was in the best interest of the German Reich. We also had to make sure that the qualifications for acceptance of the children were being met. They had to be healthy, under eighteen, and their parents had to be willing to let them go" (N. Wollheim, interview, January 1990).

Indeed, that was the question: Would the parents let their children go? As one of the former *Kinder* explains, it was Hobson's choice: "I[130] want you to imagine my parents' predicament, as well as that of thousands of other parents. Mine had to choose between putting two young children, ages eight and ten, onto a train, knowing only that they were going to England and might never be seen by them again, or keeping the children with them, thus hindering their own chances of escape. The other possibility was for all to be deported to a concentration camp." It was really no choice at all. They had to let the children go.

While some parents were informed by the Jewish Committee about the *Kindertransports*, news seems to have spread largely by word of mouth from friends or through organizations. Elli's[4] parents learned about the transports from a relative in England; Margarete's[54] heard about them through involvement with B'nai B'rith. Lotti's[165] father's correspondence with a refugee committee in England helped secure a seat for her. Franz's[15] family was advised of the new opportunity at a meeting sponsored by Quakers. Advertisements for guarantors were placed in English newspapers by the Quakers, and potential sponsors responded.[68] Beate's[59] desperate family addressed letters randomly to English families; this resulted in a sponsor and a seat on one of the transports for their daughter. Some English families based their choice of foster children on snapshots made available to them. Inga[78] was picked on the basis of a picture she had sent, and when the English family realized that she had a sister, they accepted her as well.

Besides being at the right place at the right time, it helped, as in all situations, to have connections. Ernst[141] did not even know the influential person who pulled strings for him. He reminisces: "I remember standing in line to register for emigration to the children's transports and to Palestine via the Zionist organization, Youth Aliyah. I was very much a latecomer. There were thousands ahead of me, and it seemed pretty hopeless. A friend who was already in Oxford had recommended me to someone in England. Although this person was not Jewish, he had some powerful connections, which included the chair of the Board of British Jews. My friend had described to him my particular plight [of father's incarceration in a concentration camp]. All of this was unbeknownst to me or my mother. In early May 1939, I was suddenly notified that I was to leave Vienna on the next transport in a week's time. My application had been advanced from the bottom of the pile to the top. Later, much later, I have often wondered who was displaced by me."

Bertha[105] owed her place on a transport to her little sister's alertness. One day the little girl ran home breathlessly to report that a friend was to leave for England. In response, her father hurried to the friend's home and then, upon learning about the transports, rushed to the Jewish Committee. He was given two seats for Bertha and her brother but was committed to secrecy. The transport, leaving from Munich, had only twenty places. Only older boys of fifteen and sixteen, who were in danger of being apprehended and sent to concentration camps, were being considered. Bertha knew that danger to be very real. One of her schoolmates had been taken to a concentration camp. Only his ashes had been sent back.

Officials in charge did the best they could to be fair. They tried to allocate seats to communities in proportionate numbers. But with thousands of eager applicants and merely a handful of seats, only a few hopefuls could be accommodated. The line between life and death was a narrow one indeed. Fifteen-year-old Eric[35] was among the lucky ones: "The leaders of the Jewish community in Düsseldorf were asked to choose ten children. In December 1938, my mother and I were asked to report to the community office. I can't remember what was said, but I do remember Stella. I can still see her clearly before my eyes. She had also come with her mother. It was winter. She wore a warm coat, which was embellished by a fur collar. We did not exchange a word. I looked at her and she smiled in a slightly embarrassed fashion. She did not make the transport. Later she was deported and murdered."

The trip to the offices to learn if their child's application would be accepted was indeed anguishing for parents. Trevor Chadwick, of an eminent English family and a Latin teacher at a public school, had journeyed to Prague to pick up two Jewish boys his school was sponsoring. While there, he became aware of the hundreds of Jewish children who had no prospect of leaving. After returning to London, he contacted the World Movement for the Care of Children from Germany as well as the Society of Friends (Quakers), organizations that were busy searching for sponsors. Chadwick, much moved by what he had seen, made it his private business to return to Prague and match children to potential guarantors (Anonymous, "The Pimpernel of Prague," 1988).

Gerda,[123] then eleven years old, remembers what led to her meeting Trevor Chadwick: "My mother had gone to make inquiries about the *Kindertransports*, only to be told that these were full up. We were sitting in our digs, and she mentioned the fact to my father. Subdued silence. Another failed attempt. Then my mother added with some acerbity, 'You ought to have gone; everybody feels sorry for you.' My father's face was incredibly lined, although in happier days he had been known as a joker. 'Well, perhaps I'll try again,' my father said hesitantly. 'Oh yes, please Daddy, do,' I begged; and so it was. What my mother, a plump, straight-backed little woman under an optimistically slanted beret would not achieve, my father—little, thin, and lined, and accompanied by me—could. 'Don't tell anyone I sent you but. . .' We were given the name of Trevor Chadwick's hotel. Trevor Chadwick immediately accepted me. What is more, he got his mother to guarantee for me (until the age of eighteen). My parents, and indeed I myself, chose to look on this as a compliment. Now, I am not so sure. I was an incredibly unprepossessing child, and I dare say Trevor Chadwick dared not impose me on a stranger.

"He certainly was a superman. Tall, handsome, and with strikingly Nordic looks. It seems that many others, notably the Quakers and Nicholas Winton [another Englishman], were active in bringing the children out. At the time, though, it seemed as if Trevor Chadwick almost single-handedly had killed the dragon and was wafting me away. I was accepted at once. There was to be another interview at which the entire family was to be present. . . . My mother brought my sister along for good measure, hoping that her beauty would sway the rule against over-eighteen-year-olds. We had all dressed very neatly for the occasion, my father in a formal suit. Trevor Chadwick descended the stairs of the grand hotel, dressed most casually in a woolen jersey. We fell over ourselves in admiration. There's your real gentleman. He doesn't need to dress up. So casual. So self-assured. But, of course, Trevor Chadwick could have appeared in a dinner jacket or in a grass skirt and we would have been equally impressed. My stout little mother planted herself firmly in front of Trevor Chadwick, addressing a speech of thanks to his navel (he being very much taller than she). She liked to air her English, and I suspect she thanked him 'from the bottom of [her] heart.' Trevor Chadwick shuffled his feet."

The news that they had been accepted on a *Kindertransport* came as an immense relief to children and parents alike. Particularly the older youngsters were excited at the prospect. The recollections of one such escapee highlight the happy anticipation and give a fifteen-year-old girl's point of view: "I[70] was thrilled at the prospect of going to England. A new wardrobe was purchased for me. For once, money played no role, and I got all the lovely clothes I had always admired. There was also the prospect of returning to school. I hoped to be reunited with my family in the near future."

Alan[141] had been encouraged by his mother to find a way out by himself while his mother was waiting for his father's release from a concentration camp. She would not leave without him. There was no longer an income. When acceptance for the *Kindertransport* reached Alan, youthful narcissism blotted out all but an immense sense of relief: "My reaction to the news was one of absolute elation. After six miserable months, I was to be liberated. I was greatly excited about going to England. I was thinking about nobody but myself in my joy and anticipation."

Gunther[1] also looked forward to leaving. He was familiar with being away from home; he saw it as an adventure and had been learning English to prepare himself. Anyway, he had no idea that he might never return. In addition an incident involving his sister, which had accelerated her departure, served to increase his desire to leave. A policeman had commented to Gunther's sister that perhaps she would like to "plant flowers at Oranienburg," a nearby concentration camp.

For Hans,[174] as well as for some other teenagers, acceptance on a transport came just in the nick of time: "I was seventeen years and ten months. As far as I know this was the last transport which allowed young people between sixteen and eighteen years of age to be included. Only two months earlier I had been arrested by storm troopers and kept in prison for about four days. I had signed a paper to leave the country within three months. I believe that was taken into consideration when I was accepted."

Even younger children understood the necessity of leaving. Seven-year-old Kurt[51] wanted to stay with his parents. Friends of the family impressed upon him that it would be much easier for his parents to leave alone. He knew that his parents were trying to get to England and that they would join him before long. After a few days Kurt told his parents that he wanted to go to England. Betty,[66] then only ten, recalls: "I heard my mother plan a trip to Holland. I did not feel terrible about it. I thought it would be a good change. I memorized addresses. I knew my mother was planning to leave with my little sister. They were waiting for an American visa." Some little ones displayed an amazingly adventurous attitude. Six-year-old Margarete[54] felt as if she were preparing for summer camp. There were clothing lists, name tags, departure dates, meeting places for the different groups of children, supervisors, and so on. The only difference was that she did not know her final destination. But then, she was sure that she would be seeing her parents again soon, and so she did not worry too much about where she would be staying.

Parents tried to reassure their children that the parting was only temporary and that they would follow as soon as they could. One boy[51] felt reassured when his parents explained that they had only one visa missing and that they would meet in Southampton and from there leave together for the United States. Thirteen-year-old Marietta[153] did not want to leave her parents, her sister, and her dog, Billy. She recalls her father breaking the news of her imminent departure as gently as possible. He took her for long walks and told her about the English countryside, pretty English gardens, and the English strong belief in fair play and decency. He was preparing her for her journey, as well as trying to correct the loss of faith she had suffered from recent events that had left her in a state of shock and disbelief. Elli's[4] father explained that she was going to a very nice place and that he and her mother would follow soon. He urged her to be very brave and, in order to get on well with her foster parents, to be very good and always do as she was told.

Parents tried to prepare their children in practical ways as well. Six-year-old Maritza[75] was sent to English classes, and her mother helped her with the language. Her mother encouraged her to choose some toys to take along, although once she arrived in England, the little girl felt she had made some wrong choices. Seven-year-old Steve[80] learned that he would be sent to England, to be taken care of by someone he would call "Auntie." His mother went with him to a photographer. They took a great many passport-size pictures, and Steve was allowed to pick one for his trip. He carefully chose one—and still has it. He did not know at that time that, except for one aunt, all his relatives, including his parents, would be deported. Franz[15] selected two volumes of German plays and was buoyed by his parents' reassurance that they would be able to leave in the not too distant future.

The parents tried to find ways of providing for their children. Because the children were only allowed a very small sum of money, parents packed cameras or expensive violins that, in case of need, could be sold in England. It was hard to judge what would be useful in a foreign country. Alan[141] remembers going shopping with his mother for clothes, which they could ill afford: "Most of these purchases were quite unsuitable for England. Once there, I would not wear them for fear of being ridiculed. Later in the war, when clothes became scarce, I was able to sell them." So his mother's solicitude had not been a total loss after all. Maritza's[75] mother, without telling her, took her boots to the cobbler to have the heels filled with family jewelry. Later the mother wrote to the child's guardian that the boots needed mending; since they clearly did not, the English foster mother comprehended the message.

Mothers of little girls were concerned about their children's emotional development as well as their safety. Two touching examples illustrate the desperate ways mothers tried to anticipate their daughter's needs. One woman remembers being taken to the park by her mother, who then explained the "facts of life" to her, wanting her child to be given that understanding before she left. Another mother packed a year's supply of feminine napkins, anticipating her daughter's menarche.

While the parents were preparing the children, Norbert Wollheim and other organizers were working at top speed. Norbert describes those efforts: "We frequently worked through the night. The political situation was deteriorating, and our aim was to fulfill the target of 10,000 as early as possible. We estimated that we could manage to do that within the year. It was our task to plan the transports based upon available space on trains. After the Home Office in England processed applications and returned them to us, together with the Permit Cards, parents were advised that their children had been accepted for immigration to England. We often had a situation where parents received a Permit Card for one child but not for another. In that case, we had to tell the parents that we were sorry, but we were only able to include children who already had their cards. We had no control over these. We were dealing with parents on a fair basis and tried to convince them that there was no discrimination. As soon as we had three hundred to four hundred permit cards available, we immediately set a date for a transport. The children had to assemble at a designated place, for instance, the railway station in Berlin. Children who came from the eastern part of Germany or [from] Poland had to be brought to the station in time for the transport. If they had the means, the parents accompanied them. If not, the children had to travel alone. They either arrived the same morning or had to stay with relatives or friends. We could not possibly handle that aspect; it would have been too much for us."

There was considerable variation in time between a child being accepted for a transport and the actual departure. Some youngsters had no preparation at all. A woman,[40] then only six years old, recalls that one evening in March 1939 she was dressed up with coat, hat, and gloves, given a suitcase, and taken by her father to the railroad station. Perhaps her father had wanted to spare her the fear of anticipation. Or perhaps the family had been given a place for her at the last minute. Some children had a few days notice,[59] others knew several months in advance.[74] Twelve-year-old Miriam[113] had to travel all by herself from Poland to Berlin. She remained in a hostel for almost two weeks before she caught one of the last transports. Ruth,[126] a mere four-year-old, stayed with her aunt. "I remember my aunty feeding me poached eggs on spinach, like two big eyes in a green face. I remember a stuffed toy dog taller than I was and my grandmother's very soft and elegant red plush sofa."

Mothers experienced a strong desire to embrace their children for, what many knew would be the last time. Gunther[1] recalls that the night before he left he was allowed to sleep with his mother in her bed. Ruth[70] reflects: "I cannot even think how my mother must have felt. We spent the night at my uncle's house and we shared a bed."

Maritza[75] had been instructed not to mention her imminent departure to her grandmother. Though her parents had no prospect of leaving, they arranged a little party and tried to appear optimistic in order to put their little six-year-old daughter in a festive mood for the journey. The care her parents took in disguising their true feelings is recorded in a photograph: The date was July 1, 1939, the location the garden of an outdoor restaurant on a sunny day. Grandfather, parents, and Maritza are seated at a table under a lush tree. Maritza's mother is wearing a light summer dress and a chic hat at a fashionable angle. She is smiling into the camera. Either Maritza is frowning or the sun is blinding her. Her father's face looks tense, her grandfather's thoughtful. Still, the grandfather's beer, the father's cigarette, the arms of the two men resting on the table indicate the leisurely relaxation following a meal. It is one week before Maritza's departure. It is five months before her grandfather will be shot in the streets of Prague. It is an unknown length of time before her parents will be gassed at Auschwitz.

Some parents found it too heartrending to take their children to the station themselves and avoided that last moment at the railway station. One mother preferred to stay at home, while the father took their seventeen-year-old daughter[147] to the station. The father hugged and kissed the girl. It was the first time she had ever seen him with tears in his eyes. She remembers clearly his saying, "God knows if we will see each other again. Be brave!" Ellen's[19] mother sent her son to the station with a trusted nanny. "The day we were leaving, my mother told us that our nursemaid would take us to Köln [Cologne]. It happened all very fast. I was very scared. I recall hardly any preparation, except for some packing the previous night. There was so much confusion. The maid fetched us from home. We said good-bye. My mother, after we left, was able to express her feelings at home without us seeing her. We separated from the maid, whom we loved, without the same sentiments that parting from my parents would have entailed."

The memories of the railway stations vary, as they must. Each transport involved different parents and different children; the procedures varied from city to city, from station to station. Norbert Wollheim tried to infuse the atmosphere with as much calm as possible. He managed to have a room set aside where parents were able to congregate with their children away from the public waiting room. Wollheim's desire for privacy probably suited the Gestapo quite well. They did not like to parade the scenes of departing children before the public; it is quite probable that was the reason many *Kindertransport* trains left at midnight. In order to lessen the feeling of threat, Wollheim maneuvered to get permission to handle the departures himself, without the presence of the SS. The leave-taking was the most dreaded moment of the whole procedure. A chair would be placed in the middle of the room for Wollheim to stand on. The children, standing close to their parents, wore large tags with numbers around their necks. Wollheim would call out each number. Parents would hug their children and watch them leave. One woman,[3] then only seven years old, cannot remember the journey at all, but she does remember that because her name started with *A*, she was the first in line to board the train. She and her five-year-old sister, leading a long line of children, trudged up to the train, leaving their parents behind.

Many of the older children who do remember the railroad

station have a grim recollection. Even the appearance of the railroad station itself was intimidating. The Hamburg station, for instance, was heavily decorated with swastika flags and swarming with people in uniform.[149] A clear description of the atmosphere is given by one of the youngsters:[40] "Looking back on the scene today, it appears macabre. This cold and dark railway station, the long lines of silent children; then, sitting in the train, not knowing where I was going, surrounded by hundreds of children. The little ones were crying, and the older ones quite silent. It is hard to explain the way I felt, but I was cold and numb with fear. I did not cry, and I really believed my parents would follow." The sense of confusion is echoed by Ilse:[74] "Two days after I had been told that I was going on a *Kindertransport*, I was taken to the station, where there were loads of other children with parents and relatives. It was bedlam. Everyone was in tears. I was absolutely bewildered and quite frightened. None of my friends were there. I was shy and timid and spoke to no one at all." The scene affects another former *Kind*[17] even today: "I do remember the day of departure. In fact, I will never forget it. The Nazis would not allow both parents at the station, only one. The waiting room was like a funeral parlor: parents crying, children crying, fathers blessing their children. There was a general feeling of doom. For me it was tragic. I wondered if I would ever see my parents again. I still hate stations and airports."

Sixteen-year-old Hans[174] was taken to the Vienna Westbahnhof by his mother. His father was not able to accompany him. He was at that moment attempting to cross into Belgium. Hans was affected by the desperate atmosphere at the station: "There is a harassing memory of the assembled youngsters about to be handed over to the staff of the refugee committee. Babies in their cradles and small children of tender age were surrendered by their parents, knowing that this was the only way to save their children's lives. There were parents fainting and children screaming when we realized that this might be the last time we might see each other." Hans's father did not reach Belgium; he was sent to Buchenwald and death. His mother disappeared; no information as to where she died is available.

At the Prague railroad station, Marietta[153] recalls, the organizers had not been able to free themselves of the presence of soldiers: "We were all assembled at the railroad station in Prague. Shortly after arrival, various German officials and soldiers parted the children from their parents, promising the parents they would later see their children. My next recollection is of my father climbing the side of the railway carriage so he could kiss me good-bye through the window. My mother and sister stood on the platform with the other parents, desperately waving and blowing kisses, shouting farewells that we could not hear."

To carry as many children as could possibly fit, the carriages were crammed, literally to the brim. Dorli[41] and her little sister were trying to find their places: "We were given numbers to put on and found our carriage. The train was very full. There was a seat for me and a space in the overhead luggage rack net for my four-year-old sister. Some children were under the seats, some on them, and some above. The little ones were above."

Good-byes had to be said with soldiers patrolling the platform amidst all the hubbub of sorting out the children and loading and stowing babies as well as luggage. The parents displayed remarkable restraint, disguising their anguish well. Indeed, many of the children viewed the trip with optimism and, until the last moments, were not aware of the full meaning of the parting. Of course, some parents were able to muster more control than others. But most former *Kinder* recollect their parents' intensely supportive attitude. Not one writes of parents calling attention to their own desperate, or even hopeless, situation. Sometimes their true inner feelings, hidden under a veneer of control, were revealed by a seemingly insignificant action.[70] "When it was time to leave for the station, my mother was dressed most elegantly in a suit, gloves, and a hat with a veil. At no time did she lose her composure. The tension only showed when she questioned me about a forgotten washcloth, certainly no item of great importance. When it came time [for] parting, she just kissed me and pushed me away. But after we boarded, the train made another stop in a suburb. And there she was again, with my Uncle Paul, searching for me and waving through the window. I never saw my parents or my uncle again."

Thirteen-year-old David's[149] mother found it impossible to restrain her tears. Still, one wonders how she could bear the parting at all: Her husband and other son had been taken away by the SS, and after the train pulled out of the station, she would be all alone.

Ernst[141] found himself in a situation so painful that he just wished to get away as quickly as possible. His father had been released two days before from Buchenwald. As his father stood by the train, with his thin body and shaved head, he seemed a stranger to the boy. The father was in a daze, and nothing of substance was said. The boy concentrated only on the adventure for which he was heading. He felt only relief at leaving what he considered to be a hopeless nightmare. He does not remember thinking of his parents' fate. Perhaps it was the only way he could deal with the situation.

Possibly, there was a good deal of repression practiced by a number of youngsters. But, in addition, it may also have been true that in spite of their experiences with the Nazis, their youthful, optimistic minds were still unable to absorb the total horror of it all. Many did not understand the full impact of their leaving until the last minute. Fritz[169] left his house in a sprightly mood. In order to sneak in some extra clothes that would not fit into his little case, he had donned a vest, a jacket, and a coat and topped them all with a raincoat. He took the trip in his stride; it seemed as if he were just going for a holiday. Only the return ticket was missing. Whatever emotions his parents harbored, "they did not show their feelings and put on a brave face. Finally the moment came. A last embrace, a handshake, and a kiss. Then it was 'mind the doors,' a whistle, and the train went into motion. As the train started to gather speed, I saw them standing there, waving after me. Suddenly I realized that this was probably the last time I would see them." Emmy,[129] then fifteen, also recalls the shock of sudden insight. She was traveling with her parents from her home in Augsburg to reach the midnight *Kindertransport* train leaving from Munich. They were hopeful. They talked about a swift reunion. All that in spite of her mother's illness and her father's changed demeanor since his discharge from Dachau. Suddenly, sitting on the train and looking at her parents' frozen faces on the platform, the finality of the farewell struck her full force. Beate[59] experienced a similar moment: "As the train pulled out of the station and I waved my last good-bye, I saw my mother step behind my father so I should not see her pull out her handkerchief and put it to her face. Then the realization of her pain was a shock."

Franz[15] describes the evolution of his feelings in detail: "Travel to a foreign country seemed like an adventure, for I was already an

Anglophile. Preparation for my departure included all the practical activities of gathering the few things allowed and a few pictures of my parents. The emotional preparation included expressions of reassurance that my parents would be able to leave soon. My parents did not show any distress during that time. I was too sheltered to really be aware what was happening, and therefore there was no trauma. That came much later. Of course, I did feel considerable anxiety about leaving my parents, a feeling which increased as my departure drew nearer. I finally sat on the train in the Westbahnhof, in Vienna, at around eight o'clock at night on June 13, 1939, the day after my thirteenth birthday. My mother was visibly affected. And so was I, though I managed to hide it fairly well by occasionally turning my face away from the window toward my raincoat, which I had hung up on my other side. I remember looking out of the window for my parents; other parents also standing there; waving at my parents; my mother waving back, my father nodding silently, turning away from the window for a moment as an SS man passed through the coach, then back again, fighting a few tears and the train beginning to move. The image of my parents standing silently on the platform, watching the train slowly move out, is deeply etched in my memory. The entire experience of leaving my parents remains unique in my mind. I never associated subsequent farewells with it. In fact it was unique: It signified the end of one life and the beginning of another. I think I was vaguely conscious of that at the time."

Grandparents were no less affected than parents: "My grandmother came to see me off at the Friedrichstrasse station in Berlin. That was a sad moment. I thought I would never see her again, and I loved her with all my boyish heart." Bernhard[68] was right: he never did see his grandmother again. Another parting was equally affecting: "My uncle took me to the station, but my grandmother hid behind a pillar to see me off. I still remember that today, and it haunts me."[26]

Vera's[158] parents tried to protect her as long as possible. Her last glimpse was of them waving large white handkerchiefs as the train slowly jerked into motion. As she rode through Germany, Uncle Rudolph and Aunt Elsa managed to come on the train and ride with her to the Dutch frontier. In Holland there was Great-Aunt Sara. She boarded the ship and handed Vera a doll dressed in a hand-knitted outfit. But after that, the nine-year-old was alone. Her parents could protect her no further.

At first fifteen-year-old Karl's[103] parents managed to hide their distress. But when they said good-bye to him and his sister, they began to cry. The parents told them that if anything happened to them, the children should not grieve but be happy. Karl remembers them on the platform, though they were forbidden to stand close to the train. He can only recall the faces of his parents; the other people did not matter. As the train started, his parents turned their faces away. But they were not yet willing to let the children go. They needed another look. They took the underground train to the next station, and there they were again as the train that took their children into the unknown sped past.

And for nine months the *Kindertransport* trains rumbled through the night.

### All the Leaves Have Lost Their Trees

*All the leaves have lost their trees*
Child, what tumbled words are these?
(Yet I grieve for my lost tree:
Far away the wind bore me.)

GERDA MAYER

## Chapter 12

# And Most of All— Smiles!

Not one former *Kind* remembers the journey to England from beginning to end. Each one describes specific moments and recalls various incidents and emotions experienced. Put together, a clear image of the trip emerges.

Once the train left the station, the younger children found the journey the hardest. The strain of traveling without protective parents contributed to a sense of desolation and abandonment. The tag around Maritza's[75] neck made her feel like a refugee. Dora[173] was so aware of her label that she still remembers the number of her tag today: It was 109. Six-year-old Paula[17] felt unhappy and "in a fog"; she wondered what would happen to her, and there were no adults to ask. Lea,[171] only four years, does not remember any adults either. Her only memory is of hearing her "big" sisters cry at night. Her "big" sisters were all of five and seven years old. It was not coincidental that there were so few grown-ups on the train. While the SS had authorized adults to accompany the children, the permission had a harsh condition attached to it: The escorts had to return to the Third Reich as soon as the children were delivered to the English authorities. If any of the chaperons were tempted to remain in England, the SS would cancel all future transports. In effect, the escorts were hostages. As a result, Norbert Wollheim was forced to use great caution in choosing them. He found them among former members of Jewish youth groups. Parents whose young children were departing noticed the dearth of adults and begged older youngsters to look after their little ones. Before the train pulled out, the parents of two young children, having no other recourse, appealed to fourteen-year-old Elfi[50] to take care of them. Fifteen-year-old Emmy[129] found herself entrusted with two infants in a wicker basket, which was shoved into her compartment at the last minute. Beate,[59] remembering her mother admonishing her always to be kind, comforted a little orphan girl sitting next to her. There was another little girl as well, whose presence she had only recollected recently: "The little girl was crying for her mother, and I put my arms around her and told her she would be seeing her soon." Beate, now Bea, explains how the memory reemerged: "Recently I attended a *Kindertransport* reunion. While queuing up to enter the hall, I fell into a conversation with a woman standing next to me. As she told me about coming to England on a *Kindertransport*, she started to cry. I put my arms around her and told her she was all right now, not to worry. That's when I remembered the little girl on the train." It appears that her mother's advice has lasted Bea a lifetime.

Among the older boys there were some, their heads shaved, who appeared particularly subdued and very apprehensive. They were the ones who had already been incarcerated in concentration camps. Usually, when men were discharged from a camp, the SS informed them that they had to leave within a stated time or face rearrest. The Jewish committees, which arranged the transports, tried their best to provide space for youngsters who were thus at risk.

Shy children felt themselves set apart.[167] The long trip seemed even longer if the youngster found it difficult to muster up courage to befriend other children.[74] A vivacious and bubbly personality made the trip easier. Dorli[41] recalls the journey: "There were lots of children to talk to. Many were older than I, which I liked. I have to say I was excited at the idea of the forthcoming adventure. I was thrilled at the thought of going to England and putting to use the English I had been learning." On the whole, the trip was somewhat easier for the older than for the younger children. Teenage Bernhard[68] was relaxed enough to note the sunny June weather. Franz,[15] who was able to unwind sufficiently to fall asleep, characterizes the trip as "a sorrowful parting but an adventurous new beginning." For Franz and Bernhard excitement prevailed to a certain extent over apprehension. Yet, while the boys did not experience the trip as entirely stressful, they could not have been completely sanguine. As the train approached the border, Bernhard threw the few German pennies in his possession out the window; he feared that once he crossed the border into Holland, he might be arrested for carrying foreign currency. And Franz, while looking out the window, observed prisoners in striped uniforms being loaded onto freight cars. He was also conscious of the fact that the doors of the train were sealed and would not be opened until the children reached Holland. It is only in the context of Germany in 1938 that such a trip could be characterized as not excessively stressful.

There could be no true relaxation of tension as long as the children were within the boundaries of the German Reich. The SS patrolled the trains, their manner arrogant and unemotional.[19] The extent of the SS presence varied from transport to transport. On many transports the SS made an inspection tour before the train started and continued patrolling intermittently.[15] On others, the SS physically harassed the children, tearing off little gold necklaces and confiscating watches.[174] Their heavy tread was known to children of all ages, and the fear that sound aroused is indelibly imprinted on their minds. Of her journey a woman,[3] only six at the time, is left only with images of those black uniforms and black boots and the feeling of fright she experienced then. Some youngsters had genuine cause to be afraid. Recalls Elli[4]: "My mother had accepted some jewelry from a very good friend to send to her son, who was already in England. She stitched this jewelry into the hem of my skirt. I knew that if it were found, everybody on the transport would be killed. I was very fearful until we crossed the border into Holland. It was an interminable journey." Elli's mother was convinced that the authorities should be defied in subtle ways. When the German government asked that all skis be surrendered, she and her friend soaked their skis in water, then dried them by a stove, making them too brittle for usage. Apparently, Elli's mother wanted to inculcate the same attitude of defiance in her daughter.

There was one last obstacle before crossing over into Holland: The German border guards had to be faced. Fear and tension rose again as the train approached the frontier.[41] The guards' actions were unpredictable. Sometimes they made only a perfunctory search of the trains.[35] At other times search was so extensive that they detached the carriage the children were riding in from the rest of the

train and commanded the youngsters to undress while they meticu-
lously examined their pathetic little suitcases.[169] These encounters
were particularly agonizing when they took place just yards from the
border and freedom.

Once the border formalities were resolved, the trains finally
lumbered into Holland. It was a glorious and jubilant moment. The
instant the children entered Holland, an enormous burden slipped
from their young shoulders. The contrast of what they had left
behind and the welcome they received from total strangers was
almost overwhelming. "As we[147] came into the station, ladies were
waiting for us. They gave us something to eat. I don't remember
what. I just know it was like stepping into a different world, a world
of relief. I can't tell you what it meant to us, the few hours we spent
there. It made all the difference. After worrying about the SS on our
train, I saw people who were nice and friendly and had come to help
us. It ws the difference from night to day." Dorli[41] agrees: "There
was excitement and anticipation as we crossed the border, leaving
Germany. There was tremendous joy and relief when we were met in
Holland by many ladies from a charitable group. They were waiting
on the platform as our train drew in. They gave us orange juice and
buns and made us feel very welcome, even though we were only
passing through." One aspect of the reception seemed astounding to
the children. There were no "Aryans" or "non-Aryans" on the
platform. There were just smiling women. "In the evening when
we[173] reached the border, for the first time in a long while I saw
kindness. There were Jewish and Christian ladies, with a few Catholic
nuns among them. We were received with food, drinks, sweets, and
chocolates, and most important of all—smiles. From then on, the
journey was agreeable." By the time the children had left their
homes, money had already become scarce and goods had not been
easily available. Therefore, the goodies that were being offered
struck a particularly responsive chord. In addition, their symbolic
value was not lost on the children. "Big, kind ladies came onto the
train with slices of soft white bread and butter and glasses of orange
juice. I[59] wasn't particularly keen on food in those days. But I loved
that offering."

While the vast majority of children continued their trip to
England, some were sent to Sweden and others remained in Belgium

and Holland. Betty[66] was placed in a Dutch hostel, called Driebergen, in Leur near Breda, where she was to spend the next nine months. She remembers that the home was well organized, that people were very kind, and that she was taught how to wear clogs. Betty's brother had been placed with a Dutch foster family. When her parents arrived in Belgium, her brother was sent to stay with them. In order to make this possible, he had been exchanged with another refugee child, one who was living at that time in Belgium. This exchange was a twist of fate that saved her brother's life: After the German invasion her parents and brother escaped to Morocco, but the little boy who took her brother's place with the Dutch family died, together with his foster parents, under the Nazis. Betty cannot recall why she was transferred to Amsterdam. She was housed in the Wajsenhuis Building, which was run by the Jewish community. Later, after the Germans invaded Holland, the building served as a collection point from which the Jews in Holland were deported. Betty has fond memories of her pre-Hitler stay in Holland: kind teachers, learning Dutch, going to school. But this semblance of routine in no way meant that it was a normal life. Each child owned only a very few possessions. Betty had a little box that contained her treasures: a dollar given to her by her grandparents, who had gone to the United States; a silver thimble; and a picture of her mother. The children had an awareness of the precarious reality of their lives. Betty remembers discussing strategies for survival, should the Germans arrive. The children decided they would all hide in the special laundry room that was separate from the main building and had big laundry tubs, thinking the German soldiers would perhaps not be able to find them there.

The majority of the children continued their voyage, after a brief stop in Holland, by ferry from the Hook of Holland to Harwich, England. For many, memories of the last leg of the trip are hazy. They remember that it was night and that they slept on board. They recall that the crossing was rough, and many children felt quite sick. Magie[52] sounds a bit forlorn when she says, "It was a very small ship with lots of children and very few adults. We all had tags around our necks. The boat ride was very shaky and we were all very sick."

On the ferry the children had their first encounter with English life. The good-natured crew impressed Marietta,[153] particularly after the time spent under German officialdom: "We boarded a British vessel. I was greatly relieved to hear English instead of the despised German. We could not understand what the sailors were saying to us but felt from their good-natured laughter that they were being kind." And then came the great moment, that great initiation into English life, when she was offered her first "cuppa tea," strong, sweet, and comforting. She was just as impressed when she later entered an English train, which "looked grand to all of us, with the upholstered seats and mirrors above them!" English food was another story. Alan[141] and other youngsters were given bars of Aero chocolate; they tactfully threw them overboard. It was Alan's first lesson: English ferries are not comparable to Austrian *Konditoreien* (pastry shops).

While the children kept arriving, the organizers continued working at fever pitch. As the months rolled by, the race against time became more intense. Transport after transport departed from the continent, bringing hundreds of children—and leaving behind thousands more. Meanwhile, Chadwick continued his air transports from Prague. Gerda[123] found that from the moment of takeoff, all was happiness on the plane; chocolates were passed around and the children sang exuberantly.

Norbert Wollheim drove himself harder and harder. Sometimes he performed miracles. During one of the transports he discovered that one of the youngsters, whose head had been shaved, was above the age level allowed for *Kinder* by the English immigration officials. How was he to prevent him from being turned back on arrival in England? He decided on a ruse. He would tell the passport official that the passport contained the wrong age. At passport control the boy was challenged. The passport official refused to believe that German officials could make mistakes. Well, Wollheim improvised, the new Nazi officials are so busy that they occasionally do make mistakes. And did the passport official know that this boy had been in a concentration camp? There was silence. The official played with the passport. He knew the boy's true age, and Wollheim knew that the official knew. The official did not look at Wollheim when he said, "Well, if you will take full responsibility, I will permit it." With eyes averted, he let the boy pass. Another boy was challenged as well. He had brought an expensive violin with him. The passport official explained that he could not allow any object that was salable into the country; he would have to impound the violin. "No," said Wollheim, having no idea whether the boy could really play the instrument, "this is the boy's violin. Really, it is for his personal use." "Well," said the official to the boy, "then play it." Slowly the boy took his violin out of the case. As a hush fell over the hall, he began to play. The melody of "God Save the King" filled the hall. The official consented to the violin (N. Wollheim, interview, January 1990).

War, which had been a likelihood, now became a certainty. Departures of transports were speeded up as much as possible. Siegfried's[110] boat docked in England on August 29, 1939, and his sister, still in Poland, was expected on the next transport. War broke out on September 3. His sister never made it. After Hitler's invasion of Prague in the spring, Chadwick's work became more difficult and by June 1939 his transports had to cease. Chadwick commented, "I can't say how many children were on my books, but it must have been in the thousands. Nor can I say how many I got away, but it was only hundreds. . . . I shall always have a sense of shame that I didn't get more out" (Anonymous, 1988). No wonder Chadwick was called the "Pimpernel of Prague."

Wollheim was preparing another transport for September 3 when word came that war might break out sooner. He advanced the departure date to August 30. He realized that this would probably be the very last transport to reach freedom. The escorts who were to accompany this last train suspected that they would be granted asylum in England. (Until the last trip all the escorts, except one, had faithfully returned to Germany. A man[28] sadly recalls the fate of a cousin who had served as an escort: His cousin was warned by German officials that if he failed to return from England, his old mother would be sent to a concentration camp. Mindful of his mother, the cousin flew back to Nazi Germany. It yielded him nothing; both mother and son were deported.) Wollheim himself was scheduled to be on that last train, but he did not avail himself of the opportunity; he gave his ticket to an adult who did not have any Jewish relatives left in Germany. Having helped so many others, Norbert Wollheim could not help himself. He survived the war years, but at a cost: He spent them in concentration camps.

As war drew nearer, Mrs. Wijsmuller (1961) redoubled her heroic efforts and managed to do the impossible. She organized

*Kindertransport*s from Vilna and Riga to Sweden and then chartered seven planes to fly the children to England. She, together with others, had managed to get an immigration ship out of Marseilles to Palestine. When the German–Dutch border was already closed, Mrs. Wijsmuller snatched a few hundred Jewish youngsters before the trap closed entirely: She contacted officials to get a release to bring them across the frontier at Bentheim into Holland. From there they could be transported to England. Being informed that another 150 Jewish refugees were marooned in Kleef, she hurried there, only to find an additional 300 Jews, all dressed in the traditional garb of the Orthodox. Undaunted, she managed to find a train to bring them to Vlissingen, from whose port they departed for England.

Betty[66] remained in an orphanage in Holland even after the outbreak of war. By May 1940 she noticed that more and more children were suddenly arriving. The children had to share their beds. On May 9, one day before the German invasion, the children were told that they were to go on a trip the following day. Betty was awakened around four in the morning. Her little treasure box with her grandmother's silver dollar and her mother's picture was left behind, much to her regret later. Amidst falling bombs the children were driven down to the port. Betty remembers people running, all seemingly heading for the harbor. They boarded the *Bodegraven*, which took five days to cross to Liverpool. The children slept in the hold of the ship, usually reserved for transporting animals. Betty remembers seasickness and falling bombs. It was hard for her to believe that the planes were actually trying to kill her. From the ferry a train took the children to London, where members of the Jewish Committee welcomed them.[173] The children were surrounded by confusion, noise, and the mutter of foreign languages.[70] Some of the little ones were totally exhausted. Dorli[41] marveled at her little sister, who simply fell asleep standing up. Some lucky youngsters had friends of their family eagerly waiting for them. Some foster parents arrived to pick up children they had chosen from photographs. Others simply did not show up, and new arrangements had to be improvised on the spot. For many children, particularly the older ones, there was no home waiting. Although it was winter, they were taken to Dovercourt, a deserted holiday camp.[103] Beate[59] describes meeting her foster family: "When they came to the letter *S* for Siegel, a lady, who seemed ancient to me, wearing a lilac-colored suit, approached me with a 'How do you do?' To which I answered, 'Yes.' She took me to a beautiful flat in Portland Place. We had Irish stew served by a maid. I had not ever eaten lamb before, and my mother's goulash was not so wet and runny. The next day we traveled to the country, where old Mrs. Wilson, my guardian, lived. The lady who had come to meet me was her daughter. We were driven down by the chauffeur to Brasted Hall, Brasted, near Sevenoaks in Kent." Quite an elegant start.

A similar reception only served to frighten twelve-year-old Gerda,[123] who had been rescued by Trevor Chadwick and who now entered a waiting car: "It was only at that point that a vast sense of desolation swept over me. It was my real leave-taking of Czechoslovakia. Good-bye. Good-bye forever. In the front of the car sat a couple, husband and wife. At the back, there was already one other child from the transport. . . . She was only nine, and already fast asleep. . . . It occurred to me that we might be being abducted. I cried, softly enough not to alert our kidnappers, loudly enough, I hoped, to awake my sleeping companion. It did not work. I then thought of throwing myself out of the car, making for the coast, swimming the Channel to France, making my way from France to Czechoslovakia. . . . I had no money except for a lucky half-crown piece that had been given me by Trevor Chadwick. I had no map. I knew no French. . . . The next day it was English daffodils instead of the snow and slush of Prague. It was pretty shells on the Swanage sands. It was also the day that Hitler marched into Prague."

It was a day at the end of August, and the weather in England, for once, was hot and sunny. It took a long time for some of the children to be sorted out. After their arrival in Harwich, Fritz[169] and some other boys sat on the grass, surrounded by their little suitcases. (Fritz would hold on to his for many years. It rested in the attic until his final move, when it was left behind. In later years, he wished he had kept it after all.) The boys sat, waiting for they knew not what. Then someone began to sing in German, and all the boys joined in. They sang a song—Fritz remembers it clearly—about a family of starlings that brought up their young in a nest under a high roof.

And so the children's journey ended. The last transport was dispatched. The *Kindertransport* children had arrived, but they had not yet reached their final destination. Most had yet to wander to many places and many countries before finding a permanent home. What the children and some of the foster parents had thought would be a temporary stay turned, after the declaration of war, into one that lasted many years. Many of the children would be treated with loving care. Some would find only physical shelter but little balm for their young hearts. They had completed one journey. The next one was about to begin.

# GLASGOW JEWISH COUNCIL FOR GERMAN REFUGEES
### CHILDREN'S CARE

COMMITTEES:
ADULT REFUGEE and IMMIGRATION
CHILDREN'S CARE
DOMESTIC SERVICE
HEALTH and EDUCATION
HOSPITALITY
TRAINEE and SPECIAL QUALIFICATIONS

Your Reference:
Our Reference: KC/MC/MA.
Please address your reply to

KONRAD CINA
SECRETARY
25-1-39

Mrs Maas.
    go Krisp
    44 Goltz Strasse
    Spandau Berlin.

Dear Mrs Maas.

I have great pleasure in informing you that I have successfull in placing your daughter Monica with a very good home in Glasgow. All papers etc, have been sent to London & before we will be able to bring her over here very soon. Take this letter to the committee in Berlin, and ask them to arrange for Monica to be sent as soon as possible. The family taking her are Mr. George N.W. PRIMROSE (GARAGE OWNER) 26 Milngavie Rd. Bearsden ~~Stirlingshire~~ Renfrewshire

Yours Faithfully
Konrad Cina Secy.

Letter informing her parents that a sponsor has been found for their daughter Monica.
(Courtesy Monica Sexton)

A postcard from Monica written on a *Kindertransport* train before it reached the Dutch border: "We must tidy up because now comes passport control. Greetings and kisses. Don't be sad, Mommy. I am not either." (Courtesy Monica Sexton)

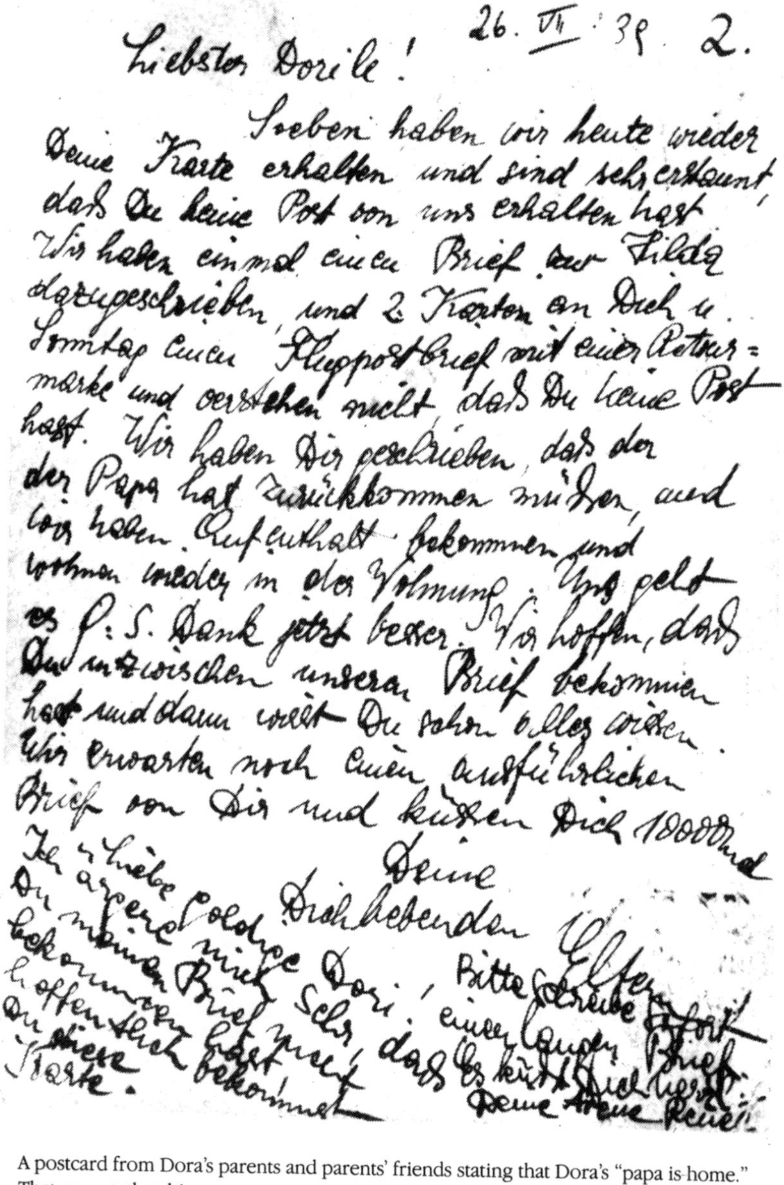
26. VII. 38. 2.

Liebster Dorile!

Soeben haben wir heute wieder Deine Karte erhalten und sind sehr erstaunt, daß Du keine Post von uns erhalten hast. Wir haben einmal einen Brief von Hilda dazugeschrieben, und 2 Karten an Dich u. Sonntag einen Flugpostbrief mit einer Retour=marke und verstehen nicht, daß Du keine Post hast. Wir haben Dir geschrieben, daß der der Papa hat zurückkommen müssen, und wir haben Aufenthalt bekommen und wohnen wieder in der Wohnung. Uns geht es G.s. Dank jetzt besser. Wir hoffen, daß Du inzwischen unseren Brief bekommen hast und dann weißt Du schon alles wissen. Wir erwarten noch einen ausführlichen Brief von Dir und küssen Dich 1000mal

Deine
Dich liebenden
Eltern

Liebe goldige Dori! Ich ärgere mich sehr, daß Du meinen Brief nicht bekommen hast, hoffentlich bekommst Du diese Karte.

Bitte schreibe einen langen Brief. Es küßt Dich Deine treue [illegible]

A postcard from Dora's parents and parents' friends stating that Dora's "papa is home." That meant that his attempt to cross the border into Belgium illegally had failed. (Courtesy Dora Vernon)

Draft of the first page of a letter written, for lack of any other paper, on toilet paper. Dora, age 16, wrote to the Refugee Committee on behalf of her parents still in Austria. As excerpted: "I left my parents in cruel circumstances. The police came to our house when we were not at home. We could not go back to our house or even to our street. My father was sent to the border and has no food or money nor a place to sleep and is close to a horrible death. My dear mother is in Vienna in despair without money or living quarters. I would beg the honorable committee to help them." (Courtesy Dora Vernon)

Ruth and Martin Michaelis before they left Germany. Brother and sister lived through difficult times in an unsuitable foster home. Ruth was severely beaten for bedwetting. They helped each other to survive. (Courtesy Ruth Michaelis)

Twelve-year-old Inga, placed in a very uncongenial home, found consolation in a diary. She still keeps one. (Courtesy Inga Joseph)

Bea, looking very English at Itchen Abbas House with its stables, theater, and gardener's and chauffeur's cottage, where she lived with a kindly colonel and his upper-class family. (Courtesy Bea Green)

Bertha, who in 1989 organized a *Kinder* reunion in England attended by about 1000 *Kinder*, showed equal resourcefulness at seventeen. Knowing that her foster father would not send for her sister in Germany if he knew she had red hair, she lied about Inge's hair color. When Inge arrived, her foster father was furious, but Inge's life was saved. (Courtesy Bertha Leverton)

Gunther and his little foster brother on the farm to which he moved from the Priory. They are still friends. (Courtesy Gunther Abrahamson)

Castle Grwych in North Wales, a home for Ruth and children without foster parents. Without beds, electricity, heat, or proper food, and with little supervision, many children fell seriously ill. (Courtesy Ruth Wesson)

Mr. Guthrie, "the gentle giant," retired shoemaker-poet, in Selkirk, Scotland, in 1990. He fixed the *Kinder*'s shoes for very little money. In spite of his describing himself "a wee bit shy," he gave me a big bear hug upon leaving. (Author's file)

Miss Pringle (seated), former assistant matron at the Priory, welcomed me at her home in Edinburgh with an open fire on a rainy summer day in 1990. She is the contact person for many of the former Priory *Kinder*. (Author's file)

*Part II*

# BEFORE  HITLER

## Chapter 13

# The Nest

The first emotion accompanying escape was one of overpowering relief. The moment the border was crossed, the plane lifted off, the ship set sail for foreign shores, an intense joy washed over the travelers. Suddenly, it was possible to walk along a street, enter a park, or meet another's gaze without having to suspect malicious intent. But there was also trepidation. After all, an uncharted future lay ahead. Nevertheless, a sense of freedom and safety, a feeling by now almost forgotten, far outweighed anxiety. One looked back only to remember and, if possible, to help those who had been left behind. It was as if memories of the recent sad and fearsome events formed such a formidable barrier that reminiscences of happier times could not break through.

But, over time, perspectives changed, and the escapees in this study are now willing to reminisce. Memories of warm and happy childhoods came flooding forth. The overwhelming majority of escapees speak with deep emotions about the close and loving family life of their earlier years. Much of life centered about the family, and the focal point of the family was the children. Families tended to be small. In Austria, for instance, 28 percent of Jewish families had no children and another 28 percent had only one child. Thus, families had relatively few nieces, nephews, and grandchildren. No wonder families valued and coddled youngsters. And those youngsters, now over half a century old, well remember their former privileged state and speak of it with affection: "I[188] had an excellent relationship with my parents. I was the spoiled baby. My parents thought everything my sister and I did was brilliant and talented, and that we were beautiful. We grew up with the idea that we were special."

Adults assumed a highly protective attitude toward children. They considered even youngsters in their teens to be quite naive and, as a result, carefully censored what kind of information should reach their well-guarded ears. Fred[39] describes the atmosphere when he was in his teens: "One must consider that at that time and in our milieu many subjects were not discussed in front of the children: first and foremost, money; certainly sex; anything negative about close members of the family; anything scandalous, as well as acts that would be considered bad manners.

"Good deportment was of utmost importance. I do not believe I ever sat at a dinner table with my parents without constant admonitions: 'You are not holding the fork correctly,' 'Your chair is so far from the table you look as if you are riding towards it,' and a million more. It seemed to us that the grown-ups surely believed that if you put your elbows on the table, you would never amount to anything. The words when out walking still ring in my ears: '*Geh voran and halt dich grad* [Walk ahead of us, and carry yourself with good posture].' In fact, I gauged the extent of my parents' anxieties after the Anschluss by the fact that they had become unaware of my transgressions, such as leaving food on my plate, unthinkable in previous days."

Adults expected children to conform, but in return they made every attempt to spare them anxiety. Gertrude,[176] then in her early teens, recalls: "My childhood in Vienna was happy and more or less uneventful. I grew up spoiled and sheltered from any unpleasant event which my mother thought might upset me." Even in Germany, under the Nazis, parents still managed to shelter their children. Lotti[165] comments: "I do not recall people being arrested during the Hitler years because my parents protected me from any such knowledge."

Protectiveness and pampering did not necessarily suggest a lack of parental strictness. Youngsters were rarely asked to give their opinions or take part in any decision making. Children were expected to be *brave Kinder* (good children). Hilde[162] characterizes herself as having been a typical Austrian child, polite with her parents and always good and obedient. Parents, and fathers in particular, tended to be somewhat authoritarian. Their rule was rarely challenged. Franz[15] describes the atmosphere well: "My family was a close one; my parents had what I still consider an ideal marriage.

They were affectionate to each other and to me, though, of course, the affection my father showed me was that of a European father: formal but nonetheless obvious and reliable." On the whole, the system was clearly two-tiered; parents and children were not on an equal level. Respect for adults was an essential part of education. Children were used to having their activities directed and choices made for them. It was far more usual than it is now to turn to parents for counsel. As a result, children were more in the habit of having faith in their parents. Fred's[39] parents gave him the impression most parents tried to achieve with their children: "To me, my parents were self-assured, competent and gave the appearance that they were able to handle whatever the future would hold in store for the family."

There were, of course, some whose childhoods were not happy, although the number is surprisingly small. Several escapees report that their fathers had left the household, leaving their mothers to make a living as best they could; apparently, single mothers are not a modern invention. One of the abandoned mothers[170] sold clothes from door to door. Another woman[189] received no alimony owing to a strange Austrian law: Divorced soldiers were not obliged to support their families. Thus, his mother, who worked six days a week, had little time for her family. Three escapees recall that their parents were excessively busy with their social life.[111] Yet these complaints are frequently mitigated by memories of the availability of a large extended family. For instance, in one family where relations were "solid but not close," the boy[6] lived near his grandparents, great grandmother, aunts, and cousins. He looked forward to frequent visits and to helping "Opi" and "Omi" in their garden.

In fact, blissful recollections about life with close and distant relatives abound: descriptions of gatherings for Sunday meals and of visits to aunts, cousins, and particularly grandparents, who frequently lived only a few streets away, almost around the corner. Religious families gathered on Shabbat. Ten-year-old Anitta[43] and her family would join her grandparents for dinner. Afterward, settled in his rocking chair with Anitta at his feet, her grandfather would put on his earphones to listen to the radio, philosophize, or tell stories from the Talmud. Grandmother liked to entertain Anitta with singing and funny stories. It was a beautiful world, which suddenly ended on March 11, 1938.

In addition to blood relatives, there were the honorary aunts and uncles. Most accounts of childhood refer to the parents' active social life and wide circle of friends. The children not only played with their school friends but also spent a great deal of time with the children of their parents' friends. Children usually addressed their parents' friends as *Onkel* and *Tante*, and the families shared vacations and outings. These frequent visitors became a strong part of the children's lives, and friendships tended to last for many years. A description from Germany: "We[54] had a large family, my parents had many friends, and I had many school friends as well. We had large family gatherings. Friends of my parents visited, making a fuss over the children and bringing many little presents." From Austria: "We[141] had an active social life with family and friends. I was very much a part of this in typical Central European style. I had a circle of friends and all lived in the same neighborhood and had gone to the same schools since first grade. We are friends to this day, though thousands of miles apart."

One reason for those long-lasting friendships was the structure of the schools. When a youngster entered school, he or she was likely to spend the next four years with the same children. At age ten there was a change of school, and students entered the *Gymnasium*. During those years there were, of course, different teachers for different subjects. But it was the teachers who went from classroom to classroom; the constellation of students within the classroom never changed. Thus, young people remained together for eight of their most formative years; friendships solidified and frequently lasted a lifetime. Standards in school were authoritarian and rigid. Children who attended *Gymnasium* were held to uniformly high standards, with no allowances for individuality. When students failed to fulfill expectations, teachers regarded their failures as purposeful and deserving of scolding. It was not that children were actually punished in some cruel way; it was the admonition that they dreaded, and it whipped them into line. Nevertheless, for most youngsters the exalted position of teachers was simply taken for granted, and the cohesiveness among schoolmates was a strong compensatory factor.

The feeling of being sheltered and cared about came, in no small measure, from the household help, particularly the ever-present *Kinderfräulein*. The *Kinderfräulein* was the German version of the English nanny. But while the latter has a reputation for formality and rigidly good manners, the *Kinderfräulein* was usually a fairly young girl, frequently from the countryside, who joined the family when the children were very small and remained for years and years. Usually, her good humor, warmth, and informality provided a sanctuary for the child from the more formal atmosphere and emphasis on good manners insisted on by parents. Children were surrounded by adults almost continually. It was unthinkable for a child to play in the streets. Outdoor play, accompanied by mothers or, more frequently, by the *Kinderfräulein*, took place either in private gardens or in parks. The adults sat on green wrought iron chairs, for which one paid by the hour, which were placed beside carefully manicured lawns, glorious flower beds, trickling fountains, and statues commemorating kings, queens, generals, and composers. On Sundays children usually accompanied their parents rather than visit each other. Children frequently were well into their teens before they pursued activities independently of adults.

It comes as no surprise that in many accounts of the Hitler period the loyalty of household employees figures prominently. Their kindness stands out in a period that was mostly bereft of humanity. Escapees write about the maids and cooks who so faithfully served them over the years and about the mothering received from their *Kinderfräulein* and the many years spent together. "Our[139] *Kinderfräulein* came to our house when I was three weeks old and stayed until we left. She tried to follow us later. She was a faithful woman who, in Vienna, had really been my mother. I still write to her." Escapees remember the practical help they received: "A young woman, who cleaned my[14] brothers' apartment once a week, was there when the Gestapo came. She immediately phoned and warned us not to go back to the apartment and then in small bundles brought out our personal belongings." Religious convictions made many reject Nazism. "Our[73] maid had become a part of the family. She was a devout Catholic and shared our unhappiness." Some devoted servants—one hesitates to call them servants—rose to extraordinary heights: "Our[42] household help was wonderful. While my colleagues at the university did not know us after the Anschluss, our cook took a heroic stand. She was honored by the Yad Vashem as a 'Righteous Gentile.'" An intense bond of affection sometimes tied employer to employee: One correspondent[22] recalls that her aunt's maid remained as a companion to her employer. When the aunt was deported at the age of 81, the companion committed suicide.

I myself have the fondest memories of our *Kinderfräulein*, Hella. She joined our household before I was even born. The cook, Mitzi, came shortly thereafter. I spent as many hours in the kitchen as I did in the living quarters with my parents. Hella and Mitzi doted on me. If my parents were dissatisfied with my behavior, Hella and Mitzi always sided with me, hiding misdemeanors from my parents and buying me whatever little treats my parents forbade. Among these were delicious rolls piled high with Hungarian salami. My roly-poly shape demonstrated that I really did not need them. It was not only the extra treat that gave me pleasure but also the knowledge that I was surrounded by so much love. This spoiling did me no harm. I knew quite clearly that this relaxation of the rules was only transient and that in the long run my behavior had to be modeled according to my parents' standards.

I lost contact with Hella during the war. On my first return to Vienna I was more than eager to find her again. She had no telephone. To search for her and to be sure to find her in, I went to her prewar address rather late at night. But would she remember me? It had been almost twenty years since our last contact. With some trepidation I rang the bell. After a pause a voice asked in German: "Who is there?" How was I to answer this question? I was no longer the same person. I had forgotten most of my German. Even my name was different: *Dorli* had become *Dorit*. The door opened cautiously. Recognition was immediate on both sides. There were hugs and there were kisses and there were tears. I looked around the apartment where Hella lived with her family. The walls of the room were covered with pictures of my mother, father, sister, and me. For twenty years there had been no contact, and still the walls were covered with photographs of us! Hella spoke of my mother as if she were present: "Mama says. . . ." Alas, my mother had been dead many a year, but for Hella she was alive. After that meeting we wrote and kept in touch. Not long ago I received a letter. "I am 81 years old," it read. "If it were not for Hitler, I would still be with you." I hurried back to Vienna to see her again and learned that she was in the hospital. When I entered the sickroom, she stretched out her arms toward me and exclaimed, "*Aber du bist doch mein Kind* [But you are still my child]!"

Of course, not all domestic help was able to withstand temptation. The same writer[14] who tells about his brother's dedicated housekeeper adds: "A maid who had been with my paralyzed uncle and his wife for many years took all their jewelry and silver. When my aunt tried to stop her, she pushed her to the floor and, cursing the Jews, left." And my family and I lived in fear of Mitzi, who had turned into an ardent Nazi.

On the whole, the escapees reminisce lovingly about parents, grandparents, aunts, uncles, cousins, and the *Tanten* and *Onkeln* of an honorary nature, as well as schoolmates, *Kinderfräulein*s, and cooks. Yes, many of the escapees had been enveloped by love. The nest had been amply feathered, and its warmth would not be wasted. During the years to come Maritza[75] frequently remembered how her mother had taken her out to interesting places, had pampered her, and had rarely been angry, even when Maritza tried to swing from the belt of her mother's coat. She also remembers her grandmother's extreme devotion. Those memories nourished Maritza in later years when she was deprived of loving care. Her mother's great strength of character and indulgent love stood Maritza in very good stead when she was alone and forlorn. The feeling of having once been loved "by all and sundry" carried many—old and young alike—through the years.

## Chapter 14

# A Certain Style

They had a certain lifestyle. It was one that many in middle Europe, Jewish or non-Jewish, adopted at that time. Most of the escapees in this study knew and felt that they were Jewish, but, on the whole, their mode of living tended to be worldly and secular. A minority were orthodox in their outlook. How do the escapees characterize the years before the great debacle? How do they think and feel about that period of their lives?

The recollections are surprising in their unanimous enthusiasm and glowing descriptions of the past: "Life was lovely and blissful";[140] "I am grateful for my Austrian cultural background";[172] "When I came to England, I thought I had been cast out of Paradise!"[158]

Are such exclamations mere hyperbole? A yearning for lost youth? A looking back with rose-colored glasses? One might suppose so, but careful study of the descriptions seems to indicate otherwise. The escapees do not speak in vague generalities but detail their recollections. Moreover, there is a consistency from person to person. The same elements that made for happy memories recur from report to report.

As already indicated, social life in Germany and Austria was active and a large circle of friends was common. Vienna, in particular, provided endless opportunities for socializing. It was easy to meet friends in cafés, which proliferated throughout the city. Cafés were ideal for whiling away time. They were usually high ceilinged, with large windows, and the customer would seat himself at one of the small marble-topped tables. The habitué would rarely look out at the busy streets, lined with baroque buildings; there was too much activity within the café. Newspapers, backed by wooden frames, hung from the wall. The waiter's duty was to know which newspaper was customarily desired by his "regular," and he would long ago have committed to memory which of the innumerable coffees would be desired by that customer and whether it was to be with *Schlag* (whipped cream). After selecting from one of many luscious-looking cakes, one could sit without great expense for hours with a cup of coffee or two, reading, watching people, or meeting friends. Cafés specialized in attracting people of various philosophies or professions. Or one could form one's own group, as Norbert[14] did: "Many of the cafés in the center of Vienna were meeting places for groups of all shades of the literary and political spectrum. I was too young to belong to such a crowd, but a few of my medical colleagues and I formed our own group, to which we added a few outsiders."

One must not forget the *Konditoreien* (pastry shops). Glass cases exhibited a profusion of cakes, which testified to the baker's limitless imagination. The waitress, in a black uniform, a crisp white apron, and a starched white headband, would place the selected item and the accompanying cup of coffee or hot chocolate on a plate of fine china of attractive design. The customer would never be addressed merely as "you"; instead, one would hear "Would the honored lady care for another portion of the *Sacher Torte*?" or "Would the gentleman wish more whipped cream?" As one respondent[172] points out: "The café played an extremely important role in our lives. It was sinful, fattening, but oh, so good."

While there were many excellent restaurants, one could also frequent a *Gasthaus* (modest and folksy restaurant). They were available on almost every corner (and even on mountaintops) and served excellent but unsophisticated food at moderate prices. The famous *Heurigen*—establishments that served the new wine, accompanied by sentimental Viennese music—were not as popular with the Jewish population. On the whole, those places were looked upon with a certain sophisticated sneer.[172] A great deal of entertaining was done at home. Apartments were spacious, and even households of moderate means were likely to employ domestic help. And no wonder. First there was a breakfast of coffee and delicious rolls with jam. Then this small meal was followed by a midmorning snack consisting of a succulent sandwich of cold cuts between thick slices of dark bread. Lunch was no small matter, what with cream soup and a rich meat course, which on Sundays tended to be fried chicken or wienerschnitzel; the meal usually ended with a rich dessert. Still, no one was expected to go without eating until the evening meal. Before the day ended with a light supper, there was afternoon coffee with freshly baked cake. No wonder a Viennese cookbook included a special chapter of instruction to the *Hausfrau* of the small bourgeois household who had to manage with just one servant.

Household help made entertaining at home easy. The hostess set an elegant table with a white, hand-embroidered tablecloth and fine china. Generally, the children were not included on these occasions. At best, they were allowed to put on their party frocks or their blue knee pants, appear (frequently accompanied by their *Kinderfräulein*), make a curtsy or a bow to each guest, and leave. (Curtsying became such second nature to me that if while running at full speed I happened to pass an adult, I was able to curtsy without missing a step, a feat I can still perform today.) While the children made the rounds, the guests, frequently honorary *Tanten* and *Onkeln*, would wax rhapsodic about the charms and brilliance of each child. In my childish innocence I thought they really meant every word of it. After cheeks had been kissed, the children made their good-byes and went into the kitchen to eat leftovers and listen to the help discuss the generosity of each guest's tip. It was usual for guests to tip domestic help—and rightly so, with all the extra work parties required.

An important aspect of life was enjoying the outdoors, not surprising with the picture-postcard beauty of Austria and parts of Germany. Hiking in the mountains—amid meadows bounteous with wild flowers, vineyards, and lakes—exerted its magical charm on even the most sedentary person and was accessible to rich and poor alike. There were well-kept paths for the beginner and trails for the hardiest souls. At the end of each trail, no matter how long or short, a little hut with outdoor tables welcomed the wanderer with hearty, delicious food. Remarks Annie,[172] who had to wait many years before she could hike again in California: "The influence of nature's beauty on our lives cannot be overestimated. It is still important to me." It was easy to spend a day surrounded by trees and flowers. Within Vienna there were innumerable lovely parks, some even providing music on Sunday afternoons. There was also the Prater, with its alleys of stately chestnut trees bursting with candlelike blossoms in spring and, to the joy of the children, dropping large chestnuts from their branches in the fall. Part amusement park, part nature sanctuary, where aristocrats once drove up and down in their horse-drawn carriages to see and be seen, it was still a place of delight. The giant Ferris wheel of the Prater and St. Stephen's Cathedral in the middle of the city are, to this day, Viennese landmarks. And since a ring of mountains, topped by the Vienna Woods, was within streetcar distance, families poured out of their houses every Sunday to make their way to the mountains. Norbert recalls: "We solved the problems of the world while walking through the silent forest or having lunch on a flower-studded meadow."

Even families of moderate means managed to afford vacations that had charm and style. One did not have to be rich to hike or even to be part of the summer exodus to the country. Bringing their pots and pans and other household goods along, families rented rooms in farmhouses for very little money. Meir[134] recalls renting rooms in an inexpensive farmhouse at the foot of high, snow-covered mountains. The children roamed freely amidst orchards of cherry, pear, apple, and plum trees. A mountain river filled with trout rushed passed the house. At times the family would stroll into Reichenau, an elegant watering place. The entire family would sit on chairs placed on well-kept lawns near the pavilion to listen to a thirty-man orchestra. (I would bet there was a *Konditorei* not far away.) Some days the family would board the rickety little wagons of the cable car, which passed over trees and snow on its way to the top of the mountain, to wander to look for edelweiss. While varied and even glamorous, such holidays were not expensive.

On the whole, German escapees write less expansively about their vacations. The reason is self-evident: They did not know where Jews were welcome. They were more hampered in their movements, and as a result their reminiscences tend to center about activities at home or at the homes of friends.

Closely tied to the love of nature and ingrained in the children at an early age was the pursuit of sports. Swimming, skating, and skiing were considered almost as basic a part of education as French and music. In fact, a majority of schools include a week of skiing in some mountainous area of Austria as part of the curriculum. Of course, there were no ski lifts in those days, and skiers had to trudge up the long track to the top of the trail, carrying their skis, only to zoom down again in minutes. With the sun on one's face, with Alpine peaks all around, every moment was bliss. Children took skating lessons too. Sunday morning on the large open-air skating rink, with background music playing, was rendezvous time for romantic adolescents. Many of the young people[39] pursued their activities with youth groups, which in an age of chaperons afforded the opportunity to travel without parents to international jamborees. Such groups provided an inexpensive way, for those from disadvantaged homes, to take part in activities otherwise not affordable.[134]

Barred from activities taken over by the Hitler Youth, the Jewish youth groups were particularly important for German Jewish youngsters,[147] who remember the weekly meetings as a forum for exchanging ideas during discussions of books and politics, as a time of singing and playing the guitar, and as an opportunity for taking day trips on Sundays. Some of the Zionist youth groups combined fun with a more serious goal: They encouraged their now-isolated members to emigrate to Israel. An Austrian, Meir[134] had already joined an activist Zionist Youth Group by 1933. Their summer camps were primitive but fun. Youngsters slept in wooden huts with straw-covered plank beds in wooded hills. During the morning parade the Zionist flag was hoisted, after which the youngsters engaged in sports and studied theories of Zionism, socialism, and Jewish history. At night they danced the hora around romantic campfires.

The escapees extol nature activities and sports, but even more striking is the passion with which they speak of their former cultural life. They reminisce about the excitement of the literary and musical opportunities that had been available to them. Over and over they mention the concerts they attended[28] and recall the theater, with its emphasis on the classics.[180] And with a particular glow, they reminisce about the opera. Children were allowed to accompany their parents to the theater and opera at a very early age. Memories of those evenings are still counted among their most precious ones. Vera[158] was only nine when she was allowed to accompany her parents to a performance of Smetana's *The Bartered Bride*. Ralph's[5] memory reaches back even further. He was only five or six years old when he was permitted to stay up so that he could hear a broadcast of *The Magic Flute*. No TV. Just radio.

Opera in Austria was associated with family occasions, glamor, and intellectual striving. In my own case, my mother played the arias for us on the piano before we attended a particular performance. I was delighted if I could recognize these during the actual performance (a phenomenon that happened only occasionally or at my mother's whispered prompting). Sometimes my incentive for attentiveness was made tangible: My father promised me five Schillings if I could decipher and remember the plot of Verdi's *Il Trovatore*. I did so at the time, but since no one has matched this offer in recent years, I am less motivated to follow the plot on videocassettes. At the opera we mounted a grand staircase to reach the boxes. On one singularly festive and glamorous occasion I was dressed in what I still remember was a light blue, hand-embroidered silk dress, with white socks and patent leather shoes; my sister and mother and I sat together on golden chairs. My father stood behind us, since there was not sufficient space for four people in the front row of an opera box. It seemed to me then that he was guarding the family—a task he never failed to perform in later and more difficult years. When I stepped out on the balcony during intermission, and saw Vienna bathed in lights, I felt like Cyrano de Bergerac looking at Paris in the moonlight.

Some of the youngsters' enthusiasm for opera tended to be greater than their financial resources, and so they attended the opera with tickets for standing room only. This was quite a usual custom among young people.[39] Recounts Norbert:[14] "At my first visit to the State Opera as a teenager, high up near the roof in the standing room section, I fainted while listening to *Tosca*, but after a couple of minutes I again gave my undivided attention to the glorious music." (He does not explain whether it was the noble sentiments in response to the music or the hot air rising to his perch that caused the lapse of consciousness.)

A cultural background was consistently emphasized by parents. Franz[15] was given a prose translation of Homer's *Iliad* and *Odyssey*, which he devoured not once but repeatedly. (My father read these works to my sister and me in nightly installments.) Franz also knew large chunks of the libretto of Rossini's *Barber of Seville* practically by heart, as well as bits of plays by Austrian playwrights. I myself liked school but sometimes felt the urge to miss a day. I played hooky while still in elementary school. Unbeknownst to me, during one of those forays I was recognized at the Viennese National Art Museum by my mother's friend. Years later she told me that she knew that I should have been in school but did not report me to my parents since she considered that I was using my time well. The classics played such an important part in the lives of young people that they came together on their own for study and discussion. At the suggestion of one of his friends, eighteen-year-old Frank[137] formed a study group called "Evening for Literature," in which the members went beyond what was taught in class. For instance, they chose Goethe's *Faust: Part II* since they had only covered *Part I* in school.

This cultural life was by no means restricted to the wealthy. The insistence on raising money for cultural pursuits in even the most marginal households is impressive. One man[28] relates that although his parents were too poor for him to continue his studies in chemistry, he was able to hike in the Alps and attend the opera and concerts with enthusiasm. Alan[141] was living in a working-class apartment without toilet or running water and went to public baths once a week. His parents never took a vacation. Yet he was encouraged to read a great deal, mostly the classics, and to attend the theater and opera.

In contrast, very few German escapees speak of the theater and the opera. After Hitler's rise to power, attendance by Jews was proscribed and public places were to be avoided. Different cities in Germany produced different degrees of anti-Semitism, and the amount of freedom Jews had to come and go varied. Ruth[70] moved from Nuremberg to Berlin and found the "big city" exciting. Berlin, as a capital with many international visitors and foreign embassies, was far less repressive than her hometown had been. Jews moved about more freely, and Ruth was able to experience a kind of freedom she had not known before. But even when the Jews were unable to attend public performances, they still managed to have satisfactory intellectual lives. Lore,[139] who left Germany at thirteen in 1939, recalls that her parents hosted musicales in their home.

When Austrian escapees who at the time of escape were in their teens or older summarize favorite periods in their lives, the word *Fasching* comes up again and again.[172] That was a fun time. A month before Lent the season of balls would commence. Because being a graceful dancer was considered important, young people attended dancing school. White gloves even for the young men were de rigueur, as it would have been indelicate to touch a young lady with bare hands—at least in public. The young people learned all the correct dance steps, how to waltz to the right and to the left; they learned etiquette; and they flirted, which they did not have to learn. On Saturday nights balls were held for young people. In this baroque city of Vienna it was easy to find many beautiful ballrooms. During the carnival season almost every trade and profession had its own masked ball. The city lived up to the reputation given it by Metternich at the Congress of Vienna in 1815, when foreign dignitaries were meeting to redraw the map of Europe after Napoleon's defeat. The various officials danced all night and slept all day. Remarked Metternich of the slow progress: "The Congress dances, but it does not move."

From 1933 to 1938 the lives of many German Jews had become increasingly difficult. But, astonishingly, many were still able to manage their lives with moderate comfort within a restricted circle. Paul[91] acknowledges that his diary, written in 1938, discloses a not unpleasant life in Wiesbaden while the family was waiting for its U.S. visa: "My calendar for 1938 reflects normal activities, such as acquisition of roller skates in late spring, receiving Uncle Josef's bike in May, a full schedule of violin lessons, sport activities, religious school, private English lessons, helping out at the store, attending services on Friday nights, spending Saturday afternoon with Lothar and excursions on Sundays. Summer vacation starts with a glorious stay in Westfalen. Back home, preparations begin for my Bar Mitzvah scheduled in December. In September there is much excitement about Sudetenland and talk of war. In October peace in our time has been secured by the British and French, and Hitler has prevailed. Late October we enjoy the annual festival day. . . . Early November continues normal. . . . We know of course what happened in November: Kristallnacht."

In Austria life continued in its usual course right up to the abyss. Let us choose two reports. One from a wealthy young man:[180] "We had many acquaintances. We were enmeshed socially in a large group of assimilated upper-bourgoisie Jewish friends. I was especially involved with a clique that was sportively inclined: skiing, swimming, mountain climbing, etc., together with ball playing and social dancing. The happiest years of my life were my years at the University of Vienna. I absorbed a great many ideas in jurisprudence (Hans Kelsen and his school), economics (Ludwig Mises and his school), and Freud. Many of Freud's disciples were my friends and acquaintances, and we spent much time in intellectual discussions with prominent intellectuals and professors at the university before the Nazis came in the middle thirties. I read the German classics (Schiller, Goethe, Lessing, etc.) but also much philosophy, history, sociology, jurisprudence, and economics. And a good deal, if not all, of Freud. Thomas Mann was and is my ideal writer."

The following report comes from Annie,[172] whose family was of moderate means: "My family and our friends were all part of the incredibly rich intellectual life of pre-Nazi Vienna. Much has been written about it, but we took it for granted. Dance school, opera, theater, museums, of course. (I remember the first Van Gogh exhibit in Vienna. It blew us away.) *Fasching* was great, especially the masked balls. My husband was a member of the Schönberg and the Schlick circles, where he met and admired Wittgenstein. At all our social occasions and even at dinner there were discussions, lively, full of humor and wit. My parents were not typical of the older generation. But most Viennese, at least all I knew, were atypical. We were not rich. Few people owned cars. We did not, but public transportation was very good. We did have a maid, which gave us the time to be cultured. We took that for granted. We had ski courses in school, skated, hiked, swam, and climbed mountains in the Alps."

In Vienna I had an "honorary" aunt who had been a music teacher of very moderate means. But she always attended the opera and concerts and, of course, participated, as did everyone else, in mountain hiking. In New York she again lived a modest life. In my whole life I had never heard her complain; she always saw the best in everything. I enjoyed visiting her. Long after my parents were dead, visiting her was somewhat like revisiting my youth. We would sit down at a table loaded with home-baked Viennese cakes. They were, of course, placed on a white embroidered tablecloth that was covered with china and silver. Though the china was not as delicate as the Rosenthal china she had had in Vienna, it nevertheless reminded me of old times. We always talked of music, books, and politics. She seemed totally content. One day I said to her, "Aunt Gusti, do you ever miss living in Vienna?" I was certain she was going to emphasize, as was her wont, all the positive aspects of her present life. She paused for a minute. Then she said, "You know, of course, that I could never live in Vienna. But, you know, the only place I could ever live is Vienna—if I could only live there."

Eric,[35] who found no way of leaving Germany until 1939, looks back at his youth: "Yet, despite all these drawbacks and difficulties, I think back with affection to these far-off days of the 1930s when the clan was still complete and I was daily among my dear friends. Everything from those half-forgotten days seems invested with a cloak of magic, and the old figures rise up before me and I seem to see their faces quite clearly."

## Chapter 15

# Reality or Illusion?

How is it possible to combine the two images, of life before Hitler, which for many offered cultural opportunity and economic comfort, and life after Hitler, with its bestial and annihilating force? How could such a transformation occur in the briefest of time? Surely anti-Semitism so ferocious must have arisen from well-prepared, fertile soil. Surely such vicious hatred must have been there all the time without the Jewish population facing it. Were the Jews unaware of the hatred, the anti-Semitism, surrounding them? In order to make themselves feel secure, had they led a life of illusion?

It seems best to answer this question through the eyes of escapees from Austria rather than Germany. The majority of the German respondents spent the better part of their youth under Hitler and have little recollection of the pre-Hitler years. But was there anti-Semitism in Austria before Hitler? Yes, indeed there was. Most Jews were quite aware that strong anti-Semitism existed, particularly in the countryside. Yet it is striking that few escapees wrote that their lives in pre-Hitler days were seriously marred by anti-Semitism. Only a handful say they were strongly affected by it. Those youngsters living in non-Jewish areas met with anti-Semitism in the schools. The strongest experience of anti-Semitism was described by Otto,[42] a medical student in Vienna: "There was sniggering by my schoolmates in primary school whenever the word *Jew* was mentioned, particularly around Easter, when we were accused of having murdered Jesus. Strangely, while attending *Gymnasium* I did not experience any anti-Semitism. There were some Nazis in my class, but we had no trouble. One took anti-Semitism at the University of Vienna for granted." Yet it is noteworthy that those escapees who had attended the university describe their lives there as highly stimulating, both socially and intellectually, and do not regard their lives as having been particularly hampered by anti-Semitism. Otto continues: "Remarks were occasionally made in inns or drinking places. It would happen that someone would start talking about 'the stinking Jews,' ostensibly to his friends, but raising his voice sufficiently to make sure of being overheard." Another man[155] remembers spending a seemingly happy week's vacation arranged by his school only to have it end in a crudely worded diatribe against Jews by fellow students. Yet, on the whole, the escapees do not describe being disturbed to any major degree by pre-Hitler anti-Semitism. Interestingly, Berghan (1984, p. 62) reports similar results in her study of German refugees in England: of seventy-four escapees who had clear memories of their pre-Hitler years, only sixteen reported having encountered anti-Semitism.

Professionally, Jews were still restricted from entering any number of areas. Over the years they had not been permitted into the civil service, and judgeships were closed to them. They were underrepresented as professors at universities and as teachers at *Gymnasium*s. But they were able to practice independent professions, such as law and medicine; establish businesses; and work as artisans, such as goldsmiths and tailors (Pauley, 1990). The pre-Hitler professional restrictions encountered by Austrian and German Jews were not much different from those encountered by Jews in other countries. Therefore, they were accepted as a fact of life.

On the whole, there was little premonition that anti-Semitism would pose a major danger. Comments one respondent:[7] "We considered the *Illegalen* a nuisance but thought that the Austrian police were in control. This was more or less correct until March 1938." A man[39] writes: "We were aware of the '*Illegalen*.' They seemed like hoodlums—nasty, violence-prone, but nothing the authorities could not deal with." About his life in Vienna, Stefan Zweig (1964) wrote, "I must confess that neither in school nor at the University nor in the world of literature have I ever experienced the slightest suppression or indignity as a Jew" (p. 25). And Freud wrote, "The feeling of triumph on being liberated is too strongly mixed with sorrow, for in spite of everything, I still greatly loved the prison from which I have been released."

There was, to be sure, knowledge that the *Illegalen* were capable of violence, but it did not impinge on one's everyday life anymore than today's terrorists or skinheads do. Austria was full of political tensions, and not just tension due to the Nazis. After all, the workers had not forgotten that the Christian Socialist government had fired into their homes in 1934. While there were incidents of sabotage, they were experienced as directed against the government, rather than against the Jews, and it was assumed the authorities would handle such occurrences.

It should be noted that the extent of anti-Semitism prevalent which was almost taken for granted and openly displayed, was endemic not only in Austria and Germany but in democratic countries as well. For example, quotas for Jews in schools, colleges, and corporations existed all over Europe and in the United States as well. In England in pre-World War II days many of the upper classes, such as the Cliveden set, who were influential in the appeasement of Hitler, were anti-Semitic. Most English social clubs were out of bounds for Jews. Polls taken in the United States between 1938 and 1945 revealed that about 35 to 40 percent of the American population surveyed were prepared to approve of an anti-Jewish campaign while another 30 percent were indifferent to such a plan; only 30 percent were opposed to it (Wyman, 1984, p. 15). I recall my parents responding to a *New York Times* advertisement around 1945, inviting readers to join a summer country club. When my parents and I went to apply in person, the man in charge informed us in a friendly manner, without any hesitation or embarrassment, that since we were Jewish we should seek membership elsewhere.

Besides day-to-day factors, the German and Austrian Jews' sense of security was strengthened by historical factors. The Jews had lived in Germany for 1,500 years and, unlike the case in other countries, had never been expelled. Karl[69] quotes from his father's autobiography: "The Heiman family tree dates back to the early 1700s. Our ancestors migrated from Blenheim to Essingen and eventually settled in Oberdorf, a village about sixty miles southeast of Stuttgart. Our original ancestors most likely arrived with the Romans in Central Europe, who settled along the Rhine in such cities as Cologne and Mainz." The Heiman family knew that anti-Semitism existed in Germany, but since their family tree reached back over two hundred years, there was no reason for them to suspect the grotesque direction German politics would take. Germany extended equal rights to Jews around 1848. In Austria there still remained some obstacles for Jews living outside of Vienna, although they had obtained total equality before the law in 1868. The desirability of living in Austria can be measured by the fact that Jewish immigrants poured in from Hungary and Moravia. Those who could not emigrate sent their children to German-speaking schools in their own countries. In 1849 there were only 40,000 Jews in Vienna; by 1890 there were 100,000 (Bankier, 1990, p. 42). Jewish refugees from Poland, escaping pogroms, made Jews living in Germany and Austria breathe sighs of relief.

German and Austrian Jews regarded themselves as citizens, no less so than English or American Jews who identify with their country of birth. They accepted their civic duties with a sense of patriotism. They looked back with pride on the valor they had displayed during World War I. The losses experienced by the Jewish population during World War I were thought to have strengthened the bond between the Jews and their fellow citizens. A son[64] explains why his father labored under a false sense of security. "My father during World War I was decorated for bravery. This is important in order to understand why so many decent, intelligent Jews did not heed early warnings to leave Germany." I myself witnessed the waste of this sacrifice when I recently visited a small village, my father's birthplace, now in Czechoslovakia but formerly part of Austria. The gravestones in the Jewish cemetery had been vandalized or overturned. There was one tall monument still standing. It was engraved with a long list, astonishingly long for such a small village, of Jewish men who had fallen during World War I. When the memorial was erected, surely the Jews felt they had a right to assume that their relationship with the rest of the citizenry had been cemented by the common blood shed.

Besides the historical tie, there was a strong cultural tie between Jews and their fellow citizens. Berghan (1984) writes: "Enlightenment, humanism and later the stir of liberalism had created a spiritual and intellectual climate with which Jews could easily identify. As never before, Jewry found that the ideas governing society in general were related to its own creed. . . . Thus a spiritual environment was created which seemed to them hospitable and sympathetic" (p. 39).

It must be remembered that while terms such as *militarism, dictatorship,* and *fascism* come to mind when speaking of German culture, in pre-Nazi days one thought of *Dichter und Denker* (poets and philosophers). The Jewish population was attracted to the humanism of Goethe, the spirit of liberty as proclaimed by Schiller, and the principles of religious liberty as portrayed by Lessing, as well as to the works of many others who contributed in an extraordinary profusion to German culture. Indeed, it was a formidable combination of cultures with the Jews contributing playwrights, musicians, conductors, writers, and artists. In fact, the Jewish contribution to the high level of culture in Vienna was well acknowledged. Berkley (1988) points out that in cultural Vienna, Jews had become the foremost patrons of the arts. "It was primarily they who showed up in such large numbers at concerts and plays, bought intellectual journals and books, and stalked the art galleries" (p. 39). Quoting Stadler, a gentile historian, Berkley adds: "The history of Austrian Jewry in the modern age is the history of Austrian scholarship and culture, and of the country's economic and social progress" (p. 40). It would have been impossible to predict that with two cultures in such harmony one could suddenly attack the other in bestial ways never before encountered.

Critics connect the assimilation of the German and Austrian Jews into their local cultures with a rejection of their own Jewish identity, the repudiation being based on self-hatred. These critics say the Jews perceived themselves as so Germanic that they overlooked early warning signs. Had the Jews but looked and listened, they say, instead of being desirous to assimilate, they would have known that the culture they valued would betray them. And by not listening and not looking, they betrayed themselves. Thus, they lived in a fool's paradise and on illusions. Hannah Arendt (quoted in Berghan, 1984, p. 24) exemplifies these critics: "One cannot choose what one wishes oneself to assimilate to, whether one likes it or not; one cannot leave out Christianity, just as little as the contemporary hatred of Jews. . . . Assimilation is only possible, if one assimilates oneself to anti-Semitism." The astonishing implication is that incorporation of aspects of the culture one lives in must lead to becoming anti-

Semitic. Berkley (1988) also equates assimilation with self-hatred. "Finally there is the subtle question regarding . . . the nature of assimilation. In the rush to become integrated members of their societies, many Jews tried to discard everything, or nearly everything, that had made them Jews. Jews who were trying to cast aside their Jewish identity as if it were a badge of shame were only encouraging others to treat them as if they were indeed shameful" (p. 66).

It may be wise to inquire whether assimilation really led to political blindness. To do so, we must first ask: Did German Jewry assimilate to their native cultures to any large extent? The answer is that unless they held orthodox religious beliefs, they usually did. It stands to reason that those who do not live strictly by religious standards (in Austria about 90 percent of the Jews were non-orthodox) and who live in a culture other than their own will assume some local mores. Thus, Jews living in different regions assimilate in different ways. The style of living of Middle Eastern Jews is closer to that of the Arabs than to Jews living in California. Berghan (1984) rightfully notes that Judaism has undergone changes from region to region and asks rhetorically which of its forms should be considered the "genuine" one. She notes: "The traditional culture of an ethnic group will develop into something new which is shaped by both original culture and that of the larger society, but it is not identical with either" (p. 15).

The second question—whether assimilation leads to self-rejection—then arises. The Austrian historian Gerhard Botz (1990), while finding the majority of Austrian Jews assimilated, found no evidence that the Jews dropped their identification with Judaism: "Most assimilated Jews did not take the step of officially leaving their religious affiliation. In spite of not keeping the Sabbath and the ritual food preparation, they would still marry in the temple, have their sons circumcised and bar mitzva'd, have weddings and funerals attended by a rabbi, the Jewish New Year was celebrated, and instead of Christmas there was Chanukah" (p. 272).

There is also no sign that, on the whole, German Jewry exhibited signs of self-hatred. They had the choice before Hitler to be baptized or declare themselves *Konfessionslos* (without religion). Very few chose to do so. German Jews did not disassociate themselves from their culture. They created the Jewish Community Council, which was authorized to handle Jewish affairs. Its mandate, among other functions, was to establish and maintain synagogues, hospitals, and homes for the aged; keep records on births and deaths; and help "the poor suffering Jews of Galicia." A rabbinical seminary was established, and in 1893 the B'nai B'rith lodge, of which Sigmund Freud was one of the charter members, was founded (Berkley, 1988, p. 43).

There is no evidence that the escapees in my study, in spite of their identification with the culture they lived in, rejected their own. A majority characterize themselves as having been assimilated. Yet, typically, they also speak of having kept the high holidays, being bar mitzva'd, and having had full consciousness of being Jewish. Many of them rank spending Friday evening with grandparents and Passover celebrations among their favorite memories. A fairly typical response: "We[42] were fairly assimilated. But we felt strongly Jewish." Lamberti (quoted in Berghan, 1984, p. 39) comments: "I do not find it necessary to segregate myself from the society around me in order to continue functioning as a Jew and I do not have to argue myself out of my Jewishness in order to continue living as a man among other men."

The strength of the Jewish identification can be discerned by the reaction of the German escapees to the question: "Did you ever feel inferior to your non-Jewish classmates or ever desire to take part in Nazi parades or Hitler Youth activities?" The answer is a horrified "no." In fact, some considered the question a little crazy. One writes:[103] "I find this question odd. I always put up a defense towards people who wish me harm." Another astonished man[130] comments: "Joining these people never even occurred to me." But, in fact, such a question is not as peculiar as it may appear. It is not at all unusual for people, children in particular, to be impressed by a dominant group, particularly if its power is enshrined with much pomp and glory. The Jewish children were subjected by every possible means—that is, by communications, rallies, radio, newspapers displayed on street corners—to assaults about the inferiority of their race and their blood taint. They were besieged and bombarded by comparisons with vermin, misers, conspirators, biological inferiors, and worse and yet emerged from this onslaught with their identity intact. Had not their parents had a strong Jewish identification, they could not have done so.

Berghan (1984) points out that some authors "condemn the tendency of German Jews to identify with liberal, enlightened and humanistic representatives of Germany . . . maintaining that this was not the 'real' Germany, but an idealized one. The 'real' Germany, one reads, was that of the reactionaries, of the anti-Semites; in other words, many historians share the view that German history . . . has tended inevitably and with some kind of inner purpose towards National Socialism. But one may ask, does not every society contain diverse potentialities; is it really justified to maintain that the winning party in the struggle for power is typical of the whole? To say that the Third Reich was founded in the German past is true enough; to say that it was the inescapable result of the past, the only fruit that the German tree would grow, is false" (pp. 26–27). German culture had positive as well as negative aspects. It was impossible to envision that the latter would triumph. Stephan Zweig (1964, p. 364) comments that it seemed inconceivable that in Germany liberty and rights, which every citizen believed were anchored by law and secured by a solemnly affirmed constitution, could be lost.

Excessive identification with Germany was not blinding German and Austrian Jewry. It was simply a fact that the Jews could not foretell the future. This was true for the orthodox as well as the assimilated Jews. Certainly, the mostly orthodox Jews of Poland, whose destruction took place on an even larger scale than that of the middle-European Jews, had no clearer vision of what was to come. An escapee[175] who arrived in Holland just before the outbreak of war makes just such a point. He was welcomed with great hospitality by Jewish families. But his warning to them went unheeded: "Often I tried to persuade the mostly orthodox Jews in town to emigrate or at least send their children to safety overseas. There were no survivors."

No one could foretell that these Nazi brutalities could occur in the twentieth century. Not France, not Belgium, not Holland, not England, no ordinary citizen, no prime minister—no one. The Jews knew no more than anyone else. Assimilation had nothing to do with lack of foresight. Jewish life had always involved a certain amount of threat but not more so in Germany and Austria before Hitler than in other countries with their pogroms. Berghan (1984) states it well: "Those who are critical and say the German Jews should have known operate both with the benefit and the arrogance of hindsight, which has been referred to as the 'enormous condescension of posterity' " (p. 26). Hilberg, in his 1961 book on the Holocaust, speaks with equal emphasis: "Only a generation ago, the incidents described in this book would have been considered improbable, infeasible, or even inconceivable" (p. v). One might add that what cannot be conceived cannot be predicted.

*Part III*

# THE YEARS
# OF RESETTLEMENT

*Chapter 16*

# A Placement, Not a Home

There had been a certain uniformity in the *Kinder*'s lives before their arrival in England: harried parents searching for a way out, acceptance on a *Kindertransport* train, and waving good-bye. After their arrival in England the children's lives changed drastically. Even their names changed. Fritz, Hans, Dorli, and Beate became Fred, John, Dorothy, and Bea. The children's paths began to diverge immediately. Some were placed with families, some in hostels or orphanages. Some went to school, and others went to work. There were those who were placed with Jewish families, and those who were placed with gentile families. Some encountered compassionate foster parents, others spent time with callous ones, and still others had both kinds. While the parents of some of the children eventually arrived in England and the parents of others survived in foreign countries, most of the children never saw their parents again. Most importantly, there were those for whom the next few years brought security and even contentment and those for whom the next few years were steeped in misery. There were so many reasons why things could go wrong that it was fortuitous that some of the children were able to achieve happiness during the years following their arrival.

The homes the children were placed in varied from excellent to destructive. Many of the foster parents were devoted and knew just the right way to handle children. From their first greeting and over the next few years, they forged a lasting bond with their foster children. Marietta[153] was one of the fortunate children placed with such a family. Through all the confusing new impressions and foreign customs, Marietta glimpsed a normal family similar to her own. Mr. and Mrs. Jones were friendly but not overpowering. Brian, her new foster brother, and Marietta were the same age and soon became good friends. They compared their lives, parents, and customs. When she fell ill with German measles, he sneaked into her bedroom to keep her company and continue their debates, until Mrs. Jones angrily separated them. When Dunkirk was on everybody's mind, Marietta felt completely frightened. Mrs. Jones comforted her and told her that "England will never surrender." Quiet courage, a sense of humor, and camaraderie enveloped Marietta all through her years with the Joneses. Yet in spite of all the care and love she received, every night after she went to bed she conducted a one-sided conversation with her parents and sister, the moon and stars being her messengers: "In my mind, I would walk through my old home, from room to room, stroke the various pieces of furniture passed on to my parents from theirs. I would gaze at the many paintings which hung on the walls and had played such an important role in the stories I had woven around them when I was a child, and the only clouds I knew were those on the horizon. In the tall book cases in my father's study, there were all the books which my sister had read with such a voracious appetite. I was very homesick for my parents and sister."

While Marietta had found a home that in many ways was similar to her former one, Alan,[141] formerly Ernst, entered a world quite unfamiliar to him. He found himself with a family living in Oxford in a nineteenth-century atmosphere. The family, while wealthy, was not entirely "society," since its money had come from trade (horrors!) and not from land. Alan does not exactly describe the Wrights as eccentric but says they were people who were absolutely sure of themselves and of the correctness of their views, whatever these might be. Mr. Wright, then in his mideighties, was independently wealthy and never had to work. Living with him were his three daughters, all in their forties and unmarried. They belonged to the generation of English women who did not have a prayer of ever finding a husband after the carnage of World War I. All three dressed plainly, read widely, and played chamber music. The middle daughter had sponsored Alan and was responsible for his welfare. The old man had all the money and gave none to his daughters. They had inherited a pittance of a private income—as in many nineteenth-century novels—from their mother and an odd aunt.

Alan's life was very comfortable. The spacious house, which was surrounded by a large garden, was replete with servants. Alan was treated with courtesy and respect. Family members were not surprised that fifteen-year-old Alan was entirely on his own (English parents typically sent their boys to boarding school, frequently by the age of eight). They did try to spare him any embarrassment: For instance, because knickerbockers, popular with Austrian youths, were only worn for golf in England and made Alan stand out as a foreigner, they purchased him a whole new set of clothes. For his part, Alan was, as he put it, "superbly well behaved," and he assimilated quickly. He changed his eating habits overnight. A formerly fussy eater, he now ate everything put in front of him. His mother would not have believed that he ate porridge and a fat mutton joint without a murmur. From an indifferent student he blossomed into a serious one, attending school and studying for exams leading to university matriculation. The trust the Wrights placed in him served as a spur to responsible action.

When Alan turned seventeen, Miss Wright made an announcement, which, while not illogical, came as an intense shock to him. Miss Wright felt that since Alan had passed his university entrance exams, he was now in a position to find employment and continue his studies at night. Alan's transition from upper-class Englishman to tenant of a refugee hostel run by Quakers was truly unsettling. He was so traumatized that he barely remembers this period. But as was his wont, he adjusted to his new life. He delivered groceries and lived frugally. And the same good fortune that had found him a place on a *Kindertransport* through an unknown patron intervened again. Like Pip in *Great Expectations*, an unknown benefactor offered Alan money for university study. A Hungarian academic who had prospered in England wanted to help someone less fortunate than himself. He offered to lend a goodly amount of money on the condition that he need not have any contact with the recipient. Miss Wright offered to pay Alan's living expenses again, but he was responsible for his own books and clothes. Alan's luck held still further: through one of Miss Wright's contacts he received a position as a tutor at a school for the deaf. His responsibilities were simple: It was his job, since he was not hearing impaired, to listen for the air raid sirens and get the children out of bed and into a shelter. In return, he received board and lodging with one day off per week. He used the nights to earn extra money by watching the attic of an unoccupied building for phosphorescent bombs. In 1944 Alan graduated with a degree in mechanical engineering. It had taken him less than two and a half years to graduate.

The Wrights were very pleased when Alan insisted on joining the army, unlike one of the Wrights' young cousins, who was a poor student and lacked patriotic fervor. Alan achieved a high rank and was encouraged by his commanding officer to remain in the army. Alan was not so inclined. He remembers the last night before his discharge as a decisive one in his life. He was going through the last formalities. The other men could not wait to rush to the railway station to spend their first night as civilians with their families. Alan looked at the train schedule and realized that he would be arriving in Oxford so late that one of the Wrights would have to stay up past bedtime. He felt he could not possibly put them in such a position and was forced to stay at the camp. It was the most depressing night of his life. Alone in the huge barracks, Alan took stock. He was very fond of the Wrights and their perhaps somewhat quaint ways. Their home had always served as a solid base for him. His feelings for them were respect, admiration, and gratitude. In turn, they had taken quite a risk in bringing a young foreigner into their orderly world. They approved of his good manners and his scholarliness. Yet in spite of their good relationship, he was never free to be himself and always felt like a guest in their house, no matter how welcome he was. It was obvious that he did not have a home and had better do something about it. It was up to him to make a life for himself. And that is precisely what he did. He emigrated to the United States, married, and had a successful career as an engineer.

There were families who besides looking after the physical and financial well-being of their charges also dedicated themselves to the children's emotional development. Bernard's[68] foster father noticed that Bernard (formerly Bernhard) needed encouragement to blend in with English schoolboys, and Bernard welcomed his concern. His foster father accepted and understood him. He helped to toughen him sufficiently to be able to accept his peers' teasing. Bernard became a son to his foster parents. They wanted to give him the advantage of a higher education, but by that time his mother had arrived in England and would not allow them to do so. Bernard returned to his mother and shared her limited financial circumstances.

Elfi's[50] foster mother's tact and understanding were remarkable. Elfi recalls: "I discussed with Vera that if I had not lived with her and her guidance and love, who knows how I would have turned out. And she always said that I must always remember that my parents taught me all the basic values of life and that she had only taken over at a time when it was necessary."

Not every child was fortunate enough to be placed in a private home, but many of the group homes, hostels, and orphanages are remembered positively. Franz[15] recalls the National Children's Home and Orphanage, a Methodist institution in Lancashire that was staffed by local teachers and German refugees. Despite one or two canings (in accord with English custom), Franz considered the teachers to have been kind and patient and the boys congenial. In fact, one staff member became his mentor and took a personal interest in him. Betty[66] did equally well in a Manchester hostel for girls. The two competent women in charge had the gift of treating the girls as individuals and provided opportunities for private talks. The chance to confide and a close friendship with another girl eased Betty's loneliness.

There were also wealthy families who took charge of a number of youngsters and showed personal concern and generosity. James de Rothschild and his wife, Dorothy, put a house at the disposal of thirty refugee youngsters, and provided a family, brought to England to care for them.[89] The house was called the Cedars and served as the children's home all through the war. Seven-year-old Rolf, soon to become Ralph,[5] joined his twelve-year-old brother there. The Cedars boys attended local schools, and Baron de Rothschild, the moving spirit behind the enterprise, visited them frequently. Baron de Rothschild sent those boys who were qualified to some of the finest colleges in England. At the end of the war the majority of the children learned that they were orphans. In 1983 fifteen of the Cedars boys had a reunion, which Dorothy de Rothschild attended. They thanked her and she thanked them for giving her the opportunity to be of help. Ralph ranks the reunion as one of the most moving events of his life.

Most people who were in England in the thirties will have a very clear memory of the many Lyons Tea Shops. A shopping trip was made pleasanter by stopping at one of them and having a smiling waitress, clad in a black uniform with white apron and white headband, serve a cup of tea with a buttered scone. The Salmon and Gluckstein families, the chain's owners, became the guardians of over twenty children. Peter[130] and his sister Traute[131] remember the personal care they received from the "Aunties" over the years. At first the children stayed in a hostel that had been luxuriously refurbished for them. For a variety of reasons, the blitz for one, they were moved to a number of foster homes over the years. The children were able to take these changes in stride because they were continuously watched over by their guardians, who managed to keep family members in close proximity to each other. The Aunties paid careful attention to the children's emotional well-being. Not only did they correspond with their charges, but they remembered birthdays and kept a check on their school progress. Traute's guardian introduced her to a rather sophisticated world; Peter was sent to a prestigious public school and provided with a higher education. Peter entered the hotel business; Traute was able to complete a doctorate in languages. Peter reflects that what he owes his foster family cannot be described in words.

While the more fortunate children had almost ideal conditions, many others did not. On the whole, the homes the youngsters were placed in were simple ones of families with limited financial means. Because compulsory education in England ended at fourteen years of age, many of the children, to their great disappointment, had to discontinue their studies and go to work. This was true for fourteen-year-old Ruth,[24] a physician's daughter, who had to earn her own living. She was actually quite proud of the fact that she was able to save ration coupons and money to buy a coat. In fact, she was prouder of that coat than of the fur coat she purchased forty years later. But Ruth had no teenage life. Mr. Potter, her foster father, a movie theater manager, did make it possible for her to attend performances without charge, and Mrs. Potter helped her sew dresses to compensate for the limitations on her wardrobe imposed by rationing. But Ruth's social life was quite limited; while well-meaning, Mrs. Potter was strict and rarely allowed Ruth to go out on dates. Still, Ruth appreciates what the family did for her, and when

Mr. Potter died, Ruth sent Mrs. Potter the airfare to come and visit her in the United States. Ilse[74] found an even greater incongruity than Ruth did between her own and her foster mother's values. Ilse wanted to go to evening school while working as a dressmaker's apprentice. But though they were very kind, her guardians did not believe in continuing education and would not permit her to pursue further studies. Lottie's[165] education ceased because her foster placement had to be changed eight times owing to wartime conditions. In Germany she had been at the top of her class. The many moves not only led to the termination of her education, but also made Lottie a perpetual outsider. Once the daughter of well-to-do parents, she was living on charity. But with an intrepid spirit, she found a way out: She taught herself shorthand and typing, which at last allowed her to leave her sponsor and conduct her life as she wished.

Jealousy was another factor to be dealt with. One youngster's[74] foster sister developed an unreasonable jealousy of her. This forced her foster mother, who had a very sweet disposition, into an uncomfortable position with her own daughter. Such family tensions could poison the atmosphere, as fifteen-year-old Emmy[129] discovered. Because of the blitz, her foster mother moved to the country with her two children. Emmy was left alone with the man of the household. When the wife visited, she would eye the young girl with suspicion. Emmy asked to be moved to another household. There her life made a sudden turnaround. Her new foster parents treated her with such affection that Emmy still visits her foster mother, who at this writing is ninety-eight years old. Yet during all those years Emmy yearned for some physical affection, which she used to receive from her own parents. What had come spontaneously in her family seemed less customary in England. Many of the *Kinder* noted that though there was love in their foster homes, there was less physical affection and expression of emotions than they were accustomed to. The English seemed more constrained, and the children experienced this cultural difference as painful.

Many teenage escapees without parents lived in rooming houses entirely on their own. One of the places they frequented was the Austrian Center, where they found a congenial social life. They shared each other's humor and became what we would today call a support group. To outsiders they may have appeared to be secure and capable as they resourcefully organized social events and theatricals. Actually, they faced an entirely uncertain future, and they were utterly alone. Their outwardly carefree demeanor and their gallows humor hid a good deal of fear and loneliness.

Difficult though some of the problems described here were, they were still manageable. But some children encountered foster parents who were, at the very least, inept or, in some cases, suffering from severe personality problems. The younger children were least able to deal with or understand these problem parents and as a result were the most traumatized. The life of seven-year-old Stefan,[80] now Steve, was made miserable by a guarantor who was practically a social isolate. Auntie did not allow Steve any free time or to play with other children. She was not intentionally mean, and when it was pointed out to her by neighbors that a child needs playtime, she arranged for some. But by that time Steve had lost his ability to utilize it. He envied a refugee boy who seemed to lead a normal life, and he desperately missed his parents. He felt that something very important was lacking in his life, though he did not know what it was. Today he knows that what was missing was the feeling of being loved. Steve finally settled in Israel. He would have loved not to stay in touch with Auntie but somehow could not make the break. The idea that she might visit him in Israel hung over his head like the sword of Damocles. When she died, he actually heaved a sigh of relief. In a letter to me Steve puzzled why he had been unable to sever the bond that held him to Auntie while she was alive. I asked Steve whether he could be feeling guilty for despising the very person who saved his life. Possibly, the sense of gratitude outweighed the desire to be free. Steve thought my answer was correct. When I asked him if he had a picture of Auntie, he replied that if he had had one, he would have burned it when she died.

Vera's[158] foster mother wanted to appear altruistic in public. When visitors came, Vera was trotted out as the "refugee girl" whom Mrs. Fry had taken into her home out of the deep goodness of her heart. In private, with a divide-and-conquer attitude, Mrs. Fry fomented constant trouble between Vera and her own daughter, Betty. For instance, Betty's allowance was cut in half and the other half given to Vera; Betty could hardly look kindly on Vera after that. Because

Betty's birthday fell during school holidays, preventing her from bringing a cake to school, Vera was not allowed to bring a birthday cake to school for her own birthday, since "it would not be fair for Vera to have one when Betty didn't." Mrs. Fry became increasingly resentful of Vera and, as a result, outrageously aggressive. When war broke out and Vera began to cry, Mrs. Fry accused her of being selfish, thinking only of herself and not of the soldiers who had to go to war. Vera was dealt a final, devastating blow when a British soldier was killed in Palestine: Mrs. Fry hissed at Vera that perhaps Hitler knew what he was doing when he killed all the Jews.

Tension between foster parents made life miserable for some *Kinder*, particularly if these tensions were displaced onto the foster child.[70] Julie's frustration with her life made her an unpredictable and erratic foster mother. Only thirty-two years old, she was angry at being married to a man she considered a nonentity and felt thwarted by her limited financial means. But Julie was pretty and had charm. Ruth adored Julie and craved her affection. One moment Julie would hug and kiss the fifteen-year-old, as well as her own two-year-old son, and the next moment she would berate and scream at them. Besides being capricious, she was also lazy. Wet diapers were hung by the fire to dry—unwashed. She assigned innumerable chores to her ward. Each morning Ruth was the first one up; she served Julie tea in bed, cleaned the fireplace, and dressed and fed little Roger. Then she went to work in a dress factory for ten shillings a week. After work she ironed, did the chores, and took care of the little boy. Ruth knew her status in the house and never complained. She was alone (she was to be haunted by a loneliness that would not leave her for years). She needed to be loved. And so the endless quest to please Julie continued.

After some months Julie, Ruth, and Roger were evacuated to escape the bombings. Once away from home, Julie quickly took a lover and went out evenings, leaving Ruth to care for Roger. By good fortune, a trunk of new clothes sent by her mother had reached Ruth before the war started. Julie saw all those lovely new outfits and could not contain herself. She left Ruth nothing but a quilt. Needless to say, Ruth never objected. She had been reminded often enough how lucky she was to have been rescued from Germany.

Ruth's stay with Julie ended abruptly. In the spring of 1940, a policeman came to the house and informed Ruth that she had been declared an "enemy alien" by the British government. Since she was living in a "restricted" area, she was considered a threat to the safety of the country and had to be removed. Ruth was sent to the Isle of Man, where she stayed for a few weeks before she was allowed to join a second foster family in London.

Julie's new family was not much of an improvement. While the foster father was kind, and she enjoyed the companionship of one of the three daughters, she remembers her second foster mother running her white-gloved fingers over the furniture to see if it had been properly dusted. But even worse were the Sunday mornings when the girls of the family were still asleep and Ruth would polish the red brick hall on her knees. She remembers serving at table once when a nephew, a handsome captain in uniform, was being feted with his fiancée. As she was serving him soup, he turned and asked, "Well, little girl, what do you think of Hitler?" At that point Ruth dropped the plate in his lap, not entirely by accident, and left the room in tears.

It must have been extremely difficult for Ruth to cope with her unstable foster mothers. But at least she was fifteen years old. Maritza[75] was only six and a half when she was placed with a foster mother whose behavior was such that one might debate whether it could be considered to be within normal limits. She was totally neglectful of the child's well-being. Even strangers were astonished to see a child who was living in a doctor's home look so strangely shabby and poor. They did not know, however, that Maritza was frequently hungry as well. But while her foster mother neglected her physically, she was extremely demanding emotionally: After school Maritza's foster mother would launch into tedious, self-centered monologues, which the little girl was compelled to listen to by the hour. They ended only when it was time for Maritza to begin her manifold chores. Maritza was not expected to experience any emotions that were not connected with her foster home. For instance, she was not allowed to feel sad or remember her former home. One day her foster mother told Maritza that her parents had been gassed. While her foster mother did seem somewhat shocked at the news, she did not suppose that Maritza should be upset. Maritza's gratitude for surviving and being allowed to live with the family was supposed to supplant all other feelings. In fact, her foster mother considered that Maritza barely deserved to remain alive. She compared her unfavorably to her domestic animals, creatures she had chosen, she said, "not like you who was pushed onto us." Sensing her precarious position, Maritza refrained from ever being naughty.

Maritza did not show hate for her foster mother. Her need for love and approval prevented that. She had an overpowering sense of frustration and anger that her guardian should find her so unlovable when she was trying so hard to be a good daughter. She never stopped trying to win her foster mother's approval. Just breathing could get her into trouble. But there were some compensatory factors: Maritza noted that her foster mother was almost equally abusive to her own children. That realization gave her a sense that the outbursts were not targeted exclusively at her. But while her foster siblings also led miserable lives, at least they, for better or worse, belonged. Maritza felt that her foster father was basically kind and seemed to like her, but he was unable to stand up to his wife. She was a frightening woman who could maintain a tirade for many hours if he intervened. Had he had the strength, he would have left; since he did not, he kept quiet. (For my own opinion about quiet, kind spouses who stand by and do nothing, I will merely offer a comment made about Czar Nicholas II: "He is not treacherous, but he is weak, and weakness fulfills all the functions of treachery".)

When Maritza was sixteen years old, she was asked to leave and earn her own living. Yet at the same time her foster parents paid for a boy, relatively unfamiliar to them, to study medicine. As she struggled on her own, Maritza visited occasionally, hoping against hope for some emotional support. It was never there. In fact, her foster mother accused her of only coming home for a free meal—and charged her for the food! Maritza came to realize that her stepmother was vicious. Still, she continued to visit her until her death three years ago.

From the survey of placements, it is apparent that foster homes ranged from excellent to horrendous, with many of them being at neither extreme. Since the children often changed foster homes, they frequently had experiences with various kinds. It might be said that Gerda's[40] life as a *Kindertransport* child encompassed the best and the worst conditions that children who depended on "the kindness of strangers" encountered.

When Gerda arrived at her foster home, she was greeted by a kindly-looking man, two boys, aged twelve and fifteen, and a not very friendly woman (just how unfriendly she was about to find out). When Gerda awoke the next day, no one paid any attention to her. She wandered about aimlessly. And she remained isolated in the months to come. When Gerda was not in school, her foster mother ignored her and made no bones about not having wanted to take her in the first place. In order to avoid offending anyone, Gerda tried to copy her older foster brother. For example, once when he helped himself to an apple in a bowl, Gerda did the same. Her foster mother sternly told her to put the apple right back and accused her of stealing.

Things went from bad to worse. Every night at seven o'clock, right after supper, Gerda was put to bed. One evening she noticed that her bedroom door had been locked. She was frightened. She had no idea why she had been shut in. In response to her frantic shouts, her foster mother arrived and coolly informed Gerda that she was being confined for loitering on the stairs at night and listening to the adults' conversation. Gerda's protest that she had left her bedroom only to go to the toilet was not accepted. The door remained locked. Not only did Gerda hate being locked in, but there was a more obvious problem: From seven in the evening till eight the next morning was a long time to refrain from going to the toilet. Gerda grew quite desperate until she hit on a solution. Her mother had given her a very pretty white celluloid box that contained a comb and brush. She now emptied it and used it as a potty. This was all very well, but what to do with the contents? On a sudden impulse she opened the window and emptied the contents into the garden below. This arrangement worked, but only for a time. Gerda had not realized that directly below her window was a magnificent rosebush, her foster mother's favorite. After a couple of weeks this lovely bush began to die. When one morning she heard her foster mother shouting at the poor gardener for neglecting the rosebush, Gerda realized that there was a connection between her own actions and the sickness of the rosebush. That night she had a discussion with God. She pointed out that she had not meant to do anything wrong. She promised that if the gardener was to be punished or lose his job, she would confess that it was her fault; but if nothing happened, she would keep mum. The next day the gardener replanted the rosebush in another part of the garden, where it once again blossomed into the most beautiful bush in the whole garden.

Gerda was rescued two years later when her foster father died of a heart attack. Her sponsor took this opportunity to ask for Gerda's removal on the grounds that she could no longer afford to keep her. The reason was blatantly untrue since she continued to employ servants, a chauffeur, and maids. Nevertheless, her foster mother's request was probably a lifesaver for Gerda, who was then placed in the home of three sisters and a brother who were of very moderate means but who had hearts full of love. The change in Gerda's life can be illustrated by one incident: Gerda had come to believe that English children were not allowed to go to the toilet at night. On a particular night when Gerda felt the urge she quietly got up and found her way to the bathroom. So far, so good. But she had forgotten the dog. He had heard someone moving about and now sat outside the bathroom waiting for the burglar to come out. Gerda was trapped. She could hear the dog breathing on the other side of the door. She sat down on the floor and fell asleep. When she awoke, all the lights were on and her new Aunts and Uncle, and even the dog, were fussing over her. They carried her back to bed, and Gerda told them why she had gone to the bathroom secretly. Everyone was moved to tears. They made her a big pot of tea and explained that she was perfectly free to move about the whole house, whenever and wherever she liked. With this Gerda understood that at last she had found a loving home.

Some of the correspondents were grateful to the Refugee Committee, others were critical that foster parents were not more closely supervised. From a reading of the many requests from just this group of *Kinder*, it is hard to envision how the committee managed at all. It had been suddenly faced with organizing an influx of 10,000 children. Homes had to be found and hostels had to be organized under wartime conditions. Foster families were frequently in flux: Some fell sick and died; others were evacuated, and their foster children had to be resettled in other homes. The needs of the children varied: some were in orthodox homes and wanted to go to less restrictive ones; other made the opposite request. The smallest details had to be thought about, such as providing money for stamps and toothpaste. Many local members of the committee were volunteers, not trained social workers. Thus, even when committee members visited homes, they did not really know how to investigate conditions. In addition, few people at the time even had the concept of middle-class parents either physically or emotionally abusing children. And no one at the time ever considered interviewing children about the adequacy of caretaking adults. Even if the members of the London committee themselves had wanted to visit the children, it would have been almost impossible since travel conditions during wartime were highly restricted. From the individual's point of view, the committee was not always effective. Thus, one escapee writes about being in a mediocre home, asking to be changed, and being refused. But from the perspective of the committee, which had to find hundreds of homes, a mediocre one was probably the best it could do. Some of the *Kinder* were upset because they had been unable to continue their education, but funds were extremely limited. When I consider all the money that was necessary to reimburse foster parents and to provide for the children's most basic needs, I must admit to a feeling of awe and respect for the committee's achievements.

It is obvious that the quality of the home the *Kinder* were placed in was a primary factor in their level of adjustment. However, there were legions of other contributing factors, both major and minor. One might say that a good home was only a necessary, not a sufficient, condition for contentment. Some of the other factors need to be considered as well.

## Chapter 17

# So Many Reasons

There were new habits to acquire, new customs to adjust to, new attitudes to be formed. The *Kinder* had to cope with their new experiences by themselves. The kindest guardian was still a stranger to them. A good foster home was of immeasurable value, but it was only a base. It was a bit like emerging after an earthquake. Things were considerably calmer, but they were different, confusing. Nothing was in its usual place. One feels strange in a new country because all its inhabitants are acting in a strange fashion—strange, that is, compared to one's own culture. For example, when I arrived at the English boarding school Westgate-on-Sea, almost all matters, from the first call in the morning to the last good-night, were conducted differently from what I had been used to. According to the English view of preventive medicine, bedrooms were considered healthier when unheated. Thus, we started the day by chopping the ice in the water pitchers in order to brush our teeth. Leopold, now Bob,[189] who went to a boy's school, also remembers the health benefits the English ascribed to being cold: "I remember those morning showers. There was only one spigot, cold naturally, and the upperclassmen in charge of us stood by with stopwatches to make sure one was under the icy stream for exactly three minutes. I still shiver when I think of it."

One's own customs are so taken for granted that it takes time to become aware of their inappropriateness. It was a while before Gunther[1] realized that the way he greeted people must seem odd. There was no need to make a slight bow while clicking one's heels, as he had been taught in Germany; a simple "How do you do?" would suffice. New table manners had to be absorbed: After having such etiquette drilled into me for years, in England I found that my knowledge was inadequate. In English boarding school I was taught to say "I am sorry" if my neighbor asked me to pass the salt or the bread. Her request meant that I had been neglectful; I should have been aware of her wants before I had to be reminded.

Sometimes the food presented a problem. In school, we were obliged to finish all the food on our plate. At certain regular intervals the doors would open to the dining room and that most dreaded of English desserts would appear—suet pudding. Only recently did I look up the definition of *suet*: "the hard fat about the kidneys and loins in beef and mutton that yields tallow." I don't know for sure whether it yielded tallow, but I know that it yielded dread for me. The dessert was a yellow-grey, shaking mass covered with treacle, a particularly heavy syrup. As I sat with my spoon, rather than with the European dessert fork, I knew that this was a three o'clocker. It would take me that long to finish it. Had I been able to eat it right away, it would merely have wobbled, but as time passed, that shaky pudding congealed into a ghastly lump. Only those to the manner born could possibly enjoy it.

Ignorance of customs also makes for misreading friendly intentions. I recall a girl who, realizing that I could not speak English, tried to put me at ease with a friendly wink. I averted my glance. No one winked in Vienna. I thought the girl was suffering from a nervous tic, and I tactfully looked away. Possibly, she thought I had rejected her friendly gesture.

The English concepts of sportsmanship and modesty were entirely new to most of us. It was very bad taste to praise oneself. During games we were taught to say "Jolly good shot" if our opponent made a fortunate shot and "Bad luck" if she failed to score. Those habits have stayed with me. I still cringe when personalities on American TV comment that theirs is the best film with the best director, expressions unthinkable in England at that time. Occasionally, I am the target of raised eyebrows from doubles partners in tennis who find it odd when I call out "Bad luck" to a double-faulting opponent.

The formal courtesy prevalent in England at the time had to be mastered. I soon learned to follow the amenities at tea time in school when offered a goodie by a friend. Girl offering: "Would you like some?" Required answer: "Can you spare it?" Girl: "Yes, I can. Please have some." Retort: "Are you sure you can spare it?" Girl: "Yes, I am." Final acceptance: "Thank you so much." I learned the routine before I even knew what the words meant. There was a strong emphasis on self-restraint and a calm demeanor. Ruth[126] wrote that when her mother, who lived in South America, came for a visit, she asked her daughter if she was always so polite with her children; having been brought up in England, she was. Alan[141] rather liked the calm and cool behavior, so unlike some of the family set-tos he had been accustomed to at home. But when that cool self-restraint broke down, it could take strange forms: Ruth[70] still recalls the first air raid: "I remember feeling sick and almost fainting. Our British neighbors came over after the siren sounded. Mr. Ashford seemed completely unperturbed, except that his usual pipe was in his mouth unlit and upside-down. Mrs. Ashford took off her coat and apart from a little apron was stark naked. They were nudists and she had forgotten to dress."

There were all kinds of subtle differences in values and attitudes. Alan[141] observed some of these in his very upper-class British foster family: "Self-indulgence is a characteristic frowned upon. For instance, it would be self-indulgent to draw a luxurious hot bath with water up to the rim when five inches of tepid water was perfectly adequate. Or taking more than one chocolate out of the box or eating part of the main course at dinner, like the meat by itself, rather than eating the vegetables at the same time. It was all very strange—the food; the formal, quite unemotional relationships; the even tempers. I strove mightily to imitate it."

Not all the *Kinder* were able to adapt as quickly. Those who were very young, less flexible, or less observant or who were in the care of intolerant guardians were considered odd and uncooperative. Certainly, many of the former *Kinder* speak of having felt strange, alien, foreign. Maritza[75] describes her feelings: "I felt alone, isolated, and very unusual. I felt exotic." Betty[66] also felt disoriented: "I did not feel like my life had any permanence. We were refugees. We were outsiders. Everything was so different from what it had been."

Feeling like an outsider could bring with it a loss of confidence. The feelings of self-doubt typical of adolescents were added to the sense of alienation engendered by being an outsider. Watching the local youngsters with their sense of belonging and English good looks proved to be quite disheartening to many an adolescent *Kind* in a strange home. Ruth[70] remembers: "My mood varied from childish enthusiasm to despair. I thought of myself as unattractive and loathed my kinky hair, did battle with it constantly. I was gaining weight from the starchy food available in wartime. The loneliness was worse than any fear of air raids. Suicide entered my mind. I felt that if I got killed, it would not matter to anybody. But I was young and wanted to have fun. Rosalind [foster sister] was younger than I, and I envied her greatly. She was attractive, clever, and socially very popular. On occasion she took me along, and I felt like a fish out of water: shy, unattractive, ill dressed, and alienated from these young and carefree people. I worried about my future. I had no idea what to do and felt too old to be a burden to anybody. It took me many years to regain my confidence."

Many of the *Kinder* realized that they had lost their former middle-class status. Franz[15] evaluated his situation objectively: "I was a mechanic's helper at thirty shillings a week, of which twenty went for lodging. England at the time was a class-ridden society, and this did affect me. I don't remember to what extent. But I do remember that I felt conscious of being a social inferior. At the same time I was grateful for being readily accepted by other social inferiors, such as the workmen at the cement works. I do not think that I missed my old life. The happy times of childhood had been too thickly overlaid by fifteen months of Hitler."

One might suppose that the *Kinder*'s lack of fluency in English presented a serious problem. Only one or two refer to it or mention it as a passing problem, but none dwell on it. What contributed to feeling different was the absence of parents. For a while the children received mail from home. But while parents tried to sound reassuring, bad news seeped through the veiled words anyway. Dora[173] received a letter in which her mother wrote: "Thank God we are doing better. Papa had to return." The postcard actually revealed to Dora that her father had been unsuccessful in his effort to cross the border into Belgium. Dora did not guess that her father's frustrated attempt would ultimately lead to death in Buchenwald concentration camp. Dora's letters were addressed jointly to her and her friend and written by both sets of parents. The girls valued the letters so much that they divided them between themselves: One would keep the envelope and the other the letter; the following time it was the other way around. In their letters parents poured out all their love. They tried to guide their children to behave well in order to earn the affection of their foster parents. The following are excerpts from a letter to Marietta:[153] "My dear sweet Marietta: You are constantly in our thoughts. We still see your face before us in that window of the railway carriage. You were so good and brave. You are my clever and wise little girl. It is very lucky that such a nice family has enabled you to come over. Thank God for that. Continue to be good, grateful for everything. Be nice and decent to everyone. Be careful and diligent, and I am sure you will make your way. I know we don't have to worry about your behavior and manners. Did you lose anything? Was the journey very tiring? Was the country beautiful? Were you able to sleep at night? Did anyone else come with you from London? Do you need anything? I await your letter anxiously and look forward to reading all about your trip and who was waiting for you. Please write us everything, your impressions about your new surroundings, your family. Don't forget to thank them for taking you in. Write soon. Your letters will ease the wounds caused by our parting. Lots of kisses and hugs from your ever-loving Mama." And a postscript: "We miss you and await your letter. Stay well, my dearest child. Kisses from your Papa, who is homesick for you."

When the children received the Red Cross letters—twenty-five words, including the address, per letter—many had no idea what to think while a few children suspected the worst. When thirteen-year-old Marion[85] received one from her parents, stating that they were doing well, she no longer believed them, but most children kept up hope to the very end for a reunion. To their great relief, a few of the children learned that their parents had been able to escape even after the war started. Not that the good news necessarily relieved them of all their worries. Alan[141] learned that his parents had somehow managed to board the last ship from Trieste to Haifa before Italy joined the war. They were absolutely destitute upon their arrival in British Palestine. In addition, there was the worry about Rommel's Afrika Korps poised at the gates of Cairo. Being young and optimistic, Alan never doubted the outcome of the war, but he did recognize that he would have to try to help his parents survive. He did so by saving his meager pocket money until he accumulated one pound sterling, which enabled him to send off a postal order for that amount. He adds, somewhat bemused, that his parents never forgot about his filial devotion and to the end of their days talked about it to anyone who would listen. He himself, in true English fashion, did not consider that it merited praise.

Financial support from one's parents is usually taken for granted; from others, no matter how generously given, how tactfully managed, it becomes a favor. The fear of being a burden troubled many of the older children even in homes where the foster parents never implied in word or deed that they begrudged the children anything. For instance, teenage Gerda,[40] boarding with a family of moderate means, constantly worried about being a financial burden. The family did nothing to contribute to such a feeling. Nevertheless, Gerda had to struggle with herself whenever she needed to ask for money for essentials such as stockings or books for school.

Besides all their personal concerns, the *Kinder* also had fears related to war conditions, just as the English children did. One former *Kind* remembers her school being bombed to bits, but fortunately no one was there at the time. Henry[170] recalls sleeping in air raid shelters every night and emerging each morning to see the damage done to the surrounding houses. When land mines were dropped, whole blocks were annihilated. Transportation was limited for the whole population, but because refugees were considered aliens for a time, they were under further restrictions. Elli[4] was training as a nurse. Many times she saved her weekly day off until she accumulated sufficient days to visit an aunt in London. She had to report to the police within twenty-four hours of departure and arrival and do the same on her way back; there was hardly any time left for the actual visit. Young children had to get accustomed to war measures. All citizens were issued gas masks and were expected to carry them at all times. The ones for younger children were made to look like Mickey Mouse masks, but that did not disguise the smell of rubber or prevent a sense of suffocation. Air raid shelters were dug, procedures for evacuating schools were learned, and drills practiced. Kurt[51] recalls the Morrison Shelter that replaced the dining room table: It was about the size of a double bed; the top, the legs, and the bottom were made of heavy steel, and wire netting covered the sides. Even if the house collapsed during an air raid, the occupants of the shelter would be safe. Kurt and his foster brother slept in this contraption during the worst of the bombings. When the shelter was not used for its original purpose, the boys would make believe that they were caged lions, snarling through the heavy wire mesh sides.

It is sad to report that incidents of sexual abuse did occur. One shudders to think of a youngster in a strange home, without a confidante, pursued by her own guardian! One woman, then about ten years old, reports that her foster father pulled down her panties and fondled her while putting her to bed. Shortly afterward she was sent to boarding school. That was fortunate, but the situation had already gone far enough to make her avoid all sexual contact with men until after she was married. A twelve-year-old received a declaration of love from the father of the family she lived with. The youngster did not really comprehend the meaning of the incident and innocently related it to the daughter of the family. The latter told her mother, who sent the twelve-year-old away. Another incident will be referred to later. In all, three women revealed their experiences to me. Of course there is no way of knowing whether there were more.

On the whole, the *Kinder* refrained from discussing with anyone their concerns about themselves or worries about the families left behind. In most cases the atmosphere in their new home was drastically different from that of their former one. Mostly, they felt themselves to be guests, strangers, or secondary, rather than central, members of a family. Even when youngsters liked their guardians, they rarely revealed their apprehensions. Franz[15] remembers his teachers with gratitude. "But as far as discussing my specific problems or feelings with anyone other than a friend of mine, it never entered my head. And certainly none of the staff ever volunteered for such a discussion. Why my problems? There were lots of other boys who no doubt had problems. And even had a member of the staff voiced an interest in my problems, I doubt if I would have been willing to be more than polite in return. Somehow this whole notion [of confiding] did not fit the environment. After all, psychologists were still a rarity then." Few people at the time thought of questioning children as to their internal lives. It was assumed that if children were provided with a benevolent environment and if they were kept busy with wholesome pursuits, their troubles would soon straighten out.

It was not necessarily indifference that prompted this lack of inquisitiveness on the part of the adults. For one, there was a much greater distance between children and adults as compared to today. There was no familiarity between a matron, a teacher, or even most guardians and their charges. Lore[139] resided with the principal and two of the teachers of her school. She was fond enough of them to continue visiting them long after she had left them, yet she never considered leaning upon them emotionally. "At various times during my three years, one or the other would become my favorite. But there was never anything you could call intimacy." At the time, privacy was a highly valued commodity in Britain. Coming from the continent, many *Kinder* were struck by the fact that what was considered ordinary conversation back home seemed to be considered out-of-bounds in Britain. People did not inquire into the more intimate feelings of others or even into their day-to-day affairs. When I was evacuated after the war started and placed with an English family, I did not know during my year's stay what the man's occupation was. I surmised he was in the building trade, but I sensed that it might be impolite to ask.

Children and foster parents sometimes came from very different settings. Writes a former foster mother:[109] "Herbert must have longed for his parents. But his whole demeanor was admirable. He showed no overt sorrow and was ready to be amused at any small stroke of good fortune." Herbert was most devoted to his foster parents. A young couple with a baby, they had taken him into their home because they felt they owed fate a debt of gratitude for their own happiness. To the present day, Herbert visits his former foster family. His foster mother comments enthusiastically, "I wish there were more Herberts around." Why then, one might ask, did Herbert never speak about his emotional life to them? In part, it may have been because the foster parents asked no direct questions. But perhaps it was also due to a subtle difference in backgrounds, in Weltanschauung, between foster parents and foster son. The foster mother writes: "My sons quite fondly refer to Herbert simply as 'our good German.' When Herbert and his nice Jewish wife visit, we always rejoice." These are indeed kind and loving words; still, the phrases "our good German" and "his nice Jewish wife" do speak of two different worlds.

Quite striking is the fact that, on the whole, the *Kinder* in hostels refrained from exchanging confidences with each other. Gunther,[1] in Scotland, describes the extent of this reluctance. Not too long ago he went to a reunion of members of his former hostel. One of the men at the reunion, a former close companion, was terminally ill. It was only at this point that this friend confided to him how difficult it had been for him at the hostel. He had labored under a double burden: He was isolated from his family but also felt isolated from the boys he was living with. Though he had been able to understand German, his mother tongue had been Czech; contrary to appearances, he had felt thoroughly alone since all the boys spoke German among themselves. "I mention this," writes my correspondent, "in the context of suppressing feelings. It took my friend fifty years to tell me about how he had felt in that situation at that time." Other correspondents remarked that they never discussed with their siblings the extent to which they missed and worried about their parents.

It cannot be a coincidence that so many children did not discuss their past lives, their parents, their loneliness, or their worries with anyone. Perhaps there was unconscious wisdom in the avoidance of such emotion-laden topics, topics that might have aroused anxiety, fear, and possibly intense panic. For instance, conjuring up thoughts of what might be happening to one's parents might have resulted in unbearable fear. It might be hypothesized that the possibly harmful consequences of suppression are preferable to facing a catastrophic reality. There were too many imponderables in the lives of the *Kinder*, and their sense of helplessness was too great to allow them to come to any conclusions, let alone optimistic ones. The striving was to become ordinary, to fit in. Conjuring up the past and unsolvable worries about the future only got in the way of reestablishing a routinized life.

Beset by so many problems—strange customs, the sense of being an outsider, no one to confide in, worries about parents, concerns about the future, efforts to please foster parents, potentially dangerous war conditions—children responded in different ways. Some children developed symptoms of emotional problems. One child[40] suddenly began to sleepwalk; several others suffered the embarrassment of bed-wetting;[126] another developed horrifying nightmares.[6] Several older children expressed their distress through negative behavior.[1] Marion,[85] who had been placed in a hostel she disliked, recalls: "We all had duties and had to conform. I must have been a terrible teenager and no doubt quite a bother, but by this time I was angry. I no longer got what I thought was my right as a child."

In their misery two children misunderstood their parents' motives in sending them to England. Marion[85] felt rejected by her parents, and Vera[158] searched her mind for what she might have done wrong to be dispatched from home. Lea[171] and her sisters, all under ten years, protected themselves by clinging to each other and excluding all outsiders. The hostel that sheltered them was an impersonal place and did not permit visits from relatives. The three, however, did have an uncle, aunt, and cousins living in England. One time these relatives waited for the three girls as they went on their walk and tried to make contact with them. So unaccustomed were the children to any personal contact outside their own little circle that rather than talk to their relatives they ran as fast as they could back to the hostel.

Some children were able to draw on an optimistic spirit. With their buoyant and affirmative view of life, they managed to turn difficult circumstances into a positive experience. Of course, if they were fortunate to have been placed in a warm and friendly home, it helped matters considerably. But that was not always the case. Whether they had compassionate foster parents or indifferent ones, they managed to keep an optimistic outlook. They possessed a special joie de vivre, an upbeat quality that they were able to hold on to regardless of circumstances. Bernard[68] describes his uncomplicated feelings toward his foster family: "Yes, I loved them as any normal boy loves and trusts his parents. For that is what they were to me. My mother was in Manchester, but that was far away. Mrs. Frankland was there every day in the place of a mother who looks after her children. I did not feel uncomfortable about their paying for my upkeep. I simply accepted it and thought no more about it." Being an outsider was not necessarily perceived as a disadvantage by these confident youngsters. "No, my self-worth was not affected," explains Lore.[139] "I had always been treated as someone special and important by those around me and that continued to be my opinion of myself. Sorry, if this sounds conceited, but you asked me. There were periods of resentment when I wished I did not have to work so hard and scrimp and save so much, but I never doubted that I would 'make it.'" Dorothy[41] echoes those feelings: "I did not often feel like an outsider, because, to begin with, I had always been made to feel 'special' in a very positive way and, subsequently, as evacuees we were all outsiders together. I loved going to school. It was so much fun and more relaxed than in Vienna. And I was seen as something of a star as I spoke English and German and had long plaits and was able to swim. It was bad for a while when I became an enemy alien. But all my friends made jokes [about] how the government could be so silly as to call Dotty an enemy. That made me see the whole thing in proportion."

Among the children who had adjusted quickly, there were some who did not miss their parents. As a ten-year-old, Ellen[19] did not yearn for her parents. She felt happy with her new family and felt resettled, but in retrospect feels somewhat puzzled by her reaction: "I had a loving home. It has always puzzled me why I did not miss my parents. I am a teacher and find that even abused children have loyalty to their parents. How come this was not true of me?" Ellen seemed somewhat reassured when I told her that other children had similar reactions. Peter[130] recalls: "The headmaster called me into his study and told me my parents were safe in Switzerland. You most probably feel it is very odd and strange that this is the first time I mention my parents [in his account of his life] since my arrival in England. It should prove to you that I was very happy throughout all these years and endorses my theory that as long as children receive love and affection, they survive very well. I can assure you that my parents missed us hourly and daily far more than we missed them." It would be difficult to say whether parents or children, particularly young ones, suffered more. What the children who did not miss their parents had in common were self-assurance and a very caring foster family. They also learned fairly early on that their parents had survived. In this way the pleasant times they were experiencing were undisturbed by apprehension. Nevertheless, it took adaptability to fit into a new environment, however good, without a backward glance.

Some children were quite intrepid and decided to become masters of their own fate. Fred[169] was a shy seventeen-year-old, working on a farm. He felt lonely and isolated and had difficulty making friends: "The people I lived with were no help. To them I was just a hired hand. Then I realized it was up to me. I hung around town and started to talk to other young people. Not the most savoury type of companions, but gradually I became accepted. Although I don't drink much, I started to go to pubs and found that it was there that most of the social life took place, especially in the country. My shyness was most pronounced toward the opposite sex. I managed to overcome my reticence, and got involved in a new life." Henry,[170] seventeen years old, took a similar view: "No one showed me any affection or concern. Resettling so many times was difficult, of course, but you must remember that I was not spoiled, fully realized that that there was a war on and that the name of the game was survival. In that context I managed." Determination, resoluteness, and optimism were qualities Bernard[68] seemed to exude. "I never did feel that I had been uprooted," he reveals. "Rather, I thought that the course of my life had received a jolt, a change of language and lifestyle, but was still a continuation of the same life growing up from child to adult. Yes, I did feel like an outsider on occasion, but I worked hard at trying not to be. At the same time, I made sure that whoever appeared to be friendly towards me always knew from the outset of my origins and my situation. I was fortunate in being in Goole where no one knew any German. This forced me to learn English quickly and sufficiently well for strangers to ask me if I was Welsh. As a result of my efforts and good luck, I am pleased to be able to say that I had almost no trouble at all even in wartime with anyone because of my having been born in Germany. I had my leg pulled, of course, but that is a part of friendly relationships. I am not aware of any inferiority complex due to change of homeland. If I did have at any time, it was maybe due to having to struggle a little harder than other people in order to reach the same goal. I was often lonely and sometimes depressed but mostly I was too busy for that. It takes time to be miserable, and I was confident eventually I would lead a normal life, have my own family, make my own way in the world, which of course happened in due course."

External factors were not the only determinants of a child's adjustment. The way youngsters perceived their environment and how they managed to deal with it were important factors as well. For instance, one person[26] describes a particular hostel in warm, glowing terms while another remembers it as an inhospitable place.[85] True, children of different ages might have had different experiences at the same institution, but even identical experiences can trigger different reactions in different individuals. One child asked to be allowed to call his foster parents "Mummy" and "Daddy."[126] Another child broke into tears when the same suggestion was made to her.[113] She felt her foster mother was usurping her parents' place. Choosing a more formal manner of address probably resulted in a different relationship with her foster parents.

Another cogent example illustrates the impact of differing perceptions: Three people wrote in detail about a particular matron, whom they referred to as a "former cook." One[85] mentions her in passing: "We had two matrons who looked after us. I did not like either one. The cook was round and chubby, the other one very severe. Neither one ever had time to listen to my feelings or my confusion." Another[17] takes a more neutral tone: "We had two Viennese teachers. They were OK but not the confiding kind." Here is a third description of the cook:[26] "One of the matrons, a former cooking teacher in Vienna, a very famous personality, an author of a cookbook, had feelings for me. I was extremely fond of her. I stayed in touch with her till she died. My husband and I visited her in 1979 in California. I have her book *So Kocht Man in Wien* [That's How One Cooks in Vienna]. It is one of my treasures, as are the last letters she wrote to me." When I read the different comments I recognized the woman immediately. It was Aunt Alice, a distant great-aunt of mine. I had no idea that she had ever been a matron in England. I do remember her visit one hot July day in New York, when she was already in her eighties. She came to teach me the art of cookie baking. She baked the whole day while a friend of mine and I wilted in the steamy kitchen after a mere three hours; Aunt Alice continued her lesson for another three. At about the same time, she left a retirement home in New York because she found everyone there too old for her. She moved to California and in her nineties gave cooking lessons on TV there. It could, of course, be that all three descriptions of Alice by the *Kinder* are correct. Perhaps her bouncy manner did not suit every personality. Perhaps she formed better rapport with one type of child than another. Perhaps she did not know how to respond to one child's particular problem. The different descriptions of her are illustrative of the different impact the same person may have on different personalities.

There were, then, a number of factors that determined the degree of the children's adjustment. The best results were obtained when characteristics of the external situation, such as type of placement and the personality and expectations of the guardian, coordinated well with the personality and the value system of the child. For instance, some of Traute's[131] character traits were the kind important for success in a boarding school. She was an independent child who easily accepted responsibility; thus, in spite of being foreign, she quickly became the prefect of her class. In England her individualistic outlook was more admired than it had been in Vienna. As a result, her self-confidence actually increased. It might be hypothesized that a child with a more dependent, vulnerable personality, requiring a great deal of physical affection, might not have fared quite as well in boarding school.

## Travails of the Foster Parents

The *Kinder* had to meet many challenges and withstand a plethora of stressful situations. It must be remembered that extensive demands were made on the foster parents as well. Patience, sympathetic understanding, and a willingness to sacrifice time and privacy are only a few of the many qualities needed. Just as the children had to adjust to different customs, so too did the foster parents have to accept their foster children's foreign ways. The youngsters who walked into their house did not speak their language, did not enjoy their food, did not own appropriate clothes. Nor did their behavior always match their foster parents' expectations. There were foster parents who had taken in children on the assumption that the parents would soon follow. With the outbreak of war, they suddenly had a new family member on their hands. Some gladly consented to keep the children indefinitely, but others felt burdened. It must have been a shock to find that a gesture of goodwill resulted in a basic change in the family constellation. Some of the foster parents were very young, in their late twenties or early thirties, when they were suddenly faced with the responsibility of bringing up children they had thought would only be temporary guests. In retrospect, Kurt[51] marvels at the wise and patient way his twenty-eight-year-old foster mother handled him when his parents were unable to follow him as planned. When Kurt looks at his own daughter, now in her late twenties, he realizes what a demanding task his foster mother undertook.

Unexpected events in the lives of the foster parents also occurred: One woman who had accepted a child became pregnant and felt overburdened; in some families members went off to war; some families were evacuated because of the bombing. It is possible that there came a point for some families when the additional guest felt burdensome. And it must have been a dilemma for parents when their own child could not adjust to the newcomer.[74] Troublesome situations arose for both foster parents and children.

Whatever foster parents had imagined, not every child was charming or engaging. Writes one correspondent:[78] "I think I probably was a rather spoiled child with unpleasant ways. The abnormal circumstances did not improve me." As every parent knows, it is infinitely easier to accept the behavior of one's own children than the neighbor's.

According to their own descriptions, a good many of the *Kinder* went through periods of feeling quite depressed. In the movies depressed children touch the heart. They look up with trusting, tear-filled eyes, and after the adult whispers a few reassuring words, they skip happily away. Reality is another matter. Depressed children do not necessarily cry. Some develop eating and sleeping disturbances, some turn rebellious, and some become withdrawn. It can take a great deal of sympathetic understanding to help a depressed child. Parents often find it an ordeal. Foster parents might have found the task quite formidable.

The foster parents who volunteered to accept children into their homes were noble of action and altruistic. Not all of them were suited for the job, and some failed without any bad intentions. One of the *Kinder*[123] remembers her friend Hanna, who had been placed with most unsuitable foster parents. One day Hanna ran away and never contacted her foster parents again. Yet while her guardians had mishandled the girl, they had obviously not done so on purpose. Many years later when they sold their house, they mentioned the story of their foster daughter's disappearance to the new owners with the thought in mind that if Hanna should ever wish to contact them, they would be traceable.

Gerda,[123] one of Mrs. Chadwick's (Trevor's mother) foster children, feels that her own guarantor was a case in point. Mrs. Chadwick had agreed to take responsibility for Gerda. It was sheer altruism that persuaded her to do so. She already had grandchildren. Gerda does not know whether Mrs. Chadwick particularly liked her. There were some rough spots in their relationship. But Gerda comments: "Who can say if anyone could do better? Certainly I have never done anything remotely as generous myself. Even given her easy circumstances, I wonder if I would have taken on such a responsibility. Because somebody does an incredibly generous deed, it does not follow that he/she will act thereafter in a continuously angelic way. It is a hard act to keep up. I sometimes think that people like Mrs. Chadwick were possibly even more heroic than those who did the actual rescuing. This letter will probably be swallowed up in some archive, but if it should ever resurface, I should like the descendants of the Chadwicks to know of my indebtedness."

Well spoken, Gerda. The foster parents were there when it counted. That must always be remembered. It is true that there were some foster parents who seemed to have been emotionally disturbed. But on the whole, the majority provided competent care. And there were many whose dedication was exemplary. Good or bad, all the foster parents were instrumental in helping the children survive. They were not always able to compensate for the extraordinary losses the children had suffered or the emotional stresses they had to withstand, but with the myriad obstacles the foster parents themselves faced it is extraordinary that the children did as well as they did. They not only survived, but they went on to successful adulthood. There were so many reasons why it could have gone the other way.

## Chapter 18

# Fragments of
# the Children's Lives

### Sunnymead: Excerpts from an Account by Fred Stevens

*The Refugee Committee's task of placing children could not have been achieved without the help of many people. Fred's journey to his first placement suggests the large number of participants, now long forgotten, who without expecting any reward, helped smooth the path to the new life the children were to travel.*

I will never forget the day I came to Thirsk and stepped from the old station bus onto the cobblestones. So this was my journey's end, and quite a journey it had been.

I had been in England for about three months in a refugee camp. The only work permit I was able to obtain was for farm work. There was nothing for it. Farm work it had to be. They gave me a train ticket and a label so that I could be identified at my destination and a tag with an address on it. I still remember it. It said "MRS. DITCHAM, THE ELMS, YORK."

This was the reason why one morning in May 1939 I found myself on a platform at Sandwich Station, boarding the train for London. I felt quite conspicuous in my German raincoat, which looked so different from everybody else's. As I left the train at Charing Cross, the people slowly melted away. There I was in that big station hall all on my own. Then I noticed him, the old man peering down the platform. He was looking for someone. It could be me. It had better be me. I went up to him and cleared my throat. To my delight it was the man from the Refugee Committee. We boarded a double-decker bus to Kings Cross, where, after putting me on an express train heading north, he said good-bye. A man pushing a refreshment trolley asked if I wanted a cup of tea, which I accepted gladly. There was little time left and the tea came in proper china cups and saucers. I asked what to do with it after I had finished. "Just put it under the seat," he said. "It will be all right." It seemed to be another quaint English custom. To this day I don't know if it was the right thing to do.

I left the train at York. I expected the farmer to meet me. Instead, a formidable, elegantly dressed lady approached me. She was definitely not a farmer's wife. She was Mrs. Ditcham, the representative of the local Refugee Committee. She put me on a local train with a ticket to Thirsk. The countryside looked very deserted. My spirits began to sink. At last the train slowed down and the sign on the platform tallied with the name on my ticket. An elderly lady awaited me who introduced herself as Miss Winifred Hall. She looked a great deal more countrified than Mrs. Ditcham, with her plump, pleasant, round face and her hair gathered in a bun. We boarded a bus for Thirsk. I glanced about me, and my spirits immediately received a sharp boost. The town looked quaint, what with its picturesque shop fronts, one of which bore the legend, "B. Smith, Britain's Oldest Draper." Not bad, I thought, not bad at all.

I followed Winifred until we reached a high stone wall. In it was a little gate, on which was written "Sunnymead." At the other side was a lovely, tidy garden and a fair-sized house, looking over a big expanse of meadow. There Winifred's sister, Isobel, greeted me. She was elderly, rather frail, with a wrinkled, pleasant face and clear, piercing blue eyes. When she talked she hardly seemed to move her lips. I could not understand her. I just said yes or no or smiled whenever I guessed it might be appropriate. The table was set for tea. The sitting room, while a little old-fashioned, was pleasantly furnished. Large oil paintings of the ladies' forebears hung on the wall. I realized that the sisters were trying to make me comfortable, but I was decidedly ill at ease. Everything around me seemed different, unfamiliar. Everything was done with a certain formality, from mending the open fire to pouring the tea.

Presently, a smallish sort of gentleman in clerical garb entered. It was the Reverend Peterson, soon to be joined by another clergyman. The Reverend Jones was a big, burly chap, with a speech defect that made him entirely incomprehensible to me. We were soon joined by Mr. Craven, a retired gentleman. They all seemed to take a great interest in me. Lastly, but rather grandly, Miss Fawcett made her entrance. She was a plain, middle-aged lady dressed in tweeds with a haughty air. She represented nobility. She did not shake my hand but simply held hers out for me to touch. The group constituted the Thirsk Refugee Committee. I was their first success. They seemed a motley crowd, like something out of a comic opera, yet as more refugees came to work on the farms, they helped us a great deal. Over time, members of the committee dropped out, but I always kept in close touch with the Misses Hall. I visited them every week, and we would have a chat and a cup of tea. They were like elderly aunts, someone to go to if I needed advice or help. They belonged to the Society of Friends and were deeply involved in charity work. For them religion had no trappings, no ceremony, yet they would help anybody they thought to be in need, without expecting any reward.

Isobel fell ill about 1942 and died, but Winifred went on un-daunted. Though I had moved away from Thirsk, I still went to see her from time to time. The war was at its height. She was a pacifist and could not reconcile herself to it. "All this killing, it's terrible!" she would exclaim. "We must do something about it!" When the war ended and she was already very frail, she still headed the appeal for clothes for the displaced people swarming over Europe. As I moved from the district, my visits decreased. Still I kept in touch until one day I got a card saying she had passed away. It is not often that I get to Thirsk now. The last time I was there the high wall was gone. The garden was no more. One solitary apple tree was left. A hospital had been built on the grounds. The house itself was still there but empty and neglected, ready to be pulled down. There is no longer room for such houses, nor perhaps for the charity that came from it. I felt rather sad. It had been a home for me. It has been a long time since I first arrived at Thirsk, but the day I came to Sunneymead remains clearly etched in my mind.

## My Diary: Excerpts from the Diary of Inga Joseph

*Inga[78] had an unusual gift. She was able to put into words exactly what she felt. She could describe to her diary what it means*

*to be unloved, melancholy, and homesick. There must have been
many little girls who felt just as she did, without anyone or anything
to speak to.*

*June 30:* I am 12-year-old Inga Pollak and you are my darling
diary to whom I'll tell everything and you'll of course keep it all to
yourself. I'm in Falmouth, Cornwall, to be precise, at the house of Mr.
and Mrs. Robert. The house is large and very nice. But something is
my constant companion. It is homesickness. It seems to me that I've
been torn out of my own warm nest, and it hurts terribly, but nobody
must know this, only you and I.

Now I must explain to you the meaning of the word *melancholy*.
It is when one doesn't feel like doing anything anymore and believes
that nothing will ever make one happy again. It is wanting to cry
all the time. It is looking forward to nothing and suffering from
homesickness and memories of the past.

*July 2:* I don't like Mrs. Robert, but Mr. Robert is nice.

*July 3:* I'm in a foreign country and no longer at home. If
someone corrects me I immediately think the worst: They want to
annoy me, they hate me. Then I tell myself: "These people are
strangers. What have they got to do with you?" But then I feel a bit
guilty and ungrateful. After all, the Roberts have done a wonderful
deed, taking two strange children [Inga and her sister, Lieselotte].
If you are miserable, you see everything in a bad light.

How I envy English children! They're able to live at home with
their parents. If Mummy had the slightest suspicion, how upset she'd
be. It hurts me to lie to her in my letters.

*July 5:* We were very worried because Mummy's letter was three
days late. I thought she might have been taken to Dachau. When her
letter came I cried with relief.

*July 7:* I've become indifferent to everything here and just keep
thinking of the future and longing for my mother to join my father in
Paris, so we can all be together again. Is everything really so terrible, or does it only seem like it to me, consumed as I am with
longing for my family and home?

*July 8:* Mrs. Robert was in a very bad mood yesterday. She always
asks me where my handkerchief is, and she keeps correcting my
English in front of other people.

*July 11:* When I die I want written on my tombstone: "Here lies a child who perished miserably from homesickness." I've no pleasure in anything. I've lost my sense of humor. I just want to go home. What worries did I have when I lived at home? School, friends, dolls, films, food, boys. I've lost my youth now. Mr. Robert took me to the doctor because of my blocked nose. Perhaps the Roberts do care about us and just can't show it?

*July 12*: Do you know how I feel today? I feel like lying on the floor in some dark corner where nobody can find me and staying there till this ghastly period ends. I can't stand Mr. R. anymore either.

*July 15*: I have a new and terrible fear: that I may be here for years, that I may have to finish school here, that I won't see my parents for a long long time.

The Roberts keep on about my blocked nose. I must try and breathe through my nose and not through my mouth. "Inga, your mouth is open!" Mrs. R. says to me the whole time. I know that the doctor, the medicine, breathing cures, all are useless. And why will nothing help me? BECAUSE I AM UNHAPPY! Can you hate somebody, and yet be a little in love with them? Well I have another confession to make to you—that's how it is with me and Mr. Robert!

*July 16*: The Roberts say I can't take my entrance exam to High School until next summer. Next summer! Another year! You just wait, one more year and you will have a sickly child on your hands, not just a healthy one with only a blocked nose.

I love Mr. Robert. He can be so charming. I think both Mr. and Mrs. R. prefer Lieselotte to me. She is a much less naughty girl than I am.

*July 17*: Last night I dreamed that my dearest wish came true—I was together with my parents and grandparents again. I didn't tell you that Mr. Robert was annoyed with us because we made a noise in the evening. Listen carefully. This is what Mr. Robert said: "Even the dogs know that there is only one master in the house, and I hope I won't have to show it to you in the way I did to them." These words pierced my heart. True, he regretted them afterwards, but I can never forgive him, even though I love him.

Yesterday we spoke about Hitler and Germany with the Roberts. Mr. R.: "Why did you come to England if you had enough to eat?" Lieselotte: "But we could not live there. Haven't you heard about November 10?" Mr. R.: "Oh I see." He found it impossible to understand, but looked sad. I wouldn't believe it either if I hadn't experienced it.

*July 19*: My fleeting love for Mr. R. has disappeared, though sometimes when I look at him it comes flooding back for a moment. When he is not here for meals, I hardly say a word, but when he is, I chatter away all the time.

*August 17*: When I was alone at home I saw an open letter from Mummy to Mr. Robert. I read it. I shall never love Mr. Robert again, never, never! I read the following: "Dear Sir, I am very glad that my children are well and happy with you. I am pleased that you like Lieselotte so much and I hope this will soon be the case with Inga too. She is an affectionate, bright and cheerful child and usually very popular." How could Mr. Robert write to my mother saying he didn't like me. It must have hurt her terribly. Am I such a bad specimen of humanity?

Mrs. R. actually said today that I have begun to speak English well. I hope she will write and tell Mummy. My heart is so heavy that it feels as if a gigantic stone was attached to it. All my sorrows are in that stone: Will I ever see my parents again? Will I pass the entrance exam? Shall I ever speak English properly? Will the Roberts ever like me? These worries feel as if a million worms are gnawing away in my stomach.

*August 19*: But I do love him still! He is so charming when he smiles. The Rs' relations said: "You are their adopted nieces." Please never say that again! We are not your children. We belong to our parents, and they won't give us to you, not ever.

*August 20*: I have very bad manners. I am spoiled. That is my observation for today.

*August 21*: The present is a luminous ball. Behind it—the past; in front—the future. The whole soars in total darkness and reels to and fro. Below there is an abyss, above—vapor. It is pitch-dark. Either the ball crashes, then all is lost. Or it glides into the future and that means hope. Which way is it going? We mortals can't influence it. We await our fate.

All the Roberts ever think about are dogs, garden, and weather. Think of it—a 12-year-old girl has more worries than the grown-ups. When I was at home. Mummy always kissed and comforted me when I had something on my mind (what on earth could I have had on my mind?). But now there is nobody.

*August 25*: Lieselotte has become homesick. She says she has had enough of living in strangers' houses. The further the good old days slip back into the past, the more vivid their memory becomes. I am still in love with Mr. Robert—but not all the time.

*September 4*: I was too upset to write yesterday. I went downstairs and met Lieselotte running up to our room. "Do you understand what has happened?" Mr. Robert asked me. "No," I said. "War has been declared," he said. I ran out of the room. In the bedroom Lieselotte was lying on the bed, crying hysterically. I began to cry too. We talked for a long time and looked at the photograph of our parents. I marked the date on the calendar with a black ring.

*September 8*: The Roberts took me to the optician yesterday. There may be something wrong with my eye muscles. Mr. R. says it's my fault because I don't move my eye muscles enough and always turn my head instead of my eyes. To think that a forty-year-old man can talk such nonsense.

*September 17*: Dear Diary, we must say goodbye. I am sorry I had to begin and end in such an unhappy mood. I am starting school at Miss Davis, so I won't have much time to write. Lieselotte has decided to speak only English from now on. I don't know when I will continue to write, but one day I will. I have loved you very much and am sorry I had so many sad things to relate.

Inga never saw her parents again. However, she is happily married and has a family of her own.

## The Throw of the Dice

### First Impressions

*When the children left the ferries in Harwich, they were without parents, money, or language; all more or less equally helpless. Their happiness in the next few years would to a large extent depend on the kind of home in which they were placed. There was no favoritism shown. It all depended on the throw of the dice. Luck, which had been an important factor in getting away from the Nazi menace, would again be pivotal in determining each Kind's destiny. Four children, all between fourteen and fifteen years of age, arrived within a short period of each other. Owing to their widely different placements, their experiences would soon materially diverge and their lives would have little in common. In some ways their initial reception fore-shadowed events to come. However, the signs were too subtle for the children to discern. Their expectations were based on their previous experiences with their own parents. Sometimes slowly, sometimes quickly, they realized that they had been transported into a different world.*

*Bea's*[59] first contacts with her foster family occurred with style. Fourteen-year-old Bea was met by her sponsor's daughter, Estelle, and was driven by a chauffeur to Brasted Hall in Kent. Arriving at a large house, she was greeted with a formal kiss by her sponsor, dignified Mrs. Wilson. The billiard room had been converted into a suite of rooms for Bea. She was conducted there by the chamber-maid, who addressed her as "Miss." For a girl from a middle-class Jewish Austrian home, this was heady stuff.

*Bertha*[105] and her brother, who had been brought up in a religious family, had left their parents and little sister behind. At fifteen years of age, Bertha felt responsible for her twelve-year-old brother, Theo. The two had been placed with a couple in Coventry. When Bertha arrived, her heart sank. She noticed that there was no mezuzah (Jewish symbol) on the door, and she knew she was not in a Jewish family. She did not want to stay. Having neither the address of the Committee nor any knowledge of English, she had no option. She felt lost. How lost became evident with time.

*Eric*[35] took his journey in stride. He had a wonderful capacity for quick adjustment. Quartered at Dovercourt, he noted that there was a capable staff in charge and that he had a roof over his head. He appreciated being invited to tea by a local family, though he felt strange throughout—what with his not understanding the lady of the house and sandwiches, so unlike the ones in Germany, served on white bread with, would you believe it, asparagus on them! In a composition called "My First Impression of England" Eric wrote: "My first impression of England was a very foggy one." He was not sure why the lady smiled as she read his story.

*Ruth.*[184] After arriving in Harwich, all the children on the train were picked up by ladies from the Refugee Committee, put on a train to London, and then separated into groups. Those children who were to live with families were quickly picked up by them. Ruth's group of about twenty children continued their journey on a blacked-out train to Abergale, located in Wales near the Irish Sea. Hours later they arrived, exhausted, and were met by a Jewish doctor who led them in the dark up a long, winding, hilly road to their new home. It was a castle! A genuine castle from the year who knows what. But it had no furniture, no water, no toilets, no electric lights. The children lay down on the floor to sleep. They woke up to total bedlam.

### First Adjustment

*A new era was now about to begin in the children's lives. For good or ill, they would be required to make a great many adjustments.*

BEA: First there was the food to get used to. Bea felt it strange to hold her fork upside down and push food onto it, to keep her hands on her lap between mouthfuls, and to eat spaghetti or drippings on toast. Tea time with buttered toast or crumpets was a nice new experience. One had to remember never to ask for anything at the table; that was considered rude. Bea insisted on going to school immediately, though there were only a few weeks left before the summer holidays, and so she was sent to a small private school. Of course, she did not own the typical English schoolgirl uniform: white shirt, pleated black or dark green jumper, and tie. Bea was undaunted. She wore a dirndl and good-naturedly accepted the smiles of her fellow classmates.

In spite of the glamor and adventure of the new setting, Bea felt homesick. She hoped her homesickness would wear off quickly. It didn't. But she had made a start in her new life, which was as much as could possibly be hoped for.

BERTHA: While Bea was absorbing upper-class English life, Bertha's early weeks were discouraging. Aunt Val's and Uncle Willy's crude comments set a very low tone in the house. Bertha refrained from commenting. She was eager for her foster parents to sponsor her sister Inge, who was still in Germany. Her foster father was willing to do so, provided Inge did not have red hair. He had a redheaded daughter by his first marriage and did not want to be reminded of her. Bertha assured him that her sister's hair color was similar to her own. When redheaded Inge arrived, Uncle Willy was furious and told Bertha off in no uncertain terms. Bertha merely answered, "I was not truthful, because I did not want to endanger my sister's life."

Bertha was treated fairly adequately in the beginning. But little by little her situation worsened: "One gets to be a slave slowly. First I was treated like a guest. The lady did the dishes and I wiped. The next day I washed and she wiped. The next day I washed and I wiped. Soon I was doing all the housework." Bertha was not allowed to go to school nor to fraternize with Jewish children. She was sent some clothes by relatives, clothes Aunt Val immediately appropriated. Bertha's wardrobe was getting threadbare, but she did own a winter coat. When it got soiled, Aunt Val forbade Bertha to send it to the cleaners. Over the girl's objections, she insisted the coat be washed. From then on, Bertha had no coat. Occasionally she was permitted to attend religious services. When she was invited by a Jewish family for Passover, she was reminded of her former home and found it painful to return to her new one.

Uncle Willy and Aunt Val were unable to have children of their own. While they treated Bertha as an indentured servant, they were more receptive to her younger brother, Theo, and to Inge. They even wanted to adopt the little girl, but Bertha would not permit it. Bertha would have liked to leave but she could not abandon Inge. Bertha was trapped.

ERIC: Eric meanwhile was moving toward a position of greater stability. He was assigned a job and a family, in Wellingborough, a small industrial town. On their arrival Eric and his friend Eddie found a very friendly couple, Mr. and Mrs. Weedon, who welcomed them to their small cottage. Sleeping quarters were a bit uncomfortable, with the boys having to share a bed. A job in a shoe factory had been arranged through the committee that looked after the refugee children. The family could not have treated the boys more solicitously, but there were always little signs that they were not in their own homes. Every morning motherly Mrs. Weedon lovingly prepared an English breakfast consisting of porridge, salty bacon, and eggs. The boys were not used to such fare but were too polite to seem anything but grateful. They finally found a solution: "We carefully secreted the bacon into a paper bag, which we held open under the breakfast table. We then stuffed it into our pullover and on the way to work threw it into some bushes. One morning we were caught red-handed." It speaks volumes for Mrs. Weedon that, far from being angry, she was highly amused—and so was the rest of the family.

RUTH: It soon became evident that the castle was to be more than a temporary home to the children. Besides the doctor, who could not yet practice legally in Britain, there were few adults around. Mostly, the 150 children had to do everything themselves. Ruth was among the older ones. The children began by investigating their romantic setting. They found a huge antiquated kitchen in the bowels of the castle and a large number of rooms upstairs, which became their bedrooms.

Meals consisted mostly of bread, butter, and the unfamiliar but ever-present porridge. Although the boys foraged for twigs and wood for the fireplaces, the indoor temperature remained chilly. They had brought very few clothes with them. Through the committee they received some old clothes; they salvaged a sewing machine from somewhere and fashioned new, though not necessarily warm, clothes out of the old.

Ruth assisted the doctor, who ran a dispensary. Sadly, some children became seriously ill. They developed infections caused by the unsanitary conditions and a deplorable water supply. David, a boy of fourteen, became sick with rheumatic heart disease and died in a Liverpool hospital. Ruth too was struck down by rheumatic fever. Since no antibiotics existed, the only treatment was bed rest. In spite of David's death, it never occurred to Ruth that she too might die. She merely felt immense relief at being able to stay in bed to overcome her intense fatigue.

## The Passing Years

*As the months went by, the lives of the children remained in constant flux owing to wartime conditions and problems in the foster families. The four youngsters were developing in markedly different directions.*

BEA: Bea's foster mother, Mrs. Wilson, became ill. As a result, Bea was shifted from day pupil to boarder at school. She had minor complaints: The dormitories were cold and the food was awful. There were also aspects that were quite different from her former school in Germany. For instance, the English children always sang jolly songs. Bea missed classical music and thought it did not exist in England. Her main task was to adapt to English life of a fairly privileged nature. When Mrs. Wilson died, her oldest son, Colonel Wilson, and his wife took responsibility for Bea. She went to live with them at Itchen Abbas House near Winchester. To Bea, Uncle's and Auntie's manner of talking sounded somewhat as if they were in a stage play. In addition, Auntie was a bit of a snob, but because she thought Bea had come out of top drawer, albeit a German Jewish one, the young girl passed muster. One day the school in Kent suffered a direct bomb hit. Fortunately, there were no injuries, but the pupils were evacuated to Wales. The girls took turns cooking, cleaning, and teaching the smaller children. The older children proceeded with their studies mostly by correspondence. Bea absorbed Welsh country life. The farmers liked the girls, and in turn Bea liked them. She cycled to the farms to round up extra butter to add to the students' rations. One farmer showed his affection by naming two kittens after the girls. A high point for citified Bea was rescuing an abandoned lamb and carrying it to a farmhouse.

Bea worried about her parents, particularly when the letters she had been receiving through the Red Cross stopped coming. In 1941 she received a telegram from Irkutsk that her parents had left Germany on the Trans-Siberian Railway and were on their way to Peru. They were safe, after all! Bea resumed living with Auntie and Uncle and found life was pleasant. She remembers the big house, her freedom to run everywhere, and hiding in an apple tree with a book and staying there all morning. She could be herself and her foster family found her charming. Of course, she was not ever really naughty. The only naughty thing she ever did was to read a Somerset Maugham book Uncle had forbidden. She felt secure with her guardians but not exactly with the same unquestioning confidence she had felt with her parents. Looking back she reflects, "I suppose I hoped I was in their good books in a way one doesn't think about it with one's parents. One knows one is in one's parents' good books."

Still, the rhythm at Itchen Abbas House was a very satisfying one. In spite of the rationing, there were few food problems. They had trout from the river Itchen and salmon from Scotland, and Uncle also shot partridge and pheasants. They also had cooked English vegetables. (The less said about those, the better.) Bea also did her best to help the war effort: She sorted wastepaper and gathered wild daffodils, which she sold in bunches, sending the proceeds to headquarters for the war effort.

Bea's best times were with Colonel Wilson. He taught her to fish. She was not very good at it. No matter. She was quite happy to watch Uncle tie flies, carry the net, and ask him questions about life, such as "How do you decide between right and wrong?" Uncle's practical answer: "Make a list with two columns, for and against. Put the moral points at the head. Then look at the list and weigh them up and decide." Nice man. Bea liked the colonel and knew it was mutual. While she was not as close to Auntie, she got along quite well with her. In fact, once, when the Wilson's younger son was killed while serving in the air force, Auntie actually said to her that she considered Bea like a daughter.

Auntie and Uncle continued to pay for Bea's education. Mrs. Wilson had left some money in trust for good works, and Bea's university fees came under that category. Bea wrote her foster parents from the university to tell them how much she appreciated their help. In turn, they appreciated being thanked by Bea.

BERTHA: Bertha's life seemed to be the diametric opposite of Bea's. Life with Aunt Val and Uncle Willy became increasingly oppressive. Refugee Committee members called on the family once a year, but they spoke to the children in front of their foster parents and the youngsters were too terrified to reveal their true circumstances. Conventry was being bombed, and while Aunt Val and Uncle Willy repaired nightly to a bomb shelter, they insisted that the children, being German, would not be accepted there and should remain at home. Theo accidentally stepped into a hole made by an incendiary bomb and injured his ankle. Aunt Val called him a crybaby and refused to take him to a doctor. It was not until Val's mother finally insisted that Theo be examined that it was determined that his ankle was broken. The family was bombed out twice and subsequently evacuated to Yorkshire. The children did not profit by that change. In fact, they—and Bertha in particular—were by now reduced to a Cinderella status. They ate in the kitchen except when visitors came. Aunt Val harassed Bertha in many ways, for example, by insisting that the girl only bathe in Val's used bathwater. And Bertha was not allowed to use the house toilet but was sent to use one located across a field.

Bertha started to work in a cotton mill. She was a good worker and earned a good wage. Because Aunt Val always "borrowed" from her, Bertha gave up keeping any money. Val also told the children not to tell the Refugee Committee about Bertha's pay. What happened to the money sent by the committee was not discussed. When Bertha's clothes wore out, she was reduced to stealing some panties from Val. She no longer had shoes but wore wooden clogs. She used rags for sanitary towels. Once, when their foster parents went away, money had to be left with the children; the three went out and bought themselves a delicious meal of eggs and beans, which they devoured in style.

Luck had been most unkind to Bertha by placing her with Val and Willy. But she had won in the most important lottery of all—the one that fate was playing with the lives of millions of Jews. Bertha learned that her parents were alive and in Portugal, but she had no money even for stamps. She began to darn socks for lodgers in order to be able to correspond with her parents.

Bertha missed the kosher food and the candles on Friday nights. She now realized how much religion meant to her and never doubted the existence of God. She decided that until she was reunited with her parents, she would make sure that her brother and sister would remember the traditions. She talked to them about how the holidays used to be celebrated, recited the holy prayer *Shema Israel* with them, and taught her sister to read Hebrew.

There was one excruciating aspect of living with Uncle Willy: He showed an excessive interest in Bertha. The teenage girl was turning into a pretty young woman. There was friction between husband and wife. Bertha found it odd when Val told her how much Uncle Willy liked her. Bertha answered, "Well, I don't like him," but she began to watch out for her little sister and told her brother of her apprehensions. He assured her that from now on he would sleep with his scout knife at his side and would come immediately if Bertha called him.

ERIC: Eric was far luckier than Bertha. He was in a solid household that blended well with his optimistic personality. Mr. and Mrs. Weedon could not have been nicer had they been family. It was true that in spite of his foster parents' solicitude, he still missed his parents, his mother in particular. But it helped to know that his father had escaped to Holland. The Dutch interned his father at Westerbork, but he was not mistreated there. Eric felt gratified that he was able to send his father money from time to time. When the Germans invaded Holland, Westerbork was turned into a concentration camp. News from Germany and from his father ceased.

Eric's life had a sober, bourgeois quality. He and his friend Eddie left their house at seven in the morning. They stomped to work through the dark and the snow, reaching the factory just in time to don their working aprons. When the foreman pressed the button, the entire system was set in motion with a dull, ominous roar. Every ten to twenty seconds a hideous screeching whine was produced, which still echoes in Eric's memory. When war started, the working day increased from eight to twelve hours, including Sundays; most weeks the boys worked seventy-two hours. The Weedons continued in their friendly way. The more Eric got to know them, the better he liked them. Mr. Weedon would take the boys to the pub and teach them to play darts. On Sundays the family would take walks together. The boys felt they could turn to Mrs. Weedon for advice and talk to her on any subject whatsoever. Eric needed that. He was, after all, only fifteen. Eric's life with the Weedons ended suddenly in June 1940. The area Eric was living in had become restricted to "friendly aliens." Mr. Cheney, Eric and Eddie's boss, called the boys into his office. He was sorry he said, but he could no longer employ them. In his opinion sending foreigners away from Wellingborough was nonsensical. Nevertheless, he paid them their last wages and let them go.

The boys decided to return to London, where the Movement for the Care of Children had its offices. Eric felt sorry but, to his surprise, also relieved to leave. Wellingborough was a small, backward industrial town; London promised to open up new vistas. The boys were in London only three weeks when the police phoned and told them that they were going to be interned; they were to pack their belongings and be ready to leave the next day at 2 P.M. Punctually at the appointed time a paddy wagon drew up, and the young men climbed in. Eric did not know it, but he was about to be deported on the high and heavily mined seas to Australia. The story of Eric's arduous trip to Australia and his lengthy confinement there under the most primitive conditions will be told in a later chapter. Suffice it to say that Eric, with his usual good-natured and optimistic outlook, took in his stride even this sudden change, which seriously upset a good many other deportees.

RUTH: Ruth continued her solitary struggle. She was on her own, and, as she had always done, she marshaled her resources and carried on. Fortune had been consistent: She had been in an orphanage in Germany, and she continued to live in one in England. The difference was the absence of her brother and sister. They had not qualified for the *Kindertransport* on which Ruth had left Germany. They and the matron had been the only ones to accompany her to the train. When her sister said good-bye, she presented Ruth with her most prized possession: her watch. Ruth still has it after all these years. Ruth missed her sister and her brother dreadfully.

Ruth continued at the castle for two years. The boys and girls, except for separate sleeping quarters, lived a communal kind of life. The adults seemed preoccupied with their own difficult affairs; they gave only minimum guidance, certainly none that dealt with the youngsters' emotional lives. No schooling was provided. The young people spent a great deal of time together, and strong emotional and sometimes physical relationships resulted. There was one pregnancy; it is a wonder there were not more. Ruth had lived in an orphanage in Germany and had learned how to handle herself. She did what she had always done: She lived in a group, but at the same time she lived by herself. She had one friend, Mary, who was much like her. The two girls started to read whatever they could lay their hands on. This helped them both a great deal.

Ruth was sixteen when the community at the castle was dissolved; she was sent to a hostel in Birmingham. Ruth had become a dressmaker, but since material was rationed there were no jobs available. She was now living on her savings. She limited herself to one real meal a day, which was dinner, usually fish and chips. Breakfast was tea and a slice of toast. There was rent to pay for the room. Ruth managed to make a little money by doing alterations. Her financial position was worrisome but survivable. She partook of cultural events when inexpensive tickets could be obtained, but she felt disconnected and lonely. Her emotional center was missing. Ruth did not know whether that stemmed from her difficult childhood in the Munich orphanage or from her present life. Perhaps both played a part.

## The Later Years

BEA: The war was over. In 1947 Bea's mother obtained passage to England. When Bea went to meet her, she felt apprehensive. After all, she had left her parents as a child and now she was a married woman. She took her mother to Itchen Abbas and worried whether her guardians would like her. Bea felt embarrassed. Her mother seemed out of place.

Bea's marriage did not last; she felt sure that her reason for having married was the desire for a home of her own. She joined her parents for a two-year stay in Peru and got to know them as an adult. She had a wonderful time with them, telling them about her youth, and helping to build a bungalow for themselves, the first decent housing they had had since they left Munich. Her father began to practice law again and represented clients from Peru in Germany. He was also the acting rabbi of the German Jewish community in Lima. The change in roles from a foster child of Itchen Abbas to a rabbi's daughter in Lima was quite a challenge for Bea, but she was happy with the change. She liked the social aspects of going to the synagogue.

After her mother died and her father came to visit her in England, Bea got to know him well and found that they had a very similar cast of mind. Bea remarried, studied languages, and worked as a translator. She is now retired from her position as senior lecturer in the communications department of a college. She also became a magistrate and sits with professional judges in Crown Court on appeal cases.

BERTHA: In the winter of 1943/1944, on her twenty-first birthday, Bertha's parents suddenly appeared at Aunt Val's house from Portugal, filled with gratitude and loaded with presents for the foster parents. Not wanting to worry her parents, Bertha had never written about her difficulties. At first nothing negative was mentioned. Bertha shared her bed with her mother that night, and they began to talk and talk. Suddenly, all of Bertha's emotions burst forth, and she told much of the story to her horrified mother. There was a terrible scene the next morning. The parents took the children away, and Bertha felt she had been saved. She never told her parents about Uncle Willy; she was afraid of what her father might do if he knew the full situation.

ERIC: When Eric was released from internment, he joined the Australian army. After discharge he remained in Australia. As an ex-serviceman, he was entitled to a living allowance and free tuition. In the course of his studies at the University of Melbourne he met Judith, an Australian girl, fell in love with her, and married her. They both became teachers.

RUTH: At war's end Ruth hoped to hear from her brother and sister. She felt sure at least one of them had survived, but she was unable to obtain any information. She took some tests and qualified for a job in Germany as a civilian employee with the U.S. State Department. She immediately got in touch with the Munich authorities. Within two weeks Ruth had a reply from the then-elderly doctor who had issued her a health certificate when she left Germany in 1939. He himself had survived the camps. He informed her that to his great sorrow none of her relatives had survived. It was the worst day of Ruth's life. She had been so sure that at least one of them would make it. Ruth was so disturbed by the news that she wanted to leave Germany immediately, but she was obligated to remain by contract. By chance, she met some young Jewish refugees who had been hidden in Holland by gentiles during the war years. Ruth and these young people emigrated to the United States. In New York Ruth first worked in the garment district, then for a Dutch company on Wall Street, and subsequently in a hospital. Ruth married one of her Dutch friends and had a son.

## The Aftermath

Though the *Kinder*'s paths had diverged sharply when they arrived in England, as Eric, Bertha, Ruth, and Bea settled into middle age, their styles of living were not as disparate as before. They had all achieved middle-class, comfortable lives, had families, and in one form or another still valued cultural pursuits. And in one more aspect, a very important one indeed, there is a similarity: Emotionally, they are not entirely free of the consequences of their experiences. Some traces still remain. These appear more or less strongly at different times with each of them.

BERTHA: When Bertha reminisces she can still experience that intense hopelessness she felt when she lived with Aunt Val and Uncle Willy. She has never quite regained a sense of total trust toward others. A feeling of being "different" accompanies her. Yet it was Bertha who organized the first *Kinder* reunion in 1989, the fiftieth anniversary of the *Kinder*'s arrival in England. This reunion renewed her sense of belonging. She remarks, "I had not realized how many of the former *Kinder* did not have a proper identity [until the reunion]. At the reunion we proclaimed it, were proud of it, and now feel that we belong to a band of people."

ERIC: Eric could not put his past to rest. In 1958 he took the unusual step of finding a temporary job in his city of birth, Düsseldorf. He felt odd and apprehensive upon his arrival, hearing German spoken all around him. Over time his sensitivity decreased somewhat, though he never felt comfortable in the company of those over thirty years old. He already knew that twenty-seven of his closest relatives had been deported and murdered during the war. He found an aunt, sixty-seven years old, who recalled the exact day his mother and all the Jews of Düsseldorf had to assemble. It was November 8, 1941. Tante Röschen, at great danger to herself, accompanied her sister, Eric's mother, to the appointed place. His mother adopted a positive attitude, "Ach," she said, "they are only sending us to work somewhere in the east." Tante Röschen had been deeply impressed by her sister's courage. Since it is estimated that little more than half the deportees reached Minsk, Eric could not determine whether his mother was still alive on her birthday, February 2, 1942; she would then have been forty-two years old. Tante Röschen gave Eric the letters his father had sent her from Holland, in which his father still held out some hope of seeing his family again. He did not know that his wife was already dead; he himself was deported in 1944 to Auschwitz. Eric's account ends with these words: "I shall never forget my beloved parents as long as I live."

RUTH: When Ruth thinks of the past's effect—and she does this quite often—she concludes that her self-confidence was shaken because at crucial times in her life she did not have any emotional backing. She often thinks of her brother, who was murdered in a concentration camp at 14. She cannot fathom this loss. Whenever she goes to a new city, she still looks in the telephone book for his name. Recently, she received an unexpected phone call from a woman who said her name was Inge. Ruth's heart stood still. Her sister's name had been Inge, but it was not her sister calling. When Ruth reflects on her past it brings back disturbing thoughts. In spite of this, and at her son's urging, Ruth wrote a detailed account of her past at my request. Her son has made her life worthwhile.

BEA: And what about Bea? Her life had been relatively very easy. Did she get off scot-free? "I always thought that I had been very fortunate, till my sons reached the age of fourteen when I was appalled at thinking that I had to leave home at that age." In 1983, on a brief visit to Germany, she was suddenly overcome by profound anguish and began to weep. She explains: "In writing it all down, I think I gained insight into that deep sadness that overcame me in the *Bierkeller* [beer hall] in Munich in 1983. I think I wept over an irretrievable loss in adolescence that was twofold: the loss of normal growing up and becoming independent from one's parents, and for me 'home' being an idea rather than a place. When you feel like being a bit nostalgic, you are retrieving a part of your past. But with our experiences, there is a gap in our normal development that has to be accepted. It cannot be retrieved, because there is nothing there to retrieve. I do have a very good Welsh woman friend and spoke with her. 'Ah,' my friend said, 'There is a word for that in Welsh. It is *hiraeth* and it means a longing for things past. It is not equivalent to nostalgia, which is usually a deliberate indulgence of sorts, but it steals upon you, does *hiraeth*. And it isn't grief. And it's nearly always associated with a place rather than people. But it could be people.' We decided that the Welsh soul and the Jewish soul must have something in common. Irretrievable loss is what I felt. I think it was perhaps brought on by the smell and the familiar sounds as much as by the sights at the time."

*Hiraeth*. Yes, that's it. For those of us who have had irretrievable losses, there is no escaping *hiraeth*.


## We Two:
## Excerpts from Accounts by Ruth and Martin Michaelis

*Placement was a vital factor in the children's adjustment. Equally important were the children's personalities. The same events were interpreted by the children in highly individualistic ways and in turn triggered diverse reactions from their caretakers. The stories of Ruth and Martin, who left their parents together and lived with the same families, illustrate this point. The two children sifted events through very distinct personalities. Therefore, their separate accounts are at once similar and yet quite different. I have woven their stories together, while allowing them each to speak their own words.*

The journey had been endless and confusing. Four-year-old Ruth, seven-year-old Martin, and their mother had ridden on a *Kindertransport* train. Then the big ship was so loaded with passengers and suitcases that Ruth was sure it would not float. She remembers being put in the upper bunk. When she exclaimed that she felt sick, her mother peeked out from the lower bunk and Ruth threw up all over her. Through the train window she saw big buses. They frightened her because she had never seen red ones before. Aside from those buses, England seemed no different from Germany to Ruth. So why had they not just stayed home?

Their mother delivered Martin and Ruth to a strange house. Martin's first impression was of a wall calendar in the home of his future foster parents. The names of the weekdays were strange, and Martin recalls thinking "Funny country. But if that's what they want me to do, I will have to learn new ways." Ruth's mother put her to bed and explained that she was going back to Germany to settle some business affairs. All Ruth understood was that her mother was leaving her. Soon her brother and she would be alone with their foster parents.

There was one more contact with the family. Their father passed through England and took Martin to London with him. Ruth felt panic: Her mother had disappeared; now her brother was gone. She was sure Martin would not return. Martin did return, but their father traveled on to Shanghai. Their mother, who was Christian, remained in Germany.

The children had been lodged with Reverend Strang, the rector, and his wife. The rector was a kindly man; Ruth always felt safe on their long walks together. Ruth liked her English lessons. They made sense to her, and she could understand what was wanted of her. The rest of the time she was puzzled as to why everyone was continually cross with her.

And, indeed, they were very cross. Mrs. Strang had never taken care of children; she had none of her own. It was true that she kept the children clean. But she became ruthless when she perceived infractions of her rules, and punishment was unusually severe. The children were beaten, not in a rage, but in the sincere belief that such punishment was just and necessary to train children to behave properly. When Ruth wet her bed, Mrs. Strang would beat her with a leather strap. Ruth had to sleep on her stomach because of the welts on her back. She did not want to wet the bed. She would walk to the toilet, feeling the cold floor under the soles of her feet and the cold rim of the toilet seat. And then she would wake up and realize she had dreamed it all. And the bed would be wet again.

It must have been very difficult to keep the bed dry. Martin remembers the Strang's rule about going to the toilet: "It was considered naughty not to do this immediately when getting up in the morning or to want to do it at any other time. Since we had the greatest difficulty complying with this most peculiar concept, we were given a mug of senna pod tea against constipation every morning, which simply made us chronically ill. We constantly had the urge to go to the toilet but were unable to produce anything once there, which led to more punishment. I resolved to secretly pour away my tea every morning and did the same with my sister's. We began to go to the toilet secretly in the garden, mainly out of sight near the rubbish dump. For myself this rapidly brought complete recovery; for my sister, unfortunately, less so."

The problem of the senna pod tea was one of the many times Martin would take matters into his own hands and find a solution. Indeed, Ruth adored her brother and always looked to him for solutions. Frequently, he was able to provide them. There was, for example, the matter of deprivation of food for small infractions. These episodes remain etched in Martin's memory: "My sister suffered from deprivation of food more intensely than I because she was punished this way more than I was. This got to a state where I had to intervene. In the middle of the night I got up, fetched the big torch [flashlight] from the hall, went to the larder, raided it for food and drink, and had a feast with my sister. I cannot understand why we were never caught since the amount of food missing from the larder was quite large."

The children were permitted little playtime but were set to work weeding the garden for what was essentially a full working day. They were kept at opposite ends of the garden and were not permitted to speak with one another. But Martin found a way of making the tortuous hours more tolerable. His solution was directly connected with a new philosophy he had begun to evolve, one that he continued to develop for the rest of his life. Between the ages of seven and nine years, Martin made a conscious decision: He would build an inner life for himself that would be immune to the arbitrary influence of adults. He would filter all communications from the outer world, the world of his foster parents, through this inner world. And he came to a conclusion: "You must learn to fend and think for yourself. Do not expect others to spoon-feed you. Find ways of helping yourself (and others on the way if you can). Act without talking unnecessarily about it, so as not to let others know what you are really up to. Because if they find out, they will interfere to an intolerable extent, upsetting the adjustments you have achieved. Secrecy is important. Think and decide for yourself whether what you are doing is right and justified. And then just do what you have decided to do."

He began to apply his insights to the weeding problem. He became ingenious about arranging trysts without getting caught:

"The gardener showed me how to make sundials by putting bits of sticks into the soil. We soon had these sticks distributed throughout the large garden. I passed my knowledge on to my sister so that she too could read the time accurately on these sundials. Wherever we worked, there was always one nearby. We agreed to wheel our barrows to a rubbish dump at certain times of the day and meet there to play, at the end of the only dense area of trees. If anyone approached, we had plenty of early warning to get back to the barrows and emerge from the woods on different paths. My sister and I were able to meet when we wanted to throughout the day without the adults' interference.

"There was continual interference with regard to how we ought to play. This went as far as arbitrarily taking away (forever) toys they thought we were not playing with 'correctly.' The effect this had on me was simply to react by not developing any interest at all in the toys, as they seemed to be too unstable to become attached to. Instead, we developed our own toys. The adults knew nothing about these and thus could not interfere. We declared plots of soil near the hidden rubbish dump as 'our territory,' imagining roads and cities on them and playing all sorts of games related to them."

Because of the inner world he had begun to construct, Martin was able to distance himself from the unpleasant aspects of his surroundings. But there was a cost. He recalls: "There was no deliberate seclusion from other people on my part. But I was so absorbed in my inner world that any deep conscious awareness of other people and any feeling of a need to integrate with them was virtually nonexistent. This made me highly introverted throughout childhood and, as a result, for the whole of my life thereafter."

Ruth, on the other hand, had found no such solution for herself. She was miserable. She longed to be picked up on someone's lap, to be cuddled, to feel the contact of warm skin. She did not dare protest with tantrums but expressed her frustrations by gathering all the little figures from her dollhouse and putting them into the waste-paper basket. After she had done this several times, the dollhouse was taken away. Martin was aware that his sister's reactions were different from his: "My sister took accusations of being naughty seriously and went to great pains to please the adults, driven by the powerful fear of being abandoned. Her efforts were largely futile. I, on the other hand, lived more withdrawn in my inner world, which appeared odd and frightening to the families we lived with. Ruth says that she expected me to find a way to cope with every situation and that she could not have stuck it out if we had been separated."

No one ever came from the Refugee Committee in London to check on the children. But Ruth feels sure that even if they had, she would never have complained. There were many opportunities to confide in sympathetic teachers, but she feared retribution. When Ruth turned six, the Strangs sent the children to a Quaker boarding school, which became a haven for them. Ruth discovered a capacity to excel and was astonished to find that she was way ahead of the other children in kindergarten. The teachers cured her bed-wetting overnight by simply telling her it did not matter. Ruth had fun at school. She hated the holidays at the Strangs.

Martin also profited by the school placement. He always adjusted better at school than at the various foster placements. Over the years he pondered the reason: "The highly introverted nature I had developed at the Strangs enabled me to cope at school and prevented me from becoming a victim to any unbearable extent. Other pupils must have found me very odd in ways related to my introverted behavior. But in general my problems were not fundamentally different from other boys, whose backgrounds had nothing to do with the exodus from Hitler's Germany. The attention paid to the individual is less direct and less intense in a boarding school than it is in a nuclear family. In the setting of a school the individual has a greater chance of getting on without interference."

Then, quite suddenly, the children's lives underwent a radical shift. They were informed that the rector had been taken ill. The children were to spend the summer at a children's home in London until other foster parents could be found. Ruth felt immense relief.

On arrival, Ruth and Martin were quite baffled at seeing hundreds of children running all over the place. At eight and eleven years of age, they were left to look after themselves. Martin recalls: "We could do as we liked, with no supervision as to whether it was safe and healthy. There were some adults around, but they just popped in and out without any apparent influence." The extent of the dirt and neglect was appalling. Ruth soon became sick and had periodic fainting spells, which continued for the rest of the time she was there. Martin has good cause to remember: "We spent most of the first few weeks playing in a meadow flooded with water containing sewage. I gradually became extremely ill with what turned out to be severe hepatitis. Over a period of several weeks my strength gradually diminished. It could take me more than half an hour to go up a single flight of stairs to the bedroom, resting on each step. No doctor was called. For the next weeks I could only stay in bed, hardly able to move." Martin had protected Ruth in the past. Now it became Ruth's turn to minister to him. She mopped his brow and helped him to the toilet. He was convinced that if he ate an apple a day he would recover. Ruth managed to find a lady with a baby who gave her a few pennies for her two little dolls, enabling her to buy the apples. Martin has not forgotten Ruth's dedication: "My sister spent hours reading books to me, which I heard from a world gradually becoming more distant. I felt myself in a very long, dark pipe with a tiny spot of light at the far end, from which her voice seemed to be coming. At this state she or somebody finally called a doctor. His diagnosis was that I had been close to death but had coped with it through my own physical resources. Within a day or two of the doctor's visit all the other children disappeared."

As soon as Martin was sufficiently recovered, the children were sent to their second set of foster parents, the Dobsons. Ruth was pleased with her new placement. There were five children in the house, three of them girls. While the boys were under Mr. Dobson's supervision, Mrs. Dobson took charge of the girls. Ruth's new foster mother was firm and demanding, but she also had a gentle manner. The children quite frequently heard from their father via the Red Cross but never from their mother. Ruth concluded that her mother was dead. Today Ruth feels that she declared her mother dead because that belief made her absence bearable.

Mr. Dobson, a parson, was a complex person. Martin found him to be a devoted Christian and a hardworking man. The Dobsons' close family life impressed Martin deeply: "The Dobsons produced a powerful inward flow of ideas which I incorporated into my inner world. Here was born my deep desire to marry when the time came." But there was another side to the parson. Ruth noticed that he could be very harsh. Sometimes he walloped the boys. In addition, the parson could be very narrow-minded and puritanical. Martin was roughly eleven when he first ran afoul of the parson: "The oldest girl, about two years older than myself, was much more withdrawn than the other four Dobson children. Therefore there was a natural attraction for me to join her on daily long walks with the dog, just to chat. This went on for some time, until her father abruptly stopped our walks. As I learned later, he did so because of his desperate fear that my intention was to rape his daughter."

The parson continued to view Martin as a sexual threat to his children. A trivial incident cemented the parson's conviction: Martin was interested in scientific subjects and spent his pocket money on scientific books. One of these, on human physiology, contained a brief chapter on sex organs. The parson immediately confiscated the book. Martin responded by buying another copy. This infuriated the parson. Martin coolly declared that he considered the parson's attitude foolish, that he had had enough interference from adults who distorted his real intentions, and that he would no longer tolerate any interference with his scientific interests. Martin knew why he had been able to summon sufficient strength to oppose the parson. It came from his resolve to listen to his inner world when he found the external one to be unreasonable. Yet his introverted preoccupations never caused him to lose touch with reality. Martin explains: "I have always looked with interest at what the external world had to offer, gratefully accepted the things that appealed to me and weaving them into my inner world, while finding means of rejecting or just coping with the things I did not like. But during my childhood and adolescence there was virtually no communication from my inner world back to the real world. This was due to the fact that I had never been accepted. I just frightened people, especially adults."

Ruth, on the other hand, tended to deny dangers, for example, those caused by the war: "I remember at night in Kent at the Dobsons sitting on the bedroom windowsill, watching the red flares, the doodlebugs [unpiloted V-aircraft] and fighter planes, the gun battles in the air. It was exciting. I had no inkling of the danger. My brother did. He knew that the doodlebugs were coming from where our mother lived, and he became quite disturbed. I did not connect it with my parents at all. . . . I must have done a lot of denying of reality. I was a child who asked endless questions, but not about Germany,

Jews, or my parents. I do remember that Mrs. Dobson did a lot of explaining, but I was probably unable psychologically to retain much of it."

Yet there were times when Ruth was unable to repress the memory of her parents. There were a thousand reminders that other children had parents and she did not. Those thoughts made her feel depressed and "different," which in turn made her act "different." Ruth thinks she was an unrewarding child, possibly hard to comfort. She remembers yearning to be cuddled but also rejecting comfort offered because it did not emanate from the "right" person

While the Dobsons were treating Ruth as one of their own, Martin's difficulties with the parson did not lessen. On the contrary, the incident of the crystal set radio Martin had built caused his stepfather to suspect him of being a spy. Martin enjoyed building things. Technical work helped him deal with his fears during air raids. The radio Martin had built picked up a station that transmitted in German. He did not realize that the broadcast was one being sent from England to Germany, and he mentioned to the family that he had listened to a German station. The parson immediately suspected Martin of being a German spy and called the police, who concluded nothing wrong had occurred. But the level of tension in the household increased.

A new series of incidents led to Martin's being suspected by the parson of thievery. Martin used a small amount of disinfectant kept in a bottle in the bathroom for one of his experiments. The parson was outraged at the "theft." Another incident occurred: Martin was given money to replace the worn-out batteries of his flashlight, but the new batteries turned out to be defective. The parson was convinced that no new batteries had been purchased by Martin and that he had simply appropriated the money. Martin's reputation as a thief was firmly established.

The day the strictly rationed oranges were to be eaten by the family, it was discovered that the adults' ration had disappeared. Like Captain Queeg's strawberries of *Caine Mutiny* fame, the oranges became a cause célèbre. Only in this case, the parson knew exactly who had perpetrated the crime: It was, of course, Martin. It was all quite logical. Martin had stolen before; therefore, he must be the culprit. Martin thought it was undoubtedly one of the other children, who, in order to obtain an extra treat, had taken advantage of the suspicions directed at him. The scene that followed was Dickensian in quality: The family was seated around the table, and the oranges were distributed. Martin received none. He was merely to sit and watch the others eat. The parson pontificated: "This is what happens to thieves." A few weeks later another ration of oranges arrived. At the first opportunity Martin took his share and ate it. On being challenged, he explained that he was not prepared to take the risk of being deprived of his oranges again; they were distributed by the government for health reasons, and he wanted his fair share. At the eating ceremony he was again seated to watch the others eat their oranges. Again he heard the remark, "This is what happens to thieves." "That's all right," he answered. "I have had mine. Now you can enjoy yours."

Clearly, the situation could not last. The Dobsons turned to the refugee children's organization; they requested that Martin be removed from their home but offered to keep Ruth. The future foster parents, the Harrows, did not want to separate brother and sister. They would take both or neither. And so Ruth and Martin packed their few belongings and moved on.

The change was difficult for Ruth. She felt that by leaving the Dobsons she had suffered another blow: She had lost a kind foster mother, as well as friends and schoolmates. She wondered if she had done anything to be pushed out of the Dobsons' home. She resolved to make sure that she would never be abandoned again. She was too fearful to be herself and bent over backward to get approval from adults. She wanted to do so much for the Harrows that her absence would be felt as such a loss that they would not want to ever let her go. Occasionally, when rage and resentment welled up, she would deliberately seek out some job that would use up all her energy and let her fall into an exhausted sleep. After she awoke, Ruth would consider the problem that had occupied her "solved." It took her years to find out that her problems were not solved at all.

At long last, life went smoothly for Martin. He got along well with the Harrow family, and had no problems at school. The war was now over. In 1948 their parents suddenly made contact with Martin and Ruth. Ruth describes the shocking impact of their meeting in July 1949: "By the time [I heard from my mother and father,] I wanted only to be a Harrow and did not want to think about my parents. I remember when my mother came; she was a total stranger to me. I did not want to be associated with her. She was very obese, and I even found her repulsive. I was very glad that she spoke no English and I spoke no German. I did not want to speak to her. I felt that I had got my life at last on a stable basis, and I did not want her intruding and upsetting it all again. I flatly refused to go back to Germany with her. The Harrows cared for me a great deal. They even wanted to adopt me. There were furious rows between Mrs. Harrow and my mother. I did not know about these till years later. Martin had no such problems. He welcomed seeing [our] mother again. He was still able to speak German. My parents decided to leave Martin in England to prepare for a Cambridge scholarship. Of course, I felt it was unfair to ask of me what was not asked of him. My parents served the Harrows with a legal writ to get me repatriated. They did not realize what separating Martin and me meant. My real feelings were for the Harrows, but I felt they shouldn't be. I felt disloyal and trapped whatever I did."

And so Ruth returned to Germany. She lived with her mother near Lake Constance. Her father worked as a lawyer in Mainz and came home only on weekends. There were endless quarrels, which Ruth at the time believed were caused by her behavior. In retrospect, she attributes them to her parents' problems with their marriage. They must have been strangers to each other when they met again after eight years of separation; the last thing they needed was a recalcitrant adolescent. Ruth felt displaced all over again. Except now she was no longer a frightened four-year-old but an angry, stubborn fourteen-year-old. She felt overwhelmed by longings for her "original" parents and by fury that the ones who were there were the "wrong" ones. And if she could not have the ones she wanted, she preferred to be with the Harrows. She spent long hours walking by herself and fantasizing that she would walk until she reached the Channel and would then smuggle herself onto a boat for England. Knowing it would worry her parents, she deliberately stayed out late. Finally, after six months her parents allowed Ruth to return to the Harrows on condition that she and Martin visit during school holidays.

The experiences of his youth have left an indelible stamp on

Martin. He explains: "Once having become deeply introverted by the events in formative years and by constitutional predisposition, one is left with a behavior pattern for life. It is not possible to escape from it, so the only way to reach a working adjustment in adult life is to accept it, become as fully as possible aware of the advantages and limitations and make the best of it. It means that relations to other people on the individual level will always be extremely difficult. One learns to understand other people easily, but is not understood by them. Their attitude tends to be one of quick rejection because one does not behave as other people behave. It frightens people. They think I am different, dangerous, and respond to me accordingly. I am not worried about this problem because I have adjusted to cope with it and have developed a lot of healthy relationships on a personal level. I am satisfied in the sense of leading a happy life."

Ruth also feels that the early years had a profound influence in shaping her as a person. On the negative side, her experiences have imbued her with a basic sense of insecurity. On the positive side, they have also provided her with a good measure of optimism, great adaptability, and with the tenacity to "hang on no matter what happens." Until fairly recently she had felt herself to be "second-rate" or "damaged goods" for being a refugee. But, at the same time, she prided herself on her superior skills of survival. She tended to be contemptuous of others who could not perform the feats of endurance that she had been capable of. However, Ruth has been able to change most of the negative consequences of her experiences through psychotherapy. She feels strongly that without her brother she would not have survived. He made sense of the experiences for her, and even if his explanations may not always have been entirely correct, they were what she needed to carry on. In turn, she had been his raison d'être.

True to his early interests, Martin's professional life involves various scientific fields; he is involved in building sophisticated electronic equipment and running private research projects linked to various university departments. He has employed many young people, encouraging and counseling them in both their personal and professional lives.

Ruth lives in England. True to her interest in and sensitivity to people, she decided to work with adolescents as a psychotherapist.

She chose not to treat children of primary school age since she felt that they might evoke too many memories with which she was not ready to cope.

When Martin looks back at his foster home placements, he exhibits an extraordinarily tolerant attitude: "I visited all three foster parents later at a more adult stage and am perfectly convinced that ALL of them were sincere in all of their doings. None of them wantonly or for the malicious pleasure of it wanted to inflict any suffering on us. In contrast to my sister, I definitely extend the judgment of sincerity also to our first foster parents." He explains the behavior of the Strangs as follows: "Reverend Strang felt it his duty to take a child from the German exodus. They were fairly old and hardly able to cope physically with young children. The wife was opposed to their taking a child. So a hard clash, without involving any insincere intention, was fully preprogrammed." In spite of his difficulties with the Dobsons, Martin feels grateful to them. "The Dobsons became my reference comparison. There was born my deep desire to marry and raise a family of normal, healthy children. And what impressed me most at the Harrows was their hard, honest work habits and family integrity, which cemented the ideal which I had already absorbed."

Ruth is grateful to all those who took care of her, though her reactions are more equivocal: "All five of the placements certainly kept us alive. I think we have to take into account the enormous changes in understanding of children. Before researchers opened up the field, it was generally believed that as long as children were adequately cleaned and fed, they were all right. It was most unfortunate that we started at the Strangs so young and least able to deal with their cruelty. Reverend Strang was certainly not cruel, and I don't think he had any idea of what was going on. But he insisted that his wife take on children when he must have known she did not want to. The Dobsons, the Richmond staff, and the Harrows put themselves out on our behalf, and any problems were due to lack of knowledge, not cruelty. The Quaker boarding school, I think, did the most for us. It was a haven of peace in between the periods of terror at the Strangs. Psychologically, I am sure it tipped the balance of survival for us."

In spite of her bad memories of the Strangs, at one point Ruth had been willing to write to them. "Martin went to visit Mrs. Strang years later. She apologized to him for treating us badly and said that she had not known much about children. I remember Martin telling me that she wanted me to write to her in the nursing home. I did so for some time until my parents observed me writing and were furious." Ruth kept her ties to the Dobsons. A few years ago, she visited them in Tasmania, where the Dobsons then lived.

Martin and Ruth are not entirely in accord about their parents. Martin comments: "One of the saddest aspects is that my sister has strong feelings of desertion by our parents, which she cannot overcome completely even today. I do not share these feelings. I can see no objective reason whatever to suppose that our parents deserted us, but I have every reason to believe that our safety had the highest priority in their motivations and that they took considerable risks in this respect, without which we would not have been among the survivors."

Ruth expresses more ambivalent feelings. On the positive side she notes: "I know both our parents did what they could against tremendous odds and certainly saved our lives by getting us out. The anger I have isn't rational. But I have never really understood why my mother went back, ostensibly to wind up her affairs. Her sister told me after the war that my mother would never leave German soil. I have never completely understood why it took her almost three years after the war before she first made contact with us in February 1948 and then didn't come over for another year and a half, until July 1949."

The family's inability to talk about their wartime separation probably adds to Ruth's difficulties of coming to terms with her mother. At no time did the four ever discuss the ten-year gap. Ruth recalls that the family restricted its conversation to safe topics that would avoid arousing the feelings that could not be managed. Martin agrees: "My mother never talked about wartime Germany. We just do not know what happened. My father was changed by the years before the war and in Shanghai. Relationships with my parents were difficult for decades after the war and after my voluntary final return to live in Germany, right until they died."

Martin is happily married. He feels that the purpose of his life was to help his sister in their youth, promote the development of his children, and counsel the young people in his employment. Ruth is also happily married and the mother of three children. Had she not left Germany, she reflects, she might have been a lawyer like her father. But then she would never have loved anyone as much as her husband and her three children.

It would be hard to conclude that all's well that ends well. Too much suffering occurred to write the happenings off so flippantly. But it is possible to say, that when it ends well, it is better than if it had ended badly.

A postscript: All Ruth remembered of her Jewish grandmother was a stuffed toy dog taller than she was and a very soft and elegant red plush sofa. The sofa survived the war. When Ruth's father died in 1973, she rented a furniture van in London, crossed the English Channel by ferry, and drove to her father's house. She loaded the furniture on the van, returned with it to England, and had the elegant sofa reupholstered. It is in her home now.

# Chapter 19

# A Meeting of Minds and Hearts

*House parents, matrons, and foster families had an impact on the children that sometimes lasted a lifetime. But what about the effect the children had on their caretakers? I traveled to Scotland to find out. What follows are my impressions.*

The small fields were framed by stone dykes, hedges, or trees, a patchwork of color. Rounded hills rose vertically from each side of the road and were flecked with hundreds of sheep—sheep with long hair, sheep with close curly hair, sheep with black faces, sheep with white faces, running, eating, and bleating. My husband and I stopped at St. Mary's Loch and wandered around the long, deep-blue lake surrounded by steep mountains. The fluttering sea gulls presented a phantasmagoria of color: white neck and breast, brown head, gray feathers, red beak and legs, and black tail. Walking toward the castle that overlooked a green meadow, we were pursued by a goose in a bad mood. The beauty of the scenery had not surprised me. Gunther[1] had written that on his first arrival he had been much taken by the beauty of the countryside, the rolling hills, and the woods and rivers all awaiting his boyish exploration.

Our destination was Selkirk, a small town in Scotland. It was Gunther's letters from Canada that had brought us here. He had responded to my questionnaire some time ago and in one of his many subsequent letters had mentioned that he was still in correspondence with his foster family in Scotland, with whom he had lived fifty years ago. They still reside on the same farm. In fact, his former foster brother still occupies the same house. I asked Gunther if I might meet his foster family, and after getting his consent, I wrote to them. They answered that they would be pleased to meet with me.

Gunther had liked the countryside right away when he arrived in 1939 as a thirteen-year-old. I could well understand it. Selkirk lay before us and presented a charming vista. The small town consisted of two-story stone houses, each with two chimneys, one on each end of the roof; the windows were tall and narrow, and additional long windows, coming to a point on top, were placed in the steeply slanting roofs, which lent the houses a somewhat Gothic appearance. The village square boasted a pretty tea shop and two bakeries with delectable buns and cakes. One of the buildings displayed a sign indicating that Sir Walter Scott had worked there as a judge. Statues ornamented various parts of town. One was a war memorial to honor the men from Selkirk who had fallen in two world wars. The number for such a small town was startlingly high. Another statue commemorated the 1513 Battle of Flodden. All the soldiers in that long-ago battle were killed except one; he came from Selkirk and brought back the bloody flag. The town is built on a hill so that a number of stone churches, as well as the castlelike building where the local judge holds court, can be seen from afar. The color of the stone buildings stands in contrast to the green meadows encircling the town. We had just missed Common Rider Day, a festival that has been celebrated for over 400 years; riders gallop their horses around the property of the town to see that there has been no incursion. The town reminded me of something, though at first I could not put my finger on it. And then suddenly it came to me: It reminded me of Brigadoon.

I did wonder how the townspeople in their peaceful setting had ever come to hear of the needs of Jewish children from Berlin and Vienna and other such places that seem so removed from Selkirk. Or what they had thought of the youngsters once they arrived. Gunther well remembers the day: He had left Barham House near Ipswich, a former camp for training British emigrants leaving for Australia, where he and other refugee boys had been housed for a few weeks until permanent places could be found for them. His journey had taken twelve long hours and involved several changes of trains. While he had waited disconsolately for a train at a small station in Northumberland, a dear old granny, who seemed to run the station, took charge of him. He had felt ill, and she held his head and made him drink very sweet tea. Neither understood the other's language, but the woman knew a sick child when she saw one. Gunther never forgot her kindness.

Gunther's arrival at Selkirk was less auspicious. At the railway station he was met by a tall man with a white mustache and patrician bearing, who Gunther later learned was the head matron's father. As they drove from the station in his car, he warned Gunther that if he behaved himself, all would be well. Gunther did not have the vocabulary to inquire about his fate should he not behave himself. He did, however, have a premonition that he would not like the place where he was going—the Priory. That much Gunther had already told me. I felt sure that I would learn more about Gunther's life at the Priory the next day, when I would be at the home of John Millar, his former foster brother, and John's wife, Patricia.

It was time now to look for our hotel, which was situated on a small hill. From all appearances it must have been a large private home at one time. Its paneled entrance hall beckoned with a dignified welcome. Two women with a courteous manner checked us in and discreetly disappeared. I had not been able to give the Millars an exact date of arrival; my trip had taken me to a number of people who had corresponded with me about my project, and I had not been able to anticipate the length of time it would take us to reach Scotland. We had agreed that I would telephone on arrival. The hotel had only one phone, which stood in the entrance lounge on a shelf opposite the large fireplace. I made my call and cringed as my voice reverberated through the large dignified hall and up the wide wooden staircase, interrupting the discreet quiet. I reached Patricia Millar and asked if we might come to visit the next morning. There was a hesitation in her voice, and I gathered it was not entirely convenient. Then there was a quick recovery and an invitation. It was clear to me that she was changing some plans to accommodate us while trying not to betray to me the trouble she was taking. Once I got to know the Millars, this act of kindness would seem not at all surprising.

The next day we took the long road leading out of the town. A wide vista of green hills dotted with yellow and white flowers and fields edged by hedges and trees opened before us. The sky was heavy with clouds, the wind blowing stronger as the countryside opened up wider and wider. Sheep dotted the landscape. We took the Kelso road to Midlem and then turned left. The meadows were shamrock-green, and at the horizon two emerging peaks appeared like green pyramids. The road we had been traveling must have meant a long bicycle ride for Gunther when he used to bicycle from the Priory, in Selkirk, to the farm.

The high hedges that surrounded the 250-year-old house hid it from view. When we walked through a small wooden gate, I instantly recognized the house as the one in the fifty-year-old snapshot Gunther had sent me. Two sheepdogs came bounding toward us. Brightly colored flowers grew alongside the house and a tall, blond woman was tending to them. Patricia Millar extended a friendly welcome. Soon John, her husband, a soft-spoken, modest, and self-effacing man, appeared. We walked into the sitting room. It was small and low-ceilinged, so low in fact that when their tall son peeked in to say hello, he had to bend his head to enter. The shape of the room was just right for keeping in the warmth from the fireplace in winter. Gunther had written that except for some changes—such as the addition of electric power, running water, telephones, and bathrooms—the house had remained unchanged. But it was surely more sophisticated now than when Gunther had lived there. Bookcases lined the wall. Books were strewn and stacked all around, and I caught a glimpse of a title—*The French Gourmet*. We sat down in four very comfortable armchairs, which took up a good part of the room and lent it a cozy feeling. Through the window that faced the garden we observed the clouds, which varied from fluffy white to deep gray and followed each other in quick succession. Both the white and the dark clouds formed islands in a clear blue sky.

John Millar began to tell us about the time Gunther spent with his family. I was expecting to hear how his family had taken the boy in, how they had provided a home for him, and how they had aided and sustained him. But John related an entirely different story. The minister, a friend of John's father, had first brought Gunther to their home. Gunther had been unhappy at the Priory. Before the refugee children arrived, the only youngsters there had come from broken homes or had been sent there because of serious behavior problems. These were the kind of children the matron had been used to. The refugee children were there for entirely different reasons, but the rules remained the same. The matron was a very precise person who had exact rules that had to be carefully observed. In one of his letters to me Gunther had described how frustrated he felt at that time. Among the rules he thought unreasonable was one in which the matron insisted that all the children, regardless of age, had to be in bed by seven o'clock. This did not sit well with a thirteen-year-old who had enjoyed a certain independence at home. Gunther had always had trouble with authority, but he particularly resented unreasonable authority. He objected even more to the punishments that were meted out to him: The matron would order him to clean the outhouse toilets or would withhold permission for him to stay with friends. One believed in obedience, the other would not comply. Two such different personalities were bound to clash.

The minister had noted how unhappy Gunther seemed. One Saturday he took him along when he visited Nether Whitlaw, the Millar's farm. Gunther enjoyed it from the moment he saw it. He loved the work on the farm and the country life, and the Millars liked him. They asked him to come back the following Saturday, and then the next, and then the next one after that. Soon Gunther was spending weekends and holidays there. The Millars were quite poor in 1939. Fifty years ago income depended on what the farm yielded, and hill farms were marginal at best. There was not much cash around. The Millars could not give Gunther money, but they could provide food and lodging. From the time Gunther started coming regularly to Nether Whitlaw, he had a strong impact on the family and they in turn influenced his outlook. John explained: "My parents were poor and Gunther was a barrister's son. I think it was surprising that he could establish such good relations with them. My father liked to read and sometimes Gunther would select books for him at the local library. My parents were traditional conservatives, very affected by current propaganda. Gunther came from an entirely different background. With Gunther there were absorbing discussions about politics and Germany. I was very interested in history and politics. He used to teach me history and what you might call 'Kultur.' He had a most inquiring mind. The interaction between us helped me to enlarge my brain a bit." I commented that John must have been a very receptive youngster with an inquisitive intellect. But John demurred in his typically modest fashion. "I must be giving you a false impression," he said. "Gunther did broaden our horizons though."

The relationship between the two boys was by no means merely an intellectual one. John was a late child of middle-aged parents, and he enjoyed young company. He thought that Gunther was always full of fun and able to extract humor from almost any situation. They played pranks together, over which John still chuckles. "Sometimes we employed some very eccentric farm workers. Because of wartime conditions good ones were hard to find. But because of my father's arthritis we needed extra help at harvest time. Some did a good bit of drinking. When they wanted food, they would catch rabbits on the farm. We had one character by the name of McComb, who was a very lovable man when he was sober but other times would bore Gunther with endless stories of his successes in life. One day Gunther put a sea gull into one of his snares, and McComb was amazed to see that he had caught a gull." The two boys had a good-natured laugh at McComb's total bewilderment.

John had dwelled almost entirely on Gunther's assets to the family. To bring the focus back to John's parents, I remarked that they had been most generous to share their home with a child from a totally different background. "Well," John responded, "Gunther was a great help on the farm. And he was very good company for me. There was no prejudice against Jews here. Perhaps there is in big cities, but my father had never met any Jews and he had no preconceived ideas. As far as he was concerned, Gunther was just a helpful young boy, very helpful in the house." "But," I added, "caring for a young boy when the family was of moderate means was in itself a very generous act." But John played down his parents' contribution; the emphasis was entirely on Gunther's contribution. "My father was an arthritic invalid all my life, so it was of great help to have Gunther." Yet I do know from Gunther that the Millars did not merely treat him as a hired hand. The affection on both sides speaks to much more than that.

"Why did Gunther finally leave?" I asked John. He explained: "He felt in the end that he needed more income than a farm worker's income. And despite his affection for the farm and open-air life, eventually he prepared for and entered the College of Agriculture and later the University of Edinburgh. He did extremely well there. Later he left Scotland altogether. I think he took the view that the class system was too entrenched and, as a foreigner, he would not make it here. He decided that there might be a better future abroad. He sent the most amusing short notes written in a way my parents could understand. My mother still has his letters. She is now in sheltered housing and brought them all to me before she moved." John's wife added: "When Gunther comes back he fits right in. He used to play with the children when they were small and putter around outside as if he had never been away. He comes back now more than he used to. Every two or three years."

It was a weekday and John had to go to work. But first he would take us to his mother's retirement home. We followed his car through green country lanes to a modern house set in a garden. Its shape and color mimicked the stone houses of the town. A hall cheerfully painted violet led to Mrs. Millar's apartment: a small living room with a kitchen and a bedroom. The home provided privacy as well as a common room for activities with other pensioners. Mrs. Millar's sitting room resembled the one at Nether Whitlaw; comfortable chairs again took up much of the room. Wedding pictures of family members as well as pretty china and bric-à-brac were proudly displayed on the fireplace mantle. Mrs. Millar was an attractive, white-haired, slim lady with great dignity. She spoke, as she had written to me, in a matter-of-fact but decisive manner. Again I expected that she would tell me of her role in Gunther's life, and again the story was reversed.

Why, of course, she took Gunther into her home, she said. She made it sound as if it were the most ordinary thing to lodge and feed a stranger during what were hard times and meager years. "The minister brought him out from Selkirk for an outing, I think. He seemed to be quite a nice boy and I said, 'You can come out on Saturdays, if you like.' He was at school, you see, so he did that for quite a time." Yes, I knew about that. Gunther had written: "I enjoyed Nether Whitlaw from the start. I don't think I ever compared it to my life in Berlin, but I did compare it with life at the Priory, which I detested. I fitted in with the family and I loved the country life. On

Fridays, right from school, I would bike the three miles to Nether Whitlaw, summer or winter, and remain until Monday morning when I would bike back to school. On Monday evenings I always had dinner with the Church of Scotland minister who had introduced me to the Millars, and with his mother and sister. This minister bought me my first bicycle. He made no attempt to influence me in my religious beliefs. During that period I suffered three days a week at the Priory. Every Friday morning I had to ask the matron's permission to go out to Nether Whitlaw, and although she never refused it, I could never take her permission for granted. An additional irritation was the matron's insistence that I go to church on Sundays." The matron's demands did not endear her to Gunther.

At fourteen Gunther decided to quit school and move out to the farm. "Did it take you long to get used to Gunther?" I asked. "Oh, no," Mrs. Millar replied. "When he came out for Saturdays for a while we had gotten used to him and he just seemed to fit in." "Did you have any problem with the idea that you were a family and taking in a new person changed the whole constellation?" "No," was the reply again. "He was very good. I was glad to have him because John was an only child, and I think only children are often spoiled. Gunther seemed such good company. He was older and a very good influence, disciplining him when necessary. He was always very responsible. He had a very strong personality, which was developed even at thirteen years of age. He never complained about anything. He was a pleasant boy—independent but friendly." "Mrs. Millar," I asked. "How did you feel when the war broke out and you realized that Gunther might be staying with you indefinitely?" Mrs. Millar looked quite puzzled, as if I were asking an entirely nonsensical question. After a short pause, seemingly deliberating about what I could possibly mean, she answered, "I never thought about it." I am quite sure she meant it.

I wondered aloud whether Gunther ever spoke about his home or his mother, who was in Germany, to the Millars while he lived with them. Mrs. Millar replied: "No, he never spoke about his home at all. I never asked any questions, of course. I did not want to pry. He never spoke about his mother. She must have been a very devoted mother as he was very well trained. I knew he was getting letters from his mother. I used to see them come with the post. That went on for a long time and then they stopped. I did not say anything for a long while. Then I said, 'Have you heard from your mother?' And Gunther just said, 'No.' And he never heard again. Gunther never talked about things very much at all or showed any feelings of unhappiness. He must have minded. He told me years later when he came back here to visit us that he had gone back to Berlin to the house where he had lived. The person who looked after the house could not tell him a thing. He never discovered what happened to his mother. I did not discover until John told me a year ago that his father committed suicide after Hitler came to power. I think Gunther found that out only after the war. He never talked about his worries or complained about anything." And John added: "Gunther must have been under a terrific strain. But he was a very strong person. He didn't call for any support. He coped by himself."

Yes indeed, Gunther was under a terrific strain. He discussed it in his letters to me: "I wrote to my mother on Red Cross letters. Eventually her replies stopped, and I worried about her. I tried to push it from my mind. I did not know what to suspect until near the end of the war. I missed my mother and, in retrospect, was often depressed. I never thought why I did not talk to the Millars about my mother or my feelings. It was not a subject I discussed with anybody. As a matter of fact, none of the *Kinder* I was with did either. I met with a lot of kindness in Scotland and formed long-lasting relationships. I was treated like a family member and I still am. But I did have to grow up in a hurry and probably never learned to play. In those days I did feel too different to feel that I belonged."

But as John had observed, as far as his inner life was concerned, Gunther coped by himself. The fact that he loved Nether Whitlaw helped. He stayed there until 1946 and then left to study for higher degrees. While at college, he continued to work on the farm during holidays. And after he found employment in England, he still returned for visits. There were two occasions Mrs. Millar had particular reason to recall: "My husband liked Gunther very much. Gunther persuaded him to go on holiday with him, once to Cambridge and another time to Ireland. And my husband had never gone on holiday except for our honeymoon."

It was time to go. I expressed my admiration to the Millars for having shared their home for six years with Gunther. But as far as

Mrs. Millar was concerned, there was nothing to admire, nothing to compliment. Why, she said, the Millars had benefited from Gunther. If not for Gunther, her husband would have never gone on holiday, and it was really such a treat for him. Before we left, John mentioned two other people with whom I might like to talk: One had been Gunther's schoolmate; the other was Selkirk's former shoemaker, John Guthrie. He had known all the children from the Priory, and John was quite sure that he would have a great deal to tell. He was also certain that Mr. Guthrie had an excellent memory: His worktable would always be heaped with layers of shoes and boots, yet invariably Mr. Guthrie would pull out the right ones for each customer who had come to retrieve a pair.

We stopped by the roadside to use one of those clean, comfortable red telephone booths and looked up John Guthrie's number. Mr. Guthrie answered the phone, and I stated my purpose. The voice at the other end replied, "I am a right shy man." I explained that I would only like to hear his memories of the children at the Priory, and again he murmured evasively: "I'm near eighty years old." I began to feel that I was burdening him and, retreating, commented that it was really not so important that I speak with him. But he had changed his mind and told me to come. I cautiously indicated my willingness to forget all about it, but he insisted. In order to give him time, I said we would be there in a half hour and asked directions. "It's right around the Episcopal church. Folks will direct you," he said.

And indeed they did. They pointed to some neat, newly built attached houses with little front gardens carefully decorated with flowers, as only the British can; good places for retired folks to live. In response to our bell the door opened. There was a tall, broad-shouldered, white-haired, pink-faced gentleman with the broadest, friendliest smile and the warmest of greetings. No wonder they called him the "gentle giant." His handshake was a knuckle-breaker and indicated a hearty welcome. We walked up a tastefully decorated narrow staircase and entered a small sitting room, immaculately kept. Wedding pictures and family snapshots lined the mantle. The knickknacks in the room suggested a feminine hand, but we learned that that hand, alas, was no more: Mr. Guthrie had lost his wife five years ago, two months short of their golden anniversary. But then, he reasoned, since he could count the five years he had courted her before their marriage, he could, in a way, consider himself as having had a golden anniversary. The courtship had lasted so long because they had no money at the time. One of eleven children, Mr. Guthrie had had to leave school at around twelve years of age and work in his father's shoe repair business. He was the fifth generation of shoemakers, and he used to work twelve hours a day, seven days a week. Still, there was not much money, but they married anyway.

As we sank into some very comfortable chairs, Mr. Guthrie looked askance at my tape recorder, although by then I had already told this friendly, dignified man that he was the friendliest shy person I had ever met. He soon forgot the tape recorder, and we began to talk. I asked how the town reacted to the arrival of an assortment of Jewish children from foreign cities. Even now Selkirk, with its ordered pace, small-town friendliness, and conservative stores, seemed light years away from Vienna, Berlin, and Munich. "Oh," Mr. Guthrie remarked, "that kind of thing didn't matter. It was similar to being a different color. If you are blind, you would never know that someone is different." But he remembered the children's arrival well. The boys and girls lived in the big hostel, the Priory. Some were even as young as six years. The young ones did not really understand about all the troubles. The children were sort of different at first. He could not really say how. They just were. Except for one or two who might have been a bit difficult, they were all very nice children. After a while some of them could speak the language better than the Scottish youngsters. And they gave less trouble than some of the Scottish children at the Priory. They would come to his shop, and sometimes they would even get into a little mischief. But they were really very polite and very grateful. Finances were tight at the Priory. The matron only received about fifty pence a week per child for food and ten shillings per youngster for clothing and keeping shoes on them and all the rest. She did the best she could with that. That's why Mr. Guthrie charged the children little or nothing for fixing their shoes. Under the circumstances, he was glad to help out. Not so long ago the matron, now in her eighties, came to Mr. Guthrie's house for tea and they chatted about old times.

Mr. Guthrie mentioned the names of many of the children in a pronounced Scottish brogue. There were Egon and Arthur and

Gunther and big Gunther. And he remembered Susie and a "bonnie little lassie by the name of Herta." He himself had a "wee boy," but he liked a little girl so much that he wanted to adopt her. She still writes to him. Of course, she is now sixty years old. He invited her and Arthur to his house occasionally until the matron said one day, "I appreciate what you are trying to do, John, but you can't show favoritism." He could not remember the children ever talking about their parents or their homes.

I asked Mr. Guthrie if the children all left Selkirk at once. No, he said, they just sort of disappeared, one by one. Gunther was the first to go. He went to Canada, and Mr. Guthrie bought Gunther's bicycle for two pound ten. In 1965 Mr. Guthrie was asked to speak on the local BBC radio for an overseas broadcast. Gunther happened to hear it in Canada. He telephoned and said, "John, I am coming over." A fortnight later he walked into Mr. Guthrie's shop. He told Mr. Guthrie that he would be back in a month with his wife, Inge. And when they came, Inge said to Mr. Guthrie, "John, you don't need to tell me anything. Gunther has told me all about you."

Mr. Guthrie had not wasted the half hour it had taken us to reach his house. He had prepared an album with pictures of the *Kinder*, some with their spouses and children. He pointed to those who have come back to visit: Arthur and his wife, Gunther and Inge, Egon and his wife, and others. And one of the former Priory children came back one summer and took a cottage in Peebles, which is twenty-five miles away. He came to fetch Mr. Guthrie and they chatted and laughed until three A.M.; then Mr. Guthrie had to be driven back all that way early in the morning.

Before we left, Mr. Guthrie asked us to sign his autograph book. He used to keep it at his shop, and customers from foreign countries were asked to sign it. Many countries were represented, including the United States and Canada. There were also signatures of Poles, Romanians, and Hungarians who had moved to Selkirk after World War II. The book contained mementos of various kinds, such as cards and letters from former *Kinder*, which are particularly meaningful now that Mr. Guthrie does not receive as many visitors as he used to. He remembered and appreciated the *Kinder*. They gave something to him, and he gave a great deal to them. But he depicted his part in the same modest manner the Millars had used, implying that he received more than he gave.

On the way home we looked for the Priory. There it was on a side road, instantly recognizable. It was a gabled Victorian building of dark brick with a decidedly institutional look. A young woman working there came out to talk to us. Yes, it was the Priory; she had heard that some time long ago refugee children had been placed here. She had recently read an article about those days; it mentioned Gunther and a boy who later became a famous surgeon. She did not know in what country these men now lived. The Priory is now a home for adolescents with emotional problems. Just a vague memory of the *Kinder* is left. (As I was writing these words, the postman brought me a letter from Gunther. In it was an announcement: "For Sale: The Priory, Ettrick Road, Selkirk. As a Whole or in 3 Lots.")

Conflicting obligations prevented me from getting together with Mrs. Nichols, Gunther's Scottish schoolmate. But we were able to arrange a telephone conversation for early in the morning. I spoke with my face two inches from the wall, in an effort to prevent my voice from resounding through the hotel. Mrs. Nichols related that the refugee children, in spite of their strange clothes, had not seemed strange to her when they came. The Scottish children accepted them without ever thinking of why they had come or what problems they might have faced. There was no discrimination. That kind of thing only tends to come later, Mrs. Nichols reflected. She remembered that most of the children talked funny at first and that she thought they must be very brainy because they learned English so quickly while she was having such a tough time with French. She remembered Joseph, who was even able to sing "Who is Sylvia?" And there was Kurt, who had charisma; he mixed well and even joined the Boy Scouts. Gunther always went to the farm; he seemed more sullen than the others. She thought he was unhappy. She seemed to remember that he did not get along with the matron. He was a bit, well, rebellious with adults. She thought, for instance, that he pretended he could not understand English when an adult talked to him. And she thought he really could. Or he would lose himself in the back of the class. But the boys were a race apart anyway. "We gave them stares. We were interested, but of course we would not let them know it. When Gunther returned to Selkirk as an adult, he did not remember me. I told him that when he had known me as a girl, I had red, curly hair. Then he remembered. But he must have fancied other girls more, because he remembered them without having to be reminded what color their hair had been." The next day we left for Edinburgh. There was only one more person to visit: Miss Netta Pringle, who had been assistant matron at the Priory.

What is so rare as a day in June? One in which it does not rain in Scotland. Floods were cascading from the heavens, obscuring road and street signs. My husband and I had only the vaguest directions as we proceeded through the city, guessing wildly as to where to turn right or left. Knowing that Miss Pringle was past eighty heightened our desire not to keep her waiting. We pictured her as a frail, elderly lady and planned to stay but briefly in order not to burden her. We rang the bell of an attractive row house on a pleasant street. The lady who opened the door might have been elderly, but she certainly was not frail. She was perky and witty. We walked through a large square hall decorated with all kinds of attractive plates. The kitchen displayed a Canadian province's coat of arms, which Miss Pringle had designed and with which she had won a competition. In the sitting room a large fire was blazing, and comfortable chairs were pulled up around it. Miss Pringle related her story with directness and honesty, revealing a practical bent. She had come to the Priory through a coincidence. She had actually never worked before. Her mother had died when she was young, and as the oldest daughter she had been in charge of caring for the family. In 1940 she accompanied her sister to an interview for the job of assistant matron at the Priory. When her sister chose to accept another job, Miss Pringle stopped to think. Her siblings had left home; her father was remarrying. She decided to take the job herself.

When Miss Pringle came to the Priory, the first bunch of twenty-one *Kinder* was already there, in addition to an equal number of Scottish children from poor circumstances or broken homes. The refugee children had come from good homes and well-educated families. She thought the two groups would be too different to blend. She remembered the sixteen boys and five girls very clearly. Other refugee children came later, but her contact was mostly with the original group. I inquired whether any of these children, having left their parents, had exhibited signs of sadness. Did they ever seem upset? Miss Pringle thought about it. "Not really," she replied. "They were quite cheerful. They had been in this country for a few months and they were used to it. Some had been in transit in different towns before they came here. There was no alternative to adjusting. What else could they do? They were sensible and intelligent children." "Did they ever talk about their homes, or their parents?" I asked. "Sometimes," Miss Pringle answered. But in typical British fashion, she never asked. She felt that would be prying. Still, it says something about Miss Pringle that some of the children chose to confide in her.

Miss Pringle went on to tell about her recollections of Gunther. While she had been very fond of all the children, she thought the nicest was Gunther. He was so intelligent and he had an excellent sense of humor. He was the only boy to go and live on a farm. She was quite amazed that he left school at fourteen, but she knew he was not happy at the Priory. When he wanted to enter the College of Agriculture he had to pass school examinations. He had not bothered about school for some time, and the preparations were more difficult than if he had stayed in school all along. Nevertheless, he did well.

Miss Pringle did not get along too well with the matron either. She did not like the rules. For instance, she never could understand why the refugee children had to go to church every Sunday. After all, they were not Protestant; so what was the point of that? She did not like that the older children had to ask permission for every little thing. And every Sunday she had to take the children on walks, the big ones as well as the little ones. Some would always disappear. The kids from the poor families kept running away; they wanted to go back home. The matron would send Miss Pringle out on her bicycle to search for them. Miss Pringle finally got sick of it and after a year left to join the army.

From the time she left the Priory to the present, Miss Pringle has served as the center that keeps the *Kinder* in touch with each other. They write to her, and she always answers. She tells each one where the others are; she is sure they would not have been able to keep in touch with each other had she not passed the information along. Miss Pringle took out her photo album filled with past and present pictures of the *Kinder*; Herta and Gretl and Ruth and Susie and Peter and Gunther and many others. In it was also a sketch she had drawn of the matron and herself, the former rather large, she herself much smaller. She had lost track of some of the *Kinder* and asked me if I could check the names of some who might be in New York.

I knew from Gunther that after he graduated from the University of Edinburgh, he left to work his way around the world. He did not get beyond Canada. On his way to the Pacific coast a forester he met on a train crossing the prairies declared that to leave Canada without having seen the Arctic was not to have seen Canada at all. A job with a mining company took Gunther to Yellowknife, in the Northwest Territories. He had planned to stay the summer, but he enjoyed the climate, the midnight sun, and the lifestyle. He was easily persuaded to remain for several years. He lived in a cabin on the edge of Great Slave Lake. He acquired a canoe and a sailboat and spent weeks on the water exploring virtually uninhabited lakes and rivers. It was a boyhood dream come true. Later Gunther moved north to the Arctic Circle to take a job with the Canadian government managing its herd of 8000 reindeer, which forage on a twelve million-acre reserve on the edge of the Arctic Ocean. He likes to think of the reserve as one of the biggest ranches in North America. Headquarters was at Reindeer Station on the banks of the Mackenzie River, a village of about one hundred souls, most of them Eskimos and all of them connected with the reindeer project. In winter, travel about the reserve, from igloo to igloo, was generally by dogteam or tracked vehicles; in summer it was by small boat. But even ranchers need to go to the dentist. Gunther's turned out to be a young German woman, and he was her first patient. They were married in a civil ceremony in Tuktoyaktuk, on the shores of the Arctic Ocean, by a French Catholic missionary, who had to obtain his bishop's permission to join a Jew and a Lutheran. Later, when Gunther was posted to Ottawa, he remained involved with responsibilities for various aspects of the social, cultural, and economic development of Inuit. Now retired, he still serves as executive secretary of the Caribou Management Board, which brings together the Métis, the Indians, and the Eskimos in order to discuss common concerns. For his services Gunther was awarded the Canadian Silver Jubilee Medal, and in 1983 he was elected a Fellow of the Arctic Institute of North America in recognition of his significant contributions to the knowledge of the polar and subpolar regions.

Gunther never lost touch with Miss Pringle. "She remains one of my best friends," he wrote. "We used to go camping together in Europe while I was at University and I took her on a 1000-mile canoe trip down the Mackenzie River to the Arctic Ocean. She was 84 in June. I hope she lives forever." And Miss Pringle deems herself fortunate in having met the *Kinder*: "I consider I was very lucky to have had the chance to get to know and make friends with these children. Particularly considering that taking that job at first was quite coincidental. I had no training at all in child care. I have valued them ever since as friends. I only wish that I knew what has happened to some of those I lost track of."

The rain had stopped, and Miss Pringle allowed us to see her garden, which, owing to her patient ministrations, was blazing with color. She also apologized to me, quite unnecessarily I might add; she said the letter she had written me had been curt to her way of thinking. She had imagined that I was "one of those American psychiatrists who think they can poke into and fix other people's lives and problems." If she had known I was "one of them" (an escapee), she explained, she would have written to me quite differently. I assured her that her letter had been just fine. And then I apologized for at one point having referred to the local children as "English" rather than "Scottish." By then I realized what a terrible offense I had committed.

My husband and I left thinking of Miss Pringle as a friend. We thought of Selkirk as a beguiling place surrounded by a nineteenth-century landscape. We thought of the modesty, generosity, and grace of the people who had kindly given of their time, and we realized that while Selkirk on the surface exudes a spirit of long ago, it is quite involved in the modern era, with all its difficulties. During the war it gave shelter to children with problems, to English children who had been evacuated, and to the *Kinder*. After the war it had welcomed Poles, Romanians, and Hungarians. In spite of all this, it seems to have at least a facade of innocence.

On our return to New York a letter was waiting for me from Mr. Guthrie. He wrote: "It brings one down to earth when we recall old times and realize how lucky we are to be alive. Tears were in my eyes when I read your account of the terrible experiences millions of people had during those awful times. I was one of a big family, and there were seven members of it in the conflict. Two of my brothers died of wounds, and another two are still suffering yet with the same troubles. One of the latter was wounded on the retreat to Dunkirk, and after he landed here, he was patched up and sent to the Middle East to take part in the desert battles. Three of my sisters were nurses in various hospitals where they tended friends and foe alike. To end my letter on a cheery note, may I say how pleased I was with the photograph that you sent. No wonder I am sometimes referred to as a gentle giant when I see myself towering over your tiny neatness." He is also the last of five generations of shoemakers.

Mr. Guthrie had enclosed a poem which he had written in the years before his wife died. I think it reflects the spirit of Selkirk. Here it is:

> A've eaten well and peyed ma rent
> Naethin' borrowed and little spent
> Am sittin' here just quite content
> And envy naebody.
>
> Some wi' their car and braw big hoose
> Wi' a mortgage hingin' like a noose
> This for me I wadnae choose
> For I envy naebody.
>
> Gi'e me the hill and a sheltered sate
> Wi' scenes aroon ye canna bate
> Ma fellow man a'dinna hate
> Nor envy naebody.
>
> A've travelled roads baith straight and bent
> But never worry which wey I went.
> For when a' dee a'll rest content
> And envy naebody.

## Chapter 20

# The Long Way Home

While the *Kinder* were struggling to rebuild their lives, a large number of escapees were still wandering the earth, searching for a permanent haven or waiting for an American visa. The wait seemed interminable. It was necessary to find countries that would at least offer temporary asylum. A surprisingly large number of countries served for the group of escapees in this study as a temporary bridge until their final destinations were reached: Bolivia, Canada, Colombia, Cuba, Ecuador, Greece, Italy, Palestine, the Philippines, Portugal, Scotland, South Africa, Spain, Sweden, Switzerland, Turkey, and, in China, Shanghai. These countries varied greatly in their degree of hospitality, but the escapees adjusted to almost any condition. Anything seemed better than what had gone before. Still, there was no gauging how long a particular segment of life would last nor what might follow; no time frame existed for the refugees. And so they were haunted by anxiety: Will the visa come tomorrow? In five years? Will my money run out? Will I be allowed to work? Will I be considered an enemy alien?

Alice[128] remembers the confusing feelings while waiting with her family in Italy to enter the United States. The joyous atmosphere of Italy was strangely mixed with typical refugee worries: "I felt on perpetual vacation in sunny Italy. At the same time, my parents were worried about my uncle's arrest in Vienna and our lack of money. Still, they too got into the spirit of breathing freely." In spite of the blue skies, the usual refugee activities continued. Alice studied English. She accompanied her father on his regular frustrating trips to the U.S. consulate in Genoa. They would then return to the lovely little town of Nervi and "walk along the boardwalk and listen to the open air orchestra." One wonders how often Alice's parents' thoughts strayed from the music and blue waters.

It mattered greatly in which country the intermediate years were spent. However difficult circumstances were for refugees living in Switzerland or England, they were far better off than refugees living in Turkey. Germany's influence in Turkey was very strong at the time. In the 1960s, I traveled to Istanbul and visited an uncle who had been a leader of the Jewish community and was knowledgeable about political events. I learned that during the war the Turkish government imposed enormous taxes on the Jewish population, thus wiping it out financially. As soon as the Jews were able to recover, new taxes would be levied, impoverishing them once again. During the war the government also constructed concentration camps, planning to intern the Jews; it was only when the Germans were losing the war that these policies were halted.

Gertrude[86] managed to reach Istanbul with her husband. After their visa had been extended for a year, the police came several times to ask them to leave, threatening that failure to do so would result in deportation to the German frontier. With no place to go, they could not heed the warning. One day the police came and escorted them with drawn guns onto an illegal ship going to Palestine, the *Dorian II*. They were not given a chance to gather their possessions, but at least they were not handed over to the German police. The highly unstable circumstances existing in Turkey were accepted with equanimity by Gertrude and her husband. She writes: "Life in Turkey was pleasant and quiet, though a bit on the primitive side. For instance, when I came home after a ride on the tram, I would be full of fleas. I would notice them when I washed my dress and wrang it out." But what are a few fleas and irate, gun-toting Turkish policemen compared to storm troopers!

There was one group of escapees who spent particularly hard years before their final resettlement. These were the approximately twenty thousand escapees who spent the war years in Shanghai. Their reason for going there was simple: No visa was needed, only a berth on a ship and money to buy a ticket. It did not discourage the escapees that they had only vague notions of Shanghai, namely, that it was an international city known for its intrigue and "anything goes" atmosphere. All that people without visas asked was "How can I get there?"

Lola[117] remembers precisely why her family left for Shanghai: Her father had been arrested November 9, 1938. Herded through the streets of Erfurt, beaten, his ribs broken, he was sent to Buchenwald and later released on condition that he leave Germany within six months. Failure to do so would mean Buchenwald again. The family was frantic; they had no visas. Lola's father then tried to secure berths on a ship to Shanghai for himself and his family. Daily he trudged to the offices of an Italian line, only to hear the same refrain: "I am sorry, Mr. Stern. Nothing for you." One day when Mr. Stern passed the offices, too dispirited to enter, the agent gestured to him. Mr. Stern found welcome news: "I have tickets for you to Shanghai," the agent said cheerfully. "They have just been returned by a family also named Stern. They secured another passage. They are going on the *St. Louis*!" Lola's family was joyful. They knew that the years ahead were going to be hard, but at least there were to be years ahead.

Ernst[118] also had to leave to avoid rearrest. He had been incarcerated on the basis of an accusation of *Rassenschande* (shaming the German race by having sexual relations with a Jew). A woman living in his apartment house had been jealous of a married Aryan neighbor and in order to get rid of her, had accused her of sexual relations with Ernst. Ernst barely knew the woman. The accused woman's husband went to the Gestapo, testifying that his wife and Ernst had been wrongfully accused. Some time later the husband wanted to be rid of his wife. He went back to the Gestapo and explained that previously he had lied, that his wife was indeed guilty of *Rassenschande*. Ernst landed in Buchenwald and after some weeks was released on condition that he leave the country. He sailed for Shanghai on the *Conte Rosso*. The ship was loaded to the brim for the ten thousand-mile trip from Central Europe. After Italy's entry into the war, that overseas route was no longer available: Travelers went six thousand delay-ridden miles by train through Siberia and Manchuria and finally reached Shanghai by boat (Kranzler, 1971).

On arrival in Shanghai the escapees were taken to Hongkew, where the bulk of refugees lived. On entering, the refugees' spirits must surely have fallen: Parts of Shanghai had been destroyed in 1932 and again in 1937 due to fighting and bombing by the Japanese. "During the ride to their future home, the refugees were likely to come across such spectacles as screaming, deformed beggars, bodies of frozen children, and adults placed into the streets by their unfortunate families, those dying from various diseases or starvation dragging themselves to certain spots in the city to die in common resting places" (Kranzler, 1971, p. 85).

The houses were built on narrow lanes and contained about ten windowless, flimsily partitioned rooms, each meant for one family and offering hardly any privacy. Many of the refugees were unable to afford even these inferior dwellings. Lola's family, like thousands of others, was taken straight to one of the *Heime* (refugee camps). The various *Heime* held from 300 to 600 people and were usually dark, unattractive places. Men and women slept in separate dormitories, which sheltered from 6 to 150 people per room. The cots, devoid of sheets and pillows, stood in such close proximity that it was necessary to climb over one's neighbor's bed to get into one's own (Kranzler, 1971, p. 85).

Lola's family[117] was first quartered in an abandoned school. In Ernst's[118] camp there were no beds, only primitive straw mats. Eva,[177] her brother, and the rest of the family were luckier: They had a room of their own. The water supply consisted of a faucet outside the house. In order to bathe, water was bought in the water shop. The owner, in order to heat the water in a big cauldron, would simply cut a big chunk of asphalt out of a road and use it for fuel. The "ay-ho" pole man, so called because as he walked along the road he would rhythmically sing out "Ay-ho, ay-ho," would deliver the water in buckets suspended on each end of a pole carried across his shoulders. Toilet facilities were atrocious. In Eva's house, two toilets had to suffice for the twenty-four residents in the building. Gerald's[112] toilet arrangement was more distinctive: It consisted of an outhouse on the roof. At regular intervals a man came with what was facetiously called the "honey pot" and carried away the waste. He made his exit through the family's living quarters. He had a habit of appearing at mealtimes, with an unfortunate tendency to stumble. No one looked forward to his visits.

Because of the general poverty, the *Heime* fed thousands of people. How poor the community was can be gauged by the fact that although it cost only about eight cents to feed one person, even this amount became prohibitive over the years. The *Heime* had to reduce the three free meals a day to one. The Sterns'[117] poverty increased over time. For a while they lived in two rooms. The stove was in the front yard, and in the extreme summer heat and the freezing cold of winter cooking had to be done in the open. Once the war started, the family could no longer afford their own meals and had to eat in the soup kitchens. Ernst remembers eating an endless amount of eggs. For one U.S. dollar it was possible to buy one hundred eggs. It became a staple of everyone's diet. Because their own skills or professions were not marketable, many escapees were supported by American relatives or by the American Joint Distribution Committee. Most worked at menial jobs. Gerald worked in a weaving factory and as a messenger. Eva's mother, who was religious, worked in a *mikva* (Jewish ritual bath), and her father was employed to heat water with ovens fired by charcoal. Going into business posed special problems. For one thing, it was impossible to compete with Chinese merchants whose employees worked for unbelievably low wages. For instance, if Ernst wanted to buy a box of matches for six coppers, he would ask a Chinese boy to obtain them. The boy would be willing to obtain the matches for five coppers and keep a mere one copper for himself. Unscrupulous locals cheated escapees venturing into business. In addition, refugee merchants, unfamiliar with local conditions, found their goods rotting away in the extremely humid atmosphere (Kranzler, 1971, pp. 172–198). If businesses were to succeed, the refugees had to supply goods or services not offered by the Chinese. A sweater shop, for example, was successful because the Chinese did not know how to knit. Another approach was to cater to the wealthy people from outside the community by opening continental-type cafés or bakeries.

Ernst's accounting knowledge landed him a job with the Chinese Municipal Council. This put him among the few fortunate escapees with a diplomatic pass, which permitted him to leave and enter Hongkew after the Japanese takeover. Different nationalities were represented in his office. Among them was a pro-Hitler ethnic German who asked everyone where he could buy a swastika flag for his son's bicycle. Another was a Chinese who constantly pestered Ernst for the latest war news. Another was a nondescript Japanese who kept to himself. Ernst had to adjust to new customs and etiquette. He knew, for instance, that among themselves the Chinese employees referred to him, as to Westerners in general, as the "white devil." If he wanted a glass of water, he had to tell his number-one clerk, who in turn would ring the bell for his number-one boy. Number-one clerk would instruct the boy to bring the water for Ernst. After some weeks Ernst noticed that number-one boy returned with the glass of water almost immediately. The water, owing to appalling sewer conditions, had to be filtered. It then dawned on Ernst that he was drinking unfiltered garbage water. Ernst managed not to fall sick.

The Jewish community set up schools for their children. Elementary grades were usually taught by a teacher living at a *Heime* or by parents. A wealthy, longtime-resident Jewish family financed a first-class high school and staffed it with refugees. There were also schools for the more orthodox. Some of the teachers were supplied by the Mirrer Yeshiva, whose students and teachers had fled Poland and had arrived by train via Russia and Siberia. The physicians organized a hospital. Some of the illnesses were unfamiliar to the European doctors, such as various potentially fatal strains of dysentery not found in Europe, and as a result the doctors were unable to remedy them.

The escapees were ill nourished and poorly housed. They did not possess appropriate clothes for the very cold and clammy winters and the unbearably hot, damp subtropical summers. Nevertheless, a cultural life was organized: Former actors planned theater performances, musicians gave recitals, journalists issued daily and weekly newspapers, and a radio program was broadcast an hour a day from a local radio station. Religious life was available for both the orthodox and for those less so. A woman's organization, about one thousand strong, visited the sick who had no families, dispensed medicines to the poor, and prepared Sabbath and holiday meals (Kranzler, 1971, pp. 261, 269).

The influx to the Jewish community in Shanghai was enormous. From a low in 1938 of about three thousand Russian and Persian Jews, the total had risen to about twenty thousand by 1941. They all hoped that relief and freedom would come soon. What did come next was not freedom. What came next was Japanese rule.

When the Japanese entered the war in 1941, conditions deteriorated further. Relatives could no longer send money from America, and jobs were even scarcer. Sections of the Jewish hospitals had to be closed and many of the medical staff dismissed. Meals in the *Heime* could be offered only to the neediest cases. The number of people cared for dropped from eight thousand to four thousand. But the worst was yet to come. On February 3, 1943, the Japanese issued a proclamation that refugees had to live within a designated area and could no longer leave without permission. As a result, living space was at a premium. Refugees previously employed were now unable to continue working (Kranzler, 1971, pp. 287–310). Passports were confiscated and identification cards issued; in contrast to the identification cards issued to other nationals, those issued to Jews were marked with a yellow stripe. Passes were necessary to leave the restricted area. Two Japanese men, Ghoya and Okura, were in charge. Every day hundreds of petitioners lined up in the heat or cold to plead for a pass. All the escapees who were in Shanghai remember Ghoya well. An ugly, moody creature who called himself "King of the Jews," he ruled over his fief despotically. He would arbitrarily turn down requests for passes and if displeased for any reason would administer a physical rebuke. Temperamental and arbitrary, he at least did not send people to prison, which was typhus-ridden. Okura did. He jailed people for the slightest infraction. Due to prison conditions, being incarcerated guaranteed serious illness or even death (Kranzler, 1971, pp. 332–336).

Poverty became even more acute. Four hundred stalls were opened to peddle winter clothes, which people practically sold off their backs. People sold whatever small possessions they could find for a loaf of bread or a bottle of milk (Kranzler, 1971, pp. 352–353). Ernst's salary was not sufficient to buy more than one meal a day for his father. Ernst himself ate in the soup kitchens. The escapees tried to keep up their spirits. By collating news reports from the English, Russian, and German newspapers they were able to obtain a fairly accurate picture of the European theater of war. They figured out that the war was not going well for the Japanese but feared the influence of the Germans on them. While the Germans were losing the war, they were still expending manpower and effort to convince the Japanese of the necessity of the Final Solution. Cruel as the Japanese were, they refused to cooperate with the Germans in this bizarre venture. On the whole, the Japanese were opposed to Westerners, regardless of religion. They in turn were hated both by the Westerners and by the Chinese. Ernst relates that a Japanese soldier would never dare go into the Chinese district by himself; they went two at a time, or they were not likely to come out alive.

An Allied bombing raid on July 17, 1945, killed 31 refugees and wounded 250 others (Kranzler, 1971, p. 372). In spite of the devastation they experienced, the refugees welcomed the U.S. bombers that had come to destroy Hongkew's radio station. Lola recalls: "Though we were afraid of getting hit, we went and looked and loved those silver birds flying over the city." Ernst remembers picking up a wounded Chinese and suddenly realizing that he was carrying a dead body. Carnage was everywhere, but could freedom be far off now? Officially, the ghetto came to an end on September 3, 1945. Everyone—Jews, Russians, and Chinese—danced in the streets, overjoyed and unbelieving that it was finally over (Kranzler, 1971, p. 392).

After the war ended, the Jewish population of Shanghai scattered as quickly as possible to the United States, Canada, Israel, and Australia. Very few returned to their countries of birth. A handful of elderly stayed in a home for the aged until they died. Gerald's family left for Colombia and waited nine years before reaching the United States. Lola was more fortunate; she came directly to the States. Ernst waited in Shanghai for his U.S. visa. At that time he learned some astounding facts about his coworkers which were consistent with the stereotype of a mysterious East: The Chinese man who had shown such interest in European news had saved Allied air force men who had been shot down; he brought them to Pootung, on the other side of the Yangtze River, and hid them there to prevent their capture. The pro-Hitler German had been a spy and was admitted to the United States almost immediately. The quiet Japanese had worked in cahoots with the Germans.

Ernst was still waiting for his American quota number to come up. By the time he was able to leave, the Communists were already on the outskirts of Shanghai. He went to the airport during a lull between the two warring sides. In June, the Communists took Shanghai. After two and half years in Canada, Ernst gained entrance to the United States. He had taken the long way home.

# Chapter 21

# Not Yet

Waiting in England was a great deal easier than waiting in Shanghai. When my family arrived in England, friends had arranged accommodations in the lower-middle-class boarding house where they were living. The small row houses looked quaint to me, and all the boarders seated around a long table eating porridge and kippers for breakfast induced in me a strange feeling of unreality. My mother soon departed for her live-in job as a domestic. The family who had sponsored her consisted solely of a husband and wife, an upper-class couple with a conservative outlook; they were distant members of the well-known Guinness family. My mother, who could speak Latin, Greek, French, Italian, German, and some English, was the chambermaid and did the serving. Her longtime and very capable friend Camilla was the cook. The Guinnesses knew about their servants' background but never acknowledged it. My mother learned the routine quickly. Noteworthy was the evening meal, when Mr. and Mrs. Guinness dressed formally for dinner. They would sit at opposite ends of a long dining room table, and my mother would wait on them. My mother would bring in the meat on a large silver platter; she should raise the lid to display minuscule pieces of meat (though food was not yet rationed). Mr. and Mrs. Guinness would daintily choose two tiny ones and send the rest back to the kitchen. However, my mother and Camilla were not the beneficiaries of the leftovers. After the meal, Mrs. Guinness would come into the kitchen, look thoughtfully at the meat, and invariably say, "Save it. It still has some goodness left in it." We began to send food packages to my mother. For years our family quoted this phrase to characterize an action as stingy.

Nevertheless, we felt grateful that the family had accepted refugees in their household. Without their sponsorship we would never have survived. The Guinesses' rather overqualified staff came from a country where customs and cooking were quite dissimilar to English ways. I would imagine my mother and Camilla must have committed a good many faux pas. It is likely that, for their part, the Guinnesses probably had quite a few anecdotes to tell their friends about their new domestic help.

After we arrived in England, my life continued to change constantly. In order to learn English, I was first sent to a nearby convent school that extended free tuition to refugees. But since the nuns required everyone to speak French, there was not much improvement in my English. Through an agency for refugees my parents obtained a scholarship to a boarding school for me, and I was off again. I did not mind at all. Since my mother had been in Vienna the owner of a boarding school that was attended by girls from all over Europe, living away from home was not a new concept for me. To the students I was a novelty, an interesting oddity. Most of them showed an attitude of friendly curiosity. But since I did not speak English, they were not too happy to be assigned as my partner for our twice-daily two-by-two walks. No matter. I could understand their point of view. If I had been one of them, I reasoned, I would not have wanted to walk with someone who took ten minutes to stutter out a single sentence.

I enjoyed the more regulated "normal" life at school. I liked wearing the uniform of the British schoolgirl; it made me feel English. I wanted to be like the other girls. They had such a free and easy attitude; they were good in sports and they were strikingly honest, far more so than schoolchildren in Vienna. I felt pleased if they made friends with me. I felt self-conscious about the one other refugee girl in the school, who happened to be rather clumsy and gauche. I felt her shortcomings reflected on me, and I did not seek her friendship; I think I even avoided her. Since no one made any effort to teach me English, I learned through reading books, such as *The Stars Look Down*, by A. J. Cronin. Though there were no boys within miles, I liked to read the romantic novels available in the school library. Their demure love scenes were never more explicit than a tender kiss. I still remember one in which the young swain was overcome by passion as he glimpsed the ankle of his adored one as she climbed into her horse-drawn carriage. Because of my desire to feel English, I enjoyed English history. The scholastic standards were high. I worked hard and received the book *Dorothy of Haddon Hall* as a prize. "To Dorit, for Industry," says the inscription. I was so pleased with the book that I carried it across the Atlantic and still have it. There were some sad moments for me at school as well, mostly when I observed the girls' patriotism. The danger of war was in the air, and there was no mistaking where their loyalty lay. I did not miss Austria. What had happened was so despicable that I did not want to be associated with anything Austrian. I just wished I could have a country and a loyalty similar to the other girls'.

Because the school stood on the white cliffs of Dover, it was disbanded once the war started. There was the fear both of invasion and of damaging air strikes. I went back to London. Shortly after my return, my sister and I were evacuated to different parts of England as were thousands of English children. Since all the children were evacuated with their schools and mine had been disbanded, I was arbitrarily assigned to another one. My former school had been somewhat upper-middle-class and conservative. My new one, by chance, happened to be a school of Jewish children from a rather lower-middle-class setting. The change did not surprise me, however. I had gotten used to the fact that life had an ever-changing pattern, that sequences were entirely independent of each other, and that each one offered something of interest. Besides, all the other refugees I knew were in a similar boat.

A tag was placed around our necks, and we were loaded onto trains that transported us into the countryside and a safe distance from London. At each stop a particular school disembarked, and the local citizens came to select some children. When the train stopped near Atworth, a village too small to be on the map, the children from our school assembled on the platform. The lady who picked me had room for only one child in her home, and since I was standing by myself, she chose me. Mr and Mrs. Clark must have been in their late twenties; to me, of course, they were ageless adults. They had a baby son, and Mrs. Clark's sister lived with them. The house had a small, low-ceilinged sitting room with a fireplace, a small kitchen, and two upstairs bedrooms. There was no running water nor electricity. Mrs.

Clark carried all the water for washing, cooking, and drinking from the outside, including the water for the Saturday night bath. Mr. Clark was a very dignified man, whose home was his castle. We had many discussions in front of the fireplace, which was the only heating source in the house. Mrs. Clark managed everything quietly and efficiently, and I can still remember tea time, with thinly sliced bread and raisin cake baked by Mrs. Clark (before rationing put an end to that delicacy).

All of a sudden I had total freedom. In boarding school I had never been allowed to be by myself for even a minute. Sunday mornings we went to church, and in the afternoon we had lectures. One hour a day was unstructured but always under the supervision of a teacher. The evacuees in Atworth had their own school since the village school was too small to hold the new children. Classes were held in an unheated Quonset hut, which was so cold in winter that we had to interrupt our studies and run around the large room to prevent frostbite. We wore gloves, coats, and scarves during our lessons. Schooling was totally inadequate: There were too few teachers, no organization, no supervision, no homework. The children of the school had known each other and had lived next to each other since babyhood. I was definitely a double outsider. Not only had I not grown up with them, but I was also not English. I enjoyed my stay nevertheless. I liked the country life, the open meadows, the village greens. On Sundays the children would go to the village church and wait outside to watch the brides emerge with their soldier husbands. I made a few friends with some of the children who had been placed in another village, and I learned to visit them by way of little back roads and through the fields. We were supposed to knit for the soldiers, but I was as clumsy as I was uninterested. The whole village seemed to participate in helping me finish knitting the mufflers, which appeared to me to be miles long. I earned some small fame through an incident that held the possibility of danger: A number of us were playing in a meadow when wild horses suddenly came galloping toward us. Mr. Clark's sister, Ethel, happened to be in the fields with us. She called to the children to run, and she herself approached the horses screaming and waving her arms to chase them away. I had started to flee with the other children, but when I saw Ethel all by herself, I decided to return and help her. Ethel never forgot this little gesture. Over the years, whenever I returned to visit the Clarks in Atworth, she would invariably retell the story to my husband.

And so I lived from day to day; I liked being with the Clarks and never gave a thought to how or when my stay would end. It was simply another phase of a life in which nothing was predictable. The only task was to adjust to whatever came. My stay with the Clarks ended as suddenly as it had started. Because London was not being bombed at the time, many of the parents recalled their children. Again, the change did not upset me. Life was like that. Everything started and stopped without reason. I had enjoyed my life with the Clarks, and now I was going home. During my absence my mother had left her job with the Guinnesses. She had run into her former Viennese University chemistry professor, who was working in a laboratory. He offered a job to my mother as well as to my father, who was not permitted to work in England as a physician and had been unemployed so far. Since my parents did not possess work permits, they worked secretly. I was pleased that they were working, but it had never occurred to me that they would not get jobs or that our money would ever run out. I was sure that my parents would manage.

Our moderate funds were largely due to my mother's pessimism: She had always been convinced that Hitler was a menace and had the potential to cause grave danger. Therefore, my parents had deposited money outside of Austria. This second bank account now enabled us to live in moderate comfort: Our furnished apartment was attractive; we had enough to eat; we could buy new clothes if we needed them. But our funds were definitely finite. We had to watch every penny, and we were eating up our money. The fact that my parents now had an income must have been an enormous relief to them.

When I look back, I wonder that I never asked my parents how they felt about their changed circumstances. I never inquired whether we had enough money or how long the amount we had would last. There were manifold reasons for my blind faith and my expectation that all would come out right in the end. For one, I exaggerated my parents' control over our lives. I considered my parents extremely capable and knowledgeable. Over the years I had noticed the respect and admiration they received in Vienna. When I met new people and gave my name, they frequently made flattering comments about my parents: "Oh, is Dr. Bader your father? An excellent doctor and so caring! He is a true *Hausarzt* [doctor of the house]." Like most physicians during that time, my father had a dual role; as doctor and friend. My mother also had considerable renown. Her boarding school was known all over Europe as one of the finest educational facilities for girls. In fact, particularly in the Balkan countries, a girl's marriageability went up markedly if she had been educated at the Pensionat Stern, my mother's boarding school. People frequently said to me: "Oh, I know the Pensionat. Your mother is the owner, isn't she? What an outstanding woman your mother is!" Small incidents confirmed to me my parents' ability to make reasonable choices and stay in control of events. I remember once going to a luggage store with my mother to buy a camp trunk. The store owner touted the trunk that I had chosen. My mother remarked, "You know, the *Pensionat* is right around the corner. The girls frequently come here to purchase luggage. I hope that you are advising me well." "In that case," said the store owner, "I suggest you choose another trunk. Possibly the one over there." I was quite agog, not only because the owner had so blatantly lied to my mother but because my mother had been able to make her reveal her deception.

Although my parents were well respected, my perception of their control over fate was exaggerated. Nevertheless, the picture of my parents as being able to care for us remains so strongly imprinted on my mind that even today I find it difficult to imagine what would have happened had we been arrested and deported. I picture my family, accompanied by storm troopers, walking toward the cattle cars. A famous snapshot always comes to mind: It is of a little boy walking at the side of his mother with his hands up. They are among a group of people surrounded by SS troops. The grim little band has obviously been collected too fast to even allow the mother to button the little boy's coat. The picture clearly suggests that they are being marched along the cobblestoned streets to the trains. I try to picture myself, my sister, and my parents in that position. And whenever I do, I feel more sorry for my parents than for myself. I think how dreadful it would have been for them not to be able to protect us. I think how unbearable it would have been for them to be in rags, deprived of their dignity in front of the children they could no longer help and who had so fully believed in them. I wonder if my parents would have killed themselves, and perhaps us as well, since they did have cyanide at home in case of arrest. I always imagine their feelings, rather than mine. Perhaps it is because I am a parent now myself.

I also took life in stride because of my parents' stoicism. I cannot recall their ever bemoaning their fate or comparing their former status to their present one. They did not look back and lament their position as voiceless, impoverished refugees. The same was also true for most of their friends. Of course, there still was a great deal of talk about when visas would come or what kind of work would be available. But it was a looking forward, not backward, that dominated the conversation. The Nazi period blocked any look backward. It was almost as if the impact of the Nazis had caused amnesia for the period before. There was a strong urge not to be Austrian but to identify with new values. The happy years of the escapees' former lives seemed eons away. Only the time under Hitler seemed real. In contrast, anything in the present and future was better than what had just gone before. Of course, people talked about what they once had been; in fact, some were suspected of exaggerating their former eminence. A popular refugee joke went as follows: A St. Bernard dog meets a dachshund. The St. Bernard tells about his life in Vienna before Hitler. Then he asks the dachshund about his former life. Replies the dachshund, "When I lived in Vienna before Hitler, I also was a St. Bernard."

I recall being at a small gathering of my parents' friends during our stay in London. They were discussing future professional possibilities. My father talked about the fact that in the United States he would be required to take his medical exams over again. He had heard that they were very difficult and contained a great deal of material that was irrelevant to practicing physicians. Many eminent physicians had failed them. It was said that the American Medical Association had purposely constructed extremely difficult tests to prevent competition by foreign doctors. Another guest was a well-known actor. He spoke with a very strong German accent. How, he wondered, was he ever to get a part in the United States? Another friend had been a lawyer in Vienna. There were no exams for lawyers to qualify for practice in the United States. While medicine retains some similarity the world over, the concepts in law are fundamentally different in each country. He had no idea how he would make a living in New York. A businessman confessed that he really had no usable skills for employment. He could run his own business, but where would he get the capital? The talk was thoughtful and factual, rather than desperate. The underlying attitude was "But after all, we are alive."

Another reason for my unworried state was our love and admiration for England. A refreshing spirit that is hard to describe reigned in England. The atmosphere was so wonderfully different from what we had experienced before that our admiration was boundless. The whole style of life opened up entirely new vistas for us: The quiet courtesy, the freedom to express any opinion, the sincerity and honesty of the people, the ability to live undisturbed in whatever eccentric manner one preferred. We, as many others, became Anglophiles. Not all escapees agree with this view of England. Writes one of my correspondents[7]: "I was profoundly unhappy in England, depressed physically and emotionally by the weather, the alien lifestyle." And there were others who were put off by the English class consciousness. But as for our family, we felt differently.

As a result I was able to accept circumstances as they presented themselves. The only disturbing factor was my mother's pessimism. She was worried about a possible German invasion, as well as the war preventing us from ever reaching the United States. As we held only a temporary visa and no work permits, we knew life in England could only be temporary. In retrospect, I think my mother's pessimism was entirely justified. Indeed, her view was more sensible than a more optimistic one might have been. The chances of an invasion were great, and the possibility of our running out of money was even greater. But her pessimism instilled anxiety in me, and not wanting to deal with fear, I judged my mother to be wrong and substituted resentment for worry. I acquired a distance from my mother, which fortunately dissipated in the United States. My mother was considered a lifelong pessimist. It was assumed that her view of life was excessively negative and that her pessimism was a flaw in her personality. But to everybody's surprise, after we lived in the United States for a while, her pessimism largely dissipated. It became evident that it had been based on a very realistic perception of the political scene. As with Cassandra, her realistic but negative view of life had not been greeted with joy.

Just how deeply felt my mother's fear of being trapped in Austria had been even before Hitler's arrival can be deduced from a small incident that occurred while we were mountain hiking in Italy. My family, like most Austrians, had enjoyed mountain hiking. I recall the camaraderie of leaving early in the morning; stopping at the bakery for a loaf of freshly baked bread, which we munched all the way to the top, or pulling some food out of the rucksack at rest stations; and singing songs in unison. But when we were high up in the Dolomites, my mother's steps faltered and she began to cry. She felt overwhelmed and closed in, as if she were to be suffocated by the high mountains that ringed our ascent. I tried to give her courage to move on and ran ahead, calling at each bend of the road, "Here, Mother, I can see the mountain hut. We have nearly made it." She cried her way up the mountain to the hut, which typically provided pea soup, the ever-present *Würstel* (little sausages), and some delectable cake. My mother's upset was attributed at the time to "mountain fever." I am quite sure that the cause of her anxiety went far beyond the encircling mountains. For years before Hitler took over Austria she had premonitions of doom. The oppressive feelings that the mountains engendered in her were really rooted in her fear of the surrounding malevolent political forces. But in spite of my mother's pessimism, I saw her as an enterprising, creative, and spirited woman who was rarely at a loss. Her ingenuity, as well as my father's, had helped us to flee Vienna. It was what I had expected of them, and I assumed that they were able to solve almost any dilemma.

I accepted my return to London from Atworth as I had accepted all the other changes in my life. While my parents worked, I stayed home. I was supposed to clean the apartment and warm up dinner before they came home, but I found those tasks incomparably boring. I never did anything until about ten minutes before my parents were due to return home. Then I frantically threw everything into a kind of pseudo order and would resent my mother's remark that the place looked none too orderly. I recall one occasion on which I rushed to warm up a stew in time for my parents' return. I started the task about five minutes before they were due home, and in my hurry to get it on the stove, I spilled it all on the floor. I rescued the situation by spooning the spilled stew, gravy and all, back into the pot. Unfortunately, since the kitchen floor was wooden, I shoveled a great many splinters into the pot. When my father commented on the appetizingly dark color of the gravy, I bit my lip.

I spent my days reading after spending hours in bookstores selecting softcover Penguin books, which I purchased with money I had secretly taken from my parents. My newfound English honesty deserted me at times. I secretly went to the movies in the afternoon, improving my English and learning about the British Empire since the equivalent of American Westerns were movies about British outposts in one part of the empire or another. Lacking money, I found a way to walk from our house in Earls Court through all the grand London parks to Hyde Park Corner. There I listened and occasionally even debated with the speakers who stood on boxes and argued about everything from the existence of spirits to Hitler's policies. That kind of freedom of speech was overpoweringly impressive to me. I lived for the present and felt quite happy. Underneath, however, there must have been some discontent. On one occasion in a movie theater I saw Deanna Durbin act the part of a girl riding a bicycle in a Swiss boarding school, and I burst into tears. I wanted very much to be back in school.

Then suddenly one day while I was home my parents phoned to say they were coming home early from work. The police were rounding up aliens, they told me, and placing them in internment camps. I should be prepared; my father would have to report; he was to be interned. I was stunned. We were planning to leave for America as soon as we received our visa. It was to be any day now. If my father were interned, we would not be able to leave the country. And if we missed our turn, I wondered, would we ever be able to get to the United States at all? It might take years for us to get to our final goal— or perhaps never. I asked my parents what they planned to do. They said there was nothing to do; they had appealed, but this judgment was final. They said they would be home shortly and hung up. I stood by the phone speechless. I could not figure my parents out at all. Something bad was about to happen, and they said nothing could be done. But they had always done something. There must be something that could be done, I thought. And then an idea came to me. If they would not do anything, then I would.

I formulated a plan. A few months earlier, we had had a robbery. Our house was a two-family home. We never locked the door that connected our apartment to that of our charming elderly landlady; it would have seemed discourteous and distrustful of Miss Orr. Miss Orr did a great deal of charity work with disturbed adolescents. One of the girls visiting her had secretly come up to our apartment and taken some valuable items. Since theft was a very rare crime at the time, Scotland Yard had no trouble finding the culprit and the items. Inspector Scott had been in charge of the investigation. I decided I would go to see Inspector Scott and ask him for help. I consoled myself that no grown-up would refuse to lend assistance. It was past four o'clock and the offices of Scotland Yard closed at five. I ran to the Underground and stood waiting for a train for what seemed an endless time. In actuality it could not have been very long, since the English subway trains ran on a frequent and exact schedule. Despairing that I would not reach the Yard in time, I ran up the stairs and hailed a taxi. I explained to the driver that I wanted to go to Scotland Yard but that I did not have enough money. I told him the funds I did have and asked him to drive me as far as he could on that amount. The man must have noticed my agitation, or perhaps it was my request to reach Scotland Yard quickly that motivated him to drive me all the way. When I arrived, I saw a policeman guarding the archway that led into the courtyard of the building. With his legs apart and his hands folded behind his back—and seemingly ten feet tall in his blue helmet—he stated laconically that it was just five o'clock and the offices were now closed. I pleaded that I had to see Inspector Scott. "Too late," was his reply. I insisted that I would go into the courtyard and wait there for the inspector. He informed me that I could stay as long as I wanted to, but the offices were still closed. I walked past the policeman and sat down, determined to wait forever if necessary. At that moment, Inspector Scott crossed the courtyard. I ran to him and explained our dilemma. There was nothing he could do. "But," I insisted, "they are taking my father away. And we are waiting for our American visa. Can't you do something, anything?" The inspector thought a while and then said, "I give you twenty-four hours. After that, I can't help you anymore."

I thanked him and ran home (having spent all my money on cab fare to the Yard) with the news to my astounded parents.

The next day during those precious twenty-four hours, the hours we had been granted by Inspector Scott, my parents were called to the American consulate to receive their visa. Soon afterward we sailed, not long before America entered the war.

But many others, not as lucky as we, were interned. Their story must be told.

## Chapter 22

# Internment

One problem in being interned was the difficulty of predicting where one would end up. It could be Canada; it could be Australia. At best it would be on the Isle of Man, at worst the bottom of the sea. The first ship that carried internees, the *Arandora Star*, was sunk with a great loss of lives. Another problem was the open-endedness of it all: There was no way of knowing how long incarceration would last.

Starting on May 12, 1940, and continuing through July of that year, the British government considered all citizens from countries at war with Britain subject to internment. Jewish refugees, some recently discharged from concentration camps, found themselves apprehended together with Fascists and Nazis. To understand why the British considered internment sufficiently essential to divert army personnel, trains, and ships from other military purposes, it is necessary to visualize Britain's military situation at the time.

When Britain declared war on Germany, it was totally un-prepared. Had Hitler decided to invade England at that time, few obstacles would have stood in his way. One did not have to be a military expert to be aware of the appalling state of British military affairs. I was able to figure it out quite well by myself when I witnessed a group of new home-guard recruits being drilled in Hyde Park: Because of the scarcity of rifles, they were training with sticks.

At the start of the war there were approximately 55,000 refugees from Nazi oppression in Great Britain (Pearl, 1990). No one was particularly concerned about them then, but by September 1939 it was thought wise to classify aliens according to the potential security risk they might pose, since there were many pro-Hitler Germans and pro-Mussolini Italians in Britain. Tribunals were formed to classify aliens into three categories: A, the high security risk group; B, those who were suspect; and C, "refugees from Nazi oppression" or "friendly aliens." While the bulk of Jewish refugees were placed into the C category, standards varied among tribunals, depending on the sophistication or even the mood of the person making the judgment. Even young mothers with babies, as well as nuns, could be in found in group B.

Britain was becoming more and more isolated. By spring 1940 one country after another—Norway, Holland, Belgium, and ultimately France—had fallen. The British began not only to fear a German invasion but also the possibility of betrayal from within as well. (The word *quisling*, taken from the name of the Norwegian minister who cooperated with the invading German forces, would forever be synonymous with traitor.) Compared to the Third Reich, which was growing by leaps and bounds, the British Isles seemed very small indeed. It was a David-and-Goliath situation. How much so was expressed by the immense jubilation over the sinking of the *Graf Spee*. The German battleship had been surrounded by three small British ships. A battle raged, and the *Graf Spee* was forced to surrender. The whole country was ecstatic, and many viewed the victory as prophetic: Just as the massive *Graf Spee* was defeated by three small British ships, so Germany would be defeated by Britain. Thousands of people, myself among them, crowded into Trafalgar Square to welcome the returning British sailors. First came the sound of a military band, next a moment of anticipatory silence, and then a roar as the sailors came marching into the Square. Lost in the crowd, I would not have been able to see them had not some stranger suddenly lifted me up and placed me on one of the pedestals on which the Trafalgar Square lions rest. The proud young men, with their shining faces and slightly embarrassed smiles, marched past. It was a glorious moment, one to be remembered.

Actually, the celebration was out of proportion to the event, heroic though it had been. Germany was still sitting across the Channel, victorious and armed to the teeth. The British jubilation was in part to lessen fears of what was yet to come. And what came was Dunkirk. June 1940. Again the troops came home. But not in splendid victory. I stood on our balcony, not far from the sports arena to which the soldiers and sailors were being marched for the night. They looked dirty and tired, and some wore bandages. They had no weapons.

It was the time before the Battle of Britain. Churchill's speech "We will fight on the beaches . . ." was no mere rhetoric. It reflected the real sense of vulnerability, of imminent danger, that Britain was facing. It was in this atmosphere that the usually stiff-upper-lip British succumbed to hysteria. They had begun to fear a fifth column and were apprehensive that Nazis were disguising themselves as Jewish refugees. They considered that a pro-Nazi German looked and talked like a Jewish German. In order to prevent a security threat to the nation, it was decided that all aliens, friendly or otherwise, should be interned. The press adopted a frenzied tone, warning the nation of the danger the friendly aliens posed unless they were put behind barbed wire. Sir Neville Bland made a speech in the House of Commons, remarking ominously that the "paltriest kitchen maid" with German ties could be—and usually was—a danger to the security of the country. Another member expressed the fear that aliens might be signaling to enemy planes by the way they hung their wash on laundry lines. And Churchill, when asked which of the aliens should be interned, was said to have answered, "Collar them all!"

On May 11 it was determined that the roundup of enemy aliens between the ages of sixteen and seventy should commence along those coastal strips most susceptible to invasion. May 15 brought a cessation of fighting in Holland. On May 16 the Joint Intelligence Committee and the Chiefs of Staff agreed that all enemy aliens, not just those along the coast, should be interned. All through May the newspapers had provided a steady drumbeat encouraging internment. Wrote the *Daily Mail* on May 24: "Act! Act! Act!" (Shirer, 1962, p. 41). By May 28 the House of Commons was informed that all those in category B between sixteen and sixty years of age had been picked up. One worried member was still not satisfied. He reasoned that since the Prime Minister was over sixty-five and a danger to Germany, would not an alien of about the same age pose a serious threat to Britain? By June the roundup was in high gear for women as well as men. Roadblocks were set up all over Britain, and road signs were disguised to mislead the Germans should they invade. Leaflets instructed each household how to react in case of invasion.

On May 31 the Home Office declared that the time had come to intern German and Austrian men and women in category C, the category originally designated for "refugees from Nazi oppression" or "friendly aliens." The fear of saboteurs hiding among the Jewish refugees overshadowed all other considerations. Internees were picked up with such haste that almost no time was given for preparation; thus, women were frequently forced to leave their children behind. No regard was paid to an internee's potential for valuable war work. The aliens were to be interned in the dominions of Canada and Australia and on the Isle of Man, but until this could be arranged, they were to be placed in transit camps. The refugees were off once again, carrying the same small suitcases they had carried before.

## Those "Dangerous" Aliens

Mrs. Lange's[98] transit camp turned out to be the Holloway Women's Prison. A paddy wagon transported her to the fortresslike prison. As the gates clanged shut behind her, she felt as if she were being conveyed into the Tower for beheading. The holding cell was not a cheery place; it contained only an open toilet, which seemed to be in constant use by the shoplifters, prostitutes, and drunks who had arrived before her. Mrs. Lange's clothes and suitcase were searched, and the three ten-pound notes she had hidden were confiscated (though returned to her at a later date). After being searched for lice, she was conducted to her own cell; because of an ongoing air raid the door was only closed, not locked. In the blackout darkness she tapped her way along the wall, listening to the flak aimed at the airplanes. Alone, separated from husband and son, she burst into tears. A kindhearted guard allowed her to join a Viennese woman in the next cell, and sharing the narrow cot, the two women fell asleep.

The next day Mrs. Lange studied her cell. It consisted of a dirty mattress, a rough blanket, a table, a chair, a washstand, and a chamber pot. Mrs. Lange set about to improve her lodgings. She cleaned her cell, covering the little table with a kerchief she had worn; converted the mattress into a backrest; and used the government-issue blanket as a carpet. In the trash she found some discarded but usable flowers a visitor had brought and decorated her cell with them. She volunteered for prison work in order to make a few pennies, learned to knit, took out books from the library, and nursed the Viennese lady, who had fallen sick. Mrs. Lange was allowed to take daily walks in the courtyard. There she met one woman who had been arrested for murdering three people; the Fascist leader Oswald Mosley and his wife, Diana Mitford; and one young, jilted pregnant girl, who was greatly distressed that her incarceration prevented her from getting a timely abortion. It was indeed a motley crew.

Days turned into weeks. It was only when another wing of the prison suffered a direct hit in an air raid that the internees were put on a train to Liverpool to embark for the Isle of Man. The trip was agonizing. The train was attacked from the air (standing on the tracks, it made a perfect target). Of all the exigencies of emigration, Mrs. Lange dreaded the bombings the most. She found herself unable to fight her terrible fear. The next morning the internees were marched through Liverpool to the port. The pedestrians, thinking the group to be saboteurs, behaved hostilely to the point of spitting at them. Mrs. Lange took a look at the bombed-out buildings and felt sympathetic toward the inhabitants. While relieved to get on board, she was worried about being torpedoed. Next to her was a young French soldier who was being interned for refusing to join the Free French forces under General de Gaulle. He said he did not want to. He had had enough fighting.

Herbert,[109] a sixteen-year-old youngster, was to be sent to the Isle of Man but, like Mrs. Lange, passed first through transit camps. His first stay was a holiday camp in Devonshire. The feeling of being incarcerated was triggered by the soldiers standing guard to prevent the internees from escaping. Food was scarce and conditions were primitive. For the first four weeks, Herbert did not even have a towel; he used his shirt to dry himself, washed it, and wore his other shirt the next day. It was fortunate that he owned two shirts. The next camp was in the Midlands. Herbert did not want to be hungry anymore and volunteered for kitchen duty. Now he had plenty to eat. There were ten men to each tent, and it rained practically every day for four weeks (since that time Herbert has categorically refused to take a camping vacation).

## On the Isle of Man

When the first boatload of male refugees arrived on the Isle of Man, the army officer assigned to receive them was flabbergasted. Instead of cunning saboteurs, a ragtag group of men, varying in age from very young to over sixty, disembarked. They carried suitcases, bundles, parcels, and even an occasional fishing rod or typewriter. There were young men and frail old men. Some were well dressed, but others were poorly dressed, wearing only canvas shoes. The officer looked aghast at the men, who were not paying the slightest attention to him. He could not make himself shout a command, such as "Forward march!" Crestfallen, he looked at them and finally said, pleadingly, "Now, *please*, get going" (Chappell, 1984, p. 34).

Once the internees arrived on the Isle of Man, they saw a peaceful vacation island. The Victorian boarding houses and hotels that lined its shores had been appropriated by the government for the internees. In the men's camps, pro- and anti-Nazis and Fascists were mixed. In the women's camps these factions were kept separate. Until a camp was designated for married couples, husbands and wives were brought together once a month for an hour. In the fall the children who had been left behind by their mothers were brought to the island.

The camp rules were very simple. Each house was autonomous, and chores were divided equally among detainees. In the women's camps swimming under guard was permitted, and if money was available, shopping in the camp area for moderate amounts of food was possible. The internees could not leave their compound except under guard, and there was a curfew. Conditions were adequate. What was difficult was the separation from one's family, the uncertainty, the lack of money, the idleness, the boredom, the worry about overseas relatives. To bridge the time until their release, the Jewish escapees set about creating a cultural and intellectual life in the camps. It has been said that Germany and Austria suffered the loss of a great part of their cultural wealth by the departure of the Jews. While the Jewish refugees had to leave everything they owned behind, no one could deprive them of their cultural life, and in the internment camps they fell back on these resources to the fullest.

The internees began by first organizing a kindergarten; later there were classes for adults. In the women's camps courses in philosophy, languages, and mathematics were offered, as well as classes in English, which were the best attended. A library was set up, and welfare organizations contributed books. The men's camps launched an "open university." Among the camp members were many scientists, engineers, physicians, lawyers, writers, clergymen, and teachers; they participated in the courses both as lecturers and students. The number and range of courses offered were truly staggering. In the first half of the year, thirty courses were organized and 4500 classes held. They were attended daily by about 600 students. Fred Uhlman, a well-known artist and internee, wrote in his memoirs about the daily scene in his camp: "Every evening, one could see the same procession of hundreds of internees, each carrying his chair to one of the lectures, and the memory of all these men in pursuit of knowledge is one of the most moving and encouraging that I brought back from the strange microcosm in which I lived for many months" (Chappell, 1984, p. 63).

There were a great many musicians in the various camps. Hans Schidlof, the founder of the Amadeus Quartet, made the acquaintance of two future members of the quartet among fellow internees. The music classes taught by the older musicians were of such high quality that the younger musicians, professionals themselves, benefitted by attending. There was no shortage of artists either: Ten of the refugee artists in the camp were good enough to have their work exhibited at the Royal Academy in London in the summer of 1941.

The internees set up their own economic system: Each participant received tokens for labor contributed and could exchange these for services needed. All kinds of useful shops sprang up: beauty, tailor, shoemaker, laundry, and handicraft; and there were services such as wood-chopping and salvage collecting as well. The relationship between internees and guards was excellent. Herbert[109] recalls one guard falling asleep on his rifle and shooting himself in the arm.

Mrs. Lange found it easier to adjust to the Isle of Man than to Holloway Prison. Her camp was located at Port Erin on a picturesque bay of striking cliffs, dunes, and bathing beaches. Though the women were now free to visit the shops, movies, and cafés, they were reminded of their incarceration by the barbed wire outlining the camp. To make a little money, Mrs. Lange used her new knitting skills to produce socks, warm vests for soldiers, and shopping bags, which she sold to the local population. She took language courses and attended concerts arranged by internees, who had managed somehow to obtain a large number of records.

In spite of all this enterprise, life was not easy. First and foremost, the fact of being detained was grating. Living quarters had to be shared with other internees. In winter the cold was extreme. There was only one fireplace in Mrs. Lange's house, and it was lit only in the afternoon. Radios were forbidden, and lights-out was at nine o'clock. Although Mrs. Lange spent her fiftieth birthday peeling potatoes for all the women in the requisitioned hotel, she decided to make the best of things. At least she was not being bombed. Her biggest hardship was her inability to see her adult son, Hans, in a neighboring camp, but she knew that in a month's time both of them would be brought to Derby Castle, together with separated husbands and wives. On the appointed day all parties were excited. Men picked wild flowers to bring to their wives. Mrs. Lange had knitted some socks for Hans and purchased some food, since men did not have access to shops. Hans came to the reunion with a pair of hand-carved cats, reminiscent of the ones his mother had left behind.

Herbert had left his transit camp and was now on the Isle of Man too. In order to make money he darned socks for other internees. Since he could now buy such articles as toothpaste, shoelaces, soap, candy, and fortunately towels, his moderate needs were met. He could now use his two shirts for their original purpose. He was permitted, under the supervision of guards, to join an internees' work party building a local airport. It was heavy physical labor, but the job did get him out of camp and allowed him to earn a little money. Taking advantage of the lectures and entertainment provided by camp mates, Herbert took camp life in stride. He kept telling himself that it was better than being in Germany.

By July 1940 cooler and more rational minds in England had begun to prevail over the mass hysteria. Voices in Parliament were being raised, insisting that desperately needed brainpower and skilled labor were being left idle on the Isle of Man. It was to the government's credit that, even though on July 10 the first daylight raid took place over Britain, the House of Commons spent six hours in debate questioning the value of the internment system. At the end of the month a directive was issued listing twenty categories under which internees could be discharged. Among these internees were those known for their anti-Nazi stand; those who could contribute to science, literature, and art; and those who were willing to join the Pioneer Corps, a noncombative unit (Pearl, 1990, p. 44). As time went on, more and more categories for eligibility for release were added until, finally, practically all of the refugees had been discharged. But what was done was not quickly undone. It took eighteen months before Herbert was finally freed.

## The Infamous *Dunera*

When the internment policy was instituted, Eric[35] and Walter[45] could not foresee that their next few years would be most adventurous, far more so than Mrs. Lange's and Herbert's internment on the Isle of Man. When the two boys were picked up at their homes by the local British police, they had no idea that their internment would involve a long, frustrating, and at times dangerous trek. Eric, who had recently returned to London from his stay with his foster parents, the Weedons, was sent to a transit camp located at the Kempton Park race course. The men had to sleep on the bare floor, and there was only one plate for every six people and no eating utensils. The younger men were amused, the older ones grumbled. Fortunately, Eric was there only a day and a half. On July 3, 1940, Eric was sent to Huyton, another transit camp. Apparently, no one there was young enough to have anything good to say about Huyton. A partly finished housing estate made up the camp. The men were quartered—or, rather, stuffed—into the unfinished houses or into small tents. But somehow two pianos were located somewhere on the former estate, and Rawics and Landauer, duo pianists and fellow internees, gave a recital.

The internees in their crowded living space began to irritate each other. Eric, apparently, had never heard one of the most important rules to follow when dealing with bureaucracy: "Never volunteer for anything!" When a call came for those who wished to sail to Canada, he stepped forward. He considered that crossing the Atlantic would bring him closer to the United States, which might improve his chances of immigrating there. He had no relatives in Britain; there was nothing to hold him back.

July 10, 1940, found Eric and over a thousand other men carrying small suitcases and waiting under heavy guard at the bottom of the gangway to board the ship *Dunera*. The first inkling Eric received that this was not going to be a pleasure trip came as the man in front of him turned and whispered, "Watch out when you get on board. You'll be searched and there are a lot of *ganiffs* [Yiddish word for "thieves"] among the guards. Pass on the message." Eric placed the watch he had received from Tante Adelheid for his bar mitzvah into his right sock; the ten-shilling note, the only money he owned, he hid in his left sock. As the line moved slowly ahead, Eric shoved his suitcase forward with his toes, now curled around his possessions. The NCO in charge frisked Eric without discovering his secret. His suitcase was picked up and tossed on top of a stack of others. Eric had gotten off lightly; other men had money, watches, and jewelry taken from them. The guards even pocketed such small items as razors and soap. But worst of all was the seizure and destruction of private letters, documents, emigration papers, and testimonials. A manuscript of a novel carried by its author was thrown overboard. The soldiers either enriched themselves or vandalized the internees' possessions. On August 21, Jacob Weiss, whose passport with an Argentinean visa had been torn up, jumped overboard and was lost at sea.

The HMT (Hired Military Transport) *Dunera* was overcrowded by an excess of a thousand people. The ship carried almost 2,542 internees, including 200 Italian Fascists and 251 German prisoners, plus the crew and the escort guards. The latter were under the command of Lieutenant Colonel Scott and First Lieutenant O'Neill. The selection of internees was chaotic. A group of 320 men destined for Huyton Camp was accidentally delivered to the *Dunera* and shipped off. The reception center at Huyton had 320 uneaten dinners on their hands and no knowledge of what had happened to their incoming internees. Two refugee boys were startled at finding themselves aboard. One boy's father was a parachutist in the Royal Air Force, and the other's father was fighting with the British army. Renowned people were hastily deposited on board without even being able to say good-bye to their spouses; among them was the dean of one of the best-known art colleges in England and a pianist whose recital had won rave reviews only two months previously.

The internees descended into the bowels of the ship, and sentries were posted at all the exits for the next twenty-four hours. Even the latrines were out-of-bounds, and only a few buckets were put at the men's disposal. An insufficient number of hammocks were distributed and many of the men had to sleep on the floor. The men were tormented by diarrhea and violent seasickness. Soon the buckets began to overflow. It needs little imagination to picture what happened to the men sleeping on the floor.

While the crew on board showed no animosity toward the Jewish refugees, the behavior of the guards under Lieutenant Colonel Scott did not improve over time. Eric made himself scarce during the daily exercise period. The guards amused themselves by jabbing the internees with rifle butts or by smashing bottles on the floor and forcing the men to run up and down the deck barefoot. Repeated searches of belongings were conducted, which resulted in the disappearance of whatever valuables the soldiers were still able to detect. Walter comments that nothing was pinched from him simply because he came on board with nothing.

The crossing during wartime brought the specter of German torpedoes. That this was not merely a vague possibility was suggested by the presence on board the *Dunera* of the survivors of the *Arandora Star*. On July 2, 1940, that ship, on its way to Canada and loaded with mostly German and Italian prisoners as well as with Jewish refugees, was torpedoed with the loss of 729 lives. The survivors were promised not to be sent out to sea again, but within ten days they were on board the *Dunera*. Within the first twenty-four hours, the *Dunera* suffered a torpedo attack by the German U-boat U-56. Two torpedoes were fired. The ship rocked sharply, but the torpedoes seemed to have passed under the *Dunera*, which was extremely fortunate since it is most unlikely that many internees could have been saved if the torpedoes had found their target. Besides the overcrowding there were insufficient staircases for an escape, particularly since the internees were being held in the bottom of the ship (Cesarani, 1990; Pearl, 1990).

As the journey proceeded, the internees began to organize themselves. Peter G. Lasky (1990) and two other men drew up a constitution. As the only paper available was toilet paper, it became known as the Toilet Paper Constitution. Since there were a number of experts on board, the men played bridge twenty-hours a day to make the time pass. Eric passed up the philosophy lectures but took French lessons from Dr. Königsberger. The orthodox Jews suffered because of the nonkosher food. Even more painful was the fact that many of their prayer books and religious objects had been thrown overboard by the escort troops on the *Dunera*. Nevertheless, this group continued their studies and devotions and seemed oblivious to the hardships.

The hygienic conditions remained appalling.[45] On one deck there were only twelve latrines available for 1600 persons. The German war prisoners appointed themselves guardians of the facilities by placing themselves in front of the latrines and directing traffic. The command of "Three men to the right, run and . . ." still rings in Walter's ear. It was continually dark below deck, and the air became increasingly fetid. The internees had no change of clothes for the eight weeks of the journey. Since all washing had to be done with salt water, the garments were soon reduced to rags. Captain Caffyn and Lieutenant A. Brooks, a Scottish physician, did all they could to ease the lot of the abused passengers, but their power was limited since Scott and O'Neill were officially in charge of the internees and of security. As a result the latter were able to rationalize their inhumane measures in the name of safety precaution. Dr. Brooks found himself ministering to 2500 passengers with just one assistant. He asked three internee doctors—a distinguished heart specialist and two refugee medical students—to assist him. His impressions on his arrival at the *Dunera* were quite telling: "The first thing that struck me on the wharf at Liverpool was a colonel—it was Scott—standing on the bridge like Nelson, or some other admiral, taking the salute, supervising a crowd of civilians with battered suitcases as they trooped on board. I wondered, what the hell is this?" (Pearl, 1990, p. 37).

An additional worry began to occupy the detainees. The weather became increasingly warmer, suggesting that they were not heading for their promised destination, Canada. Those internees who had families in Canada felt devastated. Since they were headed south, the men believed that their destination was likely to be South Africa.

One day Eric could see what turned out to be Table Mountain, near Cape Town, through the small porthole of the toilet. However, the *Dunera* sailed on, and the men realized they were heading for Australia.

Around this time an incident took place on the ship. One evening music drifted down from the deck where the soldiers were being entertained. An internee recalls that "all at once someone began to bang a tin mug against a stanchion, someone else followed suit, then another and another, and soon all of us added to the din. Hundreds of tin mugs and plates were being beaten on steel, the holds resounded, and the singing on deck was drowned. We kept beating on steel, louder and louder, and suddenly darkness fell, darkness at noon—the guards had lowered the hatches—and we knew, all of us knew, that we would now remain damned to twilight and stale air until we reached the shores of Australia."

On September 5, the internees disembarked in Sydney. The Australian soldiers in their big slouch hats were planted a few feet from each other, rifles with bayonets fixed. The internees boarded the train for a seemingly endless journey across a landscape devoid of hills and trees. The escort soldiers on the train eyed the raggedy men. They had now worn their clothes for fifty-eight days straight. The soldier in Eric's[35] compartment soon fell into conversation with the internees. The deportees, finding themselves addressed in a reasonable manner, poured out all their pent-up frustration to this not very important member of the Australian army as if he were capable of setting things right. But perhaps he served a good purpose. His remarks of "Well, I never!" or "I'll be blowed" provided sympathy and therefore relief. However, his low level of importance became evident when he remarked before he left: "If anyone asks you whether the sentry talked to you, say no." But his cheerful farewell, typical for Australia—"You'll be right now that you're in old Aussie! Look after yourselves, and we'll see you later!"—heralded a pleasanter atmosphere than the one the internees had just left.

The internment camp, Eric noted, was an unprepossessing place surrounded by barbed wire with four armed watchtowers fortified with machine guns. It was situated near Hay, a small one-street country town of about 3000 souls. In winter the cold was intense, and because of a scarcity of blankets the men slept on their palliasses

fully dressed. In spring the ground turned into mud, which penetrated shoes and boots. Father Koenig, a Jesuit priest and internee,
describes the summer: "Gradually the heat rose, and the summer we
feared began. Strange mirages built up around us. Toward midday
we clearly saw the Murrumbidgee overflow and with its blue waves
play around trees on the river banks. Toward evening, the mirage
disappeared. Then suddenly ghostlike 'willy-willies' (aboriginal
name for a rapidly rotating column of air) whirled through the camp
and subsided in the distance. With summer came duststorms that
changed day into night and temperatures of 100 degrees (in the
shade) and more. Enormous masses of black topsoil and red sand
suddenly filled the air, were torn in a whirl high into the air, and were
carried thousands of miles away. The fine sand penetrated our huts
and was in everything—clothes, books, and palliasses. We thought
we would suffocate. . . . At night we lay on the ground to get air."

The camp was divided into two sections, Camp 7 and Camp 8,
each holding about one thousand men. The men had their
suitcases—or whatever was left of them after the *Dunera* guards
had finished enriching themselves—returned to them. Eric was
fortunate. His suitcase had not been tampered with. (There were
some men who had been told at the time of the roundup that they
would only be detained for one night. Like Walter, they owned no
possessions at all.) It did not take long for the internees to begin
organizing the camp and their lives.[35] The physical aspects had to
be dealt with first. In their long trousers the men were becoming
increasingly uncomfortable in the hot weather. Three men set
themselves up as tailors and busied themselves cutting off trouser
legs, shirt collars, and sleeves. Some men became cobblers and
manufactured shoes out of rubber tires. Amateur cooks, as well as
those who had been professionally trained in the Continent's best
tradition, managed to prepare meals ("*Dunera* Days Recalled,"
1990). Leon Kohn, later Jimmy King, had been an apprentice chef in
England. Now he was in charge of meals for a camp of a thousand
men. Moreover, with very few and primitive utensils, the cooks also
had to produce kosher meals for the orthodox internees. The meals
won general acclaim. A watch repair shop sprang up to fix those few
watches that had not been stolen by the guards. The fine red dust
continually ruined Eric's watch. The soil was prepared for planting,

and ground was leveled for ball fields. All this, of course, had to be done with a minimum of equipment.

A self-government was set up by those who were particularly politically minded. This group included the men who had worked illegally against Hitler as well as those who had drawn up the Toilet Paper Constitution on board the *Dunera*. Politics was of no particular interest to Eric, who was one of the youngest in the camp. By chance, he stumbled into one of the meetings held in the mess hall, which was attended by about three hundred men. They were deep in debate, and the air was fetid, thick smoke rising from cigarettes and pipe tobacco. A democratic form of government was decided upon.

The camp's intellectual life was soon set in motion. In spite of the oppressive heat and the dust storms, the internees began teaching each other, based on each one's expertise. The deportees were able to find among themselves teachers for the following language classes: English, Chinese, Hebrew, Spanish, French, Italian, Czech, Portuguese, Latin, classical Greek, modern Greek, and Japanese. There were also courses on politics, art, philosophy, anthropology, inorganic chemistry, Goethe's *Faust*, poetry, filmmaking, higher mathematics, atomic physics, astronomy, and theology.

One school that developed was for the 200 Chassidim, who were orthodox Jews. They were located in separate quarters and slept and studied together. They wore their religious garb no matter how burning hot the days, studied the Talmud, and carried their prayer books with them no matter where they went. They evolved a complete schedule of Hebrew studies.

There was also a school for the group of young internees who had not yet finished high school. Academics in the camp provided courses in French, German, literature, history, mathematics, and science in order to prepare the youngsters to take the London Intermediate Examination. Tuition was free since no one had any money. Eric pondered over his English classes and still remembers being stumped by the phrase "Continue the narrative." He would be in internment long enough to become sufficiently fluent in English to enter Melbourne University. His inspiring teacher came from Eric's hometown, Düsseldorf. Striding alongside the barbed wire enclosing the camp, the students studied *Macbeth*, reciting the lines by heart in dramatic tones. Mathematics was another kettle of fish: It was taught by an Austrian teacher in what seems typical Austrian educational pedagogy. Herr Peto would wring his hands and exclaim in Austrian dialect, "*Sa kän Trottel* [Don't be such an imbecile]! *Ihr hobts ja käne Ahnung* [You don't seem to have a clue]!" (A brief personal comment: This type of Austrian pedagogy, which consisted of the teacher treating a student in whatever condescending manner the teacher chose, was totally familiar to me. I had experienced it in Austria, and when an Austrian refugee professor tutored me in New York for my college entrance exam in mathematics, he would always shout at me in exasperation, "*Sie Idiot, Sie!* [You idiot you]!" As he addressed me in the formal manner of *Sie* rather than the *Du* form used for children, I never knew whether to feel insulted for being called an idiot or flattered for being addressed in a grown-up manner.)

It is impossible within the limits of space here to survey the talent available in those camps. The list of those already renowned and those who were to become so after discharge is as lengthy as it is impressive. (Cyril Pearl's excellent book *The Dunera Scandal* needs about half a page per person to summarize each one's outstanding qualifications and achievements.) The list includes a famous poet, an art historian specializing in the Renaissance, artists, actors, writers, a concert pianist, professors of all kinds, physicians, lawyers, a film producer, an atomic scientist, an Olympic coach, and a world champion in table tennis. Of three brothers who had been fished out of the ocean after the sinking of the *Arandora Star* and placed on the *Dunera*, one became a professor of oceanography and mathematics, another the head of a department of meteorology, and the third ended up working as a highly placed technical executive. Twelve internees were to become chairmen of various university departments in Australia. Not everyone functioned on such a sophisticated plane. There were also electricians and cooks and office clerks.

Eric fondly remembers the camp entertainments, such as plays, lectures, cabarets, and concerts. The presentation of Handel's *Israel in Egypt* stands out in his memory. The music had been arranged by an internee, who had transposed soprano and alto singing parts to suit male voices. The orchestra, playing with instruments donated by voluntary organizations, accompanied a fifty-voice choir. Eric recalls:

"The sublime music of Handel's masterpiece conveys the hardships of serfdom endured by the children of Israel and later proclaims, with rousing crescendo, God's divine judgment over the Egyptian oppressor. The performance was inspiring to us as we listened in the summer of 1940, during days of unimaginable heat and all-pervasive fine reddish dust. We felt that we had been abandoned in an environment which resembled the biblical desert through which the Israelites wandered well over a millennium ago. Handel's musical representation of the travails of the Jewish people in antiquity seemed most appropriate to our situation in the Riverina District during the early 1940s."

Eric noticed that the older men, between forty and seventy years of age, suffered the most. Their style of life and daily routine differed markedly from those of the younger internees. While the younger ones mostly wore shorts and walked around shirtless, the older men were more conservative and dressed in their business suits, collars, and ties even when the weather began to warm up. Formerly professional men and heads of families, they were deprived of their position and dignity through internment. Most of them did not know how their relatives in Britain were faring. Many of the women had been interned on the Isle of Man, and all communication with them was cut. The married men realized that their wives and children would not be following them as promised. Often at a loss and depressed, they consoled themselves with the thought that incarceration in a concentration camp would have been infinitely and incomparably worse.

By contrast, many of the young people took the burning heat, freezing cold, mud, dust, lice, flies, mosquitoes, lack of possessions, confinement, and total uncertainty about the future with a certain panache and sense of adventure. Walter,[45] in his late teens, took adversity in his stride: "I worked in the kitchen, taught mathematics, played bridge with some master players, played handball, and took full part in camp life. Except for the absence of women, and the ignorance as to what had happened to the refugee women left in England, it was not particularly unpleasant. *Man war unter sich* [One was among one's own]." Ah, youth!

Most of the men lacked for everything. Until some voluntary

organizations came to their aid, they were even without tooth-brushes and toilet articles. The agencies began to work on behalf of the internees in various ways: They provided material assistance to make life more comfortable; they also contributed books, records, and musical instruments and initiated a connection with various academic institutions for internees; last, they drew up petitions urging the Australian government to reconsider its stand and pointing out that most internees had been persecuted by Hitler, that they were entitled to be screened by a tribunal, and that valuable man and brain power was being wasted. The agencies also stressed that in England the attitude of interning "friendly aliens" had long been dropped and that many of the internees in England were participating in the war effort. An agency representative who was permitted to visit the camps interviewed two survivors of the *Arandora Star*—Dr. Felix Gutmann and Uwe Radok. The survivors were wearing clothes fashioned out of their palliasses and did not even own a comb. The men emphasized that if the organizations did not have sufficient funds to send clothes and books, the internees definitely preferred books.

Dr. Sidney Morris, a representative of the Society of Friends (Quakers), prepared a lengthy report after his visit. He commented that many of the men were forced to walk around with a ten days' growth of beard due to lack of razors. He noticed that they had to brush their teeth with their fingers and sand, and he observed an internee dentist treating patients with instruments made out of nails.

While the internees were in an acute state of anxiety about their relatives on the Continent, they still used their time extremely productively. They produced furniture out of packing cases and protective sun shields out of underclothes and wire from packing cartons. Several detainees had constructed musical instruments—a guitar, a violin, and a xylophone—from pieces of wood that had been tuned with pieces of glass. Dr. Morris described evenings of reading Shakespeare and Chaucer as well as a vaudeville performance. The stage had been constructed from tables, blankets were used for curtains, and a program had been fashioned out of toilet paper with decorations printed by using a carved potato. The camp motto was "We're here because we're here," and one of the camp songs contained the following stanza (Gill, 1990):

We have been Hitler's enemies for years before the war.
We knew his plan for bombing and invading Britain's shore.
We warned you of his treachery when you believed in peace.
And now we are His Majesty's most loyal internees.

The Society of Friends quickly became active on behalf of the Australian internees. It was no surprise. The Quakers had lent a helping hand at every stage of the rescue and resettlement of the refugees. But the Australian government was not eager to heed any suggestions. The authorities were afraid that 2000 released internees would settle in Australia, a country not used to such an influx. Several factors changed this conservative attitude. One was the arrival of Major J. D. Layton, who was sent by the British government and who worked ceaselessly for the internees' betterment. He was responsible for the internees' transfer from Hay to Tartura, a much more suitable location geographically. He arranged for 400 internees willing to join the Pioneer Corps to be returned to England. Of those, 40 were drowned when their ship was sunk by enemy action (Patkin, 1979). Two hundred men who had been promised that their families would follow them and 200 more who could help the war effort in England were also repatriated. About 550 men, of whom Eric was one, joined the Australian army. They were not admitted into fighting units but were integrated into the Eight Australian Employment Company, a noncombat unit. Other internees were assigned to military intelligence, entertainment troops, or civilian jobs in industry. A few managed to get to Palestine. In order to obtain compensation for the internees, Major Layton determined the financial losses they had incurred due to the destruction of their possessions on the *Dunera*. The fall of the conservative Australian government resulted in a more liberal climate, and Japan's entry into the war highlighted the useless waste of manpower in the camps.

Before being called into the Australian army, Eric volunteered for fruit picking. Together with other internees he was driven to his new destination in a fertile valley. The soldier escorts were simple people who did not know much about the world. They knew that the internees had come from Germany, and they took pains to assure the foreigners that they had nothing against them: "I tell you, son," one told Eric, "I've got nothing against the Germans. Charlie here and me, we were in the last lot [World War I] and they are good, clean fighters." It was the first time that Eric worked alongside "real Aussies." He learned something about the proverbial Australian tolerance, which may be summed up by the phrase "a fair go." The Australian government had not been very charitable, but at least the individual Aussies were.

After induction Eric, along with many other internees, was assigned to the Eighth Australian Employment Company, a unit known more for hard work than for outstanding discipline. The loading and unloading of war materials to be shipped to the Pacific theater of war was its essential task. Many of the internees volunteered for fighting units, but aliens were not accepted. Since this unit was located near Melbourne University, some of the internees were able to enroll for higher study. Eric made contact with refugee families, who welcomed him into their homes. It was on one of those visits that he suddenly felt intensely homesick. The Salomons' domestic routine was familiar to Eric. Even the meals, cutlery, and furniture were reminiscent of home. Mrs. Salomon sang while accompanying herself on the piano. The atmosphere reminded Eric of Düsseldorf and made him long for his family and the apartment on Moltkestrasse that he had left forever.

Over fifty years have passed since the *Dunera* days. A court martial was held in 1941, and Lieutenant Colonel Scott and two sergeants were found guilty for their actions against the internees. The British government paid compensation for the losses suffered. Churchill declared the deportation "a deplorable and regrettable mistake." Many of the internees have long ago forgiven the injustices committed against them. Writes Eric of his *Dunera* experience: "Although it had been anything but pleasant, I had not really suffered any serious privations. It is certainly true that our guards' behavior was very much at variance with the spirit of the Geneva Convention. They knew full well with whom they were dealing, if for no other reason than that there were many orthodox Jews on board. Lieutenant Colonel Scott was a miserable creature and first-class liar. At the same time, being young, we didn't allow such events to get us down. By comparison with what had happened to some of us in Germany little more than a year earlier, this was small beer, and now this unpleasant interlude lay behind us." Walter[45] writes: "The British soldiers were told that we were dangerous fifth columnists, so you cannot blame them for being unpleasant."

The escapees know the difference between an outrage perpetrated by a democratic government in which the individual basically has worth and the malevolence of the whims of a death-dealing dictator. They also display a tolerance for Britain's overreaction because it occurred while the country stood alone against the Nazi menace. While individual Britons acted badly, the refugees were at all times under the protection of a government that was basically kindly disposed toward them and had, in fact, saved their lives.

September 6, 1990, brought the *Dunera* boys to a reunion at the same place where they had disembarked fifty years before: Passenger Terminal, Wharf 13, Pyrmont, Australia (Gill, 1990). One of the prime movers for holding a reunion was Jimmy King, the former cook at Hay. The speeches given on that occasion were balanced and reflective, with Governor-General Bill Hayden emphasizing vigilance against hysteria during periods of political upheaval and the need to remain alert to injustices perpetrated against minority groups. Fred Gruen, a nineteen-year-old lad at the time of the internment and now a retired professor of economics of the Australian National University and a former adviser to prime ministers, expressed his gratitude to various organizations and people who had extended generous and much-needed help to the internees. He recalled the waste of it all (1990): "No doubt many around the world had much more harrowing experiences. [But] apart from the needless cruelty suffered, one could not help but be angry at the sheer inefficiency of it all. Here were thousands of dedicated opponents of what the German Nazi dictatorship stood for, men who could have been used to help the British war effort." But he cautioned that the positive aspects outweigh the negative: "However, the *Dunera* episode also provides a good picture of Great Britain as a healthy democracy at work. The unnecessary deportations and the venality of our prison guards were vigorously attacked in the British House of Commons when all this became generally known. . . . Although World War II was then at its height, a goodly number of British MPs spoke out on our behalf. . . . The present feelings of the *Dunera* survivors are, not surprisingly, mixed. Some are still angry. No doubt many others have forgotten or forgiven and only remember with gratitude the refuge Britain offered us from the Nazis before the beginning of World War II."

Governor-General Bill Hayden (1990) drew attention to one of the striking features of the *Dunera* experience, features that were also applicable to the Isle of Man experience: "For surely it is extraordinary that in a cross section of humanity there should have been so many who were, or who later rose to be, distinguished—distinguished in the sciences, the arts, the academics and the professions—and whose contribution to the cultural, social, political, and economic life of this and other countries was to be so profound" (p. 3).

## Chapter 23

# Prison, Italian-Style

*At first I was not quite sure whether Dr. Koch[93] should be defined as an escapee. She had spent the war years in Italy, an ally of the Nazis. However, southern Italy was never occupied by the Nazis. It was a judgment call. The fact that her story was so unusual piqued my interest and swayed me in the direction of inclusion. Excerpts of my interview with Dr. Koch in Vienna follow.*

W: How did you leave Vienna?

K: Italy had opened its frontiers to Jews who had enough money to deposit in an Italian bank to guarantee they were not going to be a burden to the Italian State. Hardly anybody could go there, because most Jews were wiped out financially by the Nazis. My uncle in America sent us money, and we decided to go to Italy without knowing how it would work out or what would happen there.

W: What happened there?

K: What happened! Nothing. We had a nice life and survived!

W: How many years were you there?

K: Five years, from 1939 to 1944.

W: Where did you live in Italy?

K: First we lived in Milan. Of course, you couldn't work in Italy. We would just walk around the town, sit in the gardens, and talk. But I went to school.

W: How did you live without income?

K: Well, my uncle sent what we needed from America.

W: How did the Italians behave towards the refugees? After all, it was a Fascist government, an ally of Germany.

K: The Italians helped the Jews, assisted them at the cost of their own lives. There was no population in Europe who helped the Jews the way the Italians helped.

W: Tell a little how they helped.

K: We were well received, and we were integrated into the society without problems. The only thing that was strange was that I couldn't go to school in the morning. The Italian children went in the morning, the Jewish children in the afternoon. That was the way the Italians applied the Nuremberg Laws. There were no problems getting renewals of papers. In France every three months the Jews had to beg for an extension of stay. In Italy you never had any problems like that. You lived there. You got no permission to work, but you didn't have to ask for an extension every three months.

W: Did the refugees work secretly, without permits?

K: There was no working. But all the people had enough to survive in one way or another. This went on until Italy joined the war in June 1940. Hitler put pressure on Mussolini, and then the Italians started taking non-Italian Jewish men out of the towns and relegating them to some camp in the south. And that's when my father was taken. First my father was twenty days in a prison in Milan, which was a horrible place. The police were very friendly to my mother and me. They gave us a permit immediately so we could visit him every day and bring him things. At Christmas we went to visit him at the camp he had been sent to in Alberobella in Bari. The camp commandant arranged for the hotel room. My father was taken out of camp and stayed with us. He could have escaped if he had wanted to. They arranged festivities for us every day, and my father sat together with the commandant. They made toasts for peace and brotherhood. This went on for twelve days. When we came back to Milan in January 1941, my mother and I were sent away by the police. All the women who knew my mother were desperate for her. They said, "What is happening? She has to go somewhere to southern Italy. No one knows where! How will this be?" And my mother said, "I have nothing to complain. I don't know why you are yelling. That's the way it has to be, so I have to take my child and go." She packed and took me. And that was our salvation, because all those people that remained in the north were slaughtered by the Germans when they took over Milan.

W: Why was your mother chosen to leave Milan?

K: The authorities were aware of us. They had to comply somehow with Hitler's wishes, and so they sent us to a place in the south where we were treated like kings. The best house in the village was not good enough for us. Forty years later I was made an honorary citizen of Celico, and a special medal was coined for me in Calabria.

W: How did your stay there get revived after forty years?

K: It's a story! My mother and I came to Celico in January 1941. It is high in the mountains, with deep snow and wind. Terrible. No foreigner had ever been in that place. The moment we arrived we were brought to the secretary, the administrator of the community, who said: "What! A woman with a child alone! Where is the father?" My mother said that my father was in an internment camp. "This cannot be!" said the secretary. "I will call Rome immediately. A man has to be together with his family." He called Rome and said, "Where is Mr. Koch? Mr. Koch has to come here!" So he called many, many times until finally in March my father arrived and we were together. They gave us the most beautiful house in town—a little palace really. Very comfortable and we had magnificent conditions, as magnificent as possible in that part of the world. We were never in danger. We stayed there until the Allied troops arrived in September 1943.

W: Never in danger?

K: Oh, we had a little bit of war there too because the Germans on retreat from Africa and Sicily tried to hold their lines. We had bombs, we had Germans, we had nothing to eat. We had quite a hard time for a few months, but it was nothing compared to the other parts of Europe. And then after the war was over, my parents decided to go to a place called Ferramonti Di Tarsia. It had been a so-called concentration camp, one of the concentration camps that Mussolini built in order to please his ally. There were two thousand Jews there. We went there for the holy days and to see if there was enough space for us to live there. It would be better for us to stay with other Jews in Ferramonti than to be alone in Celico, without knowing what was going to happen.

When Ferramonti was liberated by Jewish Palestinian soldiers of the Eighth Army, the whole spirit of Israel entered into the camp.

W: When you were living in Italy, did you feel it was a temporary life?

K: Well, of course it was a temporary life. We were happy to be in this part of Italy because we were out of danger, but we were well aware that we were exiles. We were accepted by nice Italian people who were four hundred years behind our civilization. They tried their best to help us—they shared their last piece of bread with us, but still everybody was aware we were being exposed to extreme hardship. Nobody knew about Auschwitz. Everybody felt their hardship was the worst. So as long as we stayed in Milan everything was fine, but when we were moved out then everybody felt that it was exile. Somehow we knew that we would get to an end, but nobody knew what kind of end and what would come afterwards. Nobody could guess. You couldn't make a guess. So we went to Ferramonti and as I told you, the Jewish soldiers from Palestine discovered us, and I had discovered *Eretz Israel* [land of Israel] and became an ardent Zionist.

W: How did you discover Eretz Israel?

K: The youth movement that existed in Ferramonti was very well organized. They had their own small state. They had their schools, they had their Zionist youth movement. I had been living in Celico like in the wilderness. I had two years of school in Vienna, one and a half years in Milan, and from age nine to thirteen I had never been in a school. I couldn't go to school in Celico. Of course not. Education was segregated, and they couldn't make a school for one child. So there was no school. I had no contact with children of my age for so many years.

W: We end on a happy note. Tell us how you were celebrated forty years after coming to Celico.

K: Oh yes, now we are going to hear about that. It's a very strange thing. I had felt so indigenous in Celico that when I left I spoke to myself with the dialect of my village, Calabrese. Now I can't remember any of it, it's gone, you know, but it was like that. In spite of the fact that I felt nostalgia for Milan, I felt enormously attached to the village. It had been inspiring to me in every sense. It was beautiful, it was Italy, it was nature, and I had to leave again—terrible. I wrote poems inspired by the village. But I used to write a lot about the period, and somehow in 1983, forty years after Mussolini was eliminated from power, I wrote an article about what had happened in my village, how we lived through the night of the 25th of July 1943 [when Mussolini was forced out of power]. Somebody else wrote an article in an Italian newspaper about Ferramonti describing it as a concentration camp where people were not killed but where they could play football, something like that. I got enraged and said, "How can you praise a concentration camp where people are not killed, but are degraded by living like that?" Somehow all this reached Calabria. The younger generation started asking their elders, "How come there was a concentration camp here and nobody told us? How could that have been?" And then somehow they discovered me. I was giving a lecture in Milan, and a young man from Calabria who was interested in this issue came to interview me and then went and spoke to the mayor of Celico—a whole *megilleh* [Yiddish word for "involved story"]. They had a big festival for the fortieth anniversary of the liberation of Ferramonti. They invited me and gave me a medal. The mayor of Celico wanted me to come to Celico too and organized a meeting with all the people who used to know me as a child.

W: Did the enchantment last? It sounds as if it might have.

K: Well, you know the biggest event was on the site of the camp at Ferramonti where almost no traces were left. Everybody was there; people from the church, the government, everybody. It was unbelievable. All the parties met in order to honor the internees and the fight against Fascism, and I was the symbol of all this. I said it doesn't fit me. It's like putting a dress on that I don't own, because I was never in Ferramonti in camp. I came there as a free person, as a child. So I said, "What do you want from me? Why did you choose me?" But then I said, "We'll have some good speeches." And when I spoke, one of the things I said was that in forty years I always asked myself why I never came back to my village, because I wanted it to remain in my memory like something very dear. I didn't want to break the enchantment by confronting the reality as a grown-up. It was worthwhile waiting for forty years in order to come back like this. And it was a big thing. In the afternoon I went to the village of Celico. It was filled with snow, just like the day I arrived forty years earlier. And all the people were there who had loved me as a child and love me still today. Some said, "It's like having found a sister again after so many years."

The interview was over. I got up from the comfortable leather chair and walked across the room to admire the medal. We had been sitting in Dr. Koch's office, a large, very high ceilinged room. Everything in it seemed to be on a grand scale: the huge windows, the many strikingly colored Persian scatter rugs, the large table with eight chairs for conferences. The room spoke of many intellectual interests. There were atlases of ancient cultures, volumes of history, books on Jewish matters, arresting paintings, unusual vases. There were family pictures and personal mementos, which suggested that its inhabitant spent many of her waking hours at her work. Not only had Dr. Koch's story made me smile, but so had her dramatic and lively way of telling it. I imagined her father exchanging Christmas toasts with the commandant of his prison; I pictured the whole village turning out to give her a medal commemorating her stay in Ferramonti though she had never really been interned there. It was all a bit like an Italian movie. But then I reflected again about the story Dr. Koch had told me. I thought how remarkable Dr. Koch's achievements really were. She had missed four years of school. She had lived in Italy, subsequently in Israel, and now she was living in Vienna. She had achieved a prestigious position as a journalist and interpreter. Yet how close to disaster she really had been! Death had been only a few hundred miles away, up in Milan. And as I looked at the medal, placed between other awards Dr. Koch had received, I concluded that she truly deserves the medal.

Perhaps all the escapees deserve a medal. Just for surviving.

Gerald Grandston, with his father on the *St. Louis*, which was not permitted to land in Cuba. While in the harbor, Gerald's father suggested they swim ashore with Gerald riding on his father's back. Even seven-year-old Gerald knew that meant death by drowning. The vessel's passengers were forced to return to Europe, where many succumbed to the Nazis. Gerald and his father survived in England. (Courtesy Museum of Jewish Heritage, New York, lent by the Grandston family [born Grunstein] of London, England)

Lola (at right) with her sister and their Chinese caregiver. Many Jews fled to Shanghai, for which no visa was needed. Many suffered severe poverty. (Courtesy Lola Loy)

Lily Feldman pictured while a member of the English armed forces in Palestine. Because her parents were killed in Auschwitz, her paybook lists an aunt as next of kin. She was awarded the African Star and the 1939–1945 Star, decorations indicating that she was stationed in Africa during World War II. Many Jewish boys and girls served in the American and British armed forces, and after the war joined the occupation forces stationed in Europe. (Courtesy Gertrude and Charles Deutsch)

Joseph and his family moved into this run-down, vermin-ridden house in Ecuador, where he eked out a living from infertile soil. (Courtesy Joseph Rauschwerger)

**Hitachduth Olej Austria**

Tel-Aviv, Ben Yehuda Road 65

Telefon :

F ü r s o r g e s t e l l e

Die Mahlzeiten sind n u r gegen
gestempelte Gutscheine auszufolgen.

התאחדות עולי אוסטריה

ת ל · א ב י ב. רחוב בן יהודה 65

טלפון :

המחלקה לעזרה סוציאלית

נא לתת את הארוחות
רק נגד תלושים חתומים

**GUTSCHEIN No.** 879

תלוש מס'

einzulösen bei *Arch. Pataky, Ein Hered 5*

לקבל אצל :

| 1 Frühstück / | 1 ארוחת בקר | um | Uhr/בשעה |
| 1 Mittagessen/ ארוחת צהרים | 1 | „ | 7 30 / „ |
| 1 Nachtmahl / ארוחת ערב 1 | | „ „ / „ |

am 30/9

oder gegen vorherige Ansage.

(Nichtzutreffendes bitte zu streichen

ביום

או לאחרי ידיעה מוקדמת.

למען הצלחת מפעלנו מבקשים אנו לתת את הארוחות רק לפי תכן תלוש זה.
Wir ersuchen im Interesse unserer Aktion nur das auszufolgen, wofür diese Anweisung
bestimmt ist.

למקבל : דיקנותו בבואך לארוחות חובה. האינו מדיק, מאבד את זכותו לעזרה נוספת.
Für den Empfänger: Rechtzeitiges Erscheinen bei den Mahlzeiten ist Pflicht.
Wer gegen diese verstößt, verliert den Anspruch auf weitere Fürsorge.

Streng verrechenbare Drucksorte.

דברי דפוס לחשבון

Otto Fleming's meal ticket in Israel. Rather than feed refugees in soup kitchens, local families offered to share their meals. This chit was for three meals, one of which (lunch) remained unused. (Courtesy Otto Fleming)

Eric in his Australian army uniform. His capacity for adjustment helped him weather the trip to Australia on the *Dunera* and subsequent internment. (Courtesy Eric Eckstein)

# Chapter 24

# The Road Upward

It was the escapees over forty or fifty years old who had the hardest time resettling. In their quest to reestablish themselves, neither men nor women considered any job too poorly paid or too menial. They tried to market whatever skills they had, and they created opportunities to make that extra dollar or shilling or shekel that helped make ends meet. Men who had formerly been manufacturers, bankers, artists, office workers, and professionals of all sorts now worked in such jobs as gardener, door-to-door peddler, janitor, butler, and factory worker. They realized that at the moment of restarting their lives they were at the bottom of the heap. Previous degrees were mostly worthless; past experience was discounted by potential employers; and European letters of reference were valueless. Limited knowledge of the local language frequently served as a bar to better positions. In addition, in 1939 and 1940, when refugees began arriving in the United States, the Depression remained a potent factor in the economy and would remain so until mobilization of war industries went into high gear. All these factors contributed to one reality: There was little chance that the escapees could continue previous occupations or lifestyles.

Before Hitler, Mr. Weinberg[84] was a lawyer and administrator; after Hitler, he worked as a general handyman. Pre-Hitler, Mr. Hönigsberg[21] owned a factory for fine ladies' shoes; after Hitler, he inspected shoes on an assembly line. Mr. Heiman[69] had owned a textile firm; after he arrived in the United States, he peddled linings and similar merchandise to tailors. Later he obtained a loan to purchase a chicken farm. Mr. Grunfeld,[176] a business entrepreneur, accepted a menial job in a leather factory. Mr. Kosak,[106] who had owned a large men's fashion establishment, spent his time in a factory dunking men's straw hats into an evil-smelling solution.

It was easier to adapt when surrounded by one's own kind. As a result, escapees tended to settle near each other. But Mr. and Mrs. Polifka[17] had a job offer in St. Louis and tried to establish themselves there even though it was not an area settled by refugees. The local people had no concept of who these strangers were. Mr. Polifka was never accepted by his coworkers. Because he was a foreigner, he never became "one of the boys." He had lost family, business, and home, and now he felt alien in an alien place.

It was not surprising that adapting to a job devoid of prestige was difficult for Mr. Loewenthal.[114] He had been a highly respected judge in Germany. In the United States his impressive credentials and considerable knowledge counted for nothing. Mr. Loewenthal considered no job beneath his dignity. He worked as a bookkeeper, as a salesman, and even as a metal plater during the war. He put on a brave front, but his son and his wife could sense in him a feeling of depression and lowered self-esteem. His wife worked under primitive conditions as a sewing machine operator. Adjustment to the new status was easier for her, but then she was not the one who had spent years of study and work to become a judge.

The painful awareness of being a refugee could creep into consciousness in different ways. For one person it was the loss of professional standing. For another, it was the sudden dependence on others and the inability to assist one's children. Mr. Adler's[6] frustration at not being able to help his son Steve through college made him feel dejected. He had always been a very proud and independent man. Many years later he presented his grown-up son with a thousand dollar check in lieu of the college tuition he had been unable to afford when Steve needed it.

The women's lives were of course also drastically changed. Those accustomed to a comfortable, even a luxurious lifestyle before Hitler, were suddenly forced to become breadwinners. Only a few of the women had been active in professions. The majority had not worked and had no sophisticated skills to offer. However, they had been in charge of households, had brought up children, and had been trained in various domestic arts, such as cooking, sewing, and embroidering. They now set about to translate this knowledge into remunerative employment. Many began to perform jobs for which they formerly had hired a domestic staff. They worked as cleaning women, sleep-in nursemaids, and seamstresses in factories and sewed and cooked for pay. Mrs. Friedman,[49] who had learned four foreign languages from a live-in governess, now became a live-in companion to a wealthy French lady. Mrs. Grunfeld[62] did not particularly enjoy accepting the hospitality of her none-too-willing relatives. After two days she left and found a sleep-in job as a cook for seven orthodox brothers and sisters in a kosher household. Although she hopelessly mixed up the separate dishes, she avoided being fired because of her excellent cooking. She gladly accepted her duties of cleaning the dining room, cooking for her seven employers, and preparing a festive meal every Friday evening—not bad for someone who not long before had never been obliged to prepare a meal for her own family.

Mrs. Lange,[98] her son, and her sister-in-law combined forces in London and eked out a simple but manageable living (Mr. Lange, who was not Jewish, had remained in Germany): Mrs. Lange knotted macramé shopping bags for two and a half shillings each; her son worked in a war factory; and her sister-in-law, who was employed as a domestic, contributed to the rent in exchange for room and board on her day off.

In Europe the wives had been the more passive ones, with the husband making the occupational decisions. This was no longer true. In fact, the wives sometimes had to come to their husband's rescue. Nervous tension had undermined Mr. Wildman's[185] physical and mental health and had turned him into a semi-invalid. At this point in the life of the family, his wife came to the fore, protecting her brood by peddling, or doing whatever else was necessary to earn a living, and ruling the roost strictly but kindly. In the Eckstein[36] family, the parents were too old and infirm to work and had to be supported by their children. Yet the wife continued to contribute to the family by knitting and selling sweaters.

Many husbands and wives worked as a team, each one contributing in different ways. In the past Mr. Vortrefflich[162] had owned a large matzo factory while his wife had supervised the household.

In New York they decided to pool their energies and open a bakery featuring delectable Viennese specialties. He rose at four in the morning and single-handedly baked all the cookies, cakes, and strudels, and she served as saleslady, cleaning woman, and cashier. When possible, their school-age daughter, Hilde, would take over for brief periods to allow Mrs. Vortrefflich to run across the street to clean her apartment and quickly prepare family meals.

Trouble started if the husband had difficulty accepting his wife's changed role. When Dr. Bron[16] opened his office, there was a physician on practically every corner in his neighborhood. Since few refugees lived in the area, he had no natural following. He had some loyal patients, but never enough. He had to make his house calls on foot or by trolley. Although he was a good physician, he was blunt and devoid of a pleasant bedside manner. His charming wife, formerly a successful gymnastics teacher, now worked as a masseuse. Dr. Bron belittled her efforts and characterized her work as demeaning. Their daughter believes that her mother's success probably underlined her father's inability to make a living.

Other husbands understood and welcomed their wife's contribution. They regretted that their own skills were no longer effective but did not necessarily feel their self-confidence undermined. Mr. Bäuml[15] had formerly been a senior partner in an import–export firm. But refugees, unless they were of some renown, were rarely given positions of responsibility. Limited language skills, unfamiliarity with local customs and mores, and lack of connections were roadblocks to high-status jobs. Mr. Bäuml first worked as a gardener and later as a vacuum cleaner repair man. Meanwhile, Mrs. Bäuml obtained a job reweaving materials. Then she decided to start her own business: She did the reweaving while her husband dealt with customers and took charge of the bookkeeping and delivering. Their son reflects: "Were their lives as happy as they had been in Europe? No, they were certainly not as happy as before 1938. But they were certainly happier than they were after the Anschluss and, beyond a doubt, much happier than if they had not emigrated."

Most of the men accepted the loss of their former station in life without complaint. Starting from scratch was neither life threatening nor a malevolent force bent on their destruction. They would succeed by dint of their resourcefulness, flexibility, dedication, and endurance. They saw their situation as difficult but not hopeless, despite the poverty and struggle that were the norm within the refugee community.

Despite their stoic acceptance of their new station in life, many of the men missed their former lifestyle. Their careers had been part of their vital selves. They had not merely given up jobs, they had given up part of themselves. It is no wonder that some men suffered a blow to their self-esteem. It is surprising that most of them adjusted to their loss of station in life without much regret or complaint. On the whole, it was easier for women to find jobs than it was for the men. As one escapee[53] commented drily, "It is always easier to find low-paying jobs for women than for men." But there was another, even more potent reason: The large majority of men obtained jobs lower in status than the ones they held previously. For the majority of women, however, the very fact that they were now gainfully employed enhanced their self-esteem. They had created jobs for themselves, they were bringing in much-needed money, and as a result they regarded themselves as a strong force in keeping the family together. Mrs. Kiesler[186] characterized these working years as the happiest time in her life.

That husbands and wives found themselves in psychologically different positions is illustrated by a former plant director[188] and his spouse. It was not easy for the *Herr Direktor* to do menial work in a factory (he was given a job loading and unloading crates at fifteen dollars a week). He was entirely unused to physical labor (he was already fifty-three years old) and came home nightly bruised and cut. His English was poor, and he had lost much of his self-respect. At times he still liked to hear himself called "Herr Direktor," though he no longer had a job to suit the title. His wife took any job she could get and worked her way from cleaning woman to well-liked saleslady in a department store.

The bare existence, the scrounging for menial jobs, the making-do, was not necessarily a period that passed quickly. As families wandered from country to country, they managed to find fringe jobs that were unwanted by the local citizenry. The Steiner[120] family included Mr. Steiner, formerly a partner in a family-owned import–export business; Mrs. Steiner, a doctor of jurisprudence and student of psychology; and two daughters in their early teens. In Paris the

parents found a job with refugees who had set up shop sewing
knapsacks. The children were too young to realize that their daily
meals of lentils and potatoes were an economy measure. They lived
in an unheatable summer house during the harsh winter and walked
for miles to shop in a cheap outdoor market. Later, in Cuba, the
family of four shared a tiny bedroom and lived on bananas while Mrs.
Steiner earned a little money by doing translations and—in spite
of never having cooked before—by baking and selling cakes. After
their arrival in New York the Steiners found an apartment in
Washington Heights, an area frequently referred to as "the Fourth
Reich" because of its large escapee population. The apartment
consisted of one room and a combination kitchen–bathroom.
Hannah, the younger daughter, recalls having to get out of the tub
or off the toilet when the iceman came to deliver chunks of ice.
Mr. Steiner found a job for eighteen dollars a week in a glass factory.
Mrs. Steiner accepted a job as a domestic in a kosher household,
although she had never learned to cook and knew nothing about
keeping a kosher home. The venture was a disaster. Not discouraged,
Mrs. Steiner took another tack: she stayed home and contracted to do
piecework, sewing little gold stars on naval uniforms. After school,
her daughter rushed home to help her with the housework and the
sewing.

But even in cases in which immigrants arrived in the United
States directly from their former homes, poverty could be their
companion for years. Mr. Bader,[13] an Austrian scientist, had been
sufficiently renowned to have been honored by the Swedish government. When the Baders arrived in Seattle, Mr. Bader worked at any
menial job, by the day or by the week. During his first year he
worked at more than forty jobs. During his second year in the United
States he felt fortunate in finding a job with a large company, if
only as a laborer. But misfortune struck on that job: Mr. Bader
suffered a serious back injury, leaving him with permanent sciatica.
The Baders' financial crisis was not resolved until 1943, when it
became possible for aliens to work in defense industries. When the
Boeing Corporation called with a job offer, in response to Mr. Bader's
application, a neighbor, an ardent pacifist, took the call and informed
the company that Mr. Bader would not work in a war industry. The
job was lost. Then, just as the Baders were getting on their feet, a

recession set in. For four years Mr. Bader was unable to obtain any job. His wife worked as a maid, and the family picked strawberries and raspberries for survival. Finally, in 1948 Boeing was willing to hire Mr. Bader again. The family was no longer in Seattle, and they were not certain that the job would be secure. Every Sunday night Mr. Bader traveled to Seattle to stay at the YMCA, and every weekend he would return home. Max, the son, reflects upon his parents with pride: "Looking back, I realize how poor we really were. We had no car and few clothes. We had to pick berries to make money. I made more money in my first year internship after medical school than my father ever made in all his years at Boeing. Yet my parents were able to get three children through college and professional schools, and I graduated from medical school debt-free." It is no wonder that Max regards his family's achievements with pride.

I would say that my own family was exceedingly lucky and had it "easy." But what did easy mean? On our arrival in New York my mother left almost immediately for a live-in job as bookkeeper and adviser at a newly opened boarding school about an hour from New York. My father, in his early fifties, began to study for the medical exam required for practice in New York. Money was tight. When my father treated me to a newly found marvel, namely a banana split, which cost all of twenty-five cents, we considered the occasion our great and rare splurge. I borrowed the evening dress for my high school prom. To purchase a dress that could be worn only on rare occasions was out of the question.

When summer came my father joined my mother at her school as a male nurse for the camp season. That fall he took the exam to qualify for a medical license. It was a source of pride for him that he was the only one of his group to pass all parts of the exam the first time around. While my parents were looking for an office and an apartment, they were introduced to a rabbi who suggested they settle in Flushing, about a forty-minute subway ride from Manhattan. Although the rabbi promised to introduce my parents to his congregation, they never heard from him again after they settled in Flushing. My father also sublet an office in Manhattan. As soon as word got around in the escapee community that he had resumed practice, patients who had known him in Vienna began to show up.

My father also opened an office in our apartment, which was small, consisting of a large living room, a fairly large bedroom, a smaller study, and a kitchen. Because every room was off a long central hallway, the apartment appeared larger than it was. My mother converted the living room into a waiting room, and the secondhand Chinese rug and the striking oil paintings she bought gave the room an elegant air. The patients did not guess that my parents slept there at night. The bedroom and a rather large closet were utilized as the office and dressing room for patients. The smaller den became our living quarters during the day, and the couch in it became my bed at night. (My sister, after working unhappily in the garment district as a seamstress, moved to Boston where a better job awaited her.) My mother had the ability to decorate with an elegant look. Interesting prints decorated the hallway and bookcases, with indirect lighting affording the den a comfortable look. For a year my father did not have a single patient in Flushing. It was only after he gave a Red Cross course that patients first began to trickle in; sometime later they poured in. My father's schedule for many years was as follows: house calls in the neighborhood in the morning, a forty-minute subway ride to Manhattan, house calls in Manhattan by bus, office hours in Manhattan, the subway ride back to Flushing for lunch, office hours in Flushing, subway ride to Manhattan, office hours again in Manhattan, the subway ride home, and brief office hours after dinner.

Meanwhile, my mother took care of the household, served as my father's nurse and secretary, and, in order to make social contacts, lectured to various women's organizations. In addition, she bought a piano for the small study and began to give piano lessons whenever my father was in his city office. She did not do this primarily for income. My aunt, a famous piano teacher in Vienna, and my uncle were living in England and were expected in New York after the war. My mother intended to recommend my aunt to the pupils and thus provide her with a livelihood. Meanwhile, the small apartment served as a medical office, a piano studio, living quarters for my parents, and, as long as I was at school in New York, a home for me. After my father's practice had grown quite large in Flushing, he dropped one set of office hours in Manhattan; much later he confined himself entirely to his Flushing office. I think of our apartment there with great nostalgia. As in Vienna, I would walk into our building and neighbors would stop to tell me what a wonderful doctor my father was. And, indeed, the length of his office hours never varied, whether there were two or twenty patients waiting. If there were only two, my father would spend an hour or more with each one. His patients brought him many of their personal problems and respected his advice.

Although we could not afford to go to the opera, my parents were able to create the same exciting intellectual atmosphere they had provided in Vienna. My mother and I shared, among other things, an interest in biographies. While we had breakfast, my father would enter the kitchen and hear our conversation, which might have gone something like this: "But mother, you can't hold it against her. You know she was so very young when she did all those foolish things." "Well," my mother might answer, "she should have heeded her mother's warning." When my father would ask who in the world we were talking about it, we would answer, as if it were self-evident: "Marie Antoinette and her mother Maria Theresa, of course!" Books, politics, travels, school were the topics of our daily conversation—although, I might add, neither my mother nor I was above exchanging gossip. Her pessimism had largely diminished. "What a wonderful world this is!" she would say. "President Roosevelt, Mayor La Guardia, and our doorman, Sam." I knew what she meant only much later. President Roosevelt stood for our trust in the government and our newfound freedom. Incorruptible Mayor La Guardia represented our lives in New York, with all its wonderful comforts, excitement, and many-faceted atmosphere. Our doorman Sam represented the fact that we could still afford some amenities. Much of that atmosphere is gone. While still happy to be living in the United States, our trust in government is no longer absolute; some New York politicians have been highly corruptible, and there are no longer flowers gracing the courtyard of the apartment house. When on occasion I drive past, I look away in pain.

There were a number of aspects of their new lives that cheered, comforted, and encouraged the escapees. The most important was the tremendous feeling of relief in being alive. Escapees felt a great sense of patriotism and of identification with values and ideas that had previously been forbidden to them. Their new countries were now occupied in defeating the forces of darkness, and their own tribulations seemed insignificant.

The escapees encouraged each other and formed what might now be considered support groups. The stories of two widowed "honorary" aunts of mine illustrate this point. Both had been very well-to-do, and neither had ever worked in Vienna, though Mrs. Rafael held a degree in jurisprudence. Mrs. Berg, who once had lived in a sumptuous apartment, became a baby nurse and slept in the baby's room or, lacking space, in some nook hastily arranged for her. She was on duty all night and most of the day. Privacy was nonexistent. And when one job was finished, there was no knowing when the next one would begin. Mrs. Rafael, her degree in jurisprudence useless, became a cleaning woman. Both women were loved by their employers and worked for many years. The two ladies visited us frequently. Formerly our friends, they now, due to loss of so many relatives, became family. They were respected exactly as they had been before their changed financial circumstances. In fact, our respect for them rose in recognition of their valiant struggles.

I recall a former lawyer who from time to time would visit my mother to sell her some trinkets. He carried an old worn leather case from which would emerge various curios. My mother would invite him to sit down, serve him coffee on our best china, preferably with Viennese cake, and then select any items she thought she could possibly utilize for future hostess gifts, birthday presents, and the like. I must admit that when I observed this little scene, I never saw the lamentable aspects of the lawyer's life, nor was I particularly aware of my mother's kindness. I think this was largely due to the fact that there were so many escapees working in positions well below their abilities that the lawyer's predicament did not strike me as particularly unusual. Lowered status did not affect the escapee's standing within the refugee community. On the contrary, there was a great deal of admiration for the intrepid spirit of those who were exerting all their energies to stay afloat. And there were usually certain aspects of their lives that served as reminders of their former standing: discussions of music or art; the white tablecloth and silver cutlery they had managed somehow to rescue (or a less expensive version bought locally); a piece of jewelry that had been pinned on a jacket collar or blouse and had slipped past the hostile eyes of a border guard; or simply a manner of style or grace that betrayed their former stature.

Escapees' contact with the local population tended to be sporadic. A great many changes have to take place before an immigrant can be fully accepted and understood by those who have always had a firm foundation. An uprooted life has aspects that are basically different from a "normal" one. The refugee is a guest by the grace of the government, without the rights of a citizen. There is often worry and concern about others left behind; there is a lack of certainty, a need to ask for guidance and advice. For some time after resettling, the know-how is missing; recognition of what is usual and appropriate is lacking. A friend told me that when he first came to New York, his parents helped him write a letter to accompany his application for a job. They counseled him to mention their own eminent reputations as well as other extraneous content, clearly marking him as a foreigner unaware of American customs. He did not get the job, but the potential employer wrote him a note suggesting that in the future he consult an American before writing another letter of application. It was good advice, kindly given.

To a large extent, the older escapees formed their own social circle until, after some years, they assimilated. They were company for each other and flocked to places that reminded them of home. In New York two cafeterias on Broadway became a meeting place for escapees, much to the chagrin of the owner. The escapees treated the cafeteria like a café. They did not just eat a sandwich but lingered over a cup of coffee or two, read newspapers, and discussed the news, as they had been wont to do before emigrating. The owner was amazed, perhaps incensed; he had never seen people dawdle so long over coffee. They were preventing a turnover of customers. One of the escapees came to the rescue and opened a Viennese-style café, offering coffee with *Schlag*. He made a fortune in no time.

The story of the escapees who were over forty when they arrived can no longer be told through their own recollections. Alas, most of them are no longer with us. The stories in this chapter were conveyed by their children. The initial downward spiral of their parents was reversed, and there were many successes. Mr. Kosak, who on his arrival dunked straw hats, went on to make a satisfactory living by selling advertisements. Mr. Bäuml, no longer a janitor, ran a successful business with his wife. Mr. Vortrefflich's strudels became familiar to everyone in the neighborhood. Mrs. Grunfeld used her experience in cooking for the seven siblings to open a successful restaurant. Mrs. Friedman continued on a part-time basis as a companion and lived very comfortably on her earnings. Mr. Heiman, a most versatile man and originally owner of a textile firm, started off as a peddler and ended by running a very successful chicken farm. Mrs. Bron, who rather early on became a widow, earned sufficient money as a masseuse to send her son through medical school. Mr. Steiner, formerly part owner of a family business, was able to leave his job in a glass factory in New York, attended night school at Brooklyn Polytechnic Institute, and pursue his scientific interests. His wife was able to abandon the little stars she used to sew on navy uniforms and develop her career as a psychologist. She was associated with the top members of her field and practiced to her last day at age eighty-two. In fact, many of the escapees worked as long as they could. Most had lost their pensions and savings, and they were deprived of the many advantages of an unbroken career. Their children report that their escapee parents readjusted and lived out their lives in contentment. They had achieved freedom. *Freedom* was not a trite word or a platitude to them. The knew its meaning in every sense of the word. They never took it for granted. Having gained liberty for themselves and for their children, they felt well compensated for all their material losses.

## Chapter 25

# The Farmer and the Taxidermist

*The escapees were willing to try their hand at any job, however far removed from their training or experience. And if at first they did not succeed, they tried again.*

### Farming the South American Way:
### From an Account by Joseph Rauchwerger

Joseph's first inkling of future difficulties came when he saw the poverty and filth in Cristobal, Panama, while on his way to Ecuador. His brother Ernst, who came to meet him, did not have good news: None of the newly arrived refugees had been able to obtain jobs. Joseph's first destination was Quito in Ecuador. The bus traveled on unpaved and rutted roads that crossed dry riverbeds and bush country. Joseph and his family saw only dirty streets and decrepit buildings simmering in tropical heat. Continuing on, they crossed the marshes of the Guayas River delta and passed sugarcane and banana plantations; after changing to a train, they ascended slopes nearly to regions of eternal snow. Finally, they climbed the slopes of Mount Cotopaxi and arrived in Quito.

Joseph and his family shared a house with a number of other families. Each family was assigned one room containing two beds, a table, and a chair. The women learned to cook over an open charcoal pit. The water to bathe the baby was brought from the well in the middle of the yard. Formerly an electrical engineer, Joseph decided, for want of anything better, that he and Ernst would try their hand at farming. They found a 270-acre farm. Fifty acres were covered by woods; 20 had bare, infertile soil that was rock-hard; another 30 acres had sandy soil which could only be cultivated during the rainy season. The brothers paid with some money that had reached them from Europe. They could not move immediately into the adobe farmhouse since they found it to be infested by fleas and other insects. First they had to scrub the woodwork and whitewash the walls. The farm had no electricity or running water. The previous tenant had used the contaminated water from the irrigation ditch. A well had to be dug to a depth of twenty-two feet; water was finally reached after three days of work. Four mules for transport, three pairs of oxen for plowing, three cows, and two horses were purchased. The best fields were set aside for cabbage and celery, which, the brothers believed, would fetch high prices in Quito. Since blackberries were in demand, twelve hundred seedlings were planted alongside the irrigation ditches. A few acres were sown with corn, peas, barley, and potatoes. The two families were full of hope as harvesttime grew nearer. The outcome was a fiasco: A hailstorm made the cabbage worthless except for animal fodder, and when Joseph and Ernst took the celery to market, they were offered a pittance, not sufficient even to pay for the transport to town. The blackberries died, the potatoes were blighted, and the corn, which had been planted on poor soil, gave very little in return. Only the peas and barley brought in some cash.

Joseph and Ernst learned two lessons from this experience: A farm on the scale of theirs would not support two families, and farming had to be learned from the neighbors rather than by innovation or by following European ways. Ernst moved into Quito and started a bakery. Joseph hired an overseer from the village, a man who understood local conditions. The next harvest proved to be a great improvement. Joseph utilized his background in engineering to design machinery to improve the primitive local farming methods and fashioned a wooden cylinder drawn by two oxen to cut the threshing time. In addition, he built two bridges over the ravines on his property so that the mule-drawn carts could cross them.

Then Joseph fell ill with a severe case of malaria. Since his recovery was very slow, he decided he had had enough of tropical agriculture and moved with his family to Quito. After eight months of looking for work, he noticed an advertisement for an engineer to run the Ambato municipal power plant. He was interviewed by the mayor, who was enthusiastic about Joseph's credentials. He asked Joseph to leave his diploma with him so that he could show it to one of the councilmen. He refused to accept a notarized copy but promised to return the original by four o'clock that afternoon. The mayor sent the diploma by special messenger to the councilman. Unfortunately, the messenger lost it on the way. The mayor apologized and gave Joseph a signed statement accepting responsibility for the loss of the diploma, but Joseph was disconsolate. He was sure he would never get another job in his life. But luck was with him. When he returned home, he found that an oil company in Selina had contacted his wife with a job offer for him.

The saga was by no means over. There were many jobs still to come. After the Selina job was over, Joseph and his family joined Ernst, who was now living in Colombo. There the two started a coffee shop, which, owing to inadequate help and refrigerating equipment's tendency to break down at frequent intervals, turned out to be unprofitable. Subsequently, Joseph worked designing a hydraulic power plant and as a maintenance engineer for a bottling plant. Joseph's daughter became engaged, but there was no money for an engagement party. The young couple moved in with their parents. Eva worked with her father. Erich sold agricultural machinery, and Joseph's wife, Ada, looked after little grandson Ricky.

After the war was over, Joseph inquired about the fate of his family but received no answer. Later he learned that his parents were shot while hiding in the woods. Eva, Erich, Ernst, and his family were able to emigrate to America. Because Joseph would not have been eligible for immigration to America for a long time, he decided to move to Israel. However, at his age of fifty-one, he found it difficult to find a position. He returned to Bogotá, Colombia, and finally reached the United States in 1957. At first he worked in Erich's poultry business; after that he held various positions until he retired at sixty-seven. Joseph earned enough to live comfortably and to enjoy attending concerts and theater performances, skiing in winter, and golf in the summer. Now in his eighties, he continues to live a well-deserved pleasant life.

## It's Still a Job:
## From an Account by Charles Deutsch

*Charles Deutsch, who had held a highly responsible position in Austria, wrote a letter in German to a friend while working on his first American job. What follows is my translation of that letter.*

Of course, I knew in Vienna what an American office would be like. After all, what were movies for? Beautiful girls' slender fingers glide over typewriters, while bosses have the right to put both feet on their desk. The boss pushes one button, stocks go up, and the factory employs a hundred more workers; the boss's son marries the beautiful secretary, or the other way around. I would dream of being part of such a concern. I had already been five weeks in New York when I saw an ad: "Wanted: Correspondent with excellent command of English." My English was far from perfect, but I did get the job. I will now give you the benefit of my experience in an American office.

Do you know what a taxidermist is? It is someone who stuffs animals. That's where I am now working. It isn't bad. When you enter the premises, a tiger is about to jump on you. Well, not exactly. He can't exactly jump because he is stuffed. But he is hanging from a wire so that when I come in he shows his pleasure by dangling back and forth over my head. I am also greeted by an ill-humored bison, an elk, a few fish, and an owl, which are said to have parties at midnight. They don't bother anyone, and no one ever dusts them. From the shop I walk into my workroom. Of course, everything works electrically there, namely the bulb and the telephone. There is no desk. There are a few boards nailed together. The typewriter, I believe, was used by George Washington and could use a cleaning. But not with our vacuum cleaner. We use it only to freshen up the animals' fur. Its use for anything else is strictly forbidden.

Let me tell you about the life that goes on around me in this office. There is a boss. He has a desk. But it is even dirtier than mine. We have no chairs to sit on. I only have a rocker, which is constructed in such a satanic fashion that my derriere has become one big corn and my back has withered into pain. Hides are tanned around me; fat is being scraped. Recently, a nice black bear was brought in to be artistically skinned. I know I must be popular with my new fellow workers because they offered me a part of the bear.

For an additional treat, they left parts of the bear all over my desk. I told you everything we have in the office. Now I will tell you what we don't have. Dustcloths for one. But then they would be useless because we do not have water either. The boss shut it off so the pipes won't freeze. We have to fetch it in buckets from the neighbor.

My illusion about American offices has been somewhat tarnished. But around the corner there are two movie houses. And I am sure there will be a movie playing where I can admire a real American office.

But after all is said, it's still a job!

# Chapter 26

# The Energy of Youth

The youngsters who arrived in their late teens and early twenties were less rooted in the past than their elders. They were particularly eager to transform their lives, that is, to shed their recognizably foreign ways and be taken for citizens of whatever country had accepted them. It was plain that their existence had changed radically and that a formidable task lay ahead. They approached their goal with the energy and optimism of youth. There were many things in their favor: They were young and adaptable. The majority had come from solid and comfortable homes that had given them a firm basis. They had been the recipients of an excellent education, preparing them for any further schooling. Recent traumas had so alienated them from their former countries that they were willing—no, eager—to put distance between themselves and their past.

Those who were privileged enough to reach the United States directly responded with delight. Even now they wax rhapsodic about their first encounter with their new country: "I[8] loved New York in time-honored immigrant fashion from the moment the boat docked and I set eyes on the city"; "To arrive in New York was to be gripped by its strength, liberality, and freedom."[137] There were many aspects of the United States that appealed to and excited the escapees. Louis[185] liked the melting pot ideology: "I assimilated quickly into the East Bronx—an Italian, Irish, and Jewish community—and took to Bronx slang like a fish to water." They responded enthusiastically to the scenery: "I[137] drove across the country, experiencing the might of industrial America, past the endless, wavy plains of the Midwest, then south, past the rock formations of New Mexico. It was a profound experience." They were pleased to find a rich variety of cultural activities. Annie[172] practically lived in the public library. She walked in Central Park at all hours (yes, we did), loved the museums, frequented the free concerts at the Frick Gallery, and felt grateful for the English language and its literature. The new arrivals found the political atmosphere they had yearned for: "I[39] arrived at the end of 1939. FDR was our hero, and we thought of him as our savior." But most of all they resonated to the form of government: "We[172] felt so much gratitude to the Constitution. In some ways we appreciated the United States more than those born here."

The escapees who headed for Australia had hardly known what to expect. They found a laid-back, dolce vita, atmosphere.[99] "No one seemed to be reaching for perfection; it was more 'She'll be all right, mate' or 'Near enough is good enough.'" People did not ask for qualifications for a job. New arrivals managed quite well in that atmosphere. In fact, sometimes they stood out by their "pressure cooker" attitude. But then, they did have to overcome a certain xenophobia: The Australians referred to the four thousand immigrants who arrived in 1938 and 1939 as "the bloody reffos." The escapees were not discouraged. They were young and strong. They were all in the same boat and determined to overcome local prejudices.

Attitudes toward Britain, a more tradition-bound country, were not uniform. While many youngsters adjusted quickly, there were others who did not feel at home there.[49] They considered the British distant, and they feared they would never breach the barrier of British reticence. It was not that they met with hostility, but they found the style of life alien and believed there was a class consciousness that could not be surmounted. They were pleased when they were able to emigrate again.[96]

Perhaps the problem in Britain lay in part with the insecure status of refugees, who were marked as "aliens." Eighteen-year-old Nelly,[73] without money and scared of the unknown, had arrived with a work permit as a domestic in a boardinghouse. After a few weeks the Home Office decreed that it was "unsafe for aliens" to mix with so many boarders. Nelly found herself looking for a new job. She located a position an hour's ride from London but found it to be too far from the agencies she visited constantly in her attempts to rescue her family. She managed to find a position as a nanny in London. In

1940 she was finally able to embark on a nursing career. But when France capitulated, all "aliens" had to leave their posts, and Nelly was desperate for money once again. She was forced to accept a job in a nursing home she described as "ghastly." Nelly was dismayed by her inability to follow her profession. She lived with a strange family, and she was too busy to make the acquaintance of the local young people. Added to all this was Nelly's constant state of helplessness as she encountered obstacle after obstacle in her efforts to find an escape route for her family. In the end she was unable to rescue them. It took years before she felt thankful for having survived. Being tossed from pillar to post made it difficult to develop love for country. It was only later when Nelly was able to resume her nurse's training that she began to identify with Britain. She was warmly accepted by both students and patients and began to regard herself as "one of them." In later years, during her long career as nurse and cytotechnician, she almost entirely lost the feeling of being an outsider. On the whole, she had become British.

Nelly's experiences notwithstanding, many escapees felt a strong affinity to Britain from the start. The "alien" hysteria passed. Kurt,[150] already in his twenties, had received a scholarship to the University of Glasgow and was teaching there. He was particularly impressed by the community feeling that developed throughout Britain during the war. Adversity combined with courage brought out the very best in people. In fact, British mores helped shape his political outlook and his moral values. He has noticed many times when he is with a group of escapees that those who spent their war years in France remained bitter while those who lived in England were impressed by what mankind can achieve.

The young Zionists[134] who arrived in Palestine felt that their dreams had come true. To be part of or actually to found a kibbutz was to put into practice everything for which they had been preparing. The kibbutzniks shared all their possessions. They labored on jobs to earn the money for the common fund to keep the kibbutz afloat and harvested their common land. It was an occupation ideally suited for the young:[179] "We were ardent Zionists and socialists. Our practical activities, our culture, our beliefs gave us strength to weather the storm. We were all in the same boat; families left behind in Europe. It was with a slow and protracted pain that we realized we had lost them. But the effect of ideological commitment and community life helped many of us, though by no means all, to cope with our predicament."

Youth is not fond of delay. The young escapees wasted no time in their effort to get a fresh start. When teenage Fred[175] arrived in New York via Holland, he was intent on beginning to enjoy life again: "My relatives introduced me to the American way of life, helped me perfect my English, get a driver's license and a job. Of course, hardships and belt tightening continued for some time. Loneliness was also a factor, but I spent many hours with my girlfriend. I assimilated into the American society rather easily." Richard[145] in Australia was practically bursting with resolve and energy: "I went straight to Australia and started work in my trade as a tailor on the first day after my arrival. I made friends very quickly, got married a few months later, and was elated to start a new life quickly. I was happy to stand on my own two feet and to help my family escape. I was very successful as a tailor: the so-called society people were my customers. I was the first *reffo* who got a car, got married, and had a business. There were many ups and downs, but I succeeded."

A willingness to work hard was a prime requirement. Those who were old enough took any job available. The younger ones, observing their parents' struggle, contributed where they could. Thirteen-year-old Hilde[162] got up every morning before six, helped in her parents' bakery, took an hour's subway ride to the special high school to which she had won an art scholarship, returned by subway in the late afternoon, helped out a few more hours in the store, and ended her day with homework. It is gratifying to know that Hilde's dedication paid off. In later years she became an art teacher at the New York Metropolitan Museum of Art. Hilde worked hard, but in this respect she was no different from the others. Otto,[42] who had almost completed medical training in Vienna which was worthless in England, had to support himself as a peddler and as a masseur until he was able to begin medical school all over again. Ralph,[5] who now lived in New York, knew that his parents did not have the funds to support him through college; he delivered newspapers, packed prisoner-of-war parcels for the Red Cross, boxed ironing board covers for a commercial concern, worked as a stock boy in a supermarket, as a busboy in a cafeteria, as a clerk in a mail room, and finally as a claims adjuster. In later years, as a program analyst, he had every reason to look back on his achievement with pride.

Another relentless pressure on the young people was the need to rescue their families. Now! Immediately! In 1937 in Germany Ellen[92] had been employed as a maid by a Jewish family. When her employers left, Ellen saw the wisdom of their move. She decided that it was her duty to leave and rescue her parents and six younger brothers and sisters. She remembers parting from her mother. "Child," her mother said, "I will never see you again." "No," Ellen had answered, "I will bring you all to America." In New York she worked again as a domestic servant. On each of her days off she made her ceaseless rounds; she never stopped begging and pleading for affidavits. She saved money to contribute to her family's rescue. And indeed she rescued them all—her mother, her father, and her five brothers and her sister.

Some escapees were now getting past school age without too much to show for it. Frank[137] was already twenty-five and tired of the drudgery of all the menial jobs he had held. At first he worked at minimum wage in New York, packed fur coats into cartons and held an office job in a furniture factory. But there was no future in any of those jobs. Frank yearned for an academic or professional career. Sometimes a twenty-five-year-old can profit from advice. Frank's aunt, who had always been his mentor, encouraged him. "You are not too old to study," she said. "Look at your uncle. He is over fifty and took his medical boards again. If he could do it at his age, why can't you?" That's all it took. Frank immediately enrolled in night school to start on the long path to a graduate degree. He decided to give up everything except work and school. No more girlfriends for the time being. He studied every free minute he had and covered 50 percent more work than is usual in night school. He achieved the straight A average needed to obtain a scholarship. At his age this was difficult to obtain, but after a search he found that the University of New Mexico was willing to grant him one for tuition. For living expenses Frank sold linoleum at Sears to the local Indians who came from the pueblos. The army delayed his graduate work and it turned out to be useful. He was given a commission and after the war worked as an investigator for the War Crimes Commission in

Germany. That experience gave him a taste of the legal world, and Frank found he functioned well in it. Harvard Law School agreed and admitted him after he was discharged from the army. A career in law was definitely better than packing crates.

Frank's studies had been delayed by his induction in the army. The delay in Britain could be even longer owing to internment and the difficulty obtaining a work permit. The young men also lacked family and connections, which might have facilitated their reentry into civilian life. Without backing, the escapees had to be doubly dedicated to attaining their goals. It meant looking for work, searching for scholarships, and sacrificing social life. It meant being single-minded. Ernst[30] gives an overview of the years it took for him to resettle, starting with the time of his arrival in Kendal, England, at twenty years of age: "The Quakers had arranged a job for me. In June 1940 I was interned, and during that time worked on the land and in a shoe factory. In the middle of 1943 I joined the armed forces. I was three years in East Africa and nine months in Austria, and I was demobilized in April 1947. During those years my quest was to survive and to win the war. I made and lost friends, refugees and others. Looking back, no relationship was lasting; they are all forgotten. I lived for the day and never planned for past the war. After April 1947, I did not think about being assimilated. The overriding thought and aim was to improve myself. I was working and trying to pass exams as fast as possible. I was busy for sixteen hours out of every twenty-four. Again I made friends, I lost friends. The twenty years from 1938 to 1958 were very hard, though interesting. The main privation was the loss of my youth. One forfeited all the pleasures which go with being young, and while this is common to the war generation of all nationalities, being a refugee more or less doubled the span."

Ernest, Hilde, Otto, Ralph, and Frank might be impressive, but among escapees they were not unusual. Nearly all my correspondents have similar tales to tell, and they tell them without self-pity. It is hard to know whose story to relate. Should we select Susan,[53] who had planned a career as a dancer and switched to demonstrating cosmetics to work her way through college? Should we focus on the girl[99] who went by herself to Australia, starting off as a nanny and ending up as an anthropologist in New Guinea? Should I add my own story about my working as a maid, as a salesgirl in a bakery and in a five-and-dime store, as a waitress, and as a mediocre secretary? There are too many such stories. In the escapee experience they are commonplace. None of the young people I knew ever complained or nostalgically reminisced about what might have been. We were here, outside the Third Reich, and that was enough.

How well children would adjust depended to a large extent on the school officials' and teachers' ability to place them into appropriate grades, familiarize them with new customs, and help them befriend the local youngsters. If the teachers also prepared the local children to welcome the newcomers, the path to integration was made decisively smoother. Some school officials seemed entirely at a loss as to how to react to the foreign children and seemed stumped by the youngsters' lack of fluency in English. Hilde[162] was simply placed in the lowest grade of her school. No explanation was given her younger classmates, who laughed at this "big kid who didn't understand anything." Every few weeks, as she began to learn the language, Hilde was promoted to another grade, only to meet with similar taunts from her new classmates. For a shy child it was like running a gauntlet. The school's approach to Jutta's[16] placement also seems devoid of logic: She was given an intelligence test that was administered in English. No one seemed to realize that Jutta's poor performance was due to her unfamiliarity with the language. She was put in an inappropriately low grade. The teachers must have been surprised when a few years later Jutta, a child considered to have a low IQ, was the valedictorian of her eighth-grade class. One wonders if the teachers ever reflected about this seeming discrepancy.

The academic aspects of school did not pose difficulties for the children. The children's scholastic background left little to be desired. It was the feeling of being unnoticed, of being merely a faceless shadow, that was so bothersome. In the long school corridors of large city schools, the local children, involved with their friends, strolled past newcomers with barely a glance. They felt no malice or prejudice. The local teenagers were simply busy with their own world, and unless teachers or parents helped to build bridges, they remained that way.

Karl[69] experienced this isolation when he enrolled in James Monroe High School, a large school in the Bronx. The local officials were not too happy to have another "refugee kid." Since Karl's English was very limited, he was placed in a German-language class. To no one's surprise he did well in German, as did the rest of his classmates, who promptly copied from him. Other than that, Karl had little contact with fellow students. He was an unhappy youngster, feeling forlorn in a big school. When he and his cousin moved to a small town in New Jersey, life quickly became much brighter. The newcomers were received with a fine welcome. Students from the journalism club interviewed the cousins, which made them feel newsworthy. Still, the boys must have been veritable greenhorns: When they were asked by the student reporters if they had ever eaten an American hot dog, they replied (after a quick, puzzled consultation with each other) that no, they never ate dogs and they had no intention of doing so. By 1944 Karl was considerably more savvy. He participated in eight beach landings, among them New Guinea, Dutch East Indies, and the Philippines with the Forty-first Infantry Division under General MacArthur, and he was among the first Americans to land in Japan after its surrender. But that lay far in the future. Meanwhile, a little fuss had turned a sad child into a smiling one.

Sometimes the personal interest of a single person could make that kind of difference. Dorrit[188] was fortunate to find a mentor in Miss Elsner, the assistant principal of Washington Irving High School. Dorrit had been feeling lonely and moody. Miss Elsner noticed her position as a total outsider and took matters in hand. She invited Dorrit for lunch to an old-fashioned drugstore and bought her an outrageously expensive ($1.45) turkey sandwich—the first ever for Dorrit. She also made Dorrit a monitor in her office, paying her ten dollars a month from some school fund. With the first month's salary, Dorrit and her mother went to S. Klein, an inexpensively priced department store, and bought her first American winter coat for five dollars. It was blue with a real beaver collar, and Dorrit was in heaven. She loved the school, loved learning, loved the four hours of art instruction a day, and became a fine student. It would please Miss Elsner to know that Dorrit became an art teacher of renown. Since her recent retirement she spends most of her spare time helping newly arrived Russian immigrant families resettle in New York.

As for myself, I entered Julia Richmond High School, where the graduating class alone consisted of eight hundred students. I had never before attended a school where the total enrollment was more than two or three hundred children. Besides examining our credentials, no one paid much individual attention to us. This neglect was compensated for by the stimulating atmosphere of the school. Students and teachers exchanged ideas, if not on an equal level then at least with mutual respect, a practice unthinkable in Vienna. There were classroom discussions of books and ethical issues. More important was our course in American history, mandatory for all students. This course opened up a new world for me. In my school years in Vienna and England, I had learned about kings and more kings. Now I learned about the ideas of democracy, about the Constitution, the Bill of Rights, the checks and balances between government bodies. It might be trite to say that the course taught me what America means, or at least should mean. It might be even more trite to say that it helped make an American out of me. Nevertheless, I must say it, because it did.

While empathy with the country's values speeded the youngsters' adjustment, there were also factors which mitigated against a smooth transition. One of these was poverty. It is difficult enough for adults to maintain their self-esteem when everyone around them is more affluent. For youngsters, who as a rule have not yet acquired a sufficient sense of self, such a situation can wreak havoc. Children who had been on a par with their peers suddenly found themselves held in contempt and rejected for reasons entirely out of their control. Dorrit's[188] father's difficulty in obtaining a reasonably paid position forced the family to live in a shabby walk-up apartment in the Bronx. Dorrit belonged to the Ethical Culture Society, a liberal organization mostly for middle-class children. If boys asked to escort her home, Dorrit would self-consciously decline. By the time she was in college, she had formed such a close friendship with two American girls that they were known as "the threesome." The girls invited Dorrit to their well-furnished apartments, and finally Dorrit reciprocated. Perhaps prior to their visit the girls had imagined that Dorrit was a European aristocrat of some sort. After their visit they knew differently. In any case, from that time on they ignored Dorrit completely. It took Dorrit a long time to wipe out the emotional consequences of her girlfriends' thoughtless act.

Being different is hard for a teenager to take, particularly if different means poorer. Add to this the necessity of living on charity, and there is a perfect formula for misery. Jutta[16] and her brother were staying with a wealthy family until their father could pass his medical exam and support his family again. The wealthy family's children were none too happy at having to share their parents with two strangers. To win their favor, Jutta would side with them against her brother; then she would suffer with feelings of guilt. But her worst moments came on Sundays, when her parents visited. Jutta dreaded their arrival. They spoke with a heavy accent and had foreign ways. Their clothes, which had been considered chic in Europe, now looked embarrassingly unstylish. The American children snickered behind their backs.

The children certainly were pained by their poverty. Of course, compared to the children left behind, their hardships are not worth mentioning. But compared to the fate of those children, there is barely any suffering in the world that is worth mentioning. That suffering stands alone and cries out beyond measure. Even compared to most *Kindertransport* children, these escapee youngsters, having arrived with their parents, were in a more advantageous position. But misery finds little relief in the greater misfortune of others. When young people suffer, they suffer acutely. At times they may have less cause than the adults around them, but that does not stop them from despairing more. Their feelings are intense: their confusion and distress profound. Feelings can plunge from joy to misery in minutes. And since teenagers tend to live in the "here and now," tomorrow often looks infinitely far away. These teenagers were no exception. What they felt, they felt intensely. Their joy at having been saved and their anguish at being on the outside looking in existed side by side. Sometimes a feeling of misery prevailed. Alice[128] clearly conveys the depth of feeling, a mixture of sadness and anger, typical of teenagers and precipitated by her unusual circumstances: "I was fifteen when I arrived. Being a refugee was tough. We had no status; my parents did not speak English; we had no familiarity with the mind-set of this land and no knowledge of the thousands of do's and don'ts one was expected to abide by. We were an unknown and unattractive quantity. And my reaction was fierce. I distanced myself from my family, my background, from everything that connected me with the Anschluss experience. My identity crisis was intense. The trauma of being separated from my accustomed lifestyle also separated me from my inner self, my sense of peace and harmony. I felt compelled to regain my well-being, but I did not know how to begin."

Youngsters showed understanding of their parents, reflecting a maturity beyond their years. Hilde,[162] the baker's daughter, recognized her parents' position: "I think thirteen is a difficult age, full of uncertainties. But I deeply felt I could not burden my parents with my problems. I was too aware of how hard my parents were working, of how great an effort my mother was making to find sponsors to help our relatives to come over before it was too late."

The parents' changed status did not lessen the children's respect for them. Karl's[69] attitude was typical: "I accepted my parents' lower status. I knew deep down that this would only be a temporary setback. Their desire to succeed was always there. The destruction of my father's powers by the Gestapo did not influence my behavior. On the contrary, I had more respect for him. I looked upon my parents as good human beings, whom fate had dealt an undeserved blow."

Young husbands and wives pitched in together to help each other get a start. Stella[72] was a young wife intent on helping her husband. She tells her story. "My husband had talked of trying to find a better job. Living on fifteen dollars a week was not very easy. I shopped for groceries on one dollar a day. One could make a very good goulash out of potatoes and one pair of cut-up frankfurters. But my husband's face was grim, and he looked more and more unhappy.

"I called one of the Jewish organizations and inquired where jobs were available for an excellent mechanic who used to be an engineer. They told me that men like that were badly needed at the Brooklyn Navy Yard, for instance, at Bethlehem Steel. I left my small daughter with my sister-in-law and told her that I was going to try finding a job for my husband. She thought I was insane.

"With my husband's photograph in my purse, I took the subway to Brooklyn. A long line of men stood in front of the employment office of Bethlehem Steel. I joined them. I was the only female and they craned their necks. The boss was Mr. Michaelman.

"Mr. Michaelman was sympathetic. He smiled when I showed him the picture of my husband and explained that he could not come himself because he could not afford to take the day off. Mr. Michaelman said he would see him in his house on Sunday.

"On Monday my husband started his new job. He worked many, many hours of overtime. But now he earned almost one hundred dollars a week."

The young escapees have made so many outstanding contributions that it is difficult to decide which ones to write about. There is Annie,[172] a physicist who contributed to her escapee husband's research in developing a device enabling paratroopers to signal each other in the dark without enemy detection. Her husband was honored for his work. There is Frank,[137] whose law practice brought him into contact with heads of foreign governments. There is a university professor[180] whose bibliography of publications runs to four pages. There is a sculptor,[127] a painter,[36] a teacher of dance,[160] a musicologist,[76] a writer.[72] There are nurses, social workers, secretaries, teachers, physicians, psychologists, and business people. There are those who started in more modest jobs and worked their way up in offices and businesses. But it is not the professional achievements, outstanding though they may be, that are the most striking element of the young people's stories. It is the combination of fierce independence and lack of self-pity that makes their accounts so remarkable.

When I began to write the chapters on resettlement, I was worried. I was deeply impressed with the escapees' ability to establish themselves occupationally. I knew that Berghan (1984) and other interviewers[141] had found similar results in their studies of escapees. I wondered how I could write about this theme. Would the stories sound too idealized? Would I be accused of bias, of only selecting the best of the lot? Perhaps Karl[69] characterizes well the spirit of the group and their capacity to build new and successful lives: "It is perhaps not the typical struggle of the newly arrived 'huddled masses,' because we were not brought up to take no for an answer. We were determined to succeed—my parents, we ourselves, and our children. I am very confident that this will also hold true of our grandchildren as they grow up in this free country of ours."

Inga Joseph (right) and her husband in their garden in Sheffield, England, in 1990, discussing with me the diary Inga kept on her arrival in England in 1939. In it she recorded her fears about her parents' safety and her unhappiness about the unsuitable foster home she had been placed in. Inga's parents did not survive. (Author's file)

Dorrith Sim (center) came to the Glasgow airport in 1991 to show my husband and me pictures of her youth. She organized a *Kindertransport* reunion in Scotland. (Author's file)

Gunther Abrahamson (in foreground), who, on arrival in Scotland, lived at the Priory and subsequently moved to a farm, shown with his former foster brother John Miller (wearing tie) and former hostel mate Arthur Spiro. The two former *Kinder* and their wives were visiting John at his farm in Scotland. (Courtesy Gunther Graham)

Meeting in 1990 in London attended by (from left to right) Gerda Mayer, Bertha Leverton, Elli Adler, Vera Schaufeld, myself, and Bea Green. None of the women knew each other before our meeting. Within fifteen minutes, faster than one usually discusses the weather and testifying to the rapport among many escapees, each one revealed her childhood experiences. (Author's file)

# Part IV

# THE EMOTIONAL AFTERMATH

## Chapter 27

# Don't Cry, Grandma!

It took years of tenacious effort and resolute faith for escapees to rejoin the ranks of productive citizens. I recall walking into my father's office when we were quite resettled. It was after his busy office hours. He looked up from the papers cluttering his desk and commented with a broad smile, "I am happy. I am making out our income tax. I am finally paying income taxes again." Taxes were welcome. They were a sign of having become once again a contributing member of society.

After the climb up had been accomplished, did the escapees simply resume their lives as they would have been had there been no Hitler? Could it be that such bruising years exacted no lasting emotional toll? It would be a rare person who could claim to have been left substantially unchanged by the ordeal. And, indeed, in spite of individual differences, when long-range emotional consequences are considered, there appears to be a commonality of reaction among the majority of escapees. A number of overlapping attitudes characterize their adjustment.

### A Darkened View of Human Nature

When the escapees were questioned about whether they believe in the basic goodness of people and were asked to describe their view of life in general, it is hardly surprising that their answers are replete with words like *pessimistic*, *cynical*, *cautious*, and *disillusioned*. As one escapee explains, "My view of people was formed by the Hitler period, the most significant single influence during my

**375**

formative years." Another states, "Events were bound to change my tendencies and to create a more hardened, more cynical outlook on life. Events had a lasting effect on me, making me to a certain degree more distrustful and cautious of people."

A certain amount of pessimism is viewed by some escapees as a constructive attribute. It was, after all, a spur to leaving Germany. A man who speaks of his own deeply embedded pessimism postulates that the same quality in his father saved their lives. Had his family responded optimistically, they might not have left Germany in 1937. His wife speaks admiringly of her father, whose optimism she absorbed. Yet it must be noted that her father did not leave in time and died at the hands of the Nazis. Is there a connection between pessimism and safety?

A tendency toward distrust of mankind forms a salient aspect of the escapees' personal philosophy. One academician expounds his theory clearly: "I view my life as a pleasure but in constant danger from anyone for whom my life either poses a perceived threat or for whom the destruction of my security offers an increase in his. I regard people in the mass as potentially dangerous and avoid all crowds whose behavior I cannot predict with any degree of certainty. Such a crowd is any number of people in excess of one. For there is no question in my mind that a Nazi-type totalitarian regime, complete with holocaust, will recur, and in fact such regimes have recurred." And he adds, cynically, "The victims could be any identifiable group, though it will no doubt help if they are labeled Jews."

Many escapees agree with the professor that a holocaust could recur. Indeed, why should they think otherwise? The institutions in which the escapees had placed their faith had failed them completely. As a result people became suspect. A man in his middle eighties looks back and declares, "If people like the Germans of high living standard and culture could be misled by a fanatical orator, any other people can be too." The escapees who as a group had valued knowledge and cultural institutions to the highest degree now recognize that the forces underlying civilization had proved impotent in the face of aggression. The bulwark structures of reason, science and philosophy, erected over centuries, had meant nothing. Some members of the intelligentsia had been as prone to bestial cruelty as the lowest street fighter. An escapee wonders about the meaning of a public morality and solidarity that fractured so easily at the first sign of pressure. Other countries, considered to have high ethical standards, stand accused as well. An octogenarian comments, "I cannot forgive them for standing by silently and closing the escape doors while Jews were being murdered." Christianity as an institution is also questioned. "How was it possible," wonders an escapee, "for such bestial events to be tolerated by a highly cultured, Christian nation?" The escapees, who had been devoted to *Kultur* almost as to a religion, witnessed how easily that culture had been vanquished by villainy.

That reason and culture proved to be no safeguard against anti-Semitism made some escapees more cautious in their relations with non-Jews. There are of course many escapees who are entirely at ease with non-Jews and number them among their close friends. Yet there are a considerable number who feel the need to protect themselves against any possible further injury to their still-raw wounds. One woman insists that she has developed an ability to detect the most covert or subtle forms of anti-Semitism. A man who had suffered a great deal in his youth and young adulthood developed a personal technique for approaching non-Jews: "I try to analyze the thoughts of people when I first meet them. When I have doubts, I generally mention the fact that I am Jewish. In that way any unpleasantness is nipped in the bud. I have met enough non-Jewish people in my life to know what to look for and listen to." One man whose wariness is profound observes, "I have to admit that I am pretty cynical about Christians. I suspect that about one millimeter beneath their skins, they're anti-Semitic and that enough of them are capable of behaving in the same way as the Nazis did if economic conditions ever become as bad as they were in Germany in the 1920s and 1930s."

## A Longing for Attachments

One might predict on the basis of the escapees' pessimism and dour view of humanity that they would likely be a bitter, possibly isolated lot intent on avoiding close contact with people. But that would be a wrong conclusion. The escapees are more complex in their attitudes. Reading through their statements, one is struck by a particular oddity: The writers seem to contradict themselves. At first I simply ascribed this incongruity to a particular person's way of thinking, but then I found, one might say, consistent inconsistencies. The escapees seem to combine the outlook of the skeptic with a belief in people. They characterize themselves as having a gloomy view of life yet also present themselves as being optimists. They see people as capable of the worst, but at the same time they search for close friendships. For instance, a man active in the Jewish community writes about his view of life: "My memories affect my relationships with non-Jews. The memorial being erected at our temple will say, 'They perished because of the world's indifference. Never again.' I became a cynic and a realist. No more idealism." Then, surprisingly, he adds, "I am basically an optimist about life. My view of the basic goodness of people has not changed." The following respondent has an equally divided perspective: "It is hard to come to terms with such evil in people. I am basically quite insecure, always expecting the worst, not surprised by horrible events. I tend to worry." And here comes the contradiction: "But I am trusting and optimistic. I view people as basically good, but I know there are a lot of bad apples."

In fact, the evil of mankind seems to challenge the escapees to become more, not less, involved with others. For instance, a man in his seventies who is currently politically active explains: "The Hitler period has certainly influenced my thinking, making it clear to me what dreadful deeds people are capable of. I am eager to form relationships with people, because I am of the opinion that people's innate goodness must be fostered to counteract the human tendency to do evil rather than good."

On reflection, it is possible to explain why the escapees' negative evaluations of people as a whole are frequently amended by a more positive view. The cause for their grim view of humanity is obvious and needs no explanation. Rather, we need to explain how their negative view became tempered by a more positive outlook. It is simply a fact of life that there are a lot of nice people in the world. And unless a person is scarred beyond redemption, continuing contact will likely soften even an extreme point of view. The refugees received help along the way. They remembered it, and this recollection influences their view of the world. A psychotherapist who had been placed in a loving foster home describes how both good and evil converged to influence her judgment: "I learned at the age of eight that not everyone is nice. I have no illusions about people's capacity for prejudice and irrationality. At the same time, there have always been people ready to help. It is other people who made it possible for me to survive." A former *Kind* who had arrived in Sweden gives a balanced evaluation: "I have met many decent and selfless individuals during those critical years. And even the Germans of my youth were a mixture of good and bad, except the bad had the power." And a physician whose disillusionment was engendered by the German intellectuals' swift acceptance of Nazi ideology later became impressed by the humanity of the simple people he ministered to in the English working-class districts.

It seems that escapees have grave doubts about mankind in an abstract sense and about the fate of the world. On an individual basis they enjoy people and welcome close relationships. They are on guard with people en masse but very comfortable vis-à-vis individuals. A social worker who describes herself as cynical comments, "I feel I have to champion the good in a person. Not in the population at large, but with individuals." I might add that I recently had the good fortune to meet the academician who wrote that he distrusts crowds and defines as a crowd any number bigger than one. There were five people present as he discussed his well-thought-out personal philosophy. He was gracious and interesting. It is not that he does not seriously hold to his views, but there is a difference between his general world view of people and his more benevolent view of the individual.

## Time and the Wounds

That the escapees have been able to temper their negative view of the world does not imply that they have been able to wipe out the emotional wounds they suffered. The passage of time itself stirs up memories. With age there is more time to reminisce. There is no more struggle to build a career, no busy hours with small children. The daily worries are reduced. Nor is the youthful optimism there, the beliefs that all losses can be filled with other pleasures and that "time heals all wounds." Says a man whose cheerful optimism carried him through many years of youthful struggle: "I am given to musing too much about my childhood days and school friends. I am now retired and in a position to be able to think more about events from the past. I am more emotionally affected now than I have ever been."

And there are others who agree. They say they are more stirred by the events as time goes by. They remember things they had swept under the rug. It took one man thirty years until he could talk about the events of his youth. There is an escapee whose father's arrest drifts into her mind, unconnected with the moment at hand; it has happened before, but this year it is happening more often. For all these years a woman had repressed her feelings about her parents' final days; now she feels compelled to visit Auschwitz. Another escapee has been feeling increasingly anguished over her aunt, uncle, and grandmother, who perished in Theresienstadt concentration camp. In her youth, when she was in her twenties and excitedly saw life ahead of her, there had been less time to think about such things. But the limited years ahead seem to focus the glance backward. The value of life seems enhanced, and losses are recognized more clearly.

To the present day there are too many tangible reminders for the escapees and too many unhealed wounds. Memories may be strong at one moment and weak the next. They may go underground for years only to be reawakened by an encounter, a memento, a place, a word, a sound. And even if one tiptoes carefully to avoid all reminders, at some unexpected moment at some unexpected place the ghosts of the past rise again.

Though she was only twenty-five when she emigrated, a woman still feels a shock at the sudden ringing of a doorbell. Large dogs trigger a fearful reminder of the Germans in a former *Kind* who remembers the Germans bringing a hound to her door. Some men and women become anxious at the sight of a uniform. One escapee comments that even if she has done nothing wrong, she "falls apart if stopped by a policeman." Another respondent is so convinced about the possible obstructionism of officials that he is sure that if he brings a package to the post office, it will for one or another reason be refused. A former art teacher, now retired, describes her own sentiments: "I cannot step into too hot a bath without thinking of the horrible Nazi medical experiments. I think of the prisoners when the weather is icy cold. I am extremely sensitive to suffering in any person. I cannot tolerate any cruelty or prejudice toward anyone. I let nothing pass."

As for myself, I am intensely moved by the innocence of children. When my children were in elementary school, parents were sometimes invited to attend a performance. The girls and boys, led by one child carrying a flag and accompanied by music, would march onto the stage, their earnest faces scrubbed clean, their clothes freshly starched. They came in with the utter certainty that if they performed well in school, all would be well. They still held the belief and never doubted that if you are good, life will reward you. And I would sit in the audience, remembering how much could go wrong and how many little boys and little girls who were oh so good reaped no rewards but did reap something most terrible. Tears would come to my eyes, and, as always, I had forgotten my handkerchief. In order not to be conspicuous with tears, and in order not to let the tears run down my cheeks, I would begin to study the ceiling. I became familiar with every crack above me.

I have also experienced moments of profound shock on European train platforms when long trains consisting of cattle cars rumble past me. They continue through the station and roll on and on. They are usually long and block the surrounding view. All one sees is a never-ending row of cattle cars. And I think: Are these the cattle cars they rode in? Are these the very ones? They must be. I have never read that anyone disposed of the cattle cars. Who cleaned them? Who put them back on their regular route? Are there marks on them, some hidden marks somewhere that tell the story? No, no marks. As they rumble past me, people in the station continue to read their newspapers or maintain their quiet conversations or their strolls up and down the platform. No one else appears to be disturbed.

A number of escapees feel wrenching emotions at good-byes. An escapee finds she cannot say good-bye even if the parting is only for a short while without "breaking up completely." Each time she is positive she will never see the other person again. A *Kind* whose guarantor failed to pick him up at the railroad station feels a "palpable sensation" about meeting or being met at airports. One respondent writes, "When I see a reunion anywhere in the world or watch someone say good-bye for the last time, even if it is part of a comedy, I burst into tears. Just as I am doing now, as I am writing this."

Some good-byes do not merely generate sadness but evoke new insights about parents. An escapee mother recently saw her daughter holding a suitcase at a railway station. As the train pulled out, the former *Kind*, now a mother, burst into sobs and began to cry and cry and cry. Her parting from her parents in Vienna had come back in a flash. Suddenly, in her mind she had become her own mother and her daughter was herself; with this metamorphosis came the full realization of what her mother had endured. There was a second recollection as well. She remembered a close friend whose mother had not been able to part from her; subsequently, they perished together.

The occasions that trigger escapees' recollections vary from those directly related to past events, such as a visit to Yad Vashem (Israel's Holocaust museum), documentary films about the Holocaust, or the anniversary of Kristallnacht, to indirectly related occasions, such as observing the lives of normal people, funerals, family celebrations, someone being bullied, old letters and photos, a ship sailing. No wonder the life of an escapee can never be a fully quiescent one. A painful memory may be encountered around the next bend of the road. And these painful memories open up each person's vulnerabilities. "Do you have scars?" I asked the escapees. Very few answered in the negative. Most answered yes. One who escaped without parents at the age of seven replied, "I am one big scar." Another *Kind* feels that everything is ephemeral, that no relationship lasts forever, and that a time will always come when he has to move on.

For many escapees change per se is distressing. One respondent observes, "I don't feel secure in new situations. I avoid change and hate upheavals. I hate moving. It seems to me that there were constant changes, different languages, different people, different homes, different addresses. I will do anything to keep the status quo. For me to make a decision to change anything, to move away, or change a job is horrendous."

Some escapees anticipate disasters that would never occur to a non-escapee. A former *Kind*, only six on her arrival in New York, feels that the initial emergency made her emergency-hypersensitive. She is always—and she means always literally—prepared for disaster. One woman suggested to her husband during the Persian Gulf War that each family member be given some cash since no one could predict what would happen to the banks in case of war. She soon concluded that it was ridiculous to keep so much money on her person. She associated her need for preparedness with her parents' foresight; they had been fortunate enough to have some money at their disposal when they left Austria.

Excessive fear of anti-Semitism is disclosed by another escapee. "If I hear of an incident, or read about something in the newspaper that the Israelis have done which does not meet the approval of the author of the article, I am immediately worried. Are we going to have another manifestation of anti-Semitism akin to the Hitler period? I cannot conceive that if we Jews do something that is not in accordance with general world opinion or is not 200% ethical, that every non-Jew will not immediately hate us." "When I awake at night," says an octogenarian, "I often imagine myself to be with the partisans or in a concentration camp."

## "O insupportable and touching loss!" (Shakespeare, *Julius Caesar*, act 4, scene 3)

There is no doubt in most escapees' minds that of all the injuries the worst is the loss of the family. Even if some family members did survive, all too often little family cohesion or contact was left. Often even the briefest descriptions by the escapees tell all: "Whatever members of family were not killed are strewn all over the world." And again: "I have no relatives except my daughter. They are either dead, killed in concentration camps, or in Bolivia." Some families manage reunions. Thus, one couple traveled from Australia to Switzerland. The husband's sister and family arrived from New York. A niece came from Canada. A brother and his wife journeyed from Sweden. And the older brother and his family, who live in Switzerland, served as hosts.

The escapees miss having a warm family surrounding them. "I

am ashamed to confess," says one, "that my heart aches when I see large families and remember the one I once belonged to in Vienna." Many lament the lack of parents while growing up. One mother notes that the thoughts about her parents were particularly strong when her children were growing up. She missed talking about the wonderful things her babies did and the new words they were learning—the kinds of things one can tell only one's parents. Most of all she missed having their love. Similar regrets are expressed by a man who feels deprived of his parents in his more mature years; only now as an adult can he truly appreciate what noble and righteous people they were. And he feels pained that he did not have the opportunity to express his love.

There are parents who bemoan the fact that their own parents were deprived of ever seeing their grandchildren. In turn, the grandchildren grieve that they never had grandparents and some-times look through old family albums and wonder what life might have been like. Sometimes there are no family albums. One woman had trees planted in Israel in memory of her parents; the framed certificate hangs on the wall next to the pictures of her daughter and son-in-law. One day she was watching *Shoah* (a documentary of the Holocaust), and as she began to cry, her granddaughter put her arms around her and said, "Grandma, don't cry. We are your family now."

To think of those who died in concentration camps is a very difficult task. To merge the photographs taken at Auschwitz and Bergen-Belsen with the mental pictures of relatives or friends who perished there becomes almost unbearable. In my own mind I have always managed to make a mental split between the two. I think of those who perished but never imagine them in a concentration camp. I look at documentaries whenever possible. I feel I must do so out of respect for the ones who died. If they had to bear being there, I must bear remembering. Yet I am not able to combine the images. For instance, I saw a photograph once of two girls. They were naked. They had disrobed in front of SS guns and were about to walk to the ditch readied for their bodies. As they walked in their nakedness, thy had crossed their arms across their breasts for modesty's sake. I never allow myself mentally to put my dead schoolmates' faces in their place. Nor do I put my own. But one day I was talking to a friend on the phone. She knew about my work and casually mentioned that someone had presented her with a book about Theresienstadt concentration camp. I replied that my aunt and uncle had died there and mentioned their names. "Hold on," she said; she came back a few minutes later. "Yes, they are in this book. And here is the date of their arrival. And yes, here is the date of their deaths." I froze. I had known the truth for years. But somehow their names on a cold, impersonal list was too difficult to fathom. There was not even a grave. Just a name on a list.

### "The Horror of the Memory Never Left"

The escapees' lives must be seen within a framework that not only encompasses family members who lived but also those who died. Their emotional life and their view of the world must invariably be colored by those memories. And memories they have. Many and very touching ones. They touch the essence of their beings. I will let them tell what they remember; I will let some of their voices speak:

"I often think of my mother's deportation from the Düsseldorf abattoirs in November 1941. I know a good many details which were passed on to me by a relative who was an eyewitness."

"The bombing of the temple and being thrown out of the apartment. And my father being taken away. Yes, I often think about it. The bad memories come back."

"My mother's brother, brother-in-law, and my cousin were all sent to concentration camps. I think of how hard my mother had it in Germany. I still think about my fifteen-year-old cousin being dragged away. Yes, I still think about it. I won't forget."

"I was arrested with my father and uncle. We spent three weeks in the local jail together, and I was held another week by myself. One can't forget an experience like that."

"At the end of the war I got a Red Cross message that my mother had been deported to Minsk. There were no survivors. These thoughts are constantly with me. It affects me to this day."

"I went to a school reunion. My father was remembered with

tremendous affection by the girls, even though we were only eleven when we parted. He was enormously popular. One fellow pupil said to me: 'We can all remember your father. He was a father to us all.' Sometimes I think my father may have died of destitution because things were very bad. He was living from hand to mouth. He might have died or been deported but, I shall never know."

"My father's and brother's arrest. My mother crying and waving good-bye on my departure."

"When I became a mother I often used to imagine what a heartache our parents suffered having to send us away not knowing where to and whether we would ever meet again. I imagine what it must have been like for my young mother, my brother, and two little sisters to have ended their life there."

"The losses felt will never be forgotten. The mother, mainly. But I also think about my work lost. Who has my sculptures, drawings, portraits?"

"Most of the things I have of my parents came to me through Holland. Most important were my parents' wedding rings and it is only now, years later, that I realized how desperate my parents must have been to take their wedding rings off their fingers and send them to Holland. How hard it must have been for her and how little hope she must have had to relinquish that ring and so did my father. And to send them out of the country to Holland where they hoped that one day I would get them, which I did, thanks to the very good Dutch friends."

"I think back of the populace surrounding the trucks when we alighted and spitting and shouting at us. My uncle and cousins were arrested also. I was one of the youngest and helped others who had been beaten during interrogations. After entering Belsen concentration camp [as a British soldier] I knew the worst; the horror of the memory never left me."

"I remember my mother running to the *Kultusgemeinde* [Jewish community headquarters] and her face of relief at getting me out of Austria. She was holding on to me and touching me all the time. I very often do that now with family and friends. I remember her looking into the window, and when the train started moving, some children putting their arms out. And I saw the parents getting smaller, some collapsing on the ground, and then disappearing in the distance. The effect of learning about their fate was indescribable. It affects me even now. We found out that my father tried to cross the border into Belgium, was caught, sent to Buchenwald, and murdered there. My friend's father survived five years of Buchenwald, and he informed me of my father's death. My mother disappeared. I have a note that my mother was sent to a ghetto in Poland and died there, date and place unknown. The memory of losing my parents in that way is never out of my mind."

"I have recently seen a pamphlet on the history of the Jewish community from my hometown. I found it most upsetting to read about those whom I knew personally and how they all went to their deaths in the camps. Somehow after all these years, I am still able to visualize many of them, and this makes reading their history a very poignant, sad, and moving experience."

"Bad memories and upsetting scenes seem to be on my mind all the time. I cannot get away from the past. Something always crops up that reminds me. Writing this, for example. I have read many books that are associated with our past. When I read *The Holocaust* by Martin Gilbert, I actually came across the part that dealt with the transport my parents were on. Forty-five years after the event I read the report on how my parents must have died. It was as if I were meant to know. Until then I was never certain as to what had happened on that journey. You can find the report on page 229. My parents were on the train that left Berlin on the 27th of November 1941. I think of the events regularly. I haven't forgotten anything."

"After the reading of my mother's diary, sent to me from Holland after the war, I was thrown into a turmoil of grief and pain. The diary ended with the date of June 22, 1942, the day of her 'removal' to Camp Westerbork in Holland. The book rested in a drawer of my desk for thirty years, unread. To explain why is unexplainable but to me; I was unable to take much more sorrow about her death. My mother! She was loved, respected, intelligent. She looked what she was: strong and matriarchal. It did not help my heartache that she wrote about me in terms of love, in praise of me, daughter, wife, mother, artist. Her beautiful handwriting got smaller and smaller, at the end not higher than one-tenth of an inch—never mentioning 'Nazis' by name but saying so much—afraid her diary could fall into wrong hands. A friend who was in Camp Westerbork with her survived, told me that she behaved there 'like a queen' and bore everything without complaint—and proudly. She never bowed to the 'Masters' to the bitter end; seventy-four years old, she died alone.

"I shall end with a dream, not mine, which haunts me ever since a friend told it to me. It could have been my dream—or yours, ours! She was buying garden chairs, all sorts, all kinds, and then, while the salesman counted up, she said to him, 'And when shall you deliver the people who shall occupy them?'"

## Chapter 28

# The Assimilated Outsider

Inhumanity had touched the escapees' lives too closely for them to be able to completely extricate themselves from the experience. The awareness of inhumanity imposes a heavy emotional burden from which very few ever completely free themselves. It colors their outlook on life and makes it improbable for the majority ever again to feel entirely "like everybody else." It is impossible to look at neighbors who have lived their lives undisturbed in their homes, in their towns, regularly visiting their grandmothers, aunts, and cousins, and say, "That family is just like mine." When the escapees were asked "Did there come a time in which you felt totally integrated and no 'different'?" and "Are there times or ways in which you still feel 'different' or somewhat of an 'outsider'?" the escapees understood the questions only too well. A mere handful were able to say with conviction that they felt just "like everybody else," just like any ordinary citizen. An overwhelming majority hedged, modified the question, or felt compelled to qualify their answer. And many replied flatly that they never were able to relinquish the feeling of "being different."

On the surface the escapees' lives appear to be entirely assimilated. I visited an escapee journalist who lives in a small rural town. He was entirely at home in his office, what with neighbors dropping by and his absorption in local civic affairs. He seemed like Mr. Small Town America. Yet when I asked him whether he still feels different, the journalist struggled with the concept: "'Different' does not have the proper connotation, because 'different' almost means a form of alienation. But I felt right along that I am a pretty fair citizen, fair family man, fair newspaperman. I have been here a long time. But I suppose there has always been a tiny division between 'them' and 'me.' "

I was surprised by the response of a friend of mine whom I had not seen for many years. I had gone to high school with her in New York. Extremely pretty, popular, and amazingly without a foreign accent, she seemed the picture of the American teenager. She became an actress and later an airline executive. Among escapees I would have characterized her as the most integrated of all. And yet when I asked her how quickly she felt integrated into the American milieu, she replied, "On the outside immediately, on the inside never."

Even intense patriotism does not eliminate the disparity felt by new immigrants. "The first year of being in this country I belonged to the civil defense program. We saved tinfoil and newspapers and bought war bonds. I always stayed up until midnight to say the Pledge of Allegiance when the radio stations signed off and played the national anthem. I felt very good, very strong, very secure. But deep inside I felt somehow different because I had gone through some things that none of my friends had a part of. After a year I was pretty much like the others. Not entirely like the others. There is always a difference."

Even resettling at an early age fails to guarantee feeling "like everybody else." An escapee who was only seven when he joined his caring foster parents cites the many positive factors—such as a good job, marriage, and children—all of which made him finally blend in with his environment. And then he adds, "But traces of feeling like an outsider still remain."

Respondents describe this sense of being an outsider in different ways: "I was an outsider when I came, and still am"; "Once different, always different." Such comments are even made by people who emigrated as extremely young children. They remark that experience forms character, and their experiences were too different from those of other people to be like them. The loss of one's parents by murder is such an overwhelming event that it marks one forever. "Not a single day passes," says a man in his seventies, "that I don't think of my parents. My history is so different that despite superficial integration, I remain conscious of the hidden hiatus between myself and society." The consciousness of one's drastically different history erects a barrier to feeling permanently "just like other people."

## A Sense of Worth

It should not be construed that when escapees say they feel different, they mean inferior. On the contrary, while some regret or feel ambivalent about categorizing themselves as outsiders, most escapees have not only accepted their status but see it as an advantage. Because of their exposure to so many perils and changes, they regard themselves as having a broader perspective than others who have led more sheltered lives. A former Austrian who, because of a number of commitments, practically commutes between the United States and Germany explains her point of view: "It is really very difficult to put me in a pigeonhole, and a long time ago I thought that was a disadvantage. It was very clear to me when I lived in Vienna that I was an Austrian and Jewish and I had a strong feeling of belonging. Now the last thing in the world would be to consider myself an Austrian. I am an American, but I am different from American-born contemporaries. I feel like a citizen of the world and at home in different cultures. I believe this to be a genuine advantage."

This is exactly how a number of escapees respond to finding themselves perpetual outsiders. It seems that what was started by hostile forces has by now become a valued asset. The escapees value their dissimilarity because in part it reflects what they consider their rich cultural background. A musicologist stresses that his service in the U.S. army during World War II turned him into an American. Yet he does feel different because of his solid European upbringing: his excellent schooling, knowledge of languages, and cultural training. In any case he does not regret this difference. In fact, he feels good about it.

On the whole, their ordeal has enhanced the escapee's sense of self-worth. They were able to mobilize their inner resources, conquer innumerable obstacles, and acclimatize themselves to entirely new conditions; having done so, they have proved their mettle. One woman asserts, "The struggle makes one feel one has won, meaning we have survived successfully. I am proud I could cope. It adds to one's self-confidence." Explains another respondent: "My self-worth was enhanced by the Hitler experience. What we have achieved we did ourselves. To have been forced to leave penniless and construct a whole new life, which I consider a success in every way, is something to be proud of."

Many women found their self-confidence enhanced when they turned suddenly from sheltered housewife into breadwinner. One woman tells of sitting in a *Konditorei* on a recent trip to Vienna. While enjoying their afternoon cakes, two women at the next table were discussing what leftovers to prepare for dinner. The listener, once upon a time a housewife in Vienna, is now an author in New York. No wonder she comments, "When I go back to Austria today, it seems to me that the people have very limited experiences, and I am happy for my worldly insights."

There are some escapees, though they are in the minority, who found their self-worth diminished by their ordeal. That feeling is strongest among those whose education was cut short, preventing them from realizing their potential. Some of the escapees made up for this loss by going to school in later years. The study of music was commenced by an escapee at age forty; at fifty-two she obtained a college degree. And even this achievement is surpassed by a man residing in England who enrolled in a university while well into his sixties. Regrettably, not all who desired to do so were able to return to school. In addition there were some youngsters who, because of their disadvantageous foster homes, needed years to reach a level of greater confidence and regain their sense of security.

As a group, however, the escapees judge their experiences to have been character building in a number of ways. Of necessity, they were forced to develop or strengthen qualities that later stood them in good stead. Among these characteristics was the ability to face crises and withstand stress. They speak of having become more outgoing, self-assured, resourceful, experienced and tolerant and of possessing a wider scope. And having found that they were able to cope, they developed greater self-confidence. In fact, some escapees believe that the extra demands made on them during their youth imparted some unique qualities not possessed by other people. This helped them gain a worldly wisdom that they would otherwise not have acquired. One person, for instance, believes that he would be quicker than others who lacked his experience to recognize danger and take action. "My survivorship," writes a correspondent, "has given me a feeling that I understand some things others do not."

## A Special Bond

The escapees straddle two worlds. In part they are outsiders, in part they are assimilated. Life, on the whole, supports and reinforces the integrated component. By fitting in, the escapees better their existence and are accepted by a wider range of people. Yet, even while the escapees desire to be assimilated into their surroundings, the outsider part continues to exist. One would anticipate that the escapees need to make some connections with those who would understand that part of their personality, that the escapees would count among their friends a good number of other ex-refugees. And this is indeed the case.

Not only do the escapees have a relatively high number of fellow escapees among their friends, but the bonds that hold these relationships together tend to be particularly strong. That does not mean that the escapees have not acquired very close and highly valued friends among the native population. They certainly have, and in most cases they are equally fond of both types of friends. If they do not find a newly met ex-refugee interesting, the special bond is lost; that bond serves as a common starting point, but there can also be a rapid distancing if being an escapee is the only connecting link. All things being equal, there is a commonality that makes for a certain comfort in the relationship between ex-refugees. New acquaintances are interested in exploring each other's experiences, and it is likely that common memories and shared problems emerge. As one of the escapees ponders the question, seemingly for the first time, he is positively surprised at his own answer: "I am fully assimilated, but it is strange that ninety percent of my friends are Europeans and that I feel most comfortable with them!"

The long-ago adventure of journeying to Australia on the *Dunera* was shared by an Australian settler with other men. Since then he has acquired many Australian friends, but he is a little partial to his *Dunera* friends. He has a special affinity for them. Even though he and his Australian chums have a good many things in common, there is a uniqueness about the *Dunera* friends that nothing can quite equal. Together they recall the years behind barbed wire, the common uncertainty about their relatives and their own future, and now they feel the same gratefulness for these later, more content years.

Another wanderer had lived many years in England, Canada, and the United States. Along the way many people touched his life, and he explains his feelings about them: "There is no doubt that when I meet people of my own background an immediate rapport is established because of our common experiences, no matter how different the details might have been. My closest friends in the truest sense of the word are all ex-refugees, and none of them live in the U.S. or anywhere geographically close. But when we meet, usually once a year, distance and time seem to have made little difference in our relationship. When one has not shared a common experience, especially such a traumatic one, clearly one can never be as close."

Surprisingly, even escapees who arrived at a very early age still have the desire for friends with similar backgrounds. A social worker who arrived in New York at age six observes: "I always gravitated to other refugees, even as a child. Still do. What my parents expected, their value judgments, their notion of respect were more typical of a European than an American home. I was brought up in a European home in the U.S. I think unconsciously I seek out people with my background and to this day I have hardly any close friendships with anyone of a different background. It is this similarity which makes the common bond."

Immigrants were not able to keep track of many of the people they had met along the way. Escapees not only moved from country to country, but in their first few years of settling they usually moved to improved quarters. It was easy to lose touch. Nobody really thought it would be possible, after so many years, to reunite people who were geographically scattered on many continents. But fifty years after the *Kindertransport*s arrived in England, Bertha Leverton, a former *Kind*, wondered what had happened to all the former *Kinder*. She decided to organize a reunion in Harrow, England, and hoped that some of them would attend. Word spread swiftly from continent to continent. Bertha found that many former *Kinder* were most eager to see each other again. They came by train, by plane, by car, and by bus. Altogether about one thousand of them arrived. *Kinder* who had not seen each other for years either recognized each other or carried snapshots taken fifty years ago to indicate whom they were seeking. Bulletin boards were filled with notices of *Kinder* seeking an old friend, a former hostel mate, or even someone encountered only for brief moments. There was an intense desire to find anyone who might bring back memories of the past.

The little girl who had arrived in London from Czechoslovakia was now a British citizen in her fifties. But she remembered having shared a car ride then with a boy and girl from the train station to the big house where she stayed for about five weeks. The two visited her until she was moved to another place. She never saw the boy and the girl again. Now she hoped to connect with them and with what they represented of her past. She remembered that the boy's name was Kurt, and she made an announcement that she was searching for him. And Kurt was there. He had come all the way from the United States. He responded to her call, and they had a jubilant reunion. What had made it so important for the English lady to find a boy and a girl whom she had only seen a few times in her life? She explains: "I feel very close to these two people. It really meant a great deal to me to see Kurt at the reunion. I feel closer to these two people than nearly anybody else because we shared that car journey, and I suppose these were the last people to whom I ever spoke Czech."

Other people came with other hopes. A *Kind* who, on escaping to England, had served as an assistant matron traveled from Israel in the hope of locating some of the thirty-five little girls who had been her charges. She was delighted at finding nine of them. One was actually carrying a letter from some other girls in the group, received thirty-five years ago. They reminded her of how she used to sit on their beds and cuddle them when they were crying for their mothers.

A woman passed around a school photo of children of the school she had attended. Two former classmates were actually seated nearby. They recognized the picture and then there were hugs and tears. An Australian *Kind* had carried a secret hope: Perhaps someone would "rise from the dead." It did not happen. No one lost reappeared unexpectedly.

The emotional impact of the *Kinder* reunion was enormous. A great many of the former *Kinder* had not even realized until they came to the reunion that there had been 9,372 others like them; they had actually believed their own stories to be unique. By knowing others like them existed, they suddenly acquired both a past and the possibility of a fuller understanding. Stories of goodness, suffering, and resilience were shared. What was most impressive and gave the *Kinder* a sense of affirmation was how well they had succeeded with their lives. It would have been a great solace for their parents, if they had known.

The idea of escapee reunions continued to spread, and soon they were being held in many countries by *Kinder* as well as other escapees. The need to construct a past seems overriding. At a Philadelphia reunion a woman was describing how at sixteen she had traveled by herself to the United States. As she told her story, she mentioned the name of the ocean liner. Another woman suddenly jumped up and excitedly exclaimed that she had been a passenger on the same ship at the same time. The two then embraced. They had not met aboard the ship, but it was as if the coincidence provided them with a common past and had made them relatives.

The healing effect of the Harrow reunion is described by a former *Kind* who had arrived in England at age six. "I shall always feel different. But in the last eighteen months I have for the first time met other train kids, and this has brought about a cure of my feelings of isolation. It has increased my confidence to know there were close to ten thousand, a whole population I can belong to. Somehow it enabled me to give up the grief for my parents that I had been hugging to myself, almost as if it had been all I had. I found many had a far worse time than myself. I have felt most recovered and have added a new dimension to my life since I now see some of these people from time to time and have made one close friend."

## Strengthened Identification but Unchanged Beliefs

Most of the escapees, not just the former *Kinder*, experienced the desire, or even the need, to gain a stronger sense of identity, having lost part of their own when they lost family and country. It became more important to feel again a strong identification with some group that could be trusted, particularly if that group could also provide one with a past. Most of the escapees found that sense of belonging by strengthening their ties with Judaism and Jewish causes. A majority of escapees value their heritage more highly than they did in the pre-Hitler days. They speak of a newfound pride in the principles of Judaism. They feel a sense of obligation to be active in Jewish affairs so as not to allow Nazi objectives to be realized. By working for Jewish causes, they are repaying the help they had received. Some turn to the State of Israel as a result of their experiences: "However stupidly they might act," one escapee opines about Israel, "they have in my eyes redeemed the Jewish psyche, which has suffered so badly because of the Holocaust."

This almost unanimous strengthening of ties with the Jewish community is particularly remarkable because most of the escapees did not change their religious convictions. Before the Hitler era their beliefs had varied from atheist to orthodox, and their religious observances from barely any to very strict. The majority observed the High Holy Days and occasionally went to temple. To a large extent, their religious beliefs remained unaffected by events. Only a handful of people relate their beliefs in God directly to the Holocaust. Such statements as "I feel gratitude to God for sparing me" are exceedingly rare. So is the opposite view: "I lost whatever belief I had in God. I feel solidarity with all Jews, but believe Jewishness to be a tragedy, if not a curse. I was never ashamed of being Jewish but have been wondering if all these religions in the world were not causing more harm than good." On the whole, the escapees fail to raise the question asked by one of their group: "How could God have permitted this horrendous catastrophe to befall the Jewish people?"

It may be surprising that such momentous events seem to have failed to influence religious beliefs significantly. But then, one may recall an event in a concentration camp recounted by Elie Wiesel: Some of the most orthodox prisoners convened a trial to judge God for permitting the extermination of the Jews, which was taking place all around them. They found God guilty. After the trial, they all prayed.

## Another Remembrance of Things Past

This sense of being an outsider that hovers over the escapees seems to constitute some internal unfinished business. The trouble with that business is that it never gets finished. One only gets used to it. But that unfinished part stays connected with the past. And it triggers the desire to return to the place where the former life took place. The majority of the escapees have traveled back to their countries of birth, and for many it was a very affecting journey, particularly on their first return. Nostalgic sentiments of childhood, recaptured memories, precious recollections, mix with the pain of what was destroyed forever. The returnees explore the old streets, stand across the way from their former home, and look through the windows; they find the path daily taken to school and listen to the familiar sounds of music coming out of open windows.

The memories of the first thirteen years of one escapee's life return each time he visits Vienna: "I have returned to the scenes of my youth several times. Many memories, both pleasant and unpleasant, received new life; the old colors, textures, smells. And that in itself is a pleasant sensation; to stand beyond time and watch in the mind's eye a little boy who no longer exists in a physical environment remarkably unchanged. It has become an enjoyable ritual with me whenever I visit Vienna to walk down the street in which I lived and to take the walks I took as a little boy."

I, like so many other escapees, have made the same rounds, walking from former home to school, to the parks I played in, to the *Konditorei* we frequented for treats. The nostalgic memories were tinged with anger and sadness. I visited my mother's boarding school, run now by the state. I recognized the paintings and the grand piano, now shabby and neglected. My mother never received compensation. Waves of sadness came over me at the ice cream parlor directly opposite my former school. There were the same mirrors, the same small tables and white chairs. Nothing at all had changed. The establishment had survived the Nazis and the Russians. Most of the children who noisily crowded in each day after school let out are either scattered or dead.

Another escapee combines the good memories with the bad: "The hallway with its curlicue metal work was unchanged, and the staircase still had its ornate handrail. As we slowly walked up one floor to the apartment where I was born, I smelled the familiar musty odor and I was home again. A strange nameplate was on the door, but in my mind I could hear the voices of my sisters and brothers and of my mother and saw myself as a little boy coming back from play. We retraced the route to my elementary school, as well as to my high school. The smell of disinfectant in the high school was as I remembered it. We walked to Schönbrunn. The tall linden trees still lined the cobblestoned street. As soon as we entered the park, memories returned of walking there on Sundays hand in hand with my father and then in 1938 seeing the sign 'Jews not admitted.' The next visit was to the joint grave of my grandparents and my brother. The Jewish section of the Zentralfriedhof [main cemetery in Vienna] was an unbelievable sight. Big mausoleums fronting both sides of tree-lined avenues had been desecrated and were partially collapsed; gravestones were overturned; weeds had grown so tall that we could hardly get through much less read the directional markers. We searched for almost an hour before we found the grave and, as best we could, cleared some of the weeds. Our departure from the Westbahnhof brought back memories of my emigration from the same terminal. I had said farewell to my family, not knowing if I would ever see them again. This time with my wife at my side, I could afford the luxury of emotions that I had denied myself at the time. And I cried silent tears for what might have been if the Jewish culture of Vienna had not been eradicated and our family were still united."

Some escapees find only pain in returning. A former *Kind* experienced an intense feeling of fear on his arrival when he saw the police in jackboots and leather coats striding up and down the station. He never returned. Some are drawn back by relatives or friends they wish to see. Many want their children and spouses to understand their background better. Some visit former neighbors who had shown some humanity during those dark years. One returnee did just that and felt time disintegrating when she heard a woman whom she had not seen for twenty-two years exclaim, "*Na, Jessas, die kläne Elfi is wieder do* [Oh, Jesus, little Elfi is here again]!"

The escapees tend to keep a strict distance from anyone over a certain age. With respect to the local older generation, the returnees will never be able to rid themselves of the thought "What were you doing during those years?" Without some concrete credentials, such as the voice of a knowledgeable friend, no bridges can be built. Yet the escapees do not believe in collective guilt, and most show extraordinary openness to the younger generation. Since young people now outnumber the older generation, many of the escapees feel more at ease returning.

For most travelers the journey back does not lay any ghosts to rest, but it does revive memories and makes real what at times seems unreal. I remember standing in front of my former house with my husband and children and explaining that the SS once came for us but that the concierge managed to deflect them with a lie. I had the distinct feeling that I was making all this up and was inventing a story to make myself interesting. But as Dr. Robert Sugar remarked when he discussed his journey back in one of his lectures about the Hitler period, "The stories I had made up were really true."

The escapees are unfortunately not the only ones who need to integrate very diverse aspects of their lives. Salman Rushdie (Mazorati, 1989) was aware of the phenomenon when he wrote, before potential assassins forced him into isolation: "Most of the time, people will ask me—will ask anyone like me—are you Indian? Pakistani? English? What is being expressed is a discomfort with a plural identity. And what I am saying to you is that we have got to come to terms with this. We are increasingly becoming a world of migrants, made up of bits and fragments from here, there. We are here. And we have never really left anywhere we have been" (p. 100).

## Chapter 29

# I Am Glad Hitler Missed One

As time passed, the lives of the escapees became more comfortable. Of course they continued to worry about their relatives still in the Third Reich, particularly when the Red Cross letters stopped coming, but the full truth was revealed to them only after the liberation of the death camps. It was only then that most refugees realized the enormous gulf that had separated their lives from those they had left behind. The pictures from the camps were shattering, and over the years more and more horrendous details emerged. It took time to tell the whole story, the details about the *Einsatzkommandos* (the troops detailed to shoot and bury thousands until the death camps were ready), the daily selections of those who were to live or die, the starvation, the ovens, the doctors' experiments—and still other horrors. Each new revelation was a further shock to the escapees. They had survived; most others had been murdered. The question of how their own survival, as contrasted with the death of the six million, affects the escapees is often raised. Since it is often assumed that survivors suffer from "survivor guilt," it is important to examine whether this is true for this group of escapees.

### Not Guilt but Agony

The overwhelming majority of the escapees state unequivocally that they do not feel guilty. They may feel sorrow, grief, pain, even agony but most of the time not guilt. One man's brief reply is fairly typical of the group: "I feel no guilt; only regret and sadness for those who did not survive. I feel lucky and privileged to be alive." Most respondents add an explanation as to why they do not feel guilty. Some explain that they had been too young to help, that an individual could not have changed world events, that the forces against them had been too overpowering, and that they had been penniless at the time. They ascribe their survival to luck, and those who were youngsters at the time express thankfulness for their parents' foresight and sacrifice. They reiterate that when they were in a position to help their parents, they did what they could. Those who were very young at the time call attention to their parents' attempts to rescue their relatives. But even among those who were only in their teens, there were some who attempted to help. One former *Kind* still has the rough copy of the letter she carefully composed and sent in vain to the Refugee Committee in London to obtain help for her parents. She had penned it on toilet paper, the only paper she had available.

Among the many reasons escapees give for not feeling guilt is the fact that their own demise would not have benefited anyone. "I did not feel guilt, as I could not have helped by staying behind but would only have perished with them," explains a man whose own odyssey of resettlement lasted years. Others also point out how narrowly they themselves escaped destruction and document the point by giving details: "I never felt any guilt. The only reason we managed to get here was by the grace of my uncle who vouched for us or we would have rotted like everyone else. My dad was already arrested and ready to be sent to a concentration camp when our visa finally came." A man is thinking of his wife and son when he writes, "I feel no guilt for having survived or that my family was able to get out of hell before we were all sucked into it." Several respondents explain that while there was nothing they could do concretely for their families, they compensated by helping in other ways. One woman joined the armed forces, another worked for the Red Cross during the war, and a third helped resettle refugees who arrived in New York in the early 1940s. In fact, one woman emphasizes her lack of guilt feelings: "I feel glad that Hitler missed one, but I feel I must be worthy to justify all that was done to save me, especially by my mother. It has given me a goal to strive for. It made me determined to remain mentally healthy."

Several escapees explain that in their own minds they have reviewed whether they could have done more. But even if they have found some overlooked possibility after searching their memory, they still do not feel guilty. A former *Kind* wished she could have been more mature at the time. Her mother had written asking her to try and help her get an affidavit as a domestic. As a little girl she was either too young or too snobbish to do so. She regrets that she had been too childish to handle the request. She also sometimes thinks of her cousins who were a bit younger than she. They were such nice children, perhaps nicer than herself, and yet they did not survive and she did. Yet while she wonders why it went the way it did, she does not feel guilty. She knew that her parents' happiness lay in the fact that she survived.

Among the minority who do feel guilty, most characterize this feeling as not warranted. Some connect the feeling with a specific image, such as visualizing their grandmother waving goodbye. An escapee experienced a surge of guilt when she found the name of a close friend listed in the *Totenbuch* (Book of Death) at Auschwitz. Although she was only eighteen and was instrumental in rescuing her sister, a woman faults herself "for not being pushy enough." She explains: "I still reproach myself for not having done enough. I think the guilt is probably emotional in part and also justified up to a point, especially when I know that some people were more successful in rescuing others, even if they may have had more resources."

There are a few who are plagued with guilt because of decisions taken and now regretted. After the invasion of the Netherlands by the Nazis a former *Kind* stopped sending money to his father in Westerbork, Holland, where his father had been interned. He wonders now whether his father might have received the money after all. Another man suggested that his parents choose one of two possible ways of escaping; the one he suggested apparently failed them, and they perished. He cannot forgive himself to this day that they ended their days in Auschwitz. A memory plagues another woman: When she was fourteen and temporarily in France, a friend pleaded with her for an affidavit. She failed to ask her father to aid her friend, and now she is sure the friend did not survive. Her father probably would not have been able to help yet the incident remains in her mind.

Several escapees suffered a sense of guilt while they were young but managed to overcome it. A diary an escapee kept during her first years in England depicts her feelings at the time: She had been full of courage, faith, and hope as well as pain, loneliness, terrible fear for those at home, and irrational guilt. Although she had realized her family would not wish her to be unhappy, she had never allowed herself a day of joy until the war was over. Another escapee, while a youngster in Holland, felt strong guilt for feelings of jealousy: Her cousins' parents came and fetched their own children to live with them while she remained in a children's camp. She resented being left behind. However, her cousins and their parents ended up in a concentration camp, from which only three of them emerged. Now she realizes that it was all just a matter of luck.

Two men raise some particular points that trouble them about their non-Jewish relatives in Germany. When thinking about his non-Jewish relatives who lost their lives on battlefields, one respondent feels a sense of guilt. The other ponders: "If my father had not married a Jewess, I would have possibly fallen as a German soldier, as three out of my four male Aryan cousins did. Or still worse, I might have been forced to witness or even commit war crimes. Being half-Jewish, I have a divided background though my treatment in Nazi Germany made me decide to throw my lot with the Jews. All the same I feel guilt towards my dead cousins who through no fault of their own paid the Nazis the highest price."

The question of God is also brought up by another former *Kind*: "During the time when I subjected myself to all sorts of guilt feelings, I wondered whether I didn't or ought not feel guilty for escaping when six million others died. I recognized that my escape was mostly luck; it certainly was not due to any planning on my part. And if I can't take credit for it, how am I to be blamed for it? Fortunately I do not believe in a God, for if I did, I would have to cope with the problem of His guilt."

The large majority of the escapees feel obliged to explain why they do not feel guilty. It is almost as if they feel guilty for not feeling guilty. Possibly, they assume that others will not believe them, since there has been a great deal written about the pervasiveness of "survivor guilt." The fact remains that most of these escapees do not consciously feel guilty. The age factor does not seem to be the pivotal one, since most of the escapees who were old enough to take action do not feel guilt. They recognize their helplessness in the face of the enormous forces aligned against them. What does seem to be a factor in the escapees' lack of guilt feeling is their clear recognition that it is others who should feel guilty; the Nazis, for instance, or anyone who failed to extend help when they could have done so.

If it is correct that most concentration camp survivors feel survivor guilt, then one must wonder why these escapees do not. The escapees were physically removed from their incarcerated loved ones and therefore were unable to help them. Perhaps the common suffering among the concentration camp inmates made for greater identification with one another and provided more opportunities for guilt; that is, there might have been small actions that one inmate could have made for another—whether it was giving a spoonful of food or perhaps speaking a single word of comfort—that might have been too difficult to perform because of physical weakness or despair. Perhaps these are the incidents that come to mind when a survivor unjustifiably reproaches himself. The escapees, who had no opportunity to perform such actions, could not level such accusations against themselves.

## A Debt Repaid

The escapees are acutely aware that their suffering was nothing compared to those in concentration camps, and as a result they feel they owe a debt of gratitude and have an obligation to make something of their lives. This attitude, representative of the group as a whole, is well summed up by the following words, although most other escapees do not inject a religious note: "I have never felt guilt about having survived, but I have always, at every stage, felt strongly that any unpleasant experiences which I have had were trivial in relation to the sufferings of persons who did not escape and underwent tortures of the most devilish kind. Instead of feeling guilty, I have all along been concerned with the question of why I survived and what it is that God wants me to do. I have taken many actions which indicate that positive behavior towards other people has become very important for me to give meaning to my life."

The desire, or perhaps the acute need, of the escapees in this group to render services to mankind is extraordinarily high. I would venture a guess that it is the dedication to humane causes that is a factor in alleviating any guilt that the escapees might otherwise feel. In fact, the escapees filled pages not only with descriptions of what they do but also with explanations of why they want to do it. There is a passion in their voices as they describe their involvement with causes and explain the depth of their dedication. "I was a recipient," says one of them, "and now it is my turn to give."

Their own experiences have imparted to many escapees a heightened sensitivity to and a deeper awareness of other people's suffering and a strong identification with victims all over the world. They tend to be vigilant about all forms of racism and acutely dislike disparaging remarks about minority groups. They underscore the importance of high ethical standards in personal relationships. Predictably, many escapees have chosen helping professions. There are social workers, psychologists, psychotherapists, and physicians among this group of escapees. One former high school teacher became involved with the children of Nazi criminals while working briefly in a teacher program in Germany in the postwar years. In order to gain a better understanding, she returned to the United States to obtain a doctorate in sociology and political psychology and has done research in these fields ever since. A psychologist who felt an obligation to alleviate pain started a center for preventive psychiatry for young children. I need to include myself at this point, since together with two other people I founded a mental health clinic.

Some escapees try to extend help on a one-to-one basis, for example, by aiding newly arrived Vietnamese and Russian refugees. Other respondents have joined and supported various humanitarian organizations. The number of institutions they contribute to, either financially or personally, is truly astonishing. For example, one correspondent lists his affiliations: For many years he was active as a Big Brother. For thirty to forty years he supported pro-environmental, antinuclear, and antiwar organizations, and made contributions to progressive candidates, as well as to the American Civil Liberties Union, Ralph Nader Consumer Advocates, World Federalists, and others. He adds that if people think him naive for his support of so many liberal causes, his idealism tells him otherwise.

One talented escapee writes radio scripts and articles about "righteous gentiles," gentiles who saved Jews at a risk to their own lives. Others lecture to high school students to keep the memory of the Holocaust alive and have become actively involved with Holocaust museums. Some escapees utilize the political process in order to fight for what they deem to be right and fair. One respondent notes that he was only four years old when he arrived in the United States and that his family suffered a siege of poverty that lasted for many years until his father was able to reestablish himself. This experience has sensitized him to fight injustice even at a cost to himself: "My outlook on and reaction to life's events has clearly been affected in a major way by my experience in escaping Austria. It has made me more sensitive to political matters and changed my life for the better. It is also a handicap in the sense that I feel compelled to get involved in certain matters that from a purely personal perspective I would do better to leave alone. I am a letter writer and will pounce on things that I feel are wrong. I also do this on the job and have hurt myself in the process. Yet I feel driven to do this when the matter is important. My brother does not write letters, but he will go to extraordinary lengths to legally fight for something that he feels is right. In the 1960s he worked hard to prevent the federal government and the state highway engineers from building a freeway through Seattle's black community without certain safeguards. He won. I think that many survivors have risen so high in American society because they feel a need to build a monument in life for those who died."

Time had not softened the painful memories the escapees carry of the victims. A former art teacher, now retired, describes her own sentiments: "I cannot step into too hot a bath without thinking of the horrible Nazi medical experiments. I often think of the prisoners when the weather is icy cold. In many daily situations what these poor people went through comes to my mind. I am extremely sensitive to suffering, poverty, isolation, and unhappiness in any person. I cannot tolerate any cruelty or prejudice toward anyone. I let nothing pass. I am lucky in that my past career and now my retirement have given me plenty of opportunity to exercise my beliefs."

## "A New Birth of Freedom"

There is still another factor that probably helped the escapees keep their perspective. It was the new roots they began to form soon after reaching the country in which they finally settled. Once the first resettlement difficulties were past, the escapees discovered that countries like Britain, Canada, Australia, and the United States provided opportunities that would never have existed for them in Germany or Austria. These opportunities were not necessarily of an occupational or economic nature; they often involved new attitudes, a fresh political outlook, the experience of freedom of expression or action, or the possibility of setting individualized goals. Quite a few of the correspondents have not reached their former level of affluence, but most of them do not consider this a handicap. For instance, a former Viennese used to travel in a much higher socioeconomic circle than he does now. He remembers his parents' luxury apartment in the best section of the city, but he prefers his modest home in the suburbs with all its greenery and Florida with its lush tropical growth. And he is content and grateful to be living a good life, unlike millions of his unfortunate contemporaries.

True, there are some escapees who regret missing out on professions they had hoped to attain. It was too late for two women to study medicine and too late for a dancer who missed her young dancing years, which for her were the most crucial ones. A songwriter saw his career cut short, an artist had to delay her career for many years, and another artist was robbed of many of her works. But these lost opportunities were offset, at least in part by the many advantages the escapees found in their resettled lives. A man dismisses the stodginess of German middle-class life: "I might have been a different person; probably a good middle-class German burgher." Two escapees sarcastically say, "*Wir danken unseren Führer* [We thank our Führer]," a Nazi party slogan. A college professor comments, dripping with contempt for Austria: "What would have become of me had there not been a Hitler? I can only say, '*Wir danken unseren Führer.*' I would have followed my father into business. I would have led a financially comfortable life, doing all the proper things at the proper time without quite knowing or perhaps caring why. Austria would have continued to be, as indeed it has, a culturally claustrophobic environment: Mother Church uniting with the native *Lederhosen* mentality and Austro Fascism to strive for the achievement of total intellectual stagnation, which in fact they have achieved. In this environment I would have been stuck like a fly in aspic: presumably comfortable but cataleptic. I cannot imagine what my circle of friends might have been, but I also cannot imagine that it would have been what it is. Had I stayed in Vienna, I could not possibly have had the professional success I had had here." And another escapee, an outstanding jewelry artisan, speaks along the same lines: "I think in spite of many changes and difficult times I can say '*Ich danke meinen Führer*,' because I might not have ended up where I am today. Also not having been Gentile, I was able to leave Europe and not end up a corpse in Stalingrad as many young Austrians did."

Many of the women echo this sense of relief at having left. They feel that their lives in their new countries gave them a much wider scope. Had they married and settled down in their countries of birth, they would probably have become good *Hausfrauen* with a far more limited life. A nursing career would probably not have been open to a woman who realized this lifelong ambition in the United States. Another achieved her goal of becoming a social worker, a career her parents would formerly have opposed. While she feels that her circle of friends is probably smaller, she feels that her life is much less superficial than it would have been. An author provided a spontaneous answer to the question of what her life would have been like had it continued in its original course: "I have never posed that question, what life might have been like, to myself, so off the top of my head, my life is totally different from what it would have been. I don't know what I would have been, but when I go back to Austria today and see people my age, I am so glad that I got a ticket out of that environment. It seems to me confining and narrow." A personal note is added by another escapee: "I might have been more affluent, but probably would be less cosmopolitan. Above all, I would not have met my husband, and that is unthinkable."

Besides responding to new opportunities, the escapees developed a strong love and loyalty for their adopted countries. Most newcomers soon began to feel patriotic stirrings. Many began to see themselves as American or English. Even if they had not transformed themselves entirely, they certainly no longer thought of themselves as Austrians or Germans. For many of us a turning point came the day we became citizens of the country we had adopted and that had adopted us. Obtaining our citizenship was certainly the pivotal point in changing my own family's sense of belonging. I recall the day quite clearly. All activities were interrupted. My father, of course, saw no patients that morning, my mother canceled her piano students, and I did not go to school. The three of us (my sister was living in Boston) dressed in a festive fashion and took the subway downtown. Answering questions about American history preceded the taking of the oath. We waited for the judge to ask us to rise, and we lifted our hands to swear allegiance to the Constitution. I can still get teary eyed about that moment. We were not exactly in a palatial setting. For others it might have seemed a dull, bureaucratic procedure. But for us it was a glorious moment. We practically waltzed out of the building. We were citizens once again! American Citizens! We were practically like everyone else. We felt superpatriotic. By this time, five years after our arrival, we spoke only English at home. As soon as we learned about Thanksgiving, my mother made a splendid feast and, lacking family to make it a big party, invited as many honorary aunts and uncles as we could think of. We celebrated every American holiday. We all felt entirely American and did everything we could to support the country. When the American people were asked to buy war bonds, we did so whenever we could afford it. With my part-time job in a five-and-ten store, I regularly put money aside for that purpose. When we were asked to conserve raw materials or donate to the war effort, we complied. We never purchased anything on the black market or cheated on the allotted rations. Before we became citizens, we had helped the war effort under a sort of illusion; after all, we could only pretend to be American citizens. With citizenship, the present and the past were rolled into one because, in effect, we had no past. In those days it was impossible to think back about former happy days in Austria or even about having ever been an Austrian. It was as if merely thinking about it tainted us. And so we became Americans, and the American past became our past too.

In my strong feelings for my adopted country, I am joined by other escapees. A voice from Canada: "I felt entirely resettled after my emigration to Canada in 1952 at the age of twenty-six. Canada is a more open society where almost everybody at one time or another was an immigrant. A good job helped. I never encountered discrimination and had much recognition." An American immigrant feels no less at home in his surroundings: "I think I became an American within the first couple of years when I learned to play baseball in summer school. I was assimilated almost immediately. In a society where so many people are foreign-born, one becomes part of the crowd very quickly. I worked in a department of about thirty people where five of us at one time were foreign-born and two of the men had foreign-born wives. I felt like a citizen when I got my citizenship papers in 1946. I was totally integrated within a few years of my arrival." An English citizen writes, "Living in this country brings with it untold blessings as many youths have found who settled here." This identification with and full appreciation of the democratic countries the escapees live in continued to grow over the years. There is a full awareness that living under the protection of the law and being guaranteed basic freedoms can never be taken for granted, particularly when one considers how few people on this earth are fortunate enough to have such benefits.

An American settler recently celebrated a very special anniversary: "On May 5, 1991, I gave myself a red, white, and blue party. I celebrated with my husband and friends my fifty years of freedom. I hung the American flag on a pole that is attached to the front of the house and cried. I wished my parents and brother could have joined me. I do not speak a work of Czech or German anymore. It is as if it never was. I sometimes wonder if it ever existed. Maybe I imagined it all."

The question might be raised, Can you really find a new country, a new loyalty? "This depends on your interpretation of the words *my country*," wrote my own mother. "Is it the bond of common language? This has no holy ring in my ears. My earliest recollections go back to a country made up of many nationalities. My friends, my early companions, in later years my pupils, represented a babel of languages. It is not the language spoken by people around you which matters. The spirit expressed in any language makes the difference. Should I seek 'my country' within unchanging boundaries? Borders in our times have become the very symbol of instability, insecurity, and of man's folly. Borders are not providence-made. They are man-

made and how often in our times have they proved to be mad man–
made. If I was forced to change my country, I have not been forced
to change my conception of what constitutes it. To me, it means the
country where I am accepted as an equal, where I am allowed to
work and given the same chance as the next best one, where the law
protects my rights, where I can speak my thoughts, and where justice
is indivisible. There is no better way of expressing my idea of what
makes America 'my country' than by quoting the words of our great
countryman, Benjamin Franklin. This is what he said and that is how I
feel: 'Where liberty dwells, there is my country.' "

There is strong awareness among the escapees that the odds of
survival, when six million died, were certainly extremely small.
It almost seems that one's life was preserved in the most fear-
producing lottery of all times. Add to this the enormously good
fortune of ending up under a democratic form of government when
most of the world lives under one form of dictatorship or another,
and it becomes understandable that most escapees speak with strong
feelings about the country in which they finally settled.

## In Sharper Relief

When the escapees consider their lives, I wonder whether they
see their many diverse qualities, some of them quite contradictory.
If one were to describe them in broad strokes one might say that they
are people with, at best, a skeptical or, at worst, a pessimistic outlook
on life and the future of mankind. Yet they optimistically form strong
ties and welcome new relationships. They are on guard with people
en masse but comfortable vis-à-vis individuals. They adjusted exceedingly well to their new countries, yet the feeling of being an outsider
remains. While feeling different, they in no sense feel inferior but
have a strong sense of self-worth. In fact, they feel themselves to be
more experienced, possessing a wider scope and more alertness to
danger, than non-escapees. They are not particularly religiously
observant, but they have a strong identification with Judaism. They
do not feel guilty, but gratitude for survival prompts them toward an
altruism that makes them a strong contributing force to society. They
have formed extremely strong ties to their new countries. In spite of

their excellent integration, the losses they experienced have left them with an emotional pain that never quite disappears.

Perhaps finding oneself to be somewhat of an outsider might be a spur toward self-realization. The feeling of being an outsider, writes Vaclav Havel (1989), has been a lifelong wellspring of energy directed at continually improving himself and a decisive force behind everything worthwhile he has managed to accomplish.

William Shirer (1990), author of *The Rise and Fall of the Third Reich*, wrote recently of the escapees: "One of the things that has given me a tremendous amount of admiration is the indomitability of the human race. I remember the refugees from Nazi Germany who did not know what tomorrow would bring. But they had some indomitable quality. They were not weeping. They were determined. And they did."

## The Images That Haunt

I echo Shirer's view and feel the same admiration for these escapees. Some of the escapees have been kind enough to stay in touch by telephone or have even visited with me after the completion of our correspondence. That has, of course, been extremely gratifying. And I feel great pleasure in knowing that they have reestablished their lives and that many have gained stability by creating their own family. But sometimes on our first contact, I have had to catch myself for an instant as the caller speaks of retirement or grandchildren. For I have read the story of each escapee over and over again and in my mind's eye they have not grown older. I see them the way they were during those first years of peril and subsequent reconstruction of their lives. I see fearful families leaving their homes for the last time, tensely heading for the railroad station, apprehensive of being arrested before the border is finally crossed. Young people are setting out by themselves into a world unknown to them or their parents. Trains packed with children are diminishing in the distance as parents are left on empty platforms. Shadows are slipping over borders in the darkness. A mother is trying to affect nonchalance as she pushes a perambulator with her baby across a bridge and past passport control to safety. Families are hiding near borders to be guided across at nightfall. Some of the uprooted are wandering from country to country until, many years later, they finally find safety. New arrivals are scattered on every continent. Friends and relatives are perhaps never to meet again. I see the women laboring in menial jobs: Here, a girl who lost her own parents working as a baby nurse for happy, loving couples who are oblivious to her loneliness; there, a mature woman making ends meet by stitching gloves or hats or flags. I see the men—the lawyer now a door-to-door salesman and the businessman working on a chicken farm. I see the waiting for the Red Cross letters, which eventually cease and are replaced by a black curtain that falls until the terrible truth is revealed. Those are the pictures in my mind's eye, and I will always remember the escapees' fortitude and valiant struggles while still holding on to their humanity.

And I hope their stories will be remembered in the record of history.

*Epitaph*

# In Memoriam

KARL: We lost twenty-two family members, men, women, and children, not to speak of innumerable friends and neighbors. Several of my schoolmates were killed.

LEA: I lost my mother, two brothers, and one sister.

ERIC: Both my parents were deported and murdered. I lost another twenty-five relatives, twenty-three of whom were deported and murdered and two of whom committed suicide.

DOROTHY: I lost both my grandmothers, six other relatives, and many friends.

ELFI: I lost my parents and many relatives. There are probably quite a number of school friends, but I have no definite information.

INGA: I lost my mother, grandmother, aunts, and uncles, about six by suicide.

STEVE: I lost my parents and all the relatives who were alive at the time.

MARGARET: I lost at least twenty relatives and approximately thirty friends.

FRANZ: My great aunt, who lived in a home for the aged, was arrested and died en route to a concentration camp.

KURT: I did not lose anyone from my family. I don't know how many friends. My parents' friends committed suicide.

HEDI: Ten relatives, three friends definitely and probably many others, one by suicide.

NORBERT: Ten relatives. All murdered in concentration camps.

GARY: I don't know. Father committed suicide.

RUTH: I lost my mother and sister. I was too young to know about the others.

ELLI: I lost my father, a great aunt, several family friends. I don't know exact numbers.

ELLISA: My father's brother, wife, and child died in concentration camps, probably in gas chambers.

RUTH: I lost my parents, many of my other relatives, and several friends.

GERALD: I lost my parents, grandmother, and her husband, who committed suicide instead of being deported, six aunts and uncles and cousins.

MARGARET: I lost my grandmother, aunts, uncles, cousins and countless numbers of distant relatives. I don't know the exact number of school friends.

MARGA: On mother's side: grandmother and grandfather, two aunts, twin cousins, one uncle; on father's side: many cousins, two aunts, many distant relatives. Many classmates.

VALERIE: I lost a very dear friend in Vienna, who helped the elderly to leave, including my father of eighty-two. She prepared their documents and travel tickets. She was deported when war broke out.

HANNA: I lost my grandmother and her sister after the Nazis occupied the Sudentenland. Both were murdered in Theresienstadt. My uncle died after his release from Buchenwald of serious medical problems, the result of physical torture. One friend was killed by firing squad.

DORRIT: My mother's entire family of seven cousins and their children; the old aunt who brought her up as well as my father's brother—all killed in concentration camps. My little childhood playmates on surrounding streets were also wiped out with their families. I could name them if asked.

CARROLE: Both my parents committed suicide, not at the same time. I was away from home. An uncle and an aunt died in a concentration camp. My cousin told me.

ERNEST: Mother and father and many other family members. Amount unknown.

BETTY: I lost grandparents, uncles, aunts, and cousins.

And many, many, many more . . .

# Make Believe

Say I were not sixty,
say you weren't near-hundred,
say you were alive.
Say my verse was read
in some distant country,
and say you were idly turning the pages:

The blood washed from your shirt,
the tears from your eyes,
the earth from your bones;
neither missing since 1940,
nor dead as reported later
by a friend of a friend of a friend . . .

quite dapper you stand in that bookshop
and chance upon my clues.

That is why at sixty
when some publisher asks me
for biographical details,
I still carefully give
the year of my birth,
the name of my hometown:

GERDA MAYER born '27 in Karlsbad,
Czechoslovakia . . . write to me, father.

*Note*: The poet's father, Arnold Stein, escaped from the German concentration camp in
Nisko in 1939, fled to Russian-occupied Lemberg/Lwow, and then disappeared in the
summer of 1940. It is thought he may have died in a Russian camp.

# The Respondents

1. Abrahamson, Gunther
2. Ackerman, Manfred
3. Adamez, Ruth
4. Adler, Elli
5. Adler, Ralph
6. Adler, Stephen
7. Andersen, Marianne S.
8. Anderson, H. Lofty
9. Anderson, Valerie
10. Angel-Lord, Gertie
11. Argent, Hedi
12. Babich, Edith
13. Bader, Max
14. Barclay, Norbert W.
15. Bäuml, Franz H.
16. Bendremer, Jutta T.
17. Bergman, Paula
18. Bloch, David L.
19. Boehm, Ellen
20. Bregman, Eva
21. Breitbard, Ilse
22. Bresslauer, Gertrud
23. Brody, Maria
24. Brunell, Ruth
25. Burian, Elissa
26. Camis, Ilse F.
27. Carr-Gregg, Charlotte
28. Deutsch, Charles K.
29. Deutsch, Gertrude
30. Dorman, Ernest M.
31. Dornbush, Laslo
32. Drucker, Olga
33. Drucker, Rolf
34. Dyke, Susanne
35. Eckstein, Eric
36. Eckstein, Ruth
37. Egert, Ruth R.
38. Ekstein, Rudolf
39. Elmer, Fred
40. Feldsberg, Gerda S.
41. Fleming, Dorothy
42. Fleming, Otto
43. Fox, Anitta Boyko
44. Frenkel, Carole
45. Freud, Walter A.
46. Freudman, Judith
47. Friedman, Lilly
48. Friedman, Susanne
49. Friedman, Walter F.
50. Frohlich, Elfi
51. Fuchel, Kurt
52. Furst, Margaret

53. Goldberg, Susan
54. Goldberger, Margarete
55. Goldschmidt, Karl
56. Gombrich, Lisbeth
57. Gorden, Frances
58. Grandston, Gerald
59. Green, Bea
60. Grossman, Walter
61. Grubel, Fred
62. Grunfeld, Walter W.
63. Hadar, Chava
64. Harris, Frank A.
65. Harrison, Helga
66. Hauser, Betty
67. Hayman, Eva
68. Heikel, Bernard H.
69. Heiman, Karl L.
70. Heiman, Ruth K.
71. Heineman, Herbert S.
72. Hershan, Stella K.
73. Hewspear, Nelly
74. Hyman, Ilse
75. Jasper, Maritza
76. Jellinek, George
77. Johnson, Gertrude
78. Joseph, Inga J.
79. Kahn, Ely J.
80. Kala, Steve
81. Kalish, Reuwen F.
82. Kamnitzer, Marietta
83. Kane, Bertha
84. Kaplan, Lore W.
85. Karpf, Marion
86. Katz, Gertrude
87. Katz, Helga
88. Katz, Leo
89. Katz, Ralph
90. Kaufmann, Eva

91. Kester, Paul
92. Kleiner, Ellen
93. Koch, Rita
94. Konig, Karl
95. Lamb, Catherine
96. Lamet, Elsa
97. Lampert, Lilly
98. Lange, Hans
99. Lawrence, Fancy
100. Lederer, Gerda
101. Lederer, Liesel
102. Lederer, Regina
103. Leigh, Charles
104. Lerner, Armand
105. Leverton, Bertha
106. Lewin, Edith
107. Lieberman, Nina J.
108. Liebman, Lucie L.
109. Lindemeyer, Herbert
110. Lindenbaum, Siegfried
111. Lindenstraus, Erica
112. Lindenstraus, Gerald
113. Litke, Miriam
114. Lowenthal, Herbert
115. Loon, Liese
116. Low, Hannah
117. Loy, Lola
118. Lustig, Ernst
119. Marcus, Edith
120. Marlens, Hanna
121. Matzka, John
122. Maurer, Kurt
123. Mayer, Gerda
124. Meltzer, Asher
125. Michaelis, Martin L.
126. Michaelis, Ruth L.
127. Model, Elisabeth D.
128. Modine, Alice

129. Mogilensky, Emmy
130. Morgan, Peter
131. Morgenstern, Traute
132. Myller, Rolf
133. Najmann, John
134. Neeman, Meir
135. Neurath, Paul
136. O'Brien, Vera
137. Parker, Frank G.
138. Parker, Gertrude
139. Parker, Lore
140. Pengelly, Alice F.
141. Peters, Alan
142. Plank, Emma
143. Ransome, Marga
144. Rauchwerger, Joseph
145. Roberts, Richard
146. Robinson, Susi
147. Rose, Frances R.
148. Rosner, Philip
149. Ross, David
150. Rothschild, Kurt W.
151. Rothschild, Valerie
152. Rubin, Berta
153. Ryba, Marietta
154. Saeman, Henry
155. Sanders, Eric
156. Saxton, Monica
157. Schafer, Kitty
158. Schaufeld, Vera
159. Schiller, Ken
160. Segal, Kroner H.
161. Shuster, Harold
162. Sigal, Hilde
163. Sim, Dorrith M.
164. Simon, Maria
165. Spaeth, Lottie P.
166. Spenser, Anita
167. Stein, George
168. Steinberg, Henry
169. Stevens, Fred
170. Stricker, Henry H.
171. Taub, Lea
172. Ulman, Annie
173. Vernon, Dora
174. Vernon, John
175. Weis, Frederick V.
176. Weis, Gertrude
177. Weisman, Eva
178. Weiss, Hans
179. Weiss, Meir
180. Weiss, Walter
181. Werner, Oscar M.
182. Wertheim, Morris
183. Wesson, Bernard
184. Wesson, Ruth
185. Wildman, Louis
186. Winer, Eva
187. Winer, Leon
188. Woolf, Dorrit
189. Woolf, Leopold
190. Woss, Magda S.

# Questionnaire

*Please use separate sheets of paper for your answer.*

A. BACKGROUND DATA
    1. Name and sex:
    2. Address and telephone number:
    3. Occupation (if any) before Hitler advent:
    4. Occupation(s) after Hitler advent:
    5. Father's occupation before and after Hitler advent:
    6. Mother's occupation before and after Hitler advent:
    7. Any siblings?
    8. Country of residence under Hitler:
    9. Age and date of leaving:
   10. How many months or years did you live in a Nazi-occupied country?
   11. Did you lose any member of your family (parents, siblings, children)?
   12. How many members of extended family (cousins, aunts, grandparents)?
   13. How many friends, schoolmates, etc.?
   14. How many by murder and how many by suicide?
   15. If you married after resettling: Jewish spouse? An "ex-refugee"?

B. BEFORE THE ESCAPE
    1. What was your life like before Hitler came?
      a. What kind of family life? What sort of relationship with parents and relatives?

b. Did you have a circle of friends? Did your parents?

c. What was your general emotional state and outlook on life?

d. What was your socioeconomic standing and outlook for the future?

e. Was a cultural background emphasized (studies, opera, theater, classics, sports)?

f. Was your family religious? How orthodox? Assimilated? Jewish identification?

g. What were some particularly happy events you recall? Please detail.

2. What was your response to Hitler's rise to power?

a. If you lived in Germany, at what point did you and your family understand the full extent of the danger? If you lived elsewhere, did you and your family feel threatened by Hitler's rise to power?

b. If it caused anxiety, did it interfere with everyday life or did you think it was a passing phase?

c. If you did not live in Germany and Hitler invaded your country, how did the *suddenness* of the terror affect you?

d. At what point did you understand the full impact? Then or later?

e. If you were young, did the adults try to shield you from knowing the full danger? If so, was that good or bad?

f. How did it affect you when you saw the adults in your life very worried? Were family relations affected either positively or negatively by the stress?

g. How did you and your family manage? Become overwhelmed? Cope actively?

h. How was your daily life affected under Hitler? What were your (and family's) outstanding emotions? Fear, anxiety, terror, hate, sadness, depression? Others?

i. How did people behave toward you (friends, business associates, schoolmates, household help, concierge)?

j. Did events change your view of people and life? If so, were you aware of it?

k. Did the way people behaved at that time affect your present view of people?

l. Did you witness or experience any incidents of a violent or threatening nature? If so, do you still think about these and when do they come to mind?

m. Was anyone close to you arrested? How did that affect you and your family? Do these incidents still come to mind?

n. What were your feelings when you heard of or saw public humiliations or arrests of Jews? Did these events ever affect your feelings of self-worth? Did you ever feel ashamed of being Jewish?

o. Did these memories affect you in your relationship to non-Jews? Do they now?

p. If you were young, did you ever wish you could join the Nazi parades? Did that make you feel guilty?

q. Did you feel inferior to non-Jewish schoolmates or friends?

r. Any other emotional consequences?

## C. THE ESCAPE

1. How did your escape take place?

   Give a step by step description of the escape:

   a. Do you remember what papers, stamps, visas, passports, quota numbers were necessary to be able to leave the country? Give as many details as possible.

   b. How did you or your family manage to obtain them? Please detail.

   c. What were the bureaucratic difficulties, lucky breaks, close calls? Please detail.

   d. How many plans came to naught? How many countries rejected you?

   e. While you were trying to leave, did you have dangerous encounters or knowledge that someone was or would be arrested? Were they? How did you react?

   f. Did anyone outside the family extend help?

   g. What was your state of mind (afraid, in a fog, tried to repress, remained hopeful)?

   h. Do you think these events have affected your present attitude to government, authority, or bureaucracy?

   i. Did you leave with your family? If not, did you see them again? When and how?

    j. How did you feel when you or your friends left (whichever came first)? Did you, or they, say good-bye or just sort of disappear?

    k. Can you detail the day of leaving? Do you recall the events and emotions?

D. AFTER THE ESCAPE

  1. The years immediately after you escaped and before permanent resettlement.

    a. How many countries (which ones) and places did you live in before you settled more or less permanently?

    b. How many different schools did you attend and how many jobs did you have?

    c. Did you live with family, relatives, friends, strangers?

    d. Did you have anyone to lean on, help or guide you? Did that help?

    e. Were there "refugees" in your area? Did that help? Did native citizens befriend you?

    f. What was your state of mind during those first few years (lonely, anxious, lost, or relief for being alive, sense of adventure, desire to get on with it)?

    g. Did you miss your former life? Did you think of those left behind, or were you too busy with resettling? Feel gratefulness or identification with new country?

    h. Was it difficult to resettle and to assimilate? Did you feel like an outsider? For how long? Do you still feel like an outsider sometimes? If not, when did it stop?

    i. Was it easier for the men or the women in your family to find jobs and to resettle?

    j. Was your self-worth affected by being unsettled and possibly having less than before? Had your status changed? Did that affect you?

  2. What were the years like after permanent resettlement?

    a. How many years did it take to feel entirely resettled? Or did that time ever come?

    b. Were there specific occurrences that helped (army, marriage, children, good job)?

    c. In terms of occupation, contacts, socioeconomic level, happiness, are you in about the same, better, or worse position than if you had not been a "refugee"?

    d. Is your circle of relatives and friends comparable to what it might have been?

    e. Did the struggle to resettle affect you emotionally? In what way (make you feel anxious, apprehensive, more self-confident, or make you more outgoing, etc.)?

    f. Did there ever come a point when you no longer felt like an outsider and felt no different from other citizens? If so, when?

    g. During the war years did you think of those who had not gotten away? Did you repress those thoughts? What did you think had happened to them? How did you find out? How did this news affect you? Does it still affect you?

    h. If you were reunited with family members, what was that like? Did they seem like strangers, or were you able to resume where you had left off? If you were reunited with parents, was that relationship changed?

    i. What had been your religious beliefs? Did they change? Become stronger? Weaker?

    j. Was your identification with Jewish people or Jewish matters strengthened, weakened, unaffected by your experience?

    k. Did you tell your children and grandchildren in detail what had happened? Were they interested? How deeply?

    l. Can you describe your feelings if and when you went back to where you had lived? If you went back more than once, did your attitude change?

    m.Do you feel any animosity toward Germans, Austrians, Poles, etc.? In your feelings do you discriminate among generations? If so, in what way?

    n. What percentage of your friends are ex-refugees? Do you have any special bond with these? Are you just as comfortable with your other friends?

PLEASE ANSWER THE QUESTIONS BELOW IN DETAIL

    3. The emotional aftermath. Introspection on the effect of the Hitler period on you.

a. Has the Hitler period influenced or altered your *view on people, events, life*? How?

b. Was your *basic sense of security* affected (i.e., tendency to feel anxious, distrustful of fate and future, need to keep planning ahead? Or optimistic, nothing worse can happen, etc.)?

c. Do you think your view of the *basic goodness of people* changed for better or worse? Less or more trusting? Neither? More or less eager to form relationships?

d. Did you try to *substitute for lost family* with friends? Did you succeed?

e. Do you think your *basic sense of self-worth* was affected? (Did being Jewish, a "refugee" and an outsider lower your self-esteem or make you feel confident for having coped? Feel more experienced, surer for having survived? More cultured than others? Less so? How long? Up to the present?

f. It is hard to say, but take a guess: Do you think you might have been a *different person* had there never been a Hitler period? If so, how?

g. Did there come a time in which you felt *totally integrated* and no different? Are there times or ways in which you still feel "different" or somewhat of an outsider?

h. Are there aspects of *being a European* left (attitudes, food, culture, style of living)?

i. If you meet or are with other ex-refugees, do you have a *special rapport* or find quicker communality than when you meet others? Many friends ex-refugees?

j. Did you *lose the aspects of life* that made you feel happiest before Hitler? If so, did you recapture them?

k. Ever *feel guilt* that you escaped when others did not? Ever wonder whether you could have helped more? If so, is the guilt justified or more of an emotional nature?

l. When were you *most emotionally affected*: while living under Hitler, immediately thereafter, a few years later, now, or all the time?

m. Do you think there are *emotional scars* left? What kind?

n. Are there situations that bring *old thoughts, feelings, losses* to the surface (seeing large families, scenes of violence, children moving away)?

o. Are there some particular *bad memories* or upsetting scenes that return to your mind from time to time? If so, what tends to precipitate them?

p. Did you or do you have *recurrent dreams* or *unwanted thoughts* about the events?

q. Did the awareness in the media of the fiftieth anniversary of Kristallnacht revive thoughts and memories? Bring to mind *memories you had forgotten*?

r. Any other thoughts, feelings, or experiences you would like to add?

THANK YOU FOR PARTICIPATING IN THIS PROJECT

*If you have any materials such as photographs, original writing, newspaper clippings, old passport photographs, please send them to me.*

(A different questionnaire was used for those who left their home on a *Kindertransport*. Sections C and D were modified to accord with their experiences.)

# References

Anonymous, "The Pimpernel of Prague." *The Observer, Review Section*, July 10, 1988.

Bader, Lily. "One Life to Live" (unpublished autobiography). New York: Leo Baeck Institute, 1956.

Bankier, Alexander A., ". . . . auch nicht von der Frau Hinterhuber." In *Österreichishe Jüdisches Geistes und Kulturleben*, edited by Liga der Freunde des Judentums, 17–38. Vienna: Literas-Universitätsverlag, 1990.

Berghan, Marian. *German Jewish Refugees in England*. London: Macmillan, 1984.

Berkley, George E., *Vienna and Its Jews*. Cambridge, MA: Abt Book, 1988.

Botz, Gerhard. "Die Ausgliederung der Juden aus der Gesellschaft: Das End des Wiener Judentum unter der NS-Herrschaft (1938 bis 1943)." In *Eine zerstörte Kultur*, edited by Gerhard Botz, Ivar Oxall, Michael Pollack, 285–312. Buchloe, Germany: Druck und Verlag Obermayer GmbH, 1990.

Cesarini, David. "The Fear Mongers Within." In *Arrival of HMT* Dunera *at Sydney*, edited by W. Travers. Rose Bay, New South Wales: Hay-Tatura Assoc., 1990.

Chappell, Connery. "Island of Barbed Wire: Internees on the Isle of Man in World War Two" (1984, unpublished).

Dawidowicz, Lucy. *The War against the Jews 1933–1945*. New York: Holt, Rinehart and Winston, 1975.

Des Pres, Terrence. *The Survivors: Anatomy of Life in the Death Camps*. New York: Oxford University Press, 1976.

Friedlander, Vera. "Ein Kapital Jüdischer Kultur." *Weltbühne* 40(September 1991): 1221–1223.

Gardner, Muriel. *Code Name "Mary."* New Haven: Yale University Press, 1983.

Gill, Alan. "When Friends Were Enemies." *Sydney Morning Herald Magazine*, September 1990, 21–24.

Gruen, Fred. Address delivered at the Conference on the Fiftieth Anniversary of the Arrival of HMT *Dunera*, Sydney, September 6, 1990.

Havel, Vaclav. Letters to Olga, June 1979–September 1982. New York: Henry Holt, 1989.

Hayden, Bill. Address delivered at the Conference on the Fiftieth Anniversary of the Arrival of HMT *Dunera*, Sydney, September 6, 1990.

Hershan, Stella. "Memoir of Nazi Austria and the Jewish Refugee Experience in America." *American Jewish Archive*, University of Cincinnati, Fall/Winter, 1991.

Herzstein, Robert E. *Adolf Hitler and the German Trauma 1913–1945*. New York: Putnam, 1974.

Hilberg, Raul. *The Destruction of the European Jews*. New York: Harper & Row, 1961.

Hillesum, Betty. *An Interrupted Life: The Diaries of Betty Hillesum 1941–1943*. New York: Pantheon, 1983.

Jelavich, Barbara. *Modern Austria: Empire and Republic, 1815–1986*. Cambridge, Eng.: Cambridge University Press, 1987.

Jellinek, George. "The Gold Watch." *New York Times*, June 28, 1987 (and *Jerusalem Post*, December 2, 1988).

John, Michael. "Zur wirtschaftlichen Bedeutung des Judentums in Österreich 1848–1938." In *Österreichische Jüdisches-Geistes und Kulturleben*, edited by Liga der Freunde des Judentums, 39–85. Vienna: Literas-Universitätsverlag, 1990.

Kochan, Miriam. *Britain's Internees in the Second World War*. London: Macmillan, 1983.

Kranzler, David H. "The History of the Jewish Refugee Community of Shanghai, 1938–1945." Thesis, Yeshiva University, 1971.

Lasky, Peter G. Letter to the Editor, *Australian Jewish News*, July 20, 1990.

Leitner, Yecheskel. *Operation Torah Rescue*. Jerusalem: Feldheim, 1987.

Levi, Primo. "Shame." *Esquire*, January 1988, 99–102.

Lifton, Robert J. *The Nazi Doctors*. New York: Basic Books, 1986.

Marty, Martin E. Review of *News from the Land of Freedom*, edited by Walter D. Kamphoefner, Wolfgang Helbich, and Ulrike Sommer. *New York Times*, December 29, 1991.

Mayer, Gerda. "Make Believe." In Mayer, Gerda. *A Heartache of Grass*. Cornwall, Eng.: Peterloo Poets, 1988.

McPhee, John. *The Control of Nature*. New York: Basic Books, 1989.

Marzorati, Gerald. "Salman Rushdie: Fiction's Embattled Infidel." *New York Times Magazine*, January 29, 1989.

Patkin, Benzion. *The Dunera Internees*. New South Wales, Australia: Cassel, 1979.

Pauley, Bruce F. "Politischer Antisemitismus im Wien der Zwischenkriegs-
zeit." In *Eine zerstörte Kultur*, edited by Gerhard Botz, Ivar Oxall, and
Michael Pollak, 221–246. Buchloe, German: Druck und Verlag Obermayer GmbH, 1990.

Pearl, Cyril. *The Dunera Scandal*. Port Melbourne, Victoria: Mandarin
Australia, 1990.

Shirer, William L. *The Rise and Fall of the Third Reich*. New York: Fawcett,
1962.

Shirer, William. In the *New York Times*, May 13, 1990.

Turner, Barry. *And the Policeman Smiled*. London: Bloomsbury, 1990.

"Was Übrigbleibt." *Berlin Tagesspiegel*, September 12, 1991.

Wickers, Hermann, and Wacker, Jean-Claude. "Über die Grenzen, Alltag und
Widerstand im Schweitzer Exil." Eine Ausstellung der Studienbibliothek
zur Geschichte der Arbeiterbewegung Zurich in der Universität Basel,
April 23–May 5, 1990.

Wijsmuller-Meijer, Gertrude. *No Time for Tears*. (Originally published as
*Geen Tud Voor Tranen*: P.N. van Kempen, 1961.)

Wyman, David S. *The Abandonment of the Jews*. New York: Pantheon, 1984.

Zweig, Stefan. *The World of Yesterday*. Lincoln: University of Nebraska Press,
1964.

# Index

Abrahamson, Gunther, 42, 146, 230, 271–288
Actors, 36, 37
  as internees, 324
Adamez, Ruth, 150, 159, 161
Adler, Elli, 20, 62, 105, 130, 142, 147, 159, 226
Adler, Ralph, 189, 362–363
Adler, Stephen, 179, 230, 342
Affidavits, for immigration, 73, 77, 79, 86
Air raids, 223, 226, 264, 312, 313, 316
Air raid shelters, 226–227, 249–250
"All the Leaves Have Lost Their Trees" (Mayer), 9, 155
*Alsina* (ship), 114–115
Amadeus Quartet, 315
American Joint Distribution Committee, 293
American Medical Association, 303
Andersen, Marianne S., 76, 359
Anderson, H. Lofty, 76, 359
Anderson, Valerie, 414
Anschluss. *See* Austria, Germany's annexation of
Anti-Semitism
  in Austria, 29–30
  escapees' sensitivity to, 375, 381
  in Europe, 197
  in United States, 197
*Arandora Star* (ship), 309, 319, 326
*Arbeitsdienst*, 36

Argent, Hedi, 413
Arm bands, as Jewish identification, 127
Arrests, 19–22, 32
  by denunciation, 21–23
  as emigration motivation, 41
  following Kristallnacht, 95–101, 134, 135
Arson, following Kristallnacht, 96–97, 100
Artists, as internees, 315, 324
Assimilation
  escapees' difficulties of, 387–398
  into German/Austrian culture, 197–203
Atworth, 299–301, 305
Auschwitz, 1, 37, 86, 105, 108, 149
  *Totenbuch* of, 401
Australia
  deportation to, 252, 254, 312
    *Dunera* incident and, 317–330, 392
  immigration to, 76, 360, 362
Australian Employment Corps, 327, 328
Austria
  anti-Semitism in, 29–30, 33, 195–203
  Germany's annexation of, 13–32, 39
  Jewish population of, 25
    assimilation into Austrian culture, 197–203
    childrearing practices of, 177–179

Austria (*cont.*)
  Jewish population of (*cont.*)
    civil rights of, 198
    family size among, 177
    patriotism of, 198
    Nazi sympathizers in, 14, 15, 17, 29
    swastika display in, 15, 17, 18, 21
Austrian Center, 213–214

Bader, Max, 75, 346–347
Baldwin, Stanley, 140
Baptism, 79–80. *See also* Religious
  conversion
Barclay, Norbert W., 83, 181, 185, 190
Batista, Fulgencio, 77–78
Battle of Britain, 311
Battle of Flodden, 272
Bauml, Franz H., 27, 31, 82, 102, 128,
    129, 130, 142–143, 147, 153–154,
    158–159, 178–179, 190–191, 211,
    224, 227, 344
BDM, 129
Belgium
  German invasion of, 110, 113
  Jewish refugees in, 109–110
  *St.Louis* passengers acceptance by,
    118, 119
Bendremer, Jutta T., 39, 344, 365, 368
Bentwich, Norman, 141
Bergen-Belsen, 37
Bergman, Paula, 127, 151, 157, 233, 342
Betar Movement, 119–120
B'nai B'rith, 201
Bland, Neville, 311
Blood Medal (*Blutorden*), 120
Bloom, Sol (congressman), 116
*Blutorden* (Blood Medal), 120
Boarding schools, 261, 269
*Bodegraven* (ship), 164
Boehm, Ellen, 150, 231
Boeing Corporation, 346–347
Bohr, Niels, 75
Book burnings, 33, 39
Border crossings, 86–87
  illegal, 109–112

Border crossings (*cont.*)
  by *Kindertransport*, 159–160
Boycott, of Jewish businesses, 34
Brasted Hall, Kent, 165, 244
Brazil, refusal to admit Jewish
  refugees, 116
Bregman, Eva, 23–24, 71
Breitbard, Ilse, 341
Bresslauer, Gertrud, 182
Bribery
  for concentration camp release, 117,
    135
  for illegal escapes, 111–112
  for immigration, 80, 83
Brooks, A., 320
Brown Shirts, 37
Brunell, Ruth, 212–213
Buchenwald, 20, 22, 25, 28, 98, 224,
    291
  attempted escape from, 21
  children in, 137
  escapee's narrative of, 95–96
Burian, Elissa, 414
Businesses, Jewish-owned
  boycott of, 34, 39
  confiscation of, 27–28, 29–31
    economic effects of, 36
    official orders for, 102–104

*Cabo de Hornos* (ship), 115–116
Cafes, 185–186
Camis, Ilse F., 233
Canada, as internment location, 312
Caricatures, of Jews, 24, 25
Catholicism
  of Christian Democrats, 13
  conversion to, 131–132
Catholics
  attitudes towards Hitler, 15
  rejection of Nazism by, 181
Celico, Italy, 333–336
Chadwick, Mrs., 235
Chadwick, Trevor, 144–145, 162, 163,
    165
Children, 127–137

Children (*cont.*)
  anti-Semitic incidents towards, 40
  arrests of, 137
  deaths in concentration camps, 143,
    147, 256
  deportation of, 252
  evacuation to England, 237–270
    border crossings during, 159–160
    *Kindertransports*, 141, 142, 144,
      145–146, 150, 151–153, 157–166
    leave-taking from parents, 146–
      148, 149–155
    preparation for, 146–149
    provisos for, 139, 142
    Refugee Committee and, 219–220,
      237–239, 250
    sponsorship for, 143, 156
  of mixed ancestry, 128
  resettlement in England
    adjustment to, 215–236, 245–253,
      258–264, 267, 364–365
    correspondence with parents,
      224–226, 248, 250
    cultural adjustments, 221–224, 245
    education, 209–210, 211, 212, 213,
      249
    emotional problems, 230, 235
    foster homes, 207–220, 237–244
    foster siblings, 213, 214–215, 217,
      218, 224, 228, 235
    homesickness, 240–243
    sexual abuse, 227, 251
    support groups, 214
  retarded, murder of, 47
  Switzerland's refusal to accept, 111
Christian Democrats, 13, 14
Christians, escapees' attitudes towards,
  375
Christian Socialists, 197
Churchill, Winston, 311, 328
Civil service, exclusion of Jews from,
  34, 196
*Code Name Mary* (Gardner), 86
Compensation money, for
  concentration camp victims, 68

Concentration camps
  Auschwitz, 1, 37, 86, 105, 107, 149
  Bergen-Belsen, 37
  children's deaths in, 143, 144, 256
  Dachau, 19, 21–22, 25, 28, 40–41,
    48, 96, 99, 134
  first, 33–34
  in Italy, 333–334, 335, 336
  Oranien-Saxenhausen, 142
  releases from, 31, 135, 142, 158, 162–
    163
  Theresienstadt, 1, 37, 378, 383
  in Turkey, 290
Concentration camp victims,
  compensation for, 68
Concierges, 23, 26
Congress of Vienna, 192
Consulates, entry visa applications at,
  63, 71–73
*Conte Rosso* (ship), 291
Cuba
  Jewish immigration to, 77–78
  refusal to admit Jewish refugees,
    116–118
Cultural life
  of Austrian and German Jews, 189–
    191, 198–200, 202
  of internees, 314–315, 316, 323–325,
    326
  in Shanghai refugee camps, 294
Czechoslovakia
  German invasion of, 165
  illegal escapes into, 110–111

Dachau, 19, 21–22, 25, 28, 31, 40–41,
  48, 96, 98, 134
*Daily Express*, 118
*Daily Mail*, 311
Dancing, 191–192
Denmark, Jewish immigration to, 75
Deportation
  of children, 252
  of internees, 312
    *Dunera* incident, 317–330, 392
  to Poland, 136–137

*Der Schwarze Corps*, 24–25
Deutsch, Charles K., 75, 78, 107, 163, 189, 191, 356–357
Deutsch, Gertrude, 79, 107
Dog tax, 46, 51
Dollfuss, Engelbert, 14
*Dorian II* (ship), 290
Dorman, Ernest M., 23, 31, 110–111, 364
Dornbush, Laslo, 50
Dovercourt, Harwich, 140, 164–165, 244
Drucker, Olga, 109–110
Drucker, Rolf, 72
*Dunera* (ship), 317–330, 392
    Orthodox Jews on, 320, 328
    Toilet Paper Constitution of, 319, 323
*Dunera Scandal, The* (Pearl), 324
Dunkirk, 310–311
Dusseldorf, 323
    deportation of Jews from, 256
    evacuation of children from, 144
    evacuees' postwar return to, 255–256
    Kristallnacht in, 96

Easter, 195
Eckstein, Eric, 36, 38, 39, 96, 137, 144, 159, 244, 246–247, 251–252, 254, 255–257, 317–318, 321, 322, 323–325, 327
Eckstein, Ruth, 343
Ecuador, Jewish refugees in, 72, 83–84, 338, 353–355
Education. *See also* Schools
    of evacuee children, 209–210, 211, 212, 213, 249
    in the United States, 365–367
    in internee camps, 323–324
Egert, Ruth R., 370
Eichmann, Adolf, 23, 141
Eicke, Theodor, 41
Eighth Australian Employment Corps, 327, 328

Elderly persons, emigration by, 81–82
Elmer, Fred, 79, 100, 178, 179, 189, 190, 196, 360
Emigration
    bribery for, 48–50
    delays in, 34–39, 41–43
    documents required for, 45–48, 51. *See also* Passports; Visas
    obstacles to, 45–68
    taxes for, 46–47, 51
Employment, of escapees, 303–304, 341–349, 350, 353–357, 362–363
England. *See also* Children, evacuation to England; Children, resettlement in England
    anti-Semitism in, 197
    escapees' attitudes towards, 304, 360, 361
    internment policy of, 309–330
    preparation for German invasion of, 311
    *St. Louis* passengers acceptance by, 118, 119
Escapees
    altruism of, 403–405
    emotional bond among, 391–394
    emotional distress of, 373–386, 399–403
    employment of, 303–304, 341–349, 350, 353–357, 362–363
    memories of, 377–386
    new citizenships of, 408–410
    pessimism of, 373–375
    relationships with parents, 253–254, 269–270
    sensitivity to anti-Semitism, 375, 381
    survivor guilt of, 399–403
Exit papers, 50, 51, 63

Failed escapes, 19–20
    from Buchenwald, 21
Family
    extended, 179–180, 187
    loss of, 381–383
Family life, in Austria and Germany, 177–183, 187–188

Family size, 177
Famous persons, internment of, 315, 318, 324, 330
*Fasching*, 191–192, 193
Feldman, Lily, 70, 107, 338
Feldsberg, Gerda S., 129, 149, 151, 217–219, 226, 230
Ferramonti Di Tarsia concentration camp, 333–334, 335, 336
Fischbock, Dr., 29, 30
Fleming, Dorothy, 129, 130, 152, 159, 160, 162, 164, 231, 340
Fleming, Otto, 21, 51, 78, 85, 181–182, 195, 201, 339, 340, 362
Foreigners, Nazi abuse of, 102
Foster homes
    Dutch, 161
    English, 207–220, 237–244
Foster parents
    problems of, 234–236
    sexual abuse by, 227, 251
Foster siblings, 212, 213–214, 217, 218, 224, 228, 235
Fox, Anitta Boyko, 20, 46, 101, 102, 179
France
    German invasion of, 113–114
    Jewish refugees in, 113–114
    *St. Louis* passengers acceptance by, 118, 119
Frankfurt, Kristallnacht in, 96
Freud, Sigmund, 76, 193, 196
    B'nai B'rith membership, 201
Freud, Walter A., 317, 318, 320, 329
Freudman, Judith, 82, 91–92
Friedman, Lilly, 91–92, 101
Friedman, Susanne, 111–112
Friedman, Walter F., 343, 360
Frohlich, Elfi, 158
Fuchel, Kurt, 80, 131, 146–147, 226–227, 235, 291
Furst, Margaret, 127–128, 130–131, 161

Gardner, Muriel, 86
Gas masks, 226

Germany
    Hitler's takeover of, 33–34
    Jewish population of
        assimilation into German culture, 197–203
        civil rights of, 198
        historical background, 197–198
        patriotism of, 198
Gestapo
    arrests by, 20–22, 23
    bribery of, 49–50, 117
Ghoya, 298
Globocnik, Odilo, 102–103
Gluckstein family, 212
Goebbels, Paul Joseph, 18, 25–26
Goering, Hermann, 18
    economic policy of, 28–29
    on Kristallnacht, 103–104
Goethe, Johann, 199
Goldberg, Susan, 75–76, 345, 364
Goldberger, Margarete, 135, 146, 180
Goldschmidt, Karl, 78, 135, 142, 146, 180
*Graf Spee* (ship), 310
Grandston, Gerald, 116–119, 127, 337
Greece, Jewish refugees in, 121–122
Green, Bea, 37, 43, 131, 134–135, 143, 149, 158, 160, 164–165, 244, 245
Group homes, 211, 262, 284–285
Grozman, Johann, 66–67
Gruen, Fred, 329
Grynszpan, Hershel, 95
Guinness family, 297–298, 301
Guthrie, John, 280–282, 290
Gutmann, Felix, 326
Gymnasium, 180, 195
    exclusion of Jewish teachers, 196

Hadar, Chava, 87
Harris, Frank A., 96, 97, 100, 101, 101, 198
"Hatikva," 121
Hauser, Betty, 101, 146, 160–161, 163, 164, 198, 223
Hayden, Bill, 329, 330

Heikel, Bernard W., 143, 154, 158–159, 160, 210–211, 230, 232
Heiman, Karl L., 41, 96, 98, 197–198, 341, 365–366, 369, 370
Heiman, Ruth K., 37, 145, 149, 152, 164, 191, 215–216, 223, 224
Hershan, Stella K., 20–21, 23–24, 26, 27, 31, 49–50, 78–80, 82–83, 89–90, 369–370
Hewspear, Nelly, 21, 181, 360–361
Hindenburg, Paul von, 33
*Hiraeth*, 257
Hirsch, Otto, 142
Hitler, Adolf, 332
    German-Austria unification plebiscite and, 15–16
    radio speeches of, 18, 22–23
Hitler Youth, 61, 189, 201
Holloway Woman's Prison, 312–313
Holmgren, Gunner, 76
*Holocaust, The* (Gilbert), 385
Horst Wessel song, 38, 130
Hospitals, retarded children's murder in, 47
Hostels, 211, 212, 229, 230, 233, 253
Humanism, 198, 199
Huyton transit internment camp, 317, 318
Hyman, Ilse, 149, 151, 158, 213, 235

Identity cards, 295
*Illegalen*, 14, 17, 19, 22, 27, 120, 196–197
Illness, as emigration obstacle, 81
Immigration
    age factors, 81–82
    bribery for, 80, 82
    by eminent persons, 75, 76, 87–88
    English language proficiency and, 78–79
    financial factors in, 75, 77–78, 80–81
    obstacles to, 71–88
        occupational requirements, 78, 88
        quota numbers, 73, 74
        sponsorship requirement, 73, 74–75

Immigration (*cont.*)
    religious conversion for, 79–80
Innitzer, Cardinal, 19
Intermarriage, 34
Internment
    of children, 252
    by British government, 306–308, 309–330
        alien classification and, 309–310
        in Australia, 312, 317–330
        cultural activities during, 314–315, 316
        on Isle of Man, 312, 313, 314–317, 325
        reasons for, 309–312
        release from, 316–317
        transit camps, 312–313, 317, 318
    by Italian government, 332, 333
Isle of Man, internment on, 312, 313, 314–317, 325
Israel, as Jewish name designation, 64, 133
*Israel in Egypt* (Handel), 326
Italy, Jewish refugees in, 289–290, 331–336
Itchen Abbas House, 248–249, 253

James Monroe High School, 365–366
Japan, Shanghai refugee camps administration by, 294–296
Jasper, Maritza, 108, 130, 135, 147, 148, 149, 157, 182, 216–217, 223
Jellinek, George, 9, 92–94, 370
Jewish Community Centers, 37
Jewish Community Council, 201
Jewish Cultural Alliance, 36–37
Jewish Culture Center, 19
Jewish identity
    of escapees, 395–396
    of German and Austrian Jews, 199–202
Joseph, Inga J., 130, 131, 143, 235, 240–242
Joseph, Lieselotte, 240, 242, 243
Journalists
    arrests of, 20

Journalists (*cont.*)
  dismissal of, 34
Judaism
  escapees' identification with, 395–396
  German/Austrian Jews' identification
    with, 200–201
*Judischser Kulturbund*, 36–37
*Julia* (Hellman), 86
Julia Richmond High School, 366–367

Kahn, Ely J., 75
Kala, Steve, 147, 214
Kaplan, Lore W., 341
Karolinsky Institute, 76
Karpf, Marion, 128, 131, 230, 233
Katz, Gertrude, 22, 290
Katz, Helga, 100–101
Katz, Leo, 41
Katz, Ralph, 211
Kaufmann, Eva, 25–26
Kelsen, Hans, 193
Kester, Paul, 38, 98
Kibbutz, 361–362
Kibbutz Kinrot, 125
*Kinderfraulein*, 18, 180–183
*Kindertransports*. *See also* Children,
    evacuation to England
  to England, 141, 142, 144, 145–146,
    150, 151–153, 157–166, 227, 257
    border crossings during, 159
    escorts for, 157, 163
    preparation for, 146–149
    SS inspections of, 159
  to Sweden, 163–164
King, Jimmy, 322, 329
Kleiner, Ellen, 363
Koch, Dr., 331–336
Koch, Rita, 331–336
Kohn, Leon, 322
Kommissars, 27, 28, 29
*Konditoreien*, 186, 396–397
Konig, Karl, 24
Kristallnacht, 37–38, 95–108, 134
  escapees' memories of, 95–102
*Kultusgemeinde*, 140

La Guardia, Fiorello, 349
Lamet, Elsa, 34–36, 102, 360
Lange, Hans, 312–313, 316, 343
Lasky, Peter G., 319–320
Lawrence, Fancy, 360, 364
Laws, anti-Semitic. *See* Nuremberg
    Laws
Layton, J.D., 327
Leave-taking, 84–85, 89–94
  of children from parents, 87, 92–94,
    146–147, 149–155
  escapees' aversion to, 379, 380
Lederer, Gerda, 78, 80–81
Lederer, Liesel, 113–116
Legal system, exclusion of Jews from,
    196
Leigh, Charles, 131, 155, 164, 201
Lerner, Armand, 110
Lerner, Edith, 45–46, 109
Lessing, Gotthold, 199
Leverton, Bertha, 143, 244, 246, 340,
    393
Lewin, Edith, 20, 45–46, 109, 341–342
Lindemeyer, Herbert, 36, 97, 98, 228–
    229, 313
Lindenbaum, Siegfried, 136–137, 163
Lindenstraus, Erica, 179
Lindenstraus, Gerald, 292
Lingens, Ella, 86, 102
Litke, Miriam, 149, 233
Lodz, Poland, 70
Loon, Liese, 47
Looting, 16–17, 19, 20
  following Kristallnacht, 99
Low, Hannah, 110
Lowenthal, Herbert, 40, 342
Loy, Lola, 291, 292, 293–294, 337
Lustig, Ernst, 291
Lyons Tea Shops, 211–212

Mackinnon, Miss, 79
"Make Believe" (Mayer), 9, 419
Mann, Thomas, 193
Marlens, Hannah, 345–346
Maugham, Somerset, 249

Maurer, Kurt, 111

Mayer, Gerda, 106, 131–132, 144–145, 155, 162, 165, 235–236
  "All the Leaves Have Lost Their Trees," 155
  "Make Believe," 9, 419

Meal ticket, 339

Melbourne University, 328

Meltzer, Asher, 47–48

Metternich, Klemens von, 192

Michaelis, Martin L., 257–270, 289

Michaelis, Ruth L., 131, 149, 222, 230, 233, 257–270, 289

*Mikva*, 293

Militarism, 199

Millar, John, 274–277, 278, 279–280

Mirrer Yeshiva, 294

*Mischling*, 128

Mises, Ludwig, 193

Mitford, Diana, 313

Model, Elisabeth D., 370

Modine, Alice, 81, 289–290, 368–369

Mogilensky, Emmy, 153, 158, 213

Morgan, Peter, 142, 201, 212, 231

Morgenstern, Traute, 234

Morris, Sudney, 326

Mosley, Oswald, 313

Movement for the Care of Children, 144, 252

Musicians, as internees, 315, 324–325, 326

Mussolini, Benito, 332, 335

National Children's Home and Orphanage, Lancashire, 211

Nationalization, in Germany, 34

Nazi party
  anti-Semitic policy of, 35
  in Austria, 14
  illegal activities of, 14. *See also Illegalen*

Nazi sympathizers
  Austrian, 14, 15, 17, 19, 29
  British, 311
  servants as, 84–85

Neeman, Meir, 18–19, 24, 26, 71–72, 80, 119–125, 188, 189, 361

Netherlands
  child escapees in, 160–161, 164
  German invasion of, 113
  *St.Louis* passengers acceptance by, 118, 119

*News from the Land of Freedom* (Marty), 3

Nuremberg Laws, 34, 36, 39, 128, 332

Okura, 295

Opera, 188–189, 191

Oranien-Saxenhausen concentration camp, releases from, 142

Orphanages, 211, 252–253

Orthodox Jews
  as deportees, 320, 328
  foster home placement of, 220
  as internees, 322, 323
  of Poland, 202

Outdoor activities, 187–188

Pakefield, Lowestoft, 140

Palestine
  British occupation of, 122–123, 125
  deportation to, 290
  emigration to, 189
  escapes to, 119–125, 225–226, 327
  Jewish refugees in, 361–362

Palestinian Jews
  British Army service of, 338
  concentration camp liberation by, 334

Parents, rescue of, 363

Parker, Frank G., 58–60, 79, 191, 359, 370

Parker, Lore, 132–133, 134, 181, 191, 228, 230–231

Passover, 40, 201, 246

Passports, 50–51
  confiscation of, 28, 295
  difficulty of obtaining, 45–46, 48, 49–50
  "J" designation of, 64, 77

Pastry shops, 186, 396–397
Pengelly, Alice F., 185
Pensionat Stern, 302
Personal property, confiscation of, 26–27, 28, 30, 46, 47, 102, 131. *See also* Businesses, confiscation of
during emigration, 84
receipts for, 31
Petain, Henri, 113
Peters, Alan, 19, 27–28, 135, 143, 144–145, 147–148, 152–153, 162, 180, 191, 208–210, 223, 225–226, 370
*Picture Post*, 43
Pimpernel of Prague. *See* Chadwick, Trevor
Pioneer Corps, 317, 327
Plank, Emma, 28, 80
Pogroms, 198, 202–203
Poland
deportations to, 136–137
emigration from, 2, 42, 198
emigration to, 42
Jewish population of, 140
orthodox Jews in, 202
Poverty, of escapees, 367, 368
Prague, 106
children's evacuation from, 151–152
Prater, Vienna, 187–188
Pringle, Miss, 284–285, 286–287, 290
Priory *Kinder*, 284–287, 290
Prison numbers, 106
Propaganda, anti-Semitic, 40
Prussia, Austrian attitudes towards, 14

Quakers, 239, 267, 326, 327, 364
Quisling, 310
Quotas, for Jews, 197
for immigration, 73, 74

Rabbis, abuse of, 100
Racial inferiority theories, 34
Radok, Uwe, 326
*Rassenschande*, 291
Rauchwerger, Joseph, 50, 80, 81, 83–84, 85, 338, 353–355

Red Cross, 107, 225
Refugee camps. *See also* Internment
in Shanghai, 292–293, 294–296
Refugee Committee, 219–220, 237–239, 250
*Reichsfluchtsteuer*, 46–47
*Reichstag*, 33
*Reichswanderungsamt*, 35
Relatives
as extended family, 179
"hononary," 179–180, 187
non-Jewish, 402
Religious conversion, 131–132, 200–201
as emigration requirement, 79–80
Religious observances
by deportees, 320
by escapees, 395–396
by internees, 323
in Shanghai refugee camps, 294
Resettlement, 289–412. *See also* Children, resettlement in England
adjustment to, 406–410
employment during, 303–304, 341–349, 350, 353–357, 369–370
lack of assimilation following, 389–391
Residences, confiscation of, 103, 131
Retarded children, murder of, 47
Reunions, of escapees, 255, 393–394
*Rhakatis* (ship), 119
Roberts, Richard, 22, 31, 48, 76, 96
Robinson, Susi, 131, 132, 135–136
Roosevelt, Franklin D., 349, 360
Rose, Frances R., 150, 160, 189
Rosenberg, Alfred, 34
Ross, David, 108, 151, 152
Rothmund, Heinrich, 77
Rothschild, Dorothy de, 140, 211
Rothschild, James de, 211
Rothschild, Kurt W., 361
Rothschild, Valerie, 85
"Rozhinkas Mit Mandelen," 101
Rubin, Berta, 20, 97, 99, 110
Rushdie, Salman, 398
Russia, escapees in, 2

Ryba, Marietta, 147, 151–152, 161–162, 207–208, 225

SA, 20–21, 23–24, 61
Sachsenhausen, 98
*St. Louis* (ship), 116–119, 291, 337
Salmon family, 212
Sarah, as Jewish name designation, 133
Saxton, Monica, 96, 156–157
Schaufeld, Vera, 154–155, 185, 189, 214–215
Schidlof, Hans, 315
Schiller, Ken, 53–58, 79
Schonberg, Arnold, 193
Schools
    anti-Semitism in, 129
    English, 298–299
    gymnasiums, 180, 195, 196
    Jewish, 36
    in Shanghai refugee camps, 294
Schroder, Captain, 117, 118
Schuschnigg, Kurt, 13–15, 16, 19, 23
*Schwarze Corps, Der*, 24–25
Scientists
    emigration by, 75, 76
    as internees, 315, 324
Segal, Kroner H., 370
Selkirk, Scotland, 271–288
Servants, 180–183, 187
    betrayal by, 183
    as Nazi sympathizers, 84–85
    refugees as, 297–298
Sexual abuse, of children, 136
    by foster parents, 227, 251
Sexual abuse accusations, as Nazi propaganda, 24, 25
Sexual relations, between Germans and Jews, 49–50, 293
Shabbat, 179
Shanghai, Jewish refugees in, 290–296, 337
*Sh'ma Israel*, 101, 250
*Shoah* (film), 382
Shuster, Harold, 40–41, 77–78
Shuster, Rabbi, 77–78

Siegel, Michael, 70
Sigal, Hilde, 24, 78, 178, 343–344, 362, 365, 369
Signs, anti-Semitic, 24, 31, 61, 65, 60, 127
Singer, Isaac Bashevis, 38
Singer, Kurt, 37
Single mothers, 179
Slogans, anti-Semitic, 18, 19, 23–24, 30
Sobibor, 1
Social clubs, exclusion of Jews from, 197
Social Democrats, 13–14, 15
Social life
    of Austrian and German Jews, 37, 185–194
    of escapees, 351
Spaeth, Lottie P., 37, 81, 142, 178, 213
Spira, Camilla, 37
Sports, 188–189
SS, 61
    arrests by, 23, 134
    children's interaction with, 135
    *Der Schwarze Corps* of, 24–25
    *Kindertransport* inspections by, 159
*Stars Look Down, The* (Cronin), 298
Stein, George, 48, 158
Steinberg, Henry, 98, 99, 232
Steinweg, Fritz Israel, 48
Stereotypes, of Jews, 21, 25–26
Stevens, Fred, 153, 159–160, 165, 237–240
Street cleaning, as public humiliation, 23–24, 63, 101
Streicher, Julius, 24, 40
Stricker, Henry H., 131, 179, 226, 232
*Sturmer*, 24, 40
Suicide, 43, 101, 182
Sunnymead, Thirsk, 237–239
Support groups, 214, 350
Survivor guilt, 399–403
Swastika
    Austrians' display of, 15, 17, 18, 21
    display by teachers, 129
Sweden, *Kindertransport*s to, 163–164

Switzerland
  illegal escapes to, 111
  immigration policy of, 76–77
  Jewish immigration to, 89–90

Taub, Lea, 105, 157, 230
Taussig, Martha, 133–134
Taxes
  for emigration, 46–47, 51
  on Turkish Jews, 290
Teachers, 180
  anti-Semitic behavior of, 129
  Austrian, 324
  as internees, 315, 324, 324
  Jewish, 196
Theresienstadt, 1, 37, 378, 383
Thirsk Refugee Committee, 238–239
Torah, 42
Torture, 47
Transit camps, 312–313, 317, 318
Turkey, escapees in, 290

Uhlman, Fred, 315
Ulman, Annie, 19–20, 76, 86, 185, 186,
  187, 191–192, 193, 360, 370
United Kingdom. *See* England
United States
  anti-Semitism in, 197
  escapees' lives in, 341–343, 346–349,
    359–360, 362, 365–367
  sponsorship for immigration to, 73–
    75
  refusal to admit Jewish refugees, 118
University of Vienna, anti-Semitism at, 195

Vernon, Dora, 134, 137, 157, 160, 164,
  224–225, 290–291, 363–364
Vernon, John, 97, 98, 100, 146, 151, 159
Vichy France, 113–114
Vienna. *See also* Austria
  anti-Semitic activity in, 17, 18, 19, 20,
    31–32
  anti-unification plebiscite activity in, 15
  cultural life in, 199
  *Fasching* in, 191–192, 193

Vienna (*cont.*)
  Hitler's entry into, 18–19
  Jewish population of, 25, 198
    children, 140
    natural beauty of, 187–188
    social life in, 185–188, 189–194
Violence, anti-Semitic, 134–135
  towards children, 129
  in Germany, 35
  following Kristallnacht, 95–102
  in Vienna, 17, 18, 19, 20
Visas
  entry, 71–76, 80, 83
    bribery for, 117
  exit, 50, 51, 63

Wajsenhuis Building, 161
Wannsee Conference, 34
Washington Irving High School, 366
Waxman, Franz, 79
Weis, Frederick V., 202, 362
Weis, Gertrude, 178, 341
Weisman, Eva, 292
Weiss, Jacob, 318
Weiss, Meir, 361–362
Weiss, Walter, 26–27, 189, 192–193, 370
Wesson, Bernard, 102
Wesson, Ruth, 245
Westerbork, 251, 385, 386, 401
Wiesbaden, Jewish daily life in, 38
Wiesel, Elie, 395–396
Wijsmuller, Mrs., 141, 163–164
Wildman, Louis, 80–81, 343
Williams, Tennessee, 40
Winer, Eva, 345
Winer, Leon, 40, 81
Winton, Nicholas, 145
Wittgenstein, Ludwig, 193
Wollheim, Norbert, 141–142, 148, 150,
  157, 162–163
Woolf, Dorrit, 79, 82, 85–86, 177, 345,
  366, 367
Woolf, Leopold, 99, 179
World Movement for the Care of
  Children from Germany, 144, 252

World War I, Jewish military service
    during, 198
Woss, Magda S., 28, 31


Yad Vashem, 380
Youth Alliyah, 143
Youth groups
    Hitler Youth, 200

Youth groups (*cont.*)
    Zionist, 143, 189, 334
Yugoslovia, Jewish refugees in, 121

Zelig, Simcha, Rabbi, 42
Zionist groups, 37
    Betar Movement, 119–120
    youth groups, 143, 189, 334
    refugees in, 121